A BREATH AWAY
from the right decision

Authored by Van Charles Sher

A Fictional book based on a true story

Acknowledgement

This story could not have been written without the courage
and dedication of my wife, lover, and best friend, Carol.
She made incredible notes to help me organize and 'kicked
me in the butt' when I needed it, but that's what wives do!
There were other major contributors for thoughts, ideas,
suggestions and support from many people including Jerry
Diner and Harriet Leff. A special dedication goes to my
grandson, Anthony, whose strength and courage inspired me
to keep writing when my vision was emotionally blurred.
There were many others who contributed and I thank them as
well. I hope and pray that this book helps at least one more
child to live what he dreams

Biography

I have a "Street Doctorate" Degree in Life as Carol and I
have lived many years past our ages. We both enjoy work as
Commercial Real Estate Brokers and Consultants and have
done so for over 25 years. Our philosophy in life has been to
do the right thing in life and life will take care of you; it
works if you work too! You can reach us at
vansher@home.com

Copyright © August, 2000
First Edition

Printed in Canada

ISBN 0-9715122-0-5

Edited by Rose Toy
Cover design by Pam Wakeley
Made for distribution in the United States.

Chapter One

The anticipation of going into a drug district at 11 o'clock at night, facing an organized drug ring to get my son's car back, is not my idea of fun. My son, Mark, advised us that the street had everything from semi-automatics to Uzi's. The safety factor became important, and knowing that we would be on the wrong turf put us at a major disadvantage. We tried to get some rest that day, but the anticipation of facing harm prevented any distraction that could get help to get our minds off of that evening's activity. We prepared to go down to the drug neighborhood at 11 p.m. – this allowed us time to be sure that the dealer we were looking for would be there. We were told that he would be there by 10. Through the years of dealing with our son's addiction, we learned that there are regular shifts and regular corners where scheduled personnel take shifts moving the product.

Most of these people didn't live in this immediate neighborhood, but traveled to the corners to work at their designated time. Neighbors didn't mess with these people as they infiltrated the area. There was competition in the drug trade, but there always seemed to be enough business to go around and they appeared to be friendly competitors. Mark told me which corner to go to and the name of the individual to talk to about retrieving his car.

We left the house with Mark in the back seat giving him strict instructions to keep his mouth shut. I had my 38 revolver next to me, and my wife Cindy had the car phone already dialed to 911. She also had a canister of pepper gas next to her with her thumb on the trigger. The strange part was that my gun was kept hidden; when, and if, we got out of this, we didn't want Mark to know we had the gun.

It was dark and cold. The wind was gusting and my stomach was talking back to me, but I knew that if it was close to one on one, I had a shot to get out healthy, because we were not looking for trouble. They were only doing business. I had a two-door car that helped our state-of-mind, because Mark was in the back seat and couldn't get out quickly. We pulled up to the corner about a half hour after leaving home. I rolled down my window and asked for Julio. One of the runners said he would be there in about an hour. That certainly wasn't what I wanted to hear. Were they setting us up, I thought. I drove to a spot about half a block away, next to a field at the railroad tracks. I tried to find a place where we could see, but no one could walk out of a house and blow us away. We sat in the car and everyone had a direction to watch while we waited. We were amazed – this intersection had more traffic than a McDonald's drive-in window. After about twenty minutes, three guys started walking toward the car from about thirty yards away. I told everyone to sit back and let me do all the talking. When they got about ten yards away, two of the guys stopped and one continued to my side of the car which was the closest to him. As I watched him approach, my heart beat loudly. The guy had one hand in his pocket. We were the only ones there, so I knew the one walking toward us was going to either knock on the window, try to open the door, or just take a good shot. I just waited not knowing if this good strategy or just plain fear. I don't know which, but I kept a strong grip on the gun I held close to my left leg so it couldn't be seen from outside the window. When he got there, he knocked on my window. I rolled down the window about half way. He asked me what I wanted, and I told him that we were waiting for Julio to get back my car. He said that Julio would be there in a few minutes and he walked away. We waited another twenty minutes and then Mark said Julio was on the corner. I started to drive up and Julio signaled to pull over about ten yards from the corner. I could see he didn't want me that close. I figured we were very bad for business, just hanging around and blocking traffic. He came to my window, looked in, and saw my son. He told me that he had a problem with Mark and that Mark should stay out of their territory. Mark was not a good customer and caused some problems that they would not tolerate. It was a threat and he made sure we knew it. He stayed low next to the car and I didn't get out of the car. I

2

couldn't see his hands and that made me nervous. I could feel a trickle of sweat at the small of my back. After ten seconds talking to him, I knew Julio would have no qualms blowing us all away. What helped at this moment was noticing that with us parked where we were, the people in the other cars did not stop to do any drug business. I knew Julio wanted us out of there. Besides, if they shot me or damaged our car, the police would be called in and that would further disrupt their business for the night. Unbelievably, I was thinking we had a temporary advantage, for a few minutes at least!

I spoke with him through the window and he said it was $300 that we owed for Mark's car. I said $200. We were at an impasse. This negotiation went on for twenty minutes. I said if there was a dispute, we could call the police and let them handle it. Julio said that we would never see the car again if we didn't pay. I stuck to my guns and said I had $200 cash in my pocket and it was Julio's call.

Julio knew he was losing business playing around with me. I was totally out of my league. This kid was about 28 or 29 years old and I was pushing him. By this time, there were about ten people within ten feet of the car and we were nervous. Cindy was trying to be calm and doing her best to keep an eye on everything. Mark was very nervous because he knew what kind of people we were dealing with, and he knew they were bad. He had been in the trenches with them and knew to them that life was cheap. Mark understood this situation in a different light; maybe our being slightly stupid was to our advantage at this point.

Finally, Julio said that we should follow him around the corner, which we did in our car. That was also stupid, but it was difficult to make the right decision in one split second. When we got around the corner, he said he'd give me the keys and tell us where the car was if he got the $200. I asked if everything was still on the car and he said "yes." I had no choice. I didn't need the keys because we had an extra set, but I had no idea where the car was. I said that I would give him the money if he gave me the keys at the same time. He agreed.

It was a bizarre exchange. I held the money out and Julio dangled the keys into the window -- we trusted each other like a bitterly divorced couple. He told me the car was six blocks away. I thanked him and we left quickly to retrieve Mark's car. It was now 1:00 a.m. as we drove down the dark, narrow street that had a few fenced yards. I pulled up behind the car and Mark and I climbed out. Cindy slid over to the driver's seat and waited. I went with Mark to his car. He opened the door and everything looked good. I was relieved because I did not want to be stranded alone on this desolate street. I got into the car; put the keys into the ignition, thinking I can't wait to get out of here. The car didn't start, but I didn't panic —- I brought a set of jumper cables for the battery. I opened the hood and found there was no battery. Now we were screwed!

How did a nice middle-class boy like myself, from the suburbs of Philadelphia, end up in a situation like this? That's what I want to tell you. My promise to you is that this is based on a true story. So as you take this journey with me, keep in mind that fact is often more outrageous than fiction.

Why have kids, work, and set goals for the good life when you know that the minute you stop to smell the roses, somebody close to you will smell death. There is a fine line between happiness and existence, sadness and survival, and the joy we get from family and children. How many times do you go for years fighting with a member of your family for some reason that you can't remember?

You are no different from anyone else. You end up reading some bullshit from a Miss Manner's text or listen to some 1930-thinking radio talk show host who tries to impress everyone by making people feel like true idiots.

We are not sure where the gratification comes from on any of these advice givers. We do know that the problems are real and universal. Everyone knows someone who has been faced with long-term tragedy where he or she tried to seek help. Ultimately, that person with the problem was usually not able to resolve their problem. The result was either death, divorce, cheating, drugs, firings, accidents, bankruptcies, and ultimately losing whatever dignity one had left by having to contract the last hope and savior to bail you out.

Who is this savior that will take your last dime, then write you a letter saying you should call them back when you get money to continue the case? Your lawyer! By the way, don't be surprised to get a bill for that letter! If you are an attorney, you know what we mean. If you aren't an attorney, you still know what we mean. The truth is, the attorneys are a part of the system. They aren't the bad guys, usually. However, the story I want to tell you is the story about a child and his survival.

This is based on a factual story that is about you or someone close to you that you may not yet know. It is about your children's children, your best friend's child, the minister's child, the entertainer's child, and the next generation's children! You are not immune. None of us can bury our heads and say it doesn't affect us. It affects us every day. What is it? It is the aura of drugs and how they pyramid through our daily lives. This is not a soap opera; it is all of us. The first few chapters give you a background of the upbringing of Mark and how it relates to all of us. My name is Ed and my wife's name is Cindy, and this is our story.

Chapter Two

It starts out as the perfect world: elementary school, little league, camp, junior high, dating, summer jobs, high school, proms, seashore, swim club, college, job, marriage, kids, and so the cycle continues. Today, however, more ingredients must be added. This story takes into account those ingredients and the ongoing ramifications of the technology babies.

Cindy was the "perfect" girl growing up in the 40s, 50s, and 60s. Mom and dad were the proud parents of the obedient, healthy baby who listened to every word dad said, while mom made sure baby Cindy was going to get all the things that she didn't have as a child.

Cindy played sports, walked around looking very "cute," and making mom and dad proud. She went to college and met the boy she was going to marry. And yes, the boy was going to be a doctor and was the same religion. What could be finer? The only other thing would be if the boy's family were good and in this case, the father was a successful doctor. Now that was picture perfect.

Almost! Baby Cindy met another boy at college. She was attracted to him, but couldn't go out with him because he was not of the same faith. Also, baby Cindy was getting married in one month. The $2,000 wedding gown was ready, the catering plans were made, and the invitations were sent out; the start of a wonderful life that mommy and daddy planned from birth. Does this sound a little like what you did?

"Ain't gonna happen!" Teenager Cindy said, "I don't love my fiancé." (Although she loved the rock on her finger!) Daddy said, "Yes you do, and we know what's best for you!" Does that sound familiar? Has it ever occurred to parents that just maybe they don't know what is best for their kids? Maybe the kids should play with matches and learn that fire hurts. Maybe they should play with knives and see that blood, especially theirs, is not good. How many kids today will say, "Based on your experience mom and dad, I will listen to what you say so, that I do not have to get hurt or disappointed."

Yea, right! So it was obvious what baby Cindy did. She eloped with the guy from school and reluctantly left the ring on the bedroom dresser. Welcome to the rebellion of the 50s and 60s. The parents determined where we go from here. Now it was true baby Cindy was a bright girl who just did something stupid. Domination and parental rights pushed her into it; supposedly an assumed right by parents throughout a child's lifetime, which was where the term in-law has its roots, but that's another topic.

Cindy revolted and moved to another city on another coast. She learned that washing, cooking, and maintaining an apartment had to be done by someone. She learned that nothing got done until she or her husband did it. Mom wasn't around to pick up the pieces. Did anyone think Cindy could find happiness through revolt against parents? If so, put down this book because you are an idiot who won't understand the messages sent through our humble words. She stayed married to someone she never loved, had no children, and basically learned about the working world and what it took to survive rent payments, car payments, insurance payments, utility bills, clothing bills, furniture payments, medical bills, and don't forget food. Of course there were other bills, but one tried to avoid them.

All of the training that took place in growing up started to come to the surface and Cindy realized that there was more to life than being with someone you didn't love. The real problem she faced was her fear of being alone, plus the rebellion she felt from the "parental warmth" received with comments such as the witty, "I told you not to marry him," or the unselfish egotistical, "I told you to listen to me."

Loneliness was one of the factors that most partners must face in order to try to find true happiness, whatever that was. Obviously, fear was another. You can add a few and be just as accurate as us. What did she do to get out? She didn't love him, but she didn't hate him, either. She had no money because she spent it on material things that she still had. He had nothing either, but both had jobs and managed to live from paycheck-to-paycheck. This caused emotional anxiety because the mind was set in motion, and the imagination was running wild.

After two years, Cindy moved back to her east coast roots with her husband, where their marriage coasted for another eight years. They ultimately decided that being together was bad for their ten-year relationship and they agreed to an amiable divorce. What was so amiable you ask? It was rather simple: you take one car; I'll take the other. Split the $1,000 that was in the bank and let Cindy keep the furniture.

Now Cindy's life was up in the air because she was teaching, lonely, trying to rebuild the trust that was lost with her parents, but also trying to gain a mutual respect that was

7

eventually needed between generations. Did she want parents in her life, or was she afraid of being dominated again? She was 31 years old and trying to start over. How did she do it? How would you do it? There were social and psychological factors that played havoc with her mind. Please take a minute and give it some thought.

You are wrong! Unless you have done it, you are in fantasyland (which for you non-Disney buffs means good). You cannot be astute enough to deal with the reality and set your emotional goal toward a course that allows you to see an end. If you think therapy and counseling would benefit you in this situation, then it may because your attitude says, "listen to the experts; you are so lost that your mind needs some textbook direction."

Cindy said partying and clubs were the way to meet people and get companionship. Cindy was out and as usual, companionship found company. In other words, if something was meant to happen, it would. She didn't like going out to bars or clubs, but it was better than looking at the same four walls every night.

Cindy was responsible and began processing the divorce and the distribution of the cars, a very simple procedure. She went to an insurance agency that did auto transfers, showed all I.D., and signed some papers and ownership changes. This was certainly one of the easiest solutions to a problem where government had some say. At the agency, Cindy was at the window explaining her dilemma, and I was next, standing in line for some reason that eludes me now.

Anyway, I was twenty-four years old and very carefree, coming off the Woodstock era time in life. This was baby boomer times, where I was smart enough to get through school, without working too hard. This was also the time that the 'boomers' were coming off communes, free love, free speech, anti-war, peace brother, and on and on. As I was standing at the counter of the insurance agency, well, I must go back in my life to tell you how I came to be standing here at this moment in time.

I was born to a couple that started with nothing and took risk in business to make a better life for their kids. My parents both quit salaried jobs to rent a store and go into business for themselves. They sold their row home, dug up whatever equity they could salvage, and bought a store with an apartment above it for the family to live. They had two kids, including me, and I was the youngest. We lived above the store so mom could take care of the kids and also work. Was that the good old American work ethic, or what? I was in the store from the age of two months until ten, and like anyone raised in a family retail business, I learned about people. The truth is people were nicer and generally more trustworthy years ago.

At ten, the family moved to the suburbs and I went to the nice suburban schools that had grass on the ground that was 'smokeless,' rather than the three-story brick city building with the concrete playground. I went to school, but looked to play, not worrying about important school facts such as what poems Robert Frost wrote or actually trying to memorize one. I avoided trying to figure out if two trains were running at different speeds and one carried more weight than another, how much longer would it take for both to reach the same destination. I just thought these assignments were for the smart kids. All the guys I hung out with just wanted to play ball, watch television or masturbate.

I cut a lot of school because if it was a choice of studying or going down the shore with the guys, it was an easy decision. Besides, my parents were working to make it easier for me, and this certainly was easier! Obviously, I didn't see it as my time to grow up.

High school was over and what should I do next? I had no talent or skills, so I applied to college. I was accepted and lived partly at home and partly where I could shack up. In case one doesn't know it, college can be fun with the neat student center and the great card games that go on all day. It's especially fun if attendance is not taken; it's surely a sign not to go to class. Of course there was my 29 hours of work at the supermarket, and the balance of the time I juggled between my girlfriend and my buddies.

Exams proved fatal, as a 1.0 average does not put one on the dean's list. Reality now set in; the Viet Nam war was on and friends didn't come back from overseas. School and deferments were looking good and so was living in Canada. So now, school took on a new significance. This time around, at a new college who accepted me for financial reasons only (they flunked out 1/3 of their freshman class), I carried a 3.8 average in my first semester.

Everyone says motivation is a factor to succeed, but fortunately for some students, the school was motivated by money to stay afloat. It didn't matter, because now I learned how to play the college game, and it was easy. I graduated college and taught one year in a four-story, old brick, inner city high school that was enmeshed in drugs, violence, and lots of teenage pregnancy.

Once a student came into class ten minutes late and asked me if I minded that he was late. I said that he was already late and to sit down. He said that I didn't understand because "there was this girl down the hall doing the guys and he was third in line!" Being the teacher that I was, I told him to get in line sooner next time!

Another incident occurred in the cafeteria when a security guard caught two students having sex on a cafeteria table. The guard told the kids to go to the principal's office, but the guy told the guard to wait a minute because "he was almost done!"

The students walked out of school that year when the administration called in more than 300 uniformed police to line the halls. That was scary especially since I taught in sandals, jeans and tee shirts. I could have been mistaken as a student.

This job lasted one year because of the assholes in the administration who were more concerned about teaching useless facts than teaching the students how to be productive for themselves and society. Who knows, maybe they were right? From there, it was substitute teaching and grad school, which leads me back to the insurance counter and the chance meeting with my soon-to-be wife.

As Cindy was discussing her situation, I did what any red-blooded young man would do. I analyzed the situation: divorcee, with an apartment, a nice body (didn't bother to check out the face), probably horny (at least I was), and it was 2 p.m. It was the perfect time to figure out how to get laid, and all times seemed perfect to me. For those of you with a generation gap: balled, fucked, screwed, and for the straight ones, make love. (George Carlin explains this a lot better in one of his best routines.)

I set up a substitute teaching assignment in Cindy's school, wrote her a note to come to my room, and then asked her out. What a Frick and Frack operation; Cindy had been married ten years and was seven years older than me. She knew some of the finer things and was used to a different lifestyle. She paid $400 a month for her apartment, I was paying $70 per month split two ways. Cindy dressed properly for work and arrived on time. I called in to school, got my assignment at 7:00 a.m. then went back to sleep because I wasn't late if I showed up by 10 a.m. (Of course they requested my presence by 8:30 a.m.) You get the idea of my priorities at that time.

I asked her out, and since she had nothing planned on that particular school night, she figured going out was better than looking at the walls.

I picked her up at the apartment, took her to the quickest, cheapest bar/ restaurant and back to the apartment. Once at the apartment, the "free-love" spirit in me figured it would just be some easy lay. Wrong.

I said, "Let's ball."

"What's that mean?" she said.

That really takes the edge off a strong hard on. Then Cindy had the guts to insult me by saying "no", and also, she didn't even know my last name! I gave her my last name but she still said "no." With that, I thought there was no sense staying there and preceded to the door, never to be seen again.

In through the door walked Cindy's estranged husband. (She let him stay there until he could find his own place.) The "husband" said to stick around and have a cup of coffee. This whole scene was different so I figured another strange scenario was coming, so why not. It was see this play out or go back to the apartment and blow some grass. Grass you could do anytime, but this scene was interesting.

Cindy's husband was nice, and it was different, so I decided to see this through, temporarily. I came back each night and we all got friendly, but I wasn't getting any action. The only place I was getting action was at the racetrack where I knew every horse, but, unfortunately, not the order in which they would finish the race. My hormones created an idea for me. It quickly sunk in that a bath might be a place for some action. I put in a bath figuring Cindy would jump in and I would catch what I figured would be an experienced piece. Remember, it's the mystery for man that makes most things exciting.

Well, the bathtub was full and in walked her husband who thanked me for filling the tub. Before he walked in, I was thinking about sex, but after he walked in, colors came to mind, and I knew deep blue was the color of the day for parts of my anatomy. Anyway, we fucked that night after her husband left. For the religious people, as God said in the bible, it was good! It dawned on me that her husband had nowhere to sleep, so I told him to take my room at the apartment and I moved in with Cindy. Remember, after sex the first time with a particular partner, the relationship changes because the guys got what they wanted and of course, all men respected the girls in the morning (this is stated so that any young, stupid girls reading this will not deprive the guys getting their rocks off). That was one of the last times that I saw her husband as he moved away about three weeks later.

Our relationship continued for about six months, with Cindy being stable and me being loyal, but not responsible in trying to achieve anything better than companionship and good sex. A relationship was forming and a combination of personalities meshed rather quickly. After a year of night courses while I taught high school, I completed grad school and got a job selling foundations on the road. What, you ask, are foundations? The women know that means bras and girdles. What a job to keep looking at the same two cups and figure thirty ways to make breasts look attractive covered in cotton and nylon. Now that I had my first real job, I decided to see if Cindy wanted to get married. It was a great feeling to propose naked, on a pillow, and a good stiff one waiting for the right answer. If you were thinking that could be one ugly sight, then I want to know where you have been; or if you are a guy or gal or...!

When the news was brought to Cindy's parents, with whom she had developed a relationship again, her father greeted the news with, "Good, now he can move out. My daughter is not going to live in sin."

"No one's moving out," Cindy said.

"You will get married this weekend," her father said.

"We can't because my father is out of town," I told him.

My father was a traveling salesman who was away about two or three nights a week. The result was the following weekend we were married in her parent's home. Everything was fine for a short time as Cindy taught and hated it, and took advantage of the days-off system. In the meantime, I despised the regiment of some idiot sales manager for bras and girdles insisting on getting sales reports two nights a week at an exact time, which was the precise time to ruin an evening.

My job lasted one year until I said, "I was going to Las Vegas for a vacation," to which the sales manager said I wasn't. Didn't he realize that to order someone to do something he didn't want to do was a challenge to his manhood? I knew that I was one of the top producers (I did so love the bras and what filled them) so I wasn't real concerned about offending the manager. I went to Vegas and still had my job upon returning, which I quit about two weeks later in order to take a summer job running a swim club.

I took a summer job while I was deciding what to do when I grew up. Cindy was now 6 months pregnant, on maternity leave, and spending her summer at the swim club. This was cool, but I had no idea of 24 hours into the future, but fatherhood sounded like a good idea because Cindy was real happy and all four of the potential grandparents were also happy.

The swim club proved to be pivotal in our lives over the next twenty-one years. It was here that we met and became friendly with a number of the members. It was a natural occurrence for us to meet new friends; Cindy was bubbly, pregnant and generally a lot of fun to be around. I knew what I was doing around swim clubs because I was a lifeguard for most of the summers since I was sixteen. Everyone talks about the lifeguards and how the girls love to associate with them and basically give all to them. Every word of that was true! It didn't matter if the girls were sixteen, eighteen, twenty, or married. There was an aura that did exist and probably still does around any lifeguard stand on the beach. Guaranteed that there will be a slinky female torso hanging on to every intelligent word the well-conditioned god sitting high in the throne is uttering, even if he is discussing water temperature.

Back at the swim club, I was the ideal manager because I was good with the members and knew how to handle the problems quickly when they arose. Handling problems quickly was what life was about, but it was easy when problems were in your control. Chaos occurred when you had a problem and you were not the boss, because no one believed they should be resolved as quickly as you did. This swim club had two decks and the top deck was an adult's only area, which allowed for tanning of areas that usually were not exposed.

At the swim club, we became very close to a married couple that were both lawyers. They had three kids who were sixteen, fourteen, and eight. The kids were street-savvy and pretty wise for kids who were growing up in a wealthier part of the city, but they all had some emotional problems. When the summer season was over, we all stayed friends.

I actually started to grow up and was introduced to a job by

Cindy's father, to be a stockbroker. I interviewed and was asked a question at the interview, which never was forgotten, and one that probably got me the job. The manager asked if I played poker. Hell, I thought, this job would be great, thinking back to the old days of playing cards all day. I had no idea what stocks were all about, but I associated it with a poker game. That was pretty astute and accurate by all standards. In six months, I was an expert at telling people how to invest their hard-earned money. Hard to believe one could get on the telephone, tell somebody you didn't even know, that a company they never heard of was going to make them a lot of money. Greed was a wonderful thing!

Cindy was sitting in the apartment at 8 p.m. with her parents and me. The water bag broke and the ritual began.

"Grab the suitcase."

"Cindy, get into the car. I'll drive."

"Don't get into an accident. How do you feel? Should we clean the water off the sofa? Oh shit. You call ..."

We sped off to the hospital, making the trip in just ten minutes. We were stopped by a police officer, but he saw the situation and told us to continue on our way. Now came the wait. It was 10 o'clock at night, then midnight, 4 a.m. then 6 a.m. as time dragged on. By 11 a.m., and after a night of hard labor, the doctors decided to take the baby by cesarean section.

Everybody was relieved when our baby boy was born. The doctor came out in his bloodied greens, with a big smile, and told us that everything was fine. We saw the baby, who we knew was going to be named Ritchie. Ritchie was said to look like everyone in the family, then everyone focused on features that identified the child as the son of Cindy and me. Everyone always waited for the tests to be done, including the APGAR test, and we were told Ritchie was healthy. And so the visiting and feeding rituals began.

The first day the baby was in the nursery, I noticed that all of the other babies were asleep, but not ours. I told Cindy and we both kept it in mind, but brushed it off based on the doctor's seal of approval. The next day, the baby still wasn't sleeping, but the doctors said all was fine. It was time to take the baby home and all was at peace with the world. The hospital was in a beautiful suburban setting with trees all around. The staff was so friendly that you felt like they were family. I was in training for the stockbroker's exam. I spent twelve weeks in New York and came home on weekends to be with my new family. Anyway, the baby was born, I was a stockbroker, and Cindy was a mother.

Unfortunately, life was not this easy.

We kept noticing twitches in Ritchie's eyes that disturbed us. We became very concerned, so we took him back to the doctor's office. We said Ritchie was having some sort of seizures, but the response was, "Babies don't have seizures."

By the time Ritchie was three weeks old the seizures became very obvious. They were so noticeable that even the doctors acknowledged what we have feared all along. By four weeks, the problem was extremely serious. Ritchie was experiencing minor seizures every minute or so with grand mol seizures every ten minutes.

The baby would involuntarily throw his head to the right, kick his right leg all the way over his body to his left, roll his eyes to the top of his head, stiffen the rest of his body, and let out the most unsettling scream that tore out our hearts. This ritual went on 24-hours a day. Finally, after two months, Cindy flew with the baby to a research clinic in Cincinnati, Ohio, where there the ratio was one doctor for each child. This was one of two children's research facilities in the country. I flew from Wall Street by helicopter to La Guardia Airport to meet Cindy in Cincinnati. If you ever flew in a helicopter, you know how scary the experience can be. The four-passenger helicopter left from the river at the base of Wall Street in New York City. The body of the helicopter rolled from side-to-side under the propeller perched high on top. It took off almost straight upward, but with the front leaning down so that you see the ground. Then it swept out over the river toward the airport. There was a bridge that was about half a mile down the river, which I expected we were going to fly above. As the helicopter approached the bridge, we did not go higher. It got closer, closer, and still we were eye-level with it. I felt my underwear getting damp, because now I could see the bolts on the bridge. I was in a cold sweat. The pilot noticed my reaction and smiled.

"Stop squirming," he said. "We always fly under the bridge." Now he tells me! The fear factor may have been exaggerated because of my being on edge anticipating the fate of Ritchie, as some of his test results were due to be in.

I met Cindy in Cincinnati and went through the introduction of staff and doctors. The doctors continued testing Ritchie for a week. While Cindy stayed with the baby in the hospital, I had to fly back to New York.

The testing involved biopsies of the brain, liver, skin, and every other organ imaginable. The testing was agonizing to the baby and equally so to his mother. Some tests were so painful that Cindy just held Ritchie for hours to try to comfort him. A few nights, she fell asleep holding Ritchie inside her arms.

The fear of the unknown and the desire to know the truth were intense emotional factors. The fear that your child could be sickly first enters your mind. Then the doctors act as if they were guessing about treatments; now you start to worry if the baby was mentally retarded. Thoughts like, "will he ever drive," and "will he be normal when he grows up," all race through your mind.

Reality set in when the doctors said, "We don't have any idea what is wrong, but it appears that there is a missing enzyme in his system.

"Does that mean wait until you find it and then we'll make everything right? Does that mean we should make plans for his funeral? What does that mean?" we asked.

The fact was it meant they had no idea of the problem and obviously no idea of the solution. They said they were keeping the biopsies frozen to try to identify the problem, and they would call us in a week to give us their final results. I flew out again to pick up my family. We left on the Sunday so that I could be back in New York for training on Monday morning.

We arrived back at the apartment only to discover that our place was broken into and the television was gone. Most of the other valuables we had were lined up at the door, apparently the next items in line to be taken. Fortunately, one of the upstairs neighbors saw what was going on and scared the thieves away with the threat of phoning the police.

Now the day deteriorated from bad to worse. Everyone was drained upon our arrival home only to find out we were victimized, too. It was an eerie feeling to be violated – to realize you are so vulnerable. It was one of the few times in my life that I could appreciate the feeling that a woman must have, after a rape.

Chapter Three

Every emotion was hitting us, and hitting us hard. We wanted to kill the bastards who took advantage of every thing sacred to us. We were violated and now we looked to each other for support. If there was a weakness in Cindy or me that was inside or outside of our emotions, it had to be faced. The feeling of putting all the physical possessions away that we cared about created a sadness because time and thoughts were being wasted on bullshit pictures, televisions, and stereos, while our child's life should have been all that was on our minds.

This is a potent statement – but it's wrong. The strong people focus on what they can control, while the weaker people dwell on problems, not suitable solutions or paths to follow. Emotions at this point are fragile. Every hour felt like a day waiting for the doctors 300 miles away to give us the results we so eagerly wanted to hear, but were terrified to find out.

The doctors weren't living the next 60 years in their minds, but we were. The results came back and were conclusive. There was definitely a problem and the name of the problem was "Ritchie's syndrome." It was something that the doctors had never seen. The final word to us was that he may live six months, but with good care, maybe he would last a year. Cindy cared for him; she took him everywhere. By the age of five months, he was having grand mol seizures every five minutes. His only movement was the seizures. Other than that, he did not move at all.

Cindy would go to a store and lay Ritchie on a counter. People would rush over toward her, not knowing that this child was not going to fall off the counter. Those that didn't come over would just give the look to each other, questioning how stupid this woman was? When people were told that he wouldn't fall and given a brief reason why, it make it easy for Cindy because there were no lies. For the faint of heart, who, as Jack Nicholson says, "can't handle the truth" - too bad.

Feeding him was difficult, because swallowing only occurred as a reflex action. Cindy would feed him while he was lying down on his back, a good way for almost anyone else to choke. She would put baby cereal or fruit in his mouth and wait for him to swallow. Sometimes it could take hours to get a jar of food into his belly. Other times, it was amusing when he sneezed with a mouth full of green peas or carrots. The problems occurred when his organs didn't work right or he was constipated. Sometimes manual procedures were used. This may sound disgusting to the sheltered, but what do you think goes on in homes that care for people who can't care for themselves. It is part of life and it is hard. Every night, the baby screamed, but it was not pain. The sounds were erratic and there was nothing that could stop them from happening. By the way, that did not make for the best conditions for a pleasant sex life. Remember the carefree kid, who was married, with a kid on the way? In six months, he grew up and aged ten years – out of necessity. The vision of dragging a "vegetable" through life was not exciting.

The lawyers from the swim club followed the baby's progress with us. They were neat people, who since have passed away. He was an interesting guy – sensitive and jovial, and fairly carefree, while she was the meek-and-mild business lady lawyer. He specialized in criminal law and took pride in being good at his job, which he considered getting guilty people off by playing a better game than the other attorney. He told us about one case he had where he got this low-life off scot-free for writing numerous bad checks. Guess what happened to our friend, the attorney, when his client paid him by check! We believed that he wasn't even upset because it was so ironic. Her specialty, which we never even knew, was adoptions. She came to us; now knowing we had no hope of a healthy son.

"I'm getting you a healthy baby," she told us.

We had no idea or thought of adoption. We were so tied up with doctors, Phenobarbital, Dilantin, sleepless nights, working to support who knew what, and of course, some self-pity. When the idea was brought to us, we immediately said, "Great, thank you!"

Then we talked to people who adopted and began to learn about problems that many adopted parents faced. Despite the problems, a feeling of excitement was coming back to us year-old newlyweds. Within three weeks, the attorney called us and said the baby was due the next day. We thought that was impossible; people waited years for the opportunity to adopt and they were paying thousands of dollars in legal and illegal fees. Wow – a new baby six months after the first baby! It's hard to explain the type of thoughts that go through someone's head at this point.

Think about the entire situation. You are totally drained and concerned about your first-born baby. You have no idea of his future and want to give him all of your time while he is alive. You always have in the back of your mind that some miracle will happen and a cure will be found. You wonder what he will say when he really wakes up. He looks like a normal baby. You still hold out hope that this whole mess will go away, but you also know it won't.

I kept looking at Cindy to be sure she was handling everything and not going off the deep end. Cindy keeps looking at me to see where my head is because neither of us had any perception of what was in store for the future. We were still newlyweds and finding out about each other – each had our own sensitivities. Although Cindy was seven years older than me, the age gap narrowed to equality during the first 4 months with the baby. We're not sure if it narrowed upward or downward. The mind is everything in these types of situations. The mind could say to just get out of the picture and walk away from the problems.

This may sound unusual, but when the guy is young, and only looking to get laid, what is his first response to, "My period is late?" Generally it's, "Oh shit!", or the brilliant, "How did that happen?"

What a bummer, all the guy wanted to do was get his "rocks off" and the dumb bitch got pregnant! Remember guys, it was all their fault and you had no responsibility! What are we going to do? Of course one escape mechanism is that it is some other guy's baby, so that's her problem. All of those thoughts go with the immature or typical guy's mind who thinks with the head below the waist.

All of these thoughts, full of self-pity and negativity, where now mixed with the idea that another baby was coming the next day. Talk about not being able to see straight! I had a job that I was just trying to get used to. The job was a commission job, which meant there was pressure to make sales in a field I had no idea of what I was doing. I never had to make more money than I needed for the next couple of weeks. I never lived a high lifestyle considering when $50 bucks a week kept me in food, gas, and rent. The rest of the time high lifestyle only meant "high" like grass or hash. Foresight, without experience, was the proverbial pissing into the wind routine.

The baby was coming and Cindy was excited; I had no idea of anything except to try and keep everything rolling. I felt like I was in a fog, and everything was happening so fast there was no time to think.

To this day, which is twenty-five years later, I had no idea what was going on in Cindy's mind. We were together in action, but the thought process had to be so shallow. If everything were truly analyzed, I'm not sure if we would have or should have split because of all the pressure. There were other pressures; the kind most newly married couples face. That pressure was from the parents who could tell you what was best for you, even when you didn't ask or want an unsolicited opinion. Even when you politely said, "We can handle it."

Everyone has an opinion about everything, and everyone is more than willing to impose those opinions on you even though their lives are probably totally fucked up! Do you realize how much they resent you for not being grateful to them for giving you the solution that that thought you were unable to see? Don't these do-gooders realize that if you have half a brain, and four months to consider all options, that you have already looked at each scenario dozens of times and had the sense to project the ramifications and all the options? The problem is with each decision that we had to make, there were five or six effects that could occur, which were out of our control.

What if the now six-month-old baby lived longer than expected? Do we keep him, put him in a home, put him up for adoption, make him a ward of the state, etc.? If we keep him, who can take care of him 24-hours a day? Who can afford all of the extra medical bills? What about a "normal" marriage, sex, and companionship? What about getting a chance to play? Who wants to come home from work and be told it's your turn to play nurse to your non-responsive baby boy. It's depressing and not fun. It's like coming in from a storm, and instead of the sanctity and solitude of your own home, you walk into a tornado. There was a tenseness that had no escape; it was not logic that could overcome emotion when your entire life was consumed with the threat of the death of your baby and more self-pity.

The blessed day arrives and we get the call from the attorney to come down to her office to get our new baby. We still had no idea if it was a boy or girl. We went to the office, which was over 45-minutes away, and it seemed like hours. The thoughts that were going through our minds included health of the baby, cost to do all of this, what were we hoping for, and were we doing the right thing? The thought then came to mind about all the people who adopt because they can't have their own children, and then mom gets pregnant. Should we wait to try again? What would happen if Cindy got pregnant again shortly? What were the odds of another baby like the first one? Cindy's background in health answered that and it was confirmed in later conversations with doctors. The odds were 4:1 against it happening again. What would you do? The answer seemed pretty obvious to us. We made a decision right there that the odds were too great to risk another nightmare that could be another lifetime that takes six months to live through. Also, the possibility of whatever germ, disease, or missing enzyme could surface anytime throughout the child's life. That would equate to shock therapy which gave one the privilege of sitting comfortably in a chair with connectors all over your body, and waiting for someone to jolt the electric current at any time.

We finally arrived at the lawyer's office. The office was old, but had wood walls with beautiful carved decorations. We waited in the reception area about five minutes, and then we were called into her office and saw the blue blanket. The lawyer walked over to us and handed Cindy the baby, "Here's your new son."

Cindy told her his name was going to be Mark. The tears flowed from both of us and after about fifteen minutes she gave us the history of the mother, including where the baby was born and the mother's last name. That was unusual, but this was America and the world operated around who you knew. She explained the procedure of the adoption and the procedure at the orphan's court for the final decree. We listened while holding our new son and didn't hear a single word that she said. We were getting ready to leave and I asked how much we owed her. She gave us the hospital bill and all she said was, "Raise him well."

It was unique to have an attorney that benevolent when the

market was calling for thousands of dollars in fees. We tried to keep in touch with her, but time just didn't allow us that luxury or obligation since we now had two babies. She died of cancer two years later. It may sound corny, but this was one kind lady who put friendship and well being above all else. We hoped she found a comfortable place in heaven.

We got into the car with the baby and looked at each other and Cindy started to cry. I, being macho, turned away and wiped away my own tears. These were the first tears of joy in a long time. This was the light at the end of the tunnel. There was now a place to put the love and affection that was half-bottled up inside – a place where there was a future. This was a child that some day could say "I love you mom and dad." This may sound simple to those who have normal, healthy children. One cannot understand what it means to go home and look for the affectionate smile of the baby when he recognizes you, realizing that will never happen.

One should appreciate people's feelings when a tragedy involving a child occurs, and they say, "I'm going home to give my child a hug." A child does change the life of the typical middle-class suburban household because, well, because it does. Why leave out the rich and poor in those statements? The answer is, you have to be there to know, and we're not there. How badly that child was wanted is also a factor. How selfish are the parents is a factor. How grown up are the mom and dad is a factor. Dad, you have to go play a softball game at 5 p.m., but mom must be at work. Do you stay home? Get a sitter? Resent the baby because you can't play? Take the baby and hope another mom is there who will watch him for you? Which option did dad use in your family? Where are dad's priorities?

On the other side of the coin, mom wants to go shopping without taking along the baby. Does dad volunteer to watch him, go with mom so he doesn't have to change the diapers? Does he tell her to take the beeper so he can get her to come back when he needs some help? Does he call a neighbor, evoke sympathy, and eventually help? Maybe mom should take the baby even though she knows the baby should be in bed, but the choice is who comes first in the chain. Lots of options and we're sure you have already drawn some opinions. You probably faced many of the same situations.

We walked into the apartment and were greeted by all of the new grandparents. Cindy's father said he did not think adoption was a good idea. This was perfect timing, but typical of the nature of the beast. Cindy's mom was holding the baby, glowing with pride and ready to protect this child to any degree needed. Her eyes were filled with tears of joy. My parents were realists from their working class background and were cautiously happy for the kids. They were aware of the hardship and pain of the past 6 months, and they were glad to see some positive sparkles in our eyes.

You could see that everyone was concerned about taking on another responsibility since Ritchie needed 24-hour a day maintenance. Everyone knew the burden would fall heavily with Cindy. It didn't matter. Cindy started referring to this little package as her "little chicken."

Cindy was together, but experienced highs and lows with Ritchie. Did he smile or was it a seizure? Would he eat in thirty seconds or would it take three hours? This was a tough way to plan. If a person needs a rigid schedule, this was not it.

Mark was growing and Ritchie merely existing. Things settled a bit over the next six months, and more decisions had to be made. What could we do with Ritchie? He made it through the winter. Doctors said the first winter would probably kill him because he would catch a cold, which his immune system couldn't fight, and it would be over. That was one hell of a way to feel as we looked at our son every day and wondered if it would be his last. How do we value life? Maybe it wouldn't be the cold, maybe it would be an overdose or under dose of the Phenobarbital or the Dilantin. The dosage was constantly changing due to his condition in combination with his weight and food intake, which were all unpredictable. On several occasions we had to rush him to the hospitals because he was dehydrating or in a constant seizure. Have you ever seen a nine-month old strapped to a board getting an I.V. through his tiny head because his veins in his arms and legs were too small? It was not a pretty sight and the feeling in our stomachs made us nauseous when we saw it. He was alone in his fight because there was nothing to do but wait for the liquids to enter his body so that he could come home to wait to die.

Cindy spent many nights in the hospital with Ritchie waiting and hoping, knowing the results were already determined. I spent time with Mark but had no idea of what to do with him. Diaper changing was not anything that I had done or ever wanted to do. There were times when Mark had a stinky diaper and I would call Cindy to come home to change it, if she was anywhere in the area. How many husbands do you know that did the same? It does hit close to home, doesn't it? My patience level was low because I was in a place mentally that was so foreign to me that I couldn't handle the crying, which was normal. Now, there was resentment because there was no time to be alone with Cindy, and the level of our conversations was always so predictable.

What a dilemma; we had a healthy child and the normal roles of mom and dad were being redefined. Everyone should have been happy, except things couldn't be normal. It was also inconvenient when we were out with both kids because an innocent question such as "how old are they" became awkward for everyone. "One is three months and the other is nine months" was the typical response. "O.K., Ritchie is our natural, but he is sick. Mark is adopted and he's fine."

Sadly, our sarcastic responses were from frustration when the questions were innocent. Ritchie didn't look like a child who was retarded, but he didn't move and this was strange because all babies move. Cindy would take both kids shopping with her mother's help. We tried to have as normal a life as possible, with Cindy going full-force with motherhood and me establishing myself as a stockbroker starting to make a living to cover expenses, but still working from paycheck to paycheck.

We were exposed to many alternatives that were foreign to us including organizations that helped financially, helped with training and patterning, and homes that cared for these children 24-hours a day. Well, it was obvious to us that we could take care of our own child, but the patterning sounded like a good idea. After all, we still were hoping for that miracle. So Cindy took him to patterning for over a month, and soon realized that it was useless in Ritchie's case and a waste of time. Patterning was the use of people, in this case, mostly volunteers, who physically moved the body parts for Ritchie and others. The volunteers continued to pattern for hours and days, hoping to stimulate him to work the movements by himself. What was discovered was that there were lots of little children, with major deficiencies, that would be precluded from ever becoming productive, independent adults.

Chapter Four

We saw a whole new world and it was real and ugly. The terms cute and adorable do not fit. Kids like Ritchie were not pretty to look at; they could tell you a lifetime of pain through their warm eyes. You could see they were trapped in their bodies. They could show it by expressions on their faces; the joy when someone gave them that hug that said "I understand and love you."
These children had feelings that may not be understood, but they knew hugs, warmth, and the touch of caring people. We've seen kids live and die. We've seen kids with heads 10 times the normal size where you needed two people to carry the head and one to carry the body. It's not pretty in the world of the hydrocephalic. It's not pretty in the world of physical and mental retardation. The facilities always had beds that were geared for safety. There were obvious signs that these people were different. There were devices that were designed to work with each individual that included funny-looking braces, just to help kids tolerate pain by

keeping their arms and legs in the same position. There were huge balls that were used to roll the kids on stimulate their muscles. There were things that looked like they belonged in torture chambers in the medieval times, but they had a function.

We saw all of this, but Mark didn't because he was young and moving. We could put both kids on the floor and Mark would snuggle up to Ritchie, who would be propped up on a chair. It was sad because Mark was looking for some interaction, but none was to be had from the immovable object, his brother. Something had to be done because the only change taking place was time moving forward and Mark growing older day by day. The focus of the future had to stay with Mark, who was now eighteen months old. Ritchie was 2 years old.

What thoughts were going through our heads? We can't continue doing thirty-six hours of care in twenty-four. We were tired and Mark wasn't getting all of the attention that we thought he deserved. All of the love was there, but not the time needed to do the extra step. It became apparent that Ritchie was getting very tough to handle because his needs were so great. He would vomit three or four times during a meal due to reflex action. His screams were so loud that they would wake up neighbors at all hours. We were in an apartment and the walls were thin. His screams were not pain, but reaction of some unknown stimulus, and we were helpless to soothe him. We were kept wide-awake many nights by the erratic screams. There was nothing to do to stop the screams, and there was such compassion, because he was such a small, helpless, innocent child.

We decided that it would be beneficial for us to move to a home for future security, and simply because it was the next progression. We found a new townhouse (alias row home) development in the suburbs, and realized that we couldn't afford it based on the accepted financing formulas. But we did what every smart buyer does when they want something and are told they can't have it: we lied! Not only did we lie, we got a letter from my boss, which said I made double the salary I actually did. Now we qualified to purchase the home, which would be ready for us to move into within five months. While this was going on, we had to evaluate the situation with Ritchie.

Ritchie was dead weight to carry up and down the stairs. His body was skinny, but stiff. His head would flop in whatever direction was closest. It was involuntary. Mark was going full throttle, which was what kids do at age two. The combination just didn't mix. Cindy remembered that there were county advisors and counselors with whom we could discuss alternatives. She set up the appointment and met at their office. She spoke to them for over an hour and came away with knots in her stomach. The counselor said it would cost us over $25,000 per year to put Ritchie into a home, but the county would front the bill and we would pay it back from my income. I barely made the $25,000 and we needed it to live on. Our family would be allowed to keep enough of the income to live on and the county would supplement the balance. They also said it would be reviewed every year, which meant that if I had a good year, the county would take everything. That takes the incentive out of busting one's butt. Also, the expenses of the county's home went up every year as the payback increased. Then we reluctantly went to look at the county homes, which were clean, neat, and depressing. Picture twenty kids moaning aimlessly and in contraptions specifically built for their physical needs. It appeared to us that Quasimoto had his whole family at this one house. Don't let anyone tell you that it is the money that drives the people who work at these places. There isn't enough money in the world to do what some of these workers consider their daily routine. We still had decisions to make. We took Ritchie to the county association for the retarded and again, out of desperation, did patterning. In many cases, this procedure allowed for the comfort of the children who were basically waiting to die, but were not aware of it.

It was getting easier to make that awful decision each time Mark did something new and cute. We knew we had to put Ritchie into a home. We found one home two and a half hours away. The county recommended it, and had the funding for it. That meant we voluntarily move him there or they voluntarily move him there! Tough choice(sound sarcastic?), so we took him there. We were impressed -- the home was for unwed mothers and retarded children, and was run by nuns. It was a magnificent building with the most caring people that you could imagine. Every courtesy was extended and more. We felt good leaving in one way, but empty in another. The only part that made it tolerable was that Ritchie didn't know us. He didn't know our voices or probably our touch. His brain was smooth and he had a zero IQ. That was almost inconceivable, but it was true. Because of the lack of brain development, there was no message center to tell him of his senses. For all intents and purposes, he was blind and deaf. We could leave him with the hugs and kisses, but there never was a response from him. We went to see him every week for over a year, most of the time with Cindy's parents along for the ride. Every time we left him, there were tears and empty feelings in our guts. We kept wishing that there were some type of pill that would miraculously appear to make him normal. We loved him, but we were helpless. It was time for Mark.

We tried for a normal life with Mark. We bought a cute puppy, a toy fox terrier, because it was nice for a boy to grow up with a dog. It must be reminiscent of the old Dick, Jane and Spot books. We were now a typical family with nice neighbors and the little backyard. Children were playing on the cull de sac street and lots of people our age were gearing for their new lives in their new homes. Mark had his toys and his plastic tool set. He was happy and he had all of our attention.

Can you believe that after all that shit, we had found what everyone else had; a healthy family. We did all of the fun things, like the carnivals and playgrounds, and the Big Wheel. Mark played with all the little guys in the neighborhood, and appeared to be liked by all. We continued to see Ritchie but the frequency of visits lessened because of to the distance.

The county always put pressure on us as expenses at the home continued to escalate by about 5% per year. This was tough to handle. Our family's income was not stable because of having a commission job, so planning became difficult. Our home was fixed up as well as we could, with the contemporary look, including all of the imitation leather furniture. (Ecologists could say we saved some animals.) Our one-car garage was nicely packed with toys and the car that was handed down from Cindy's parents. We painted the entire house except the rooms that were papered by Cindy. Cindy liked to wallpaper in the nude. Sometimes it took longer than it should have when I helped with the cutting and pasting, but that happens when you are young. It just shows that there can be sexual activity through Mylar and grass cloth.

We paid $36,000 for the house, and were comfortable making the $400 per month payments. The utilities were all electric which took a lot of time to get used to because the temperature of the heat comes out at the setting of the thermostat, which is twenty or so degrees cooler than your body. That felt cold! Also, how many years were you programmed to "turning down the thermostat" when you left the house, just to save money. It was against our principle to keep the heat steady and not turn it down, because when you turn on electric heat, you use the emergency mode, which sends the meter in fast motion and costs much more. We had to buy storm windows and screens and we bought the wrong ones. Did you know that windows sweat? Not only do they sweat, they soak the wallboard and cause it to buckle. Ah, the joys of owning a home.

We were in the home about two years and feeling comfortable. Mark was three and a half years old. Ritchie was still alive but starting to get the look of a child with severe retardation. Our life was starting to form that "married couple with child" pattern. It didn't take long for that to change. Our next-door neighbor moved and a new young couple came in. He was a carpenter and she worked in an office as a receptionist. They had no children and were very amiable for the first two months that they were there. They moved there from a heavily bigoted area where fights were common occurrences at the corner bar. Their values were different than ours and it started to come out when he told me that he knew how to play the welfare game. He pulled up in a new car, stayed around the house at least half the week, and had a huge supply of beer within arms reach. Maybe that was the way to live. It made sense because we all work for the opportunity to be able to buy nice things and work little or not at all. We work to retire and he already has!

One night during the summer, we put Mark to sleep. His room was next door to the neighbor's playroom. Keep in mind that these were townhouses so a party wall was on both sides of us. It was now midnight on a Tuesday. All of a sudden, we heard loud bangs that were constant in thirty-second bursts. We woke up and scrambled to see if the house was falling down. After a few minutes, we realized the noise was coming from the room next to Mark's bedroom. We phoned our neighbors to ask what was wrong. They said nothing was wrong and they had a bunch of friends over and they were playing air hockey. I told them it was keeping up our entire family. I was told that they could do whatever they want, and not to bother them. But they also said to come over for a beer, because all of their friends were over and they would be doing this all night. I was pissed because of their inconsiderate attitude for a three-year old. They stopped about 3 a.m.

The next day I saw the neighbor in the backyard, and told him I thought it was very inconsiderate of them to do what they did, and I didn't appreciate it. With that, the neighbor, who was ten years younger than me, fifty muscular pounds heavier and six inches taller, said we could settle the issue right now. He said that he would beat the shit out of me and proceeded to walk toward me. This would have been suicide -- mine! I quickly said that if he came on my property, and laid a hand on me, I would have him in jail for the next twenty years. The guy bought what I said and stopped cold in his tracks. How stupid could he be because anyone with common sense knows that he would be given the benefit of the doubt in a courtroom? My jaws could be wired, ribs broken, and pain everywhere, but the law would say I provoked him and he feared for his safety. I probably would be fined and put on probation on the condition that I get counseling. This was one time that I was glad to see brains win over brawn.

About nine months after we were situated in the new home, the county notified us that since they were subsidizing Ritchie, they felt that it would be better for him to be closer to our county since a social worker periodically had to check on him. Also, they had an opening closer to home. We went out to see the facility, which physically, was very nice. We approved it, which was a mandatory approval, and the physical move was made. This facility was only twenty minutes away, which would allow us to visit weekly, which we did. After about three months, we noticed that Ritchie appeared to be in visible discomfort. We examined him thoroughly, and were horrified when we pried open his mouth. His teeth were decayed down to the exposed nerves. We went ballistic with the management. We then studied the entire situation, and watched more closely at the goings on. The caretakers for the small, immobile children were the severely mentally retarded older population that was educable. Cindy watched as the caretaker fed Ritchie. She pushed the food down his throat not realizing that she was banging the metal spoon against his teeth with tremendous force. Then she was patting him on the back to soothe him, but the force of the pats could have knocked out Mike Tyson. This was creating a dilemma. We were going to be in a war with the administration of the home and the county was torturing our child. We could not move him to another home, as there were no openings, and the county officials brushed off our request; they had far more bureaucratic things far ahead of us on the list. Also, Ritchie could have been displaced if we caused too much of a stir.

The logical conclusion was to win the lottery and take away

all of the pressure. That didn't work because I believe that you have to buy tickets to have the opportunity to win. Since that wasn't going to happen, we had to explore other steps. We decided to move back to the original county that we lived in because the financial and social treatment of kids like Ritchie was much more favorable. They gave the families more freedom to choose which home their child would go to if there were openings and they did more realistic evaluations of the family's living style in order to determine what payment would be made from their income.

It took us one week to look at homes in order to make a final decision. Cindy's father told us that we couldn't afford to move. We expected that comment since her father was from the old school that said "if you can't pay cash for it, you shouldn't have it." We put down a deposit and picked the lot right next to the sample home in a new development that was in our old county. The lots were on half an acre, and the homes were beautiful. The builder was trying to set up a reputation, so he was giving away things most builders charged for; it worked out great for us. Picking the lot next to the sample was a smart thing to do because they always build the sample homes on the best lots. The home was gorgeous and something we never thought we would be able to afford. The selling price was $68,900. The colonial home was a 4 bedroom, with 2.5 baths, a 2-car garage, and was on ½ acre. There was an option to expand the house by two feet, which would have been great, except it cost an extra $1,000. Scratch that! We had to sell our house and get financing for the new one. How do you sell a townhouse where there are hundreds already built and more new ones going up daily by the same builder? Realize that a home that is two years old that has been fixed up is usually a better deal than the brand new one, but it is hard to convince buyers of that.

Cindy wrote up a brochure and stood in front of the sample homes every Saturday and Sunday, handing out the two pages describing our home and driving people back the two blocks to see it. I would go over every few hours to take my shift, but I was not happy wasting my weekend days. This went on for about a month and finally someone wanted our house. Did we ever get that agreement typed in a hurry! The home sold for $39,000 and we were flying high. In the meantime, we applied for the mortgage for the new home. The application went in with the usual liar's letter stating what enormous income would be received through the year based on commissions received so far. This is a wonderful country that says that if a buyer wants to buy, and a seller wants to sell, everyone is a buddy to connive, steal, and cheat the banks and mortgage companies to make it happen. All was successful and the both mortgages went through. Everything now went back to ethical dealings because everyone got what they wanted. Even monopoly has a jail for landing wrong, but this is called business. I'm not sure, but this was not in economics 101 or even 102, the advanced course.

The new house was almost ready. Cindy drove over to it every other day since it was only fifteen minutes away from where we lived. It was a neat experience to see our future home being built right before our eyes. Even though it was the same home as the other 50 some odd homes being built, it was ours. We would take Mark there in the stroller and walk the muddied ground. Then we would go into the wooden frame structure trying to picture what it would look like with the walls up. It looked monstrous. Many days when we were there, we would check the studs to be sure good ones were used; sometimes studs would have big knots in them and would be useless for support. We kicked in the weak studs when we saw them just to be sure that they would be replaced the next day. The workers were there every day, and there were some characters. First there was the dog, a collie, from up the street that knew the area because he used to roam the fields when it was farmland. He came down to the work area every day about 11:30 a.m., just in time to beg for food from all of the workers. His nickname was Jaws. He was so friendly that his nose could pick your pocket while you were petting him. Then there were the carpenters. This was the first time that we learned that there were rough carpenters and finish carpenters. Don't ever let a rough carpenter do finish work. It's like watching an elephant do ballet. The only difference is the carpenter's work is supposed to last, after the performance. We can't forget the painter, Al. He was contracted by the owner to whitewash the inside of all of the new homes prior to settlement. He was scary, but he was nice. As you spoke to him, his eyes, which were spaced-out looking, got real glassy. He apparently kept inhaling the paint and enjoyed whatever planet he was on, as a result of the fumes.

The home was nearing completion in November. It was cold outside, but that didn't stop our frequent visits to our new home. We were friendly with the builder and he did things that would be frowned upon in today's market. He allowed us to go into the home and wire the alarm system ourselves before we made settlement, and before the walls were up. He also allowed us to lay the floors in the foyer and kitchen areas. We were not mechanics or craftsmen, but felt that we had to save money by doing it ourselves. Besides, how hard would it be to lay a floor? A friend of ours who had done it at his house said he would help. So Cindy, me, and our friend were laying a floor. Picture a small-enclosed area that is measured out to lay a tile floor. By the way, you start from the middle and work towards the sides to keep it centered. We learned that from our friend. What he learned was that you can't work with mastic or glue on a floor with no ventilation and not get high as a kite. It was amazing how unimportant the floor became after two hours of sniffing this stuff. The doors were closed and a space heater was on to keep the right temperature to allow the glue to dry. We decided that it was the glue or us. After much deliberation, we opened the doors and hoped everything would be all right. It was, and we were, and we shortly came out of the clouds.

We settled the home and the movers did their usual job leaving minor scratches on the walls and they completed the move that day. The ground was basically hard, mostly mud or dirt, but the floors appeared to be staying where we put them; life was again looking great. We had the usual window decor of pillowcases and sheets while we were getting adjusted, but it was great that we were in before Christmas. It will be neat to have a fireplace for the holiday season.

Our first attempt at a warm, cozy fireplace was an experience. We had no idea there is something called a flue, which must be opened before you light the fireplace. If you don't open it, and you start a fire, the house fills with smoke. After you panic and burn your fingers trying to open the damn thing, you then have to run all over the house opening all the doors and windows to let the smoke out. This is standard operating procedure for most people who never used a fireplace before. The fireplace is much easier to use the second time.

We adjusted to everything pretty well the first month. There was so many things to do when moving into a new home, like hanging pictures, arranging furniture, then rearranging it to better utilize the space, organizing all of our things, making lists for things we needed at the hardware store, etc. None of these things were a big deal since we were happy and we were where we wanted to be to raise Mark. We had him in the nice picture-perfect suburban setting. One sample home was located next door and the other was two doors away. One cold Sunday morning, when I was at the breakfast table with Mark, a man and his wife walked into the house. He was saying to his wife, as he was walking into the kitchen, that how much this house looked like the other sample home. They stopped in their tracks, and we all stared at each other for a few seconds. I think they were more surprised than I was. I was wearing shorts, but no shirt. When I told him that he just walked into our home unannounced and uninvited, the intruder looked like he wanted to crawl under a rock. Since he appeared sincere, I invited them to stay for coffee. I believed that he may have bought one of the homes, but I wasn't sure.

It was always a wonderful feeling when Cindy, Mark, and I, as a family, pulled into the driveway and at the end, sat our home. It was as if we drove up a private path and into heaven. It was only a fifty-foot double drive, but it was ours, and it was so much more than we dreamed of having.

We were so proud and that was an indescribable feeling. That sense of pride came to a halt very abruptly when the first electric bill came in the mail. My heart stopped momentarily, as I read $543 on the bill. My first reaction was to put a sale sign on the home. I calmed down and my second reaction was the same as my first. We were able to survive the shock and reality set in after that. The bills were less than half of that in the ensuing months. We learned another lesson about taking the chill out of a new house; it costs lots of money!

Chapter Five

We had contacted the social services in the new county and they remembered Cindy from before; they still had her old records. We liked this county better. The county workers sat with Cindy again and said there was an opening in one of the homes that was only one mile from our new home, and the best operator in the state ran it. We interviewed with him and it became obvious to us that this going to work out just great. We had come to the realization that miracles don't happen, and we couldn't control our own actions based on trying to gain unrealistic foresight. Ritchie was never going to improve and he would eventually die. He remained in this new home for three years. This home had fifteen children, and there were at least four people taking care of these kids most of the time. The home was a three-story building located next to a small church. There were many fire drills and the people at the church, many of them neighbors, knew they would be needed in case of an emergency. Many of them even participated in some of the fire drills.

I had discussions with the operator of the home about resuscitating Ritchie should he be in a position to need such measures. The owner, from a very religious Catholic background, believed every life had a value and a purpose. I told him I didn't think Ritchie's did. I said we didn't want any heroic measures taken should the occasion arise. We disagreed over the definition of heroic measures. Do you think tube feeding is heroic or is an IV heroic? These are questions that have various, but inconsistent answers. I kept saying Ritchie's life had no redeeming qualities, and the operator of the home disagreed. Cindy told him that Ritchie's day had turned into one major seizure from the time he woke up until the time he went to sleep. The owner disagreed. Ritchie developed a cold that winter that created complications; he had turned blue and was rushed to the local hospital. Cindy received the call when he got there. By the time he arrived at the hospital by ambulance, his color had returned and he was released that night. In the meantime, I was calling every hospital administrator saying that there was to be no resuscitation. We wanted his suffering to end. About three months later, a snowstorm kept many employees from getting to the home. The operator sat with Ritchie for six hours. He called Cindy and said that he could not believe what he saw. He lost count of the seizures and agreed that there was no quality of life. He said that Ritchie would have been better off if he just died. Everyone realized that this child was healthy except there was no brain wave activity. He was getting great exercise from the seizures, which positively affected his entire body. His heart was strong because it too, was getting conditioning during the seizures. His life was not going to be cut short the way all of the experts had predicted. He was labeled to be institutionalized until his demise.

Mark was now preschool day care because we wanted him to get that good start on learning. He was sent to a Montessori school, because we were advised that the children could move ahead at their own pace. What a great idea! We didn't want any undue pressure on our little boy. The school was only five minutes from the house and located in the basement of a local church. There was a beautiful play area and the setting was like a picture post card. Mark would come home every day and Cindy would say " what did you do today at school"? His answer was "nothing." She thought he was shy and just wanted to do his independent thing. Cindy went to the open house, met with the teacher, and asked her the same question to which she confirmed that he did nothing. We pulled him out of that system that day because he was not being motivated. We felt that in his case, more structure was needed. Cindy asked him why he didn't do anything and he said that the teacher dropped her pencil and told him to pick it up. He didn't want to pick it up, so he wasn't going to do any work for her.

How are parents supposed to realize that the little children's perspective of school was to try to please someone else? There must be thousands of incidents that affect children in some negative way, and parents don't realize what they are.

It amazes me to watch the expressions on the faces of little children; the expressions tell an enormous story. The hurt when you take something away from them, or the defiance when you say "no." The expression they give you of whether to cry or not when they fall, especially if you are watching them at the time. The concerned look they get, waiting to see what you will say when they spill their juice on the rug, especially since you told them not to be on the rug. The fear of riding their bike for the first time without training wheels; the look of question when the dog knocks him down and licks food off his face; and when you scold him and he realizes that you lost it and he feels fear from you being out of control.

We ask ourselves how important are these moments in time, and 100's of others that you share? What affect will experiences like this have on a child's future? According to the "experts," the most important time in a child's life is the first three to six years. These are supposed to be the years that determine the child's personality and temperament. How many of us who are raising children analyze each little thing that we do, in terms of the future affect it would have on our children? How many times did dad get pissed off when the young child would cry uncontrollably for no reason? Dad would scream back and brilliantly say, "stop crying," or put a strong grip on his or her tender little arm. Dad had no idea of what to do or why. In most cases, after deep analyzing, one could probably solve the problem with dry underwear, a nap or food. Now that dad is frustrated, he can probably solve his own problem with a nap or food. Hopefully, dad has not reached the dry underwear stage. Isn't it strange how problems can be solved so easily when just basic needs are considered?

Now we were faced with the problem of finding the right preschool. First of all, no one knows the real story that goes on at any of these facilities when you were not there. You assume you do, because they said you could stop in anytime to be comfortable. The children are very delicate at this stage of their lives, and what do we do? We dump them into a facility that was recommended by someone whose kids are there. Do you know for sure that the kids were not mentally abused by being put down or constantly rejected? Do you know what activities they had? Who did the colored papers that they brought home? Did they eat all of their lunch or were you told they did because that's what you wanted to hear? Did they spend a lot of the day in 'quiet time' or 'time out' or whatever they called it then? Did the preschool people ever try to explain why the child was being disciplined, or was the child just being punished and beginning to hate school and getting the feeling that he was a bad boy?

Put yourself in the teacher's position. Do you ever run out of patience? When you do, what is your attitude toward the people around you? We all are satisfied that we did the best job that we could and our baby is safe while we work. One of the questions that haven't been resolved is "why does my kid always like to be at the end of the line?" There must be a reason that he gets in line and then makes sure that he methodically works his way to the end. I was always under the impression kids were naturally selfish and wanted everything now; wanted it first before the other kids. Then we had to be sure that he was physically similar to all the

41

other kids, because we all want our kids to be like everyone else's. Now we are saying that they are being maneuvered to be followers, by dressing like the others and being told to be good like ... Are we giving mixed messages? What about height and weight? We were told Mark was short but within the limits of normalcy, whatever that means. Did we want him to be a leader or a follower? Did we want him to be creative or did we want to mold him? Did we want him to grow up happy in the way his genes told him to, or were we confused about how to raise a child? Should it be Green eggs and ham or Dr. Spock? Does anyone really know what is good for the child? Everyone agrees that we should teach kids to say " please and thank you." Everyone says to say excuse me until the children are recognized. What good are manners if we are giving the children mixed messages? Be polite and courteous, but don't let anyone fuck with you.

Chapter Six

Mark was 4-years-old and getting in all kinds of typical boy mischief. He was quiet, slightly spoiled, and demanding since in reality, he was an only child. He loved to play ball and hug mom. Mom was his security blanket. Cindy and I idolized him – he was moving and talking like a real boy. After the experiences and pain with Ritchie, there was no stopping the presents, trips, or anything that made Mark happy. I was thrilled to see that my "macho" son could throw a ball slightly farther than the other neighborhood kids. Was that me trying to relive my life through my son? Why did dads do this?

We were at the point of talking seriously to Mark because he was becoming aware of his surroundings and beginning to ask questions about family. He knew he had a brother, but why didn't he live with him. He knew that the other kids in the neighborhood lived with their brothers and sisters. It seemed easy to tell him that Ritchie was sick and couldn't do all of the things that he could, but we all loved him. Was that sending a message that if Mark couldn't do something that we would tell him that he couldn't live here either? We thought that we showed him stability, but did we? What was stability for a four-year-old? What was going on in his mind? He had to feel comfortable because we let him pick out his own clothes and sneakers. Even at four, kids loved their sneakers – thanks to television advertising. If Barney or Pokemon told kids to wear green sneakers, bet that there would be a run on them. I didn't mention price because mom paid that extra $15 to make junior happy. I bitched and said it was ridiculous, but to be honest, I'd buy them for Mark, too. I just had to teach everyone that it was hard to make a dollar and you should think before you waste it. During all of these questions and answers between parents and children, decisions had to be made about the adoption situation.

"Your mom and dad are not your real mom and dad" was the statement you feared would happen one day. It would happen because someone you knew was talking and his or her kids heard it, didn't know what it meant, but repeat it because gossip starts at a very early age.

When was the first time you started gossiping? It could have been when your four-year-old friend took a cookie, his mom told him not to take the cookie, and you told your mom that your friend took the cookie when his mom told him not to take the cookie, and you saw the whole thing.

You get the idea of the beginning of some of the bullshit that lasts a lifetime, and tends to mold your personality. Try and go through your day today and don't talk about anyone in a way that could be misconstrued or negative. Make it easy on yourself – make it four hours when you are with friends.

Now we must decide how to explain to him that we loved him from the instant he was born, and even though he didn't come out of mommy's belly, he was our baby. We must make him understand something of a concept that was well beyond his years. We must avoid his feelings of early rejection from his natural mother and father, who wasn't named on the birth certificate. We must tell him that it wasn't his fault that his birth mommy and daddy weren't together. We've got to assure him that he was a special gift from God. We must do everything to keep him psychologically in the right frame of mind and hope that genetics take a secondary role.

We start this gracious and magnanimous gesture of tenderness and warmth by lying to him about the gift from God. He was a result of a one-night stand or possibly a wild drunken stupor from his teenage mother. He was an accident and no one gave a damn about him. He was destined to be extra money on the welfare check. No thought was given to his future. He was born in the slums and pre-natal care was a foreign language to his natural mom. Remember that the object of his mother for getting a boyfriend was to have a baby. The man/boyfriends didn't want burdens like kids because that meant responsibility and child support. For many of the girls in the slum areas, they didn't know or like birth control, and it was no big deal to be pregnant. Sometimes it was a badge of honor. Anyway, either her mom or aunt would 'help' meaning do everything which would allow the young mom to go party and get knocked up again. So we lied to the child, took the easy way out, and did it for his sake. Where do you start and where do you stop? It depended on the effect it had on the child. After you explained it, it was impossible to know if it meant anything or if any of it was understood. You also didn't know how it would be interpreted in the mind of a four-year-old child.

Try and put yourself into the head of a four year old that you know. With all of the technology of today, it would appear that a solution of how, when, and where should be step-by-step easy. Whenever the mind is involved, especially two generations, it is hard to get deep into the other person's head. Even if you think that you have done the explanation perfectly, you can't be sure for years to come. Even then, there are too many variables throughout one's lifetime. The people who say it is easy are ignorant, selfish, and don't understand any thoughts other than themselves.

Mark was now six years old, and being led into an exciting picture-perfect world. He got his first taste of organized sports. We went back to the old traditions believing that kids who were involved in healthy activity were less likely to get into trouble in later years. We associated with the kind of kids whose parents were concerned about keeping them walking the straight and narrow path. These were the cute boys and girls who were coached by their dads who were reliving their childhood fantasies through the kid's eyes. There was soccer, basketball and baseball. It was amazing to watch the kids line up on a soccer field. Days were spent teaching these athletes of the future the positions and the functions of the sport. The forwards knew that they were to keep within their designated area and pass to the open teammate. The halfbacks and fullbacks learned exactly what to look for on the field, and where and when to kick the ball. The goalie knew how to dive and extend to keep the ball out of the net. This was a well-oiled, six-year-old soccer team ... until the game started. The whistle blew and eleven players, probably all dressed the same in yellow or stripes, converged on the ball like a swarm of bees kicking it wherever they could. The other team was in the same predicament, so actually there were twenty two players that were moving together with a few occasionally falling down and getting up again. All of the strategy and planning was out the window.

This was the theory of raising children. You plan and direct, but when they must play the game on their own, you stood on the sidelines laughing, crying, screaming, and yelling directions, but they didn't listen. You did the best job that you could and who knew what the results of the game would be. You called a timeout and talked to the team. The game resumed and three or four of the players now began to understand what the coach was talking about. As the game proceeded, a few more players began to understand. The game ended and some caught on completely and others still hadn't a clue. This takes us back to explaining the adoption situation. It was the same as the soccer game. Each coach used the same rules and tried to teach the basics to the kids, yet each one had similar results in realizing that the knowledge and execution of the game were at both ends of the spectrum. Doesn't it sound like the "game of life"?

The little league baseball and basketball leagues were similar. As parents, you wanted the kids to get to know each other and then have good, healthy interaction. For the most part, it worked. There were exceptions, because one parent would take it too seriously and make a fool out of himself or berate his or another child for their performance, rather than try to encourage effort. Sure, some of these kids were terrible, but everyone knew that that kids either try their best and succeed beyond their capabilities, or they don't. These kids were under tremendous strain whether or not they were consciously aware of it – peer pressure, self-pressure, and often, parental pressure. That's a lot of stress for a six-year-old. What went through their minds when they went up to the plate knowing that there were two outs in the last inning and they were the final hope? They knew they were the one the whole team was counting on to get that hit; and everyone knew that this poor individual would feel much more comfortable playing chess. What effect did it have when their teammates said either "nice try" or did they privately say, " You blew the game"? Aren't sports wonderful?

It was entirely dependent on the individual's inner feelings, the coaches and team's attitudes, the parent's attitudes, and the perception of all of those involved. It comes down to what the brain perceives of the situation and the short or long-term effects and the variables that effect the past perception. Sounds confusing because it is. There is never the perfect reaction by any individual because everyone is so different with different perceptions.

We decided that we wanted Mark to know, from us, the entire situation, even at six years old. We knew that many people were aware that he was adopted, and the many ways that he could have found out were all unpleasant to us. We sat him down and began with "you know we are your mommy and daddy, and we love you more than anything in the whole world."

This was a great start. We didn't think that we traumatized him yet.

Next, we told him that he was a very special boy because he was a gift that was chosen. We continued with how many of his friends came from their mommy's bellies but he was in another lady's belly. We told him how we were there when he was two days old and with all the babies in the world, he was the one that we wanted and no one else. We told him that we hugged him all the time that we had him and how good he was. We told him how proud we were of him because of all the good things that he did and we mentioned all of the things that could build his six-year-old ego bigger than the Empire State Building. What more could be done?

In the meantime, there was not much going on with Ritchie. He was just being cared for by the home and given love and affection in a way that no one understood. Reports came back to the family that said that he was responding well to certain stimuli such as music and stroking of his brow. In fact, it was down to a science in that the report would say he made sighs of relief three out of ten times when his brow was gently rubbed or he smiled four times out of ten attempts when a bell would ring. This was wonderful for the review sheets, but not realistic. It was very strange to watch someone who was in a semi-coma or someone in the position of Ritchie who looked retarded and had involuntary reflexes. If you looked at them for three or four hours, your mind started to play tricks on you. You started to see his eyes following yours for two or three seconds. Then you tried to figure out what you did to make him do that. The truth was that he happened to have the reflex in the same direction that his eyes were moving. You were not crazy. This happened all of the time. After you spent day after day with these individuals, it was easy to imagine that they smiled when you came into the room, when it really was a startle reflex from noise or them awakening or having a seizure. Ritchie's seizures made the left side of his face move upward, and the left side of his mouth curled upward giving the impression of a crooked smile. The caretakers looked for any positive with the kids and that probably was what kept them going. The rest of his body was strained as earlier described. Every time we visited, the time became shorter as we could do nothing except stroke his hair and talk to him with no reciprocation.

We pretty much were resolved that Ritchie would continue to be in this state of vegetation for as long as he lived. We visited him at least once a week, but stopped taking Mark as often. It was very difficult to explain all of the messed up bodies that Mark saw and explain why those kids couldn't do the things that he could. Seeing Ritchie like this was having an effect on Mark, but we didn't know to what degree. Ritchie was about twenty pounds and his hands had atrophied somewhat, even though he was wearing medical appliances to help prevent that. He also had a fungus on his hands that was peeling off his skin. Creams were being used to help stop the peeling, but the problem seemed to linger on. We couldn't tell if he was in pain or discomfort, but everyone tried to address the obvious problems and hoped to at least cure those. Everyone always tried to keep things light so they sometimes fantasized that he played with all of the normal kids. "Where would he play if the kids played baseball?" The answer was "the kids were missing second base and since Ritchie didn't move, they could lay him there."

Yes, it was sick and demeaning, and the do gooders frowned at such insensitive humor. That was how you got by; you lightened up. If you haven't walked in these shoes, you can't have the knowledge to advise someone else. Forget all the religious beliefs and moralities that were breed about the value of any life. Watch these kids for a week and then talk about quality of life. If you had a pet that you raised and that pet gave you happiness and companionship, and the vet told you that your pet may live six months, but was going to be in terrible pain, but with medication, you could keep it alive, what would you do? The answer is that if you love that pet, you don't want it to suffer. If you were in the same situation, would you want to linger with no quality of life? Our society says we must. We presently have thousands of Dr. Kevorkians in the veterinary field. Why can't we, as humans, be treated as fairly as our beloved pets? There was always the thought of taking Ritchie out of his misery, but it was not legal, even though we felt it was humane.

We were friendly with a doctor at a local children's hospital who worked it out with me that if Ritchie were brought in for treatment, and he needed help eating, if I stayed in the room, the physicians would not administer anything that would take him out of a coma, which he would go into quickly. Is this what is referred to as "estate planning?" Again, these should not be the thoughts of a young couple, but you play the cards you are dealt.

Mark was growing up and had all of his neighborhood buddies. They went to school together and all of the parents were friendly. We all met at the local sporting events and talked about how each child was maturing, and all of the same old nonsense that every suburban community had. That was fine for the next five years with some of the kids becoming students and others lacking the maturity to value the responsibility to go with the program. Some had become students, but had no idea why other than mom said they couldn't do this or that unless their work was done correctly. Other parents did all of their kid's work with them, which gave the kids confidence in doing their work. Some of the kids started playing musical instruments and others just watched television. The elementary school was typically suburban, and life was again fine.

Mark was one of the kids who fought the study system and tried to get by without working. It didn't work. He got mostly C's and had to be pushed to do his homework. He was shorter than the other children, which gave him a slight inferiority complex. He was a good athlete, but not the best in the group. He always made the local all-star teams and was liked by almost everyone. He was a practical joker and always was quickly sarcastic. He had a good background from traveling a number of times to Disney World with us, and being with adults more than he was with multi-kid families. He was worldly, but lacked confidence. He was afraid to try new things because he feared that he would fail. It's strange, but if you line up lots of children in the ten-year-old range, then watch their facial expressions as they go through some exercises, you can easily predict the ones that are already having problems or the ones that are begging for approval. You can see which ones are confident and which ones are almost there. It would be nice to be able to shake all of the problems out of the kids and tell all of them that they are as good as the next kid, and it's good to be proud. That is another pipe dream because too many extraneous factors don't allow that to happen. Loving the kids is a strong factor that helps, but what makes each kid look at himself differently in the mirror is the ingredient that we can't figure out.

Since he was an athletic type kid, we involved Mark in ice hockey because we thought it would be nice for him to learn to skate, which would also be a confidence builder. Little did we know that he would enjoy the sport and want to stay in it for the next six years. We also didn't realize that games could be three hours away or start at 6:00 a.m. We learned that ice hockey parents are dedicated and only expect the best. Also, they are more vocal than parents of other sports. In ice hockey, where checking was not allowed until eleven years old, the parents gave each other the high sign when their kid hit another kid to get even for something. Was this teaching the children rules and discipline?

While all of the actions were taking place with Ritchie and Mark, we decided to buy a timeshare near Disney World because we loved the idea of getting away from reality. We felt it was a great place for Mark to be where politeness and manners were the habit of all "cast members," who are really Disney employees. I was making a living and was able to play with some of my salary to buy the timeshare. I was established in my field and had become a valuable commodity. I was able to move around in firms for large bonuses and not have it count as income. That was a break because I was able to put away big dollars that we would need as things progressed with Mark and Ritchie.

Mark was now thirteen –a teenager. He had his own mind and decided that school was not important as he widened his circle of friends. He was in junior high school, and that meant that two local elementary schools were now passing their kids onto the one big guy's school. New relationships formed. The boys were intently "reading" the Playboy centerfold. Remember that we used the National Geographics? The boys were starting to get their pencils pointed and their hormones bubbling. The boys were hanging with the fourteen- and fifteen-year old "big guys" and were starting to imitate their older brothers. They saw the older kids talk about getting beer or hanging out or grabbing some girl.

Their imaginations were also starting to run very wild. These kids were very susceptible to the girls who were starting to fill out their blouses, and the boys were following the leader to look and feel older. As parents, your mode of influence dwindles; you could be lied to without realizing it because there had never been a reason not to trust your son. The grades from school were starting to drop and we were concerned about his study habits. There were none. He got on the phone and you heard a tone that you had never heard before. He started to talk as if he was raised like an animal. Do you tell him you eavesdropped? Do you ignore it, keep a more watchful eye on the mouth, and politely tell him how the American language is used under your roof? Do you go back and punish him for improper behavior? Remember, that in his mind, you are old and not hip. You don't understand what today is about (he may be right about that). Do you use logic or force? We could have been nasty and teased him about hearing that he carried his books in front of his pants in school because he had a hard dick. Would embarrassing him bring him down to reality? Probably not, but we were annoyed and frustrated, so weird thoughts came into our minds.

We used logic and explained to Mark that he could communicate without language that became primitive. Mark then told us to mind our own business. At that, I became primitive, lost it, and smacked Mark across his face to get his attention. It worked and he began to understand what our

51

country practices in all of its foreign policy; might means right. I was annoyed at myself for losing my temper and Mark was embarrassed that he was the object of being put down. It was a no-win situation for everybody.

Mark was now running around with 8" spiked hair, usually black, but different colors were used, and heavy black leather with chains and hanging at the mall. He looked ridicules and we couldn't help making comments to him. I said to him that I had a great idea. You see, I used to wear a hairpiece and still had it in his closet. What else could you do with it? It is not something that most consignment shops wished to resell! Anyway, I cut the hairpiece on both sides and jelled the spike the middle. I then set it on my head so we had father/son hairdos. Was this bonding or what? I asked him how it looked and suggested that we go to the mall together. Mark didn't find it amusing. He was looking for an identity and the tough-guy image seemed to fit. He would wear all black and make sure that he didn't smile because that would ruin the image. The crew he was sometimes with was doing grass and we didn't know it. We just thought that our baby was "lost." One evening, I came across a bottle of pills that did not look familiar. I asked Mark what they were. Mark said they were his, but he wasn't sure what they were. That pissed me off because not only was Mark lying, but also, he was being stupid. I took Mark to the local police station and met with one of the officers in charge. I called the station in advance to ask that they scare the hell out of Mark; maybe help wake him up to the realities of drugs. We got to the station and I took a back seat and listened. The officer couldn't identify the pills, but said he would send them to the lab. He probably could have taken them to the drug store and the pharmacist could have identified them. He was trying to scare Mark, but also be professional. I thought he did good, especially when he said that he would allow Mark to go home and get one more chance to not be identified as a criminal. That brought a sigh of relief to Mark, but usually, lessons were forgotten quickly.

The group Mark associated with were doing skateboards and

trying to have a tough image. He still kept some of his old local friends, but only to talk to, not hang out. The relationship was now a power struggle between the new teenager and dear old dad. Mom was in the middle and was torn, but made everything as smooth as possible, until the night that the local police called us to say that Mark had been picked up for underage drinking with a few of his friends. We went to the police station, sat with the officers and found out that three boys were in the local Pizza Hut parking lot drinking beer. Our initial thoughts were that it was nice to know that our thirteen-year old liked beer with his pizza. Then, I got furious when I saw him and his attitude was not of remorse. This tended to get me more upset and violence was on my mind. I wanted to beat him into obeying, but that was what emotion was about. Our son and one of his friends, who was fifteen, were in the holding tank. We saw bars and our son locked up like an animal waiting to go to the bathroom or be handed food. The officer asked if we would take the other boy home because they couldn't reach his mom, he lived ten miles and three townships away, and it was 11:00 p.m. at night. We said we would and brought both of them to our home. We put Mark in his room and the friend in the fixed up basement on the sofa, giving firm instructions for both not to leave their rooms and we would discuss the matter in the morning when the kids sobered up.

We woke up at 7:30 a.m. and the kids were gone! What were our choices at this point? The police didn't care yet. No one had any idea where to look, so we decided to wait by the phone or until Mark got hungry and tired. We didn't know whether to hug him or kill him when we caught up to him.

We waited and then waited some more. It was now 9:00 p.m. We were very upset, as each minute was more like an hour. All kinds of sordid thoughts entered our minds. I kept looking at Cindy, each other knowing each other's feelings, and knowing that there was nothing to do but wait. We said we better try to get some sleep because he will probably try to call in the middle of the night and we will be running somewhere to get him. We were drained! We both fell asleep, but it was a restless sleep. We were up at 6 a.m. We had to do something. We called all of the hospitals in the city and suburbs to see if anyone came in. Cindy called the local police who said there was nothing that came in on the wires regarding any kids about 13 years old. We waited some more. The second day, the police put out his photograph to all departments in this and surrounding states. Three more days went by and still no word from him. Our thoughts were of abduction and death. We knew he was rebelling, but he wouldn't do this to us, right. That was a dumb thought. He was doing it to himself and we were not even a thought in his mind. He was into his own problems, or adventures, and could not conceive the pain a parent goes through as part of the "wonderful world of child-rearing."

So Mark had his problems and we had ours. I went downtown to the "hippie" section of town with Mark's picture and went store-to-store, person-to-person. Cindy stayed home waiting for the phone call. I immediately got a pager and borrowed a cell phone. The area being covered was about eight blocks long. I was told that a few people thought that they saw him. Remember that the spiked hair tended to separate him from the majority. Also, he was said to have been a pain in the ass because he had a bad attitude. My response was "tell me about it." I was there for two days and gave up, feeling that he wasn't there or there were too many places to hide out. Through these adventures, I was able to find out that there was an underground group that took in runaways from all over the country, put them to work in the backrooms, and gave them food and shelter. No wonder we had very little shot of finding him. The social workers were aware of the system and tended to use it, as a source, in cases that they felt could be beneficial. They were the ones who told me that Mark definitely was in the area and obviously alive. Every day, I went somewhere in the city – just looking. For twelve days, our heads were scrambled. There were four phone calls to the house that Cindy picked up and someone was on the other end, but didn't say anything. Cindy would say, "Mark," and repeat it pleading for him to answer. "Please talk to me," but no response. He would hang up after about thirty seconds. We assumed it was Mark, but one's mind doesn't always work right in stressful times like this.

Then Cindy would say "what could I have done when I had him on the phone?" Every thought that was possible was reviewed. We talked to each other, but each of us was thinking twelve days was too long to not have communication. We kept thinking that he must be afraid by now. He was always clean, but being in the city at thirteen, maybe alone, he could be dead. If he wasn't, was he with some deviate that befriended him and had him in a basement being tortured? Was he in a dumpster and no one found him yet? If he came back alive, we promised to . . . We were trying to work at the same time and not bring the problems to business, but it was impossible. After ½ day working, one of us was out on the street trying to find him.

This was now the 12th day and Cindy received a phone call from a police department in "Hicksville" where we believe Andy and Barney were the law enforcement officers, but they did their job well! Mark and his friend took the train from downtown over thirty-five miles out to see friends of this kid who lived in a trailer near some mountain. They were walking along a country road and the officers stopped them. They were out of place; spiked hair, green and red, leathers, chains, etc. on a 90-degree day. We drove over an hour to get to the police station, which doubled as a post office. We were elated to hear that he was alive. As we got closer, we realized that we really now had a problem. What reaction should we have; see if he wanted to go home or be angry right off the bat? You have twenty other reactions, but which was right? The boys were questioned at the police station and they cooperated. Mark said he was relieved that it was over and he missed us. When they picked him up, there were no charges, but the police did give him a lecture. It looked like he missed the dinner table. He was very thin and had lost fifteen pounds that he didn't need to lose. Cindy saw him and they hugged and she cried. I was

55

cautious and hurt. Mark was anxious to find the first hamburger store that they could. He ate two burgers and was stuffed.

One of the things that he told us was that the police stopped him a few times to see if he was the missing boy; he gave them a fake name and address and they quickly dismissed him. He said he slept in an old abandoned warehouse two blocks from where most of my searching took place. He said there were homeless and runaways camping out there. Mark said he stole bread when it was delivered to the stores before the stores opened. He used old newspaper for toilet tissue. He was scared at night. He missed home, but was afraid to call. He did say he called three times, but hung up. He was lost, but he still had to face the local courts for underage drinking. At that hearing, we all went in and the judge looked at us and said how we screwed up not controlling where Mark was. I asked if I could say something prior to her giving the sentence and she said "No." The result was that he was given a citation by the local police and had to attend sessions at the local meetinghouse for minor offenders of drugs and alcohol. As we left the hearing, the Judge stopped us at the door and we figured that we would get another lecture. She smiled and said to me, " tell your mother that I said hello since I haven't seen her in years." Did we have a look of confusion on our faces! It turned out that my mother had sold the judge dresses when my mom was in business.

This punk look phase lasted about a year and then different colors other than black started to re-enter his wardrobe. Cindy always would take him shopping and buy the things that he said he would wear. That had merit because how many kids like what adults buy.

Chapter Seven

The wars had begun and were in full force! We told Mark to continue with sports because he was so good. In other words, we wanted Mark to stay healthy through athletics. He won numerous awards and even a trip to Russia and Sweden, but he dropped out of all activities. He started bringing around kids that were older and scroungy-looking. They were all the "Eddie Haskels" of their day, but when you looked closely, they had a different look about them than we were used to. I grew up in the Woodstock era and did my share of grass as did many of my contemporaries. The one thing I knew for sure was that if my kid was doing drugs, I'd know it because I did it, and I knew what to look for.

This was one of the biggest lies to myself, but I didn't realize that until a pattern had formed and the police informed me of a problem. Remember the age of thirteen as the year that the wars begin. Many wars take place in the growing-up period between the parents and the kids, and how is each battle fought? We had already seen some of the preliminary jousting and rebellion, but it was polite and reasoning was supposed to have taken place. Mark was still a kid who playfully teased Cindy because he loved his mom. He had a love, fear, and respectful approach to me, his dad.

Mark was going to public school and was not being motivated. With our background, we felt it was time to bite the bullet and send him to a private school where there was more of a tendency to watch the kid's progress or lack thereof. Mark took all of the entry tests and did poorly, but showed promise. He was behind many of the students in the 8th grade, which he was due to enter. He was accepted under the condition that he be tutored for math, which was his worst subject. He was always good with his mouth, as he would try to manipulate anyone depending on the situation. Generally manipulation turned to lies because the manipulator must win and stretching the truth may do it. How far one stretched the truth depended on one's opinion of when it became a lie.

He enrolled for the private school, which had a religious affiliation with Quakerism. We didn't consider that to be a negative, because the religion had to do with one's feelings. It didn't preach or brainwash. That was their first association with Quakerism and we didn't find it as obnoxious as many organized religions that extorted money under some mystic ruse. This gives you an idea of the religious household that Mark grew up in. We always told him that whatever belief he found viable and acceptable to him, go for it. We believe he must have read ten or fifteen books about every religion that he could conceive. The Hindu culture, Hari Krishna, Buddhism, Catholicism, atheism, and whatever-ism, were all trying to lure the insecure looking for their rightful place in life. He never, to our knowledge, was able to find security with any of these, but he conveniently took philosophies from each. When we discussed religion, we would think of Ritchie and the things that he never got to experience. Maybe our religious internal mechanism was starting to surface.

Mark was thirteen years old, and now transformed into the private school system. The price was high, but what suburban parent wouldn't make the sacrifice for their child's future. From day one, he didn't fit. He felt inferior in knowledge and struggled to try to keep up. We were told that he calmed down as the year progressed, and was actually trying, but he still was having social problems. Here was a streetwise suburban kid in a friend's school where they were trying to stress maturity and sharing, as well as honesty and integrity, and the misfit couldn't understand the importance of the principles being taught. This was a serious dilemma! Who would break first? Obviously, we were going crazy because we were looking for light at the end of the tunnel. The teachers were upset because they cared and were unable to make headway. Mark was an intelligent kid, with a great sarcastic wit, a good athlete, and he was popular in a standoffish sort of way. To the other kids, he was an enigma. They feared him, but were close to him because all of the kids were together the entire day – it was a small school. What did Mark feel like? We asked him and his reply was sort of a wimpy, "I don't care and its O.K., but it's hard."

At home, he had the phone ringing at all times. He developed the second male brain below his waist and that meant that there always seemed to be a lot of girls around. During the summer, we were asleep and were awakened by the sound of a girl giggling. We opened our eyes and glanced down the hall from the view we had from our bedroom and spotted a young lady with a towel wrapped around her running from Mark's bedroom to the bathroom. We weren't sure if that was before or after but we told her to call her father and we were dropping her off at home, which was about twenty minutes away. Can you tell anyone what a boy's father is supposed to tell the girl's father in that situation? It turned out that Cindy dropped her off at the sidewalk and left. Mark finished the year at school and began the next. He was getting frustrated, but he really didn't know how to express it. He started disrupting classes occasionally and was doing inferior work because he didn't, wouldn't, or couldn't do the work. About half way through the year, we were called into school for a conference. The conference turned out to be a message of doom-and-gloom for the future. The rules were he could stay in school temporarily until he had a series of psychological and other tests. Being the good suburban parents, we had no choice and thought it would be a good idea. The tests lasted for a week.

The results came back and had to be interpreted for us. He had attention deficit disorder without hyperactivity. He had an I.Q. of 135. His study skills were in the 27% bracket. His social skills were in the 46% bracket. His reading levels were 34 to 45% range. His language skills were from 24% to 46% and his mathematics were from 12 to 37%. The recommendation was for him to go to the psychologist starting with one visit every two weeks. That sounded fine, because we wanted to get him the guidance that he needed and fortunately, a certain number of visits were covered by insurance. This was our first introduction into the BUSINESS of medical treatment. We were naïve, thinking that the medical people took some kind of Hippocratic oath that meant they would treat people who needed treatment.

We must have confused that with some Disney fantasy.

At this point, we feel that since you are taking the time to read what we had written, we are obligated to save you the first $135 visit to the psychologist by asking you to respond to the following questions:

How do you feel about yourself?

Were you adopted?

How do you feel about your father?

How do you feel about your mother?

Do you think that they treat you with respect?

Do you feel angry?

What do you want to do when you feel angry?

Are you jealous of your sister (brother)?

Why do you think you feel angry?

What would you like to do to feel better about yourself?

When you have a dilemma, do you talk to anyone?

Have you ever wanted to hurt yourself?

How do you feel about school?

Is there anyone that you respect and admire?

Are you upset about being here?

Our time is up for now, but I think we should continue to meet for a while.

Now most kids in the above situation are somewhat intelligent and perceive this as an "I'll test you" situation. Their answers include:

I feel troubled.

Yes

Fine

Fine

I don't know

Yes

I don't know

No

I don't know

I don't know

Sometimes

Yes (the kids know this always pushes the button)

O.K.

Al Capone (another button pusher)

No

Our son just opened the door for Psych 101 to rear its ugly head. The doctor now saw a suicidal and violent child with no direction. The jerk could have spent one or two hours talking to us since we had as much education as him (but are too close to the situation) to get all of the legitimate facts. We talked to Mark after the session and he told us he was playing with the doctor because the doctor was an idiot. Many of the troubled youth are masters in their own right in the psychology field. Many of the doctors in the field are there because they were, in some way, troubled teens, but they have forgotten that and become textbook computers.

Mark started acting out some very violent behavior. He was carving up his wrists with a pocket- knife. The doctor suggested that he be admitted to the psychiatric facility for 30 days so that he could get 24-hour treatment. Like everything else, we tried it. First he was isolated from everybody on the outside for 72 hours. That was to detox him (standard procedure). Then he was told it was voluntary so that he could sign himself out on 72-hour notice. He then had to sign to give us permission to speak to the doctor so he wouldn't breech the doctor-client relationship. Wasn't that a great way to protect a child's rights? This kid, who was now fourteen years old, who knew nothing about the real ramifications of his impulsive actions, was now the decision maker for the future of his troubled life. He finished the thirty days. The reason for the thirty days was that the programs were geared for thirty days. Why you ask? The reason was that the insurance programs uniformly allowed thirty days at one time. If anyone wished to see a real legal scam in action, and a total waste of approximately $30,000 (one session), do a study of the clients after they leave. You will find a single digit success rate. Do you think someone is getting screwed without foreplay? These sessions went on for about three months until they realized that there was a problem and the doctor didn't have a clue. While he was in the treatment program, he associated with some of the local kids who were in for treatment. They all could relate and most times they gave each other their phone numbers. They had common bonds and educated each other on the ways of rehabilitation centers and the way to B.S. your way through them.

Mark was now going into 10th grade. He was fifteen years old. He was transferred to a private school that catered to intelligent kids who had a problem, or many problems. The original Quaker school recommended it. The teachers cared and were very casual and somewhat hip with the kids. They related, taught them, and were their friends. This was the school that allowed the kids to still learn academics while they worked out their problems and continued on with their lives. It was a neat idea and seemed to have very positive results. Mark was extremely rebellious against doing any work that he saw no need to do. He wouldn't listen to us if there were other things that he really wanted to do. Remember that when the kids were out of the house, there was no way that any parent knew what was happening. He was continually losing his temper and had apparently been drinking and/or using some drugs. He decided that the pressure was so great that he asked to check back into the drug rehabilitation unit. They had adolescent units at most centers so that the peer group was together. The problem that these places had was that not all of the people wanted to be straight and they taught the others the tricks of the trade on outsmarting the keepers of the institute. These people tended to stay in touch with each other and that generally could be very good or extremely hazardous. Mark checked himself out after nine days because he was straight and sober. He said he had enough of the problems and wanted to straighten everything out in his life. He said he was doing drugs but he was together now and trying to go straight. His in-and-out attitude remained the same until he was sixteen.

There was nothing we could do because this boy had rights, according to the law. We only had the insurance and made all of the arrangements because of his inability to do so, but he had all of the rights and us, as parents, had none. On the other hand, what if he destroyed someone's property? Would the parents be held responsible? It seems that in our society there are a number of conflicting and convenient idiosyncrasies. Since we felt that Mark was on the right track, we bought him a car three days before his sixteenth birthday. He was so excited because it was a new black Pontiac. He was hugging and kissing everyone. He washed the car every day and just sat in it. I didn't give him the keys for three days. We didn't believe he would have had the self-discipline to have the keys and not start the car. He still didn't have much patience. This was one of the conflicts that hit our marriage because of values. I said he should get an old junker until he learned responsibility and Cindy said it would be too dangerous for him if the car broke down in a bad area. I asked what he would be doing in a bad neighborhood. Around and around we went and it came down to trying to keep Cindy happy by giving in. One could call me a wuss, or you could say I still slept in the same bed as Cindy – your choice.

Mark enrolled in a driver-training course because we felt it best to teach him discipline and the course would be paid for in the first year savings on the insurance. He already passed his driver's test and was good for a few months. We told him that there was to be no drinking and driving. We said he must be in by midnight and he was. Maybe this was the breakthrough that would help him mature and stay straight. He knew that if he screwed around with the rules initially set forth, the car would be taken away for a period of time, if not forever. His driving was good, but he had a bad temper when other drivers interfered with him. He could actually be the male model for road rage! He would cut them off or mostly give them the one finger high sign. He would occasionally call and ask if he could stay out overnight and I checked to see if he was where he said by driving there to see if his car was there and it was. There was about a three-month period where we thought he would be OK. He had the car over the summer and there was no school. He didn't have a job, but one of his teachers from school told him that he could hire him. The teacher was renovating his older home and finishing some of the rooms. This teacher did relate to him and tried to give him some values. The teacher lived with a woman who was a free thinker as he was, and that made it easy for kids to see that adults didn't have to be like their parents. He was a vegetarian who followed the rules including milk products. Adults could be cool. He stayed there some nights. Summer ended on what all considered a positive mode, but we were cautious.

After four months, we sold his car because he was too erratic to drive it, and we were always up until we would hear the front door slam. This ticked Mark off, because although he knew he had no responsibility and no understanding of what a car was about, he still wanted it. Cindy was feeling as bad as Mark because she still pictured Ritchie and that made her want to do more for Mark. This was a conflict that allowed emotion to win out over logic every time.

In February, on a cold snowy Friday evening, we were sitting at home. Mark was out with some of his friends from the neighboring community. It seemed too peaceful. It was. We got a phone call from the neighboring police department asking us to come down to the station right away. We quickly dressed and got down to the station within about ½ hour. We were told that Mark was in a fight with two police officers in a local restaurant and he was in the cell down the hall. Mark fought a lot and had no fear, which made him dangerous. We naturally asked if anyone was hurt and the officer said no, but there was a problem with Mark. I asked what he meant and he proceeded to tell us that there was a Grateful Dead concert downtown and there was known to be a lot of LSD in the entire area and they believe Mark had some. LSD is a hallucinogenic drug that had always been somewhat unpredictable in every aspect. We asked to see him. The chief said he would take us back to see him but he would not allow us into the cell. He said it took four officers to control him enough to get him in there. I walked back, figuring that Mark really screwed up and assaulted the police and they were going to nail him good.

I figured Mark would have to humble himself and I was going to beg to avoid having him go to jail. WRONG! I got to the cell and looked in, and said, "Mark." I repeated it two or three times and he didn't respond to me. I was devastated – he looked just like a zombie. Mark was sitting on the jail single bed with his feet on the floor and he was looking straight out at the opposite wall about six feet away. His hands were in a type of prayer position and then I listened closely to his words. He said "red, blue, green, red, blue, green," and he kept repeating those words without regard to any of his surroundings. He was in a fog. I felt like it was part of the Jack Nicholson film "One Flew Over The CooCoo's Nest."

It was scary. He was alive but totally out of it. I again asked to go in to see him and was again refused admittance into the cell. The officer said that they had called the ambulance to transport him to the hospital. The ambulance came within about twenty minutes and we were told to wait outside, which we did. The officers and the paramedics had to forcibly strap him to a gurney and secure every moving part of him. They said he had incredible strength on the drug, whatever it was. Two hours passed from the time he was in the cell until he was secured in the emergency room at the hospital. He had not changed at all. He was still muttering the same words describing the colors. I looked at Cindy and we were both thinking that we were going to have another son like Ritchie. Cindy asked the hospital what we could do. The hospital put in a catheter, took some blood and urine tests, and said we had to wait and see what the tests results were.

They were honest and said it could be hours, days, or he may never come out of it. They had no idea what affect whatever he took is having on his brain. We waited along side Mark in the emergency room and kept talking to him or should we say, at him! We did that for our sanity. Within about four hours, we could start to see a different pattern of speech forming. His eyes were coming in and out of a hypnotic-type state. He was turning his head as if being very confused. He had no idea why he was strapped down. He was crying, agitated, and confused. You could see every emotion in his face and eyes over the next 90 minutes while he was coming down. The hospital was very cautious as they took off each restraint at about twenty-minute intervals. It was as though his body had gone through electric-shock therapy. He was drained!

After six hours at the hospital, he was released.

The next day, Mark and I went to the police station to see what he was getting charged with and the police said 'nothing." I asked why and they said it would have been a charge of possession if he had it on him, but since he used it all, there was no possession. Great laws, aren't they? Mark was relieved, but had mixed emotions and we believe that he wanted to know what he had experienced, but had a fear of knowing the reality of the danger he was in. I knew that he could hallucinate for long periods of time after using the drug, assuming it was LSD.

Everyone knew things were getting out of hand and the original rehab center did not help. We made phone calls to all of the local hospitals that had rehab units. The first question they asked was, "What type of insurance coverage do you have?" Cindy found one in the city that had a bed available; we went immediately.

They first interviewed all of us but focused on Mark. Cindy and I were then shown the door and Mark was in charge of his destiny and immediately put into isolation for 72 hours to detoxify and be ready to start the same old bullshit that didn't work before. The schedules were very similar at all of the places including two or three discussion groups, therapy sessions once a day or once every other day. Visitors were allowed after the isolation period for ½ hour in the evening at a specified time, if they were good. Most of the patients were extremely well educated in the plans and procedures of the rehabs. They usually played with the specialists for a few days and then decided to be serious for a while and then they get bored and started to play again and so on and so on.

These professionals had been so mired in the same routine that they didn't realize that they were the objects of levity and served no medical function other than fundraiser and clown.

There was one young, sharp, pretty psychologist who Mark saw about five or six times while in the rehab. She met with all three of us the day of final insurance, the 30th day. She had gotten written permission from Mark to discuss anything that was brought up. That never was a problem because he always was open to have us aware of what was going on. She started the discussion with "Mark has a problem." You could tell that they both liked each other and she enjoyed Mark's sharp wit. They exchanged glances that showed equality on some level, but no one knew which one. She said that Mark was a "binger." A binger was one that could be off of drugs and function normally and then get the urge to do drugs and not stop until the drugs ran out. A regular druggie got their high and was satisfied until the body craved another. A binger couldn't or wouldn't stop, and was never satisfied until they achieved the same high as the original, but it never happened. I asked what that meant. Her answer was quick and clear, "he is going to kill himself."

We were dumbfounded, but we didn't know why. We guessed we were just hit with a bolt of lightening when we should have expected it. Mark was very calm and collected as he listened and didn't make any comment at all. He didn't flinch. He didn't say she was crazy. Cindy asked the next normal dumb question which was "When?" She laughed and said she didn't know. Mark was very straight, normal, and logical. She said to us that Mark was on the border of treatment and that she could get a court order for commitment to remain or he could come back as an out patient on a daily basis and continue in his regular school. We all decided on the latter because he appeared to be doing fine. Cindy drove him to school daily and I was picking up the slack. We were running all over the city playing limo drivers, but for your kid, you tended to be optimistic and figured the experts were helping.

Mark convinced her that he was ready for another car to continue his programs and work. I was glad to have Cindy stop driving him to meetings every night. The car would give him a chance to get a job and assume more responsibility. Maybe it was wishful thinking, and parents sometimes, or should I say most times, are victims of it. My initial response was to look for a good used car that would be transportation that would work locally. Cindy looked at used cars with him and he was getting depressed. He said they were junk and Cindy felt that it would cost us a fortune in repairs. Cindy, as wives could do, convinced me that it was better to buy a car with a warranty and a car that would help build his image. It sounded good. I gave in and went to the Ford dealership. His girlfriend was with us, and both of them looked at a new beautiful teal Escort sitting on the floor. They fell in love with it. Cindy fell in love with it and tried to convince me to get it. I looked at the price and immediately said "NO!" It was ridiculous and out of the question. The dealer had the car ready the next day and Cindy never did the things she told me she would do to me! I guess they call that the joys of marriage.

He had the car about a week and he disappeared for two days. We didn't call the police, but were sitting by the phone because we figured he was on a drug binge. He called home about 3:00 a.m. and said he was in one of the major drug districts in the city and he needed us and someone stole his car. Could we pick him up? He was near a fast food restaurant that only served through a bulletproof glass. It was dirty and sleazy!

We dressed and were out of the house within five minutes realizing that we had a thirty-minute drive and had no idea what faced us when we got there. He was standing on the corner where he said he would be, wearing a shredded flannel shirt, baggy old pants that a bum wouldn't even wear, and no shoes. It was thirty-five degrees and cold. He was strung out. He said that he could get the car back for $100 at 8:00 a.m. He told us that he put the car up as collateral for some drugs. Great deal – a $13,000 car for $50 in drugs!

We waited around until eight o'clock. What a wonderful feeling to be in drug city and wait to negotiate a deal to get your car back for $100. We went to a small street and were told to go around the corner with the money and we could then have the keys. This was not a good feeling for a suburban boy who looks very out of place. Mark was remorseful and unsure of having us there. We told him to sit in the back of the car and shut up, which he did. I saw the car and five people standing around. All kinds of thoughts came to mind including "I'm dead meat." Will they trade us the keys for the money? Will they take both? Should I tell Cindy to stay in the car and take off if there was a problem? The real question hit me and that was "what the fuck am I doing here?"

I walked over with absolutely no coolness. After all, you can't be cooler than the drug dealers who were much more streetwise than me, and more heavily armed.

"Who has the keys?" I asked.

One of them said, "Me and where's the $200?"

"It's $100 and I don't want any trouble, but if there's a conflict, let's call the police."

I was lucky because the quicker I left, the quicker they could resume business. One of them said, "Give him the keys and get the fuck out of here!"

This is exactly what I did! Do you realize that they move drugs and people faster than Mc Donald's? They can have five or six cars waiting for a pick-up and have all of them moved in less than one minute, and they could have exchanged anywhere from $200 to $10,000. Put this on the New York Stock Exchange and this would be the best growth company of the year and one with figures that would make Bill Gates envious.

We called our friends to keep in touch, but we had the feeling our friends didn't want to call us back because it was the same old shit that was being discussed and complained about. It got to the point that our friends didn't want to tell us about the good things that were happening to their kids because it would make us feel bad. Actually, it made us feel good to know that our friends didn't have the aggravation that we had. In reality, we felt great that things were going well with our friends, but the friends seemed to feel guilty. It was tough on everyone.

Chapter Eight

The next month, Mark decided that he was going to start going to meetings for drug and alcohol abuse. He was going to get us off his back. That was not the way to go to get help. At almost seventeen years old, every boy is invincible, so they think. Cindy drove him to the meetings that were only five minutes from our home. The meetings were held in a church annex. There were anywhere from five to twenty young people at these meetings. The people were both boys and girls, ranging in age from twelve to eighteen years old. They all had similar problems. Some were there voluntarily, while others were there through the orders of the courts. At the breaks, everyone, with no exceptions, pulled out the cigarettes, and lit up the skies with a cloud of smoke. It appeared that smoking was encouraged at many of these facilities to calm the nerves of some very hyper individuals. The observation that bothered Cindy was seeing young children associate with the older kids and being influenced by them. They easily could develop the feeling that these guys are cool and if they see the young guys as tough, the young kids feel that they will be better accepted. Many of the problem kids do have a problem of acceptance of who they are or want to be. Mark went for three weeks, twice a week, and his interest dropped, as did the number of other people attending. Even though they were there to get help and guidance, they were still more interested in approval by their peers. They were still children!

Mark was having problems adjusting, but he was respectful to both his grandparents and us. He had a genuine love for Cindy's mom and a respect for Cindy's dad. Cindy's mom thought the world revolved around Mark, but Cindy's dad had no time or respect for Mark because he was not a model citizen and he was adopted. Being adopted, Cindy's dad felt that he was not part of the family. For that part, neither was I since it was only by injection!

We were at a crossroad because our first son was so sick, and our second son was having these problems. Should we get another car? Could he handle it? Should we make him earn it? Which came first – the chicken or the egg? We took the easy way out and were getting ready to buy him another car and Cindy's mom and dad said they would buy it. Not being stupid, we said fine. It was bought two months after his 17th birthday and we got rid of the Ford Escort. The Escort had too many bad trips to the drug zone and we were happy to start anew. Mark started his final year of high school with a history of instability and knowledge of the drug world and the rehab centers that followed. He had a girlfriend from the school that was very sharp, and to this day, no one knew why she was at this school. They always got along great and Mark did what he wanted because she said that was fine; she had a life of her own. He was seeing a local shrink who supposedly had great rapport with the students that had problems. It seemed like the shrink knew each student from this school personally. One of Mark's friends from the school stabbed his mother to death over the past summer but was released within one year because he was under the influence of drugs and was getting treatment. Another was the son of a well-known medical doctor who was prone to running away because of drugs and jealousy of his brother who was successful in school. Another was a young woman who had a tendency to screw any guy she could, whenever and wherever she felt like; at school it usually was in the bathrooms.

Guess what moms and dads – they don't just grow out of these actions because they chronologically grow older. Something must happen to change the kid's perspective about what is important in life. I don't know what is important because I am not a licensed professional psychiatrist! Did that sound sarcastic? Well, if the shoe fits

... Maybe brainwashing is not such a bad practice if it is controlled.

Mark came to us when we thought everything was going well. He told us that he was going to check himself into the rehab center. We were surprised because we didn't see his problems, but he did. He checked himself out in three days and it was never known why he went in. He just came out and continued going to high school and reading way-out books on cults and religions. It seemed to be understood in school that he was into this philosophy and they said it was o.k. because I called and questioned them. Their feeling was that if he found something interesting and diverted his attention to that, it could help him find other vents; tell that to Al Capone with his interest in taxation! Everything was quiet for about two weeks. He drove his car to school and seniors were allowed to go out for lunch, which many kids did. Cindy and I were again being lulled to sleep and getting that good feeling. We realized that good feelings were not a good thing or they were the sign of the reality that followed.

On a Wednesday afternoon, about 2:30, we got a call from the police to go to a local sandwich restaurant in a bad section of the city about two miles from the school. We got there and the place was full of police, both from the city and the suburbs. We looked at each other and knew we had a problem. As we walked in the front door, two girls, classmates of Mark, came over to us with their parents and told us that Mark had been kidnapped.

"Wait a minute, tell us what happened," I asked.

One of the girls started to rattle off the story and the other was very quiet; too quiet. The story was that Mark and the two girls were at the mall in a restaurant and finished eating lunch, which the seniors were allowed to do. They were going out to one of the girl's car, as she was the one who drove all three to lunch. As they approached the car, a man about twenty-four years old told them he had a gun and that they better get into the car with him. They got in and he told them to give him their money, which they did. He drove around for about an hour and stopped to get drugs. He then took them to a house not far from the restaurant and made them go inside. He took them all upstairs and into one of the bedrooms. He was going to rape both of the girls, but Mark said one was his girlfriend so he told Mark to take his girlfriend into the next room and close the door. He said he would shoot the other girl if he heard Mark's door open. Mark complied. In the kidnapper's room was a third girl, who was a friend of the kidnapper. He raped the girl that was Mark's friend and then made her get it on with his lady friend.

The reason Mark was not hurt was that he befriended the kidnapper who was out for a good time. He told Mark that he was just out of jail and wanted to party. Guess who was doing drugs with the kidnapper? After the episode at the house, the kidnapper drove the girls to the main street, dropped them off in front of this store, and then took off with Mark. That explanation told them why the one girl was quiet. She was afraid of Aids. The experience was very traumatic, although the girls were not always innocent. Although the girl really wasn't his girlfriend, Mark did "do her" in the bathroom at school earlier in the year as was explained to me by one of the other kids.

Now the focus was on Mark. It was going on six o'clock at night, and there must have been more than 100 police from the city and suburbs combing the area. Many were in plainclothes. They were busting their tails looking because the situation was nasty – two schoolgirls and a boy being kidnapped during the day from a mall. Everybody wanted this solved because it would have destroyed either the school or the mall. I was standing and waiting outside the store, when all of a sudden I noticed the girl's car across the street being driven by a stranger.

"There's the car," I yelled.

Officers start running for their cars to start a chase. My car was the closest and one of the cops grabbed my keys and started the pursuit. We just stood there, as there was nothing else to do. About ½ hour later, the car was brought back, we were told to drive to the police station, and that Mark was all right. We got to the station, which was only five minutes away, before the others. Every major television station had cameras rolling and microphones primed. It was the headline story on all three news stations. Mark walked in and gave us hugs and he then gave police a story that was the same as the one the girls gave. Mark was smiling sheepishly at the cameras as he was enjoying the limelight. The defendant was just out of jail and also was wanted in another county.

It took about two months for the trial to begin and it was a jury trial. The trial was at the County Courthouse, which was the site of most major hearings. The trial took three days and we sat in only for part of the testimony that included the girls and Mark. The courtroom was fairly packed and it was a scene right out of a TV show. The questions were raunchy trying to make the girls look like hookers and Mark was made to look like he cooperated to get the drugs, which may have truly been the case, but no one ever really knew.

The trial was an embarrassment to us because Mark answered the questions like he was talking on the street. Every four-letter word was used in his answers and the judge said it was fine to continue speaking that way to get answers to the questions. Cindy and I were in the room with the jury and about forty other people. As the description got detailed and the language sunk deeper, we were helpless but to sit and slump lower in our seats. We were hoping for justice and Mark's testimony showed little respect for the court, and the content appeared to be lost. Everyone was concerned that this convict would be out on bail and he would want to make sure that there were no witnesses to put him back into prison. He had little to lose. He was faced with losing his freedom or convincing all parties to back off. Legally, he wasn't allowed to contact the kids. Is that one of the dumbest statements you ever heard? Does he care if he doesn't obey the law and contacts the kids?

The effect on the kids and the parents was devastating, but I believe the effect was longer lasting for the parents as the kids bounce back quicker, at least it appeared that way. The other conclusion was that the kids didn't have a clue of the severity of the problem, or was it the parents who didn't!

In the end, the defendant was found not guilty. It was a travesty because it was obvious to everyone that this "model citizen" was guilty as sin, but the prosecutor was incapable of handling a trial. The problems were long lasting for the kids who now knew first-hand that you would not get punished if you committed a heinous crime. Second, the young girl who was raped must now continue to be tested for aids since it doesn't show up right away. Her parents and she must now endure many sleepless nights waiting and wondering when and if she will be safe or live or die. That was not a great way to plan one's future. As the Russian comedian, Yakov, said, "What a country!"

<u>Chapter Nine</u>

Mark continued with his drug escapades that now lasted only one to three days when he was away somewhere. When he called after only one day away, Cindy said she felt he was getting better since he was starting to realize the situation sooner. It was amazing how easy it was to let our minds allow itself the pleasure of positive thinking when nothing had really changed. The situation was not really improving. Every time we allowed ourselves to believe it was, Mark slipped back. He was confused and so were we. Did we trust him or not? Every time he was straight and "normal," he lost all of his self-esteem if we didn't trust him. He had done everything in his power to try to gain our support in words and controlled actions, but he had not made headway with any major decisions.

Logic told me to make the boy earn his rewards of trust. Anyone who has ever been in the world of drugs knows to throw logic out the window. Cindy kept hoping and giving in to him when he appeared to be straight. He wanted to be straight, but, like others, there was something that took over the bodies and especially the minds of the teenagers who had been on the crack-cocaine road.

They could be the perfect children and then when they were alone or in a situation that opened the door to more crack, they couldn't resist and they were out of their minds knowing the high was coming. The "thing" snapped in their heads and they were off to the races. Once they got the first high, there was no return until the funds and/or drugs ran out. The kids then began to realize that they totally "fucked up." They wanted to call home and be safe with mommy and daddy, but they couldn't handle the same old shit and more lectures. They know what they did and didn't want to hear it again. The odds were that they lost their favorite clothes, stereo, or some possession that was stolen from you. They were embarrassed and ashamed. They felt dirty. Eventually they called home and were emotionally spent. Their minds had wandered and they feared the image they had of themselves and they didn't like themselves. They were fragile at this point. They all contemplated suicide, but most gained their senses first. In reality, the kids couldn't be talked to more than they had already spoken to themselves. The only problem was they saw a very cloudy picture and the discussion they had with themselves referenced the same picture, which was hard to see, and could have been interpreted differently by each person seeing it. The last thing these kids wanted to hear was what you would have done in that situation, or what they should have done, especially when the urge to physically beat the shit out of your kid is truly overwhelming to the parents, present company included.

In early December, I got a call from Mark after he was away for another two-day stint. This call was from a sleazy motel that was mostly rented by the hour. The cashier was enclosed in a bulletproof window, which always made one feel first class. We went into the room and Mark was paranoid. He asked if anyone saw us come in. How would we know? The room was seedy and out of a 1950's detective magazine. The sheets looked like they got changed after the hooker's had a dozen tricks. The curtains were closed and the rugs were badly stained. We stood in the room for about twenty minutes after questioning him. Mark was very cooperative because he wanted to go home. We got him out of there and asked him what happened again. He said he was working for a dealer on one of the corners for drug money (and drugs) and someone dropped him off at the motel. He said his car was stolen, but knows where to find it. To me, that doesn't sound like it's lost. We said that all of us were going to the police to report it stolen, which we did. At the police station, they told me that we must go to the station district where the car was stolen, as we were not at the right station. At this time, we were standing outside the first police station and I told Mark that the police said that he must identify the dealer and who stole his car. With that, Mark defiantly said "no."

I again said that must happen and Mark said it was not going to happen. He turned his back and told us he was leaving. My blood pressure shot up and I took a running leap on Mark's back, wrestled him to the ground and rolled around on the concrete as Cindy was yelling to stop. With all of the activity, within fifteen seconds, there were ten police officers breaking us up. Cooler heads prevailed temporarily, but I was hot. Mark was just there for the ride. Cindy and I looked at each other wondering what to do in the next two minutes, let alone the next hour or day. We put him in the back seat and went to get his car, which was where he said it was, but it was out of gas. We got the gallon gas tank that we always kept in the trunk, filled it, and got the car in a position to drive, which Cindy did. Cindy always drove Mark's car and Mark always sat next to her while I followed. This was not coincidence. We figured that Mark could bolt from the car either while in motion or when it stopped so I would have a better shot of not running him over or have a chance to chase after him. Mark said he needed help again. I said that help had to come from himself, but we would make transportation available to the NA meetings. This went on for a few more weeks.

The Christmas holidays arrived, and the cheer of Santa and his friends was buzzing in the air. Mark had lots of girls that were always at his beck and call because they felt safe with him. He would have no fear to fight if someone threatened his turf (meaning the girl he was with at the time). He was very carefree when he was with the girls and they thought that was exciting. He was exciting to them. One never knew what he would do next, but usually it was clever, funny, or different. He spent a lot of time with different girls, but we never saw him treat any with much respect. He was very smooth. He knew that if he went too far, he could apologize in a sincere fashion and they would be back to him quickly.

This Christmas night, he was out with one of the girls and was due back for a Christmas dinner. He had been doing well for about a month and the family was looking forward to being together. In our minds, we were quietly celebrating the fact he seemed to be doing so well. Dinner was scheduled for 5:00 p.m. We were having a big family dinner for ten people. Mark was told to be home at 4 p.m. Four came and went, so did five and six. We knew by now what had happened. What do we do now? Do we push the panic buttons or have dinner and wait? Could we tell our stomachs that the butterflies should leave? Do we grab the antacid tablets? Do we excuse ourselves from our company and begin the trek into drug city? We are mad and disappointed. We decided to sit down and eat and hopefully, get the family out so we could begin doing something to find him. Dinner was not joyous, but it was uneventful. Mark was seventeen years old and lost in his own mind.

After dinner, we traveled the streets for about three hours looking for Mark's car. We found nothing. The next day, at about 11 p.m., we got a phone call that he ran out of gas. That was another way of saying he messed up and needed help. We figured that the car was destroyed or he had nothing left and slept in the car after running out of drugs. He met us at the car. We did bring the gas can, which was filled with one gallon of gas. Besides, we did not want to stop at a gas station in the middle of the drug zone. We also didn't want to carry a gallon of gas in our trunk in case of an accident. Either way, we were forced to do what we didn't want to do.

Mark came home by Cindy taking his keys and driving his car home. The usual routine was to get into the house, take a long shower, hit the refrigerator and fall asleep on the sofa. This was usually the time that he was most vulnerable. He was a senior in high school and just partying. I got into a discussion with him about what life was about and his future and all of the right things that parents say and the kids don't care about hearing because parents are not into today's world. We talked to him about his freewheeling sex life, and all the chances that he took in everything that he did from sex to fights to controlling people to lies to drugs. We must have pissed him off enough for him to open up about some of his escapades, which caught us by surprise.

The thing that caused society to rear its head was an adult taking advantage of children. Mark informed us that he had slept with one of his teachers. I, as the father, was in a strange position. I could say that's O.K., or was it a male or female teacher, or who was it, or any number of reactions. Frankly, I was relieved when Mark said it was a female teacher. I didn't know why I was relieved, but I was. It didn't bother me because Mark had slept with so many girls and that this one just happened to be older. I knew it wouldn't hurt his mental state any more than it already was hurt. Maybe sleeping with this teacher offered Mark some mental stimulation, but maybe that was only my fantasy or illusion.

My dilemma was not for Mark, but for the other students. I knew Mark would never say anything to the other students, but what if this teacher was making a habit of seducing the students. Did we have an obligation to report it and start a potential disaster for the school, or should we bury it and assume that it was not true? Tough decisions appear to come forward and obligate people. If this incident never happened, we just tarnished the name of a responsible teacher. We would put her on the hot seat and possibly jeopardized her job. What would you do? We decided to go to the school and discuss the situation with the principal, who was very savvy of the kids and potential situations. We approached it in a way stating that we were unsure of the facts and didn't know the teacher, but Mark said he had slept with her. It almost sounded like the same situation as President Clinton went through, except Mark didn't tell them about any distinguishing marks or idiosyncrasies of her body. I wonder if Mark ever considered smoking cigars? We never heard another word from the school about this situation, which was fine with us. We felt we gave them the information and it now was their problem if they wanted it to be.

One of his friends from the rehab, Jeff, who Mark had become very friendly with, called to say he got kicked out of his house. Mark asked if he could stay in their basement for a few days. We said it was all right with us if he obeyed certain rules like getting a job and being dependable when he had obligations. We felt everything was going fine and in about a month, Jeff's parents and he would resolve their differences and we had done a good thing. The boy had just graduated high school the year before and I couldn't see him on the street. Besides, it wasn't unusual for parents and kids not to see eye-to-eye during the transition. Jeff agreed and appreciated the hospitality. I thought that Mark would see that someone was getting responsible and would set an example for him who was in his peer group. About three weeks went by and Jeff's parents and he had a reconciliation and he moved back home and we felt that we had someone keeping an eye on Mark and keeping him straight when we couldn't. Mark later told us that while Jeff was in the basement, he brought cocaine in and they were doing it every night and many afternoons when we were at work.

Mark was still seeing a girl at school pretty regularly. He also was making a lot of friends at the school, who all had some problems. He was heavily into writing poetry. Some of the work was quite good and very deep. At times, it had a tinge of T. S. Eliot, who Mark never even heard of and wouldn't read anyway.

The next few months were typical in that he was good for three to five weeks and then off again for a few days. It got to the point that we were deciding each time whether to wait or go down to the drug zone. It depended on the moods and mentality that we had at the time. We also had to deal with frustration and disappointment that kept fluctuating. We had the fear of not knowing if this was the time he overdosed and was dumped into somebody's trash bin. His girlfriend was very knowledgeable about his actions. She was hard as far as feelings, but didn't approve of his heavy use of drugs and his escape antics.

The school administration was aware of his problems and most of the teachers were, also. Mark was liked by most of the people at the school but many were afraid of him. He socialized with many of his teachers because he had a strange maturity about him. He also had a tendency for the young hip adults to try to help him along because he seemed to be "almost there."

He would frequently get into a fight with his girlfriend's ex-boyfriend. That eventually escalated with each encounter. We had the constant dilemma of backing Mark or letting him stand alone and pay for his actions. Our philosophy was to back him when we felt he was right and back away when he was wrong. That was a great philosophy, except parents appear to be blind when it comes to their children. When he said, "why don't you believe me? I wouldn't lie to you, mom," do you believe him? Chances are you will say to him that he had better not put you into a situation where you defended him and then found out he lied to you. He could care less because he got the wolves off his back for the moment and that took all of the pressure off him. Guess what – every parent has been had on a situation similar to this.

The same bullshit persisted and Mark didn't know what to do. The logical hope and prayer of the parents were that he would mature and grow out of the drug stage and find the drive to succeed. Parents are eternal optimists when it comes to their children, because they still see them as kids who have a long way to go in learning about life. We sat down with him in order to help plan his life. This was all done based on tests that showed his aptitude and his interests. This was another great big racket! No one could plan his next hour! The tests didn't mean anything except to give a very general idea of his mood for the day.

I looked at colleges that were geared to help students get by. It was amazing to see the choices of schools and their philosophies. One school in New England allowed students to set up their own curriculum, decide how they wanted to be graded, and charged a small fortune for tuition. The idea was to allow these free thinkers to concentrate on their areas of interest instead of wasting two years re-doing high school. Others were looking at mainly B and C students who hadn't developed. There were schools for everyone and grants to go along with each school. The ads for getting help for high school seniors to find a college right for them was true, although it could be done easily without professional help. We did it ourselves. Many of these schools had tutoring set up from the start. They had college courses that were more basic than high school to get kids through. Unless one was a total idiot or didn't pick the right school, there was no reason for anyone who was diligent and with financial backing who couldn't get a college degree. We completed our searching and found three schools that were perfect. If Mark needed any help, these schools were geared for it. The school we chose only had about 2,000 students and they were mostly C students. The school was in the New England area, near Boston. Also, think about Mark being away and us having a life again. Someone, quick, slap me as I was dreaming heavenly thoughts!

We went up there for an interview and a look at the town. Everything went well except that the grades Mark had to show were D's. He interviewed well, which he always did. He was good with adults and his interaction with them. Also, it was a private school that always needed students, or should I say needed money. He got in on the premise that he take a lighter load and work immediately with a tutor to develop better study habits. He always seemed to eyeball the people he spoke to and got a compromise. The compromise was total bullshit because the adult interviewer thought that she was speaking to a responsible young adult. For the minute, she was right. After the interview, she became wrong. Unfortunately, there hasn't been nor would there be a pill that circulated through the body and disseminated responsible behavior.

The three of us walked around campus with a tour guide. There were three dormitories. One was for the guys, another for the girls, and the third was a three-story stone mansion for the senior class of either gender. The regular dorms were two and one half stories tall that were typical rooms with the toilet and shower facilities at the end of the hall. In the basement were laundry and study facilities along with the TV room. There was no cooking in the room yet all the kids had hot plates. There was a gymnasium that was very well equipped and could be equivalent to a nice high school freestanding gym. The dining room was at the front of the campus, which meant the dorm kids had to walk about two blocks to get a meal. We sampled the food, it was quite good, and there was a "great selection" of one or two hot items and a variety of cold sandwiches. The students could eat anything and all that they wanted. The drinks were self-serve and were typical with a good variety. The atmosphere was pleasant and there was seating for about 600, which was more than adequate. The building was built for this purpose. There was plenty of grass around each of the buildings and we were able to see the normal activities on the lawns including the Frisbees, blankets and people studying, and the students tossing around different balls. It made one think that this was going to be a utopia for the next four years.

We drove around the town where the campus was located and noted that there wasn't a town but a few stores along the street that connected other towns. The area was now old, but looked as if at one time it had money. One could tell because there were mansions on large pieces of ground. Some of these were converted to offices and a few had been converted to institutions such as private day care facilities or boarding schools. It was pretty and sedate, but very boring. There was public transportation all around the area, but the closest to the campus was about one mile. If you had a car, Boston was only about thirty minutes away. There wasn't a decent restaurant within five miles and there wasn't a place to stay when visiting within another five miles. There were some small towns within ten minutes drive, but they were desolate. The stores were closed by 5:00 p.m., and the only thing open was a bowling alley that also served as the town's ice cream parlor. The bowling alley intrigued me because I had never seen bowling balls that were so small or pins so skinny. The lanes appeared long, but the balls reminded me of the ones that were set in the arcade bowling machines. It just seemed strange because it wasn't the same game or it appeared to be the same game before it was modernized with the fourteen or sixteen-pound ball.

Everything again seemed to be on track as far as the natural progression of going to look at colleges and finishing out the senior year. Mark appeared happy with the thought of a place to go and the feeling that he could start over after all of the problems. He had a fear factor of something new, but everyone felt that was to be expected. We also saw some pride return to him as he told people that he was going to college near Boston. When he told his teachers in school about his being accepted, he could hardly hold back his enthusiasm of someone wanting him as a student.

Chapter Ten

At that time, we decided that Mark was OK, and we left for a vacation for four days to get away. It was time to spend a few restful nights' sleep and catch up on each other. There was a lot of love and respect for each other and each acted as a crutch for the other when situations became unbearable. That was what marriage and friendship were all about; no games, but honest feelings and respect with the goal to do the actions that were in the best interests of your partner. While we were away, we told Cindy's father to possibly expect a phone call saying that Mark needed money. What we didn't expect was for him to get conned by Mark. Mark went to his house and gave him a story that he needed a credit card to purchase something that Cindy and I ordered. Mark got the credit card, disappeared, and was gone for four days. Upon our return home, we started our investigation. The credit card was used at a gas station to buy more than $200 worth of cigarettes. The cigarettes were used to trade for drugs. The credit card was canceled immediately and Cindy's father immediately blamed the adoption and us for all of his problems. Cindy's mother was beside herself as she was looking for a way to help Mark be safe, but this was way out of anything that was ever part of her life. She was frustrated with everything and just wanted to make it better, but she was basically brushed aside because there was no time to try to explain it to her or to answer her father's continual question of "why did it happen?" Cindy just chalked it up to another slip and said, "let's move on."

With all of his positives in his life now, Mark still continued to have his drug episodes. The situation varied each time, but the results were the same, away for a day or two and then the call home. We picked him up and he said he let us down, he let his grandparents down, and he let himself down. He would go to one or two Narcotics Anonymous (NA) meetings and he would be OK. Usually, we let him drive to the meetings with the condition that he came back directly from the meetings. There were meetings at all hours of the night and places were readily available. There were probably two or three times as many meeting places as there were McDonald's, Wendy's and Burger King combined.

The programs worked for those who wanted it to work and were truly willing to give up their old lives, friends, beliefs, and almost their entire past. The members had to dedicate their near-term future to themselves, not their wives or kids or parents. They had to learn to take care of themselves. Some of these meetings would make soap operas look like a fairy tale. These meetings were real life! Emotions were spent. The addicts got out of the meetings as much as they were willing to emotionally get from them. They wanted to help themselves and help some others. It was not one upmanship or ego; it was lifesaving. Some of the people were there because it was court ordered; most were not. There were some things that went on at meetings that I think were bullshit, but then again, I am not an addict. Spirituality is a major factor in the twelve-step process. If one fought the logic and conviction, or approached the meetings with a closed mind, they were wasting their time, and the time of everyone else. Some talked their problems out while others absorbed what was going on and they may have internalized. No one cared how you beat it as long as you could stay on top and not revert back to being an active addict. There was no such thing as a former addict. The addiction was still there as it was with a reformed smoker. There was no difference. How many of us have lost weight, but couldn't stay on the new lifestyle or schedule? It was the same and even more difficult because of the stigma. If your kid was a druggie and got straightened out in some regard, you would be proud and so would he. If that kid was a friend of your child, you were harping on your child to stay away from the drug addict. That label sticks with the individuals for years or a lifetime. What's the description you would use if you were describing your friend's kid if he were a reformed addict? It probably would go something like "my friend's son was an addict and he was in trouble three years ago. He is a nice kid and very handsome." Why would the addiction word be foremost? It would be and that is our society; accept it!

Cindy went to a number of meetings with Mark, but was really a baby sitter for him. He respected Cindy enough to open up even when she was there. Mark would try to stay sober (a term used by all addicts from alcohol to drugs to any other addiction) and eventually earn his pin for being sober for 90 days. He also seemed motivated to get a sponsor who was someone you could call at any time, night or day, and they would be there to prevent you from slipping. He almost had one a few times, but never quite made it. One time he went to a meeting full of vim and vigor and met one of the other people attending the meeting and they got together after the meeting and did drugs that same night. It was a rough situation. There were stories of bikers (motorcyclists) that were at the other end of the country when someone slipped, made a call to their sponsor, who then proceeded to board a plane and be there within six hours. That's the type of dedication that was needed, but not usually found.

The only problem that we saw was Mark wanted to be with his girlfriend. She didn't have a clue as to planning for her future. She still had a year to go in high school, and was only looking forward to the next party. There was nothing wrong with that considering the age and mentality of most high school juniors, especially ones that have had problems in the past. They seemed to be more in tune for now because the future was too far away. Most adults realized that the future got closer as you got older. Anyway, the relationship with her was hot, but not serious, as was typical. The school year was almost over. The kids were starting to make plans for the proms. In this school, since it was small, the entire high school was invited to the prom, which was held in a restaurant banquet hall. The attendance that was expected and the commitments made determined at which hall it would be held. There was not your typical excitement because these kids were very blasé about school events or spirit and it wasn't cool. Mark was typical of that attitude. Also, his girl's ex-boyfriend was hitting on her again, and that made Mark furious. It was a bad situation because they all went to the same school. About four weeks before graduation, this situation was starting to get even nastier.

Mark was at her house one night, about 10 o'clock, and called us at home to tell us the ex-boyfriend was outside her house with three of his friends. Mark said the four of them had baseball bats and they were looking for trouble. I didn't know whether to believe him or not. I now had the dilemma of calling the police, her father (who didn't live in the area) or going to her house, which would take me fifteen minutes. I chose to get in the car and go to the house. I also took pepper spray. I had learned that it was better to be safe than sorry when dealing with irrational people.

I got to the house and no one other than the kids were home. The girlfriend lived with her mom. Her parents were divorced, but her dad still took an interest in her. Her father was tough and street smart from time spent in prison, and was apparently aware of some friction that was happening with the two boyfriends.

I spoke to the kids and told Mark not to get into a battle unless it was one on one. I said that because I couldn't prevent a fight, but if there was one, maybe it would be less brutal and maybe one would give up after a few blows. With that, I went home. I called her dad to tell him what happened and maybe alert him to the situation and maybe he could talk his daughter into talking sense into the boys. And maybe there really was an Easter bunny!

Who knew why responsible people tried to give advice and talk sense into people who didn't want to hear it because "we are told we don't understand." Nothing else happened that night, except Mark left her house and never came home. We were figuring either there was a battle somewhere or he was so pumped up that he went down and did drugs. By morning, we figured it was drugs. We got a call later the following day that he screwed up again because of the problems at his girl's house. There was always a new excuse. We had to go down and buy gas for his car so he could get it home. We did this and the routine began. I was pissed that he screwed up and Cindy tried to talk to Mark without me losing my temper and kicking Mark's ass out of the house. I usually calmed down after about an hour and then started to think logically.

Two weeks later, we got a call from school that we should come down to meet with the principal, which we did. We were informed that they took a switchblade knife from Mark, who said he was using it for protection against the former boyfriend, who Mark said threatened him with a baseball bat again. Cindy and I just sat and listened because in this type of situation, it was not easy to have a response. Being logical, we figured that the school had a better handle on this than we ever possibly could. Mark was sitting in on this whole conversation. Everyone wanted to know where the bat was and he said it was in the boy's car. One of the teachers went out to the car and did not find any bat. The principle asked Mark to wait outside the room because she wanted to speak with us alone.

Picture this situation; a senior in high school, a weapon with about six inches of sharp blade, no obvious threat against him, graduation coming in two weeks, college acceptance, a $20,000 investment in his education on the line, and we had nothing to say. We couldn't defend the situation and obviously couldn't justify or rectify the situation. We almost felt like we were students in the principle's office hoping that our parents wouldn't be called in. That was a strange sensation. We weren't sure if the police were going to be called in and we just weren't up for more problems.

The shoe dropped and we weren't sure how to react. We were advised that we should take Mark home and not return to school. He was not permitted to be anywhere near the graduation ceremony and would be mailed his graduation diploma. Cindy was sort of in shock. We guessed that meant he would still graduate. We then had to figure what to tell the grandparents because they were looking forward to seeing their grandson succeed and start his life without any more problems. We also had planned a graduation party for him with all of the friends and neighbors, especially since there was such good news about the future and college. We did what all good responsible parents would do in that situation; we lied!

We told the grandparents that he had a little problem in school and we wanted to teach him a lesson that would be significant and maybe help him in the future. They thought that was harsh, but if Cindy felt that we were right, what could they say. That was the position that Cindy tried to put them in so we would not have to go into detail. The people at the party never asked and we never volunteered. The party had about 80 people as it was an open house and we were used to large-group entertaining. We even brought in a psychic to take individuals in for five and ten minute conferences to predict their future. It was amazing how popular this was and there were people lined up all night to see her. I asked a few of the people who met what they thought of the reading with her, and they said she was great. I couldn't believe how many people take these psychics seriously. She told me everything was about to straighten out with Mark and things were going to get much better. That sounded good which I guessed was supposed to, since I was paying her fee for the evening. Aside from the surreal, the party went well and it was generally a very upbeat evening.

The school year ended and I wanted Mark to get a job. He worked at a construction job for a cash salary. He also learned that you could drink on the job and blow a joint if you want, and there is no reason for stress. The last part was a good lesson, but was it worth the sacrifice? Unfortunately, I found all of this out after the summer and past actions that we learned about were past actions. We knew we were just part of the training program like all parents in this situation. I don't know why there weren't classes that teach parents how to cope with kids on drugs. The only ones that I knew were the support groups for the people with a vested interest in the addicts and they all said the same thing which was " if they can't or don't help themselves, you can't help them. You can give them moral support, but don't be an enabler. Understand that they did it to themselves because they wanted to, and they must get their problems under control because they want to." The meetings only showed that you were not alone and you could relate to others who had the same problems. The problems were all the same and yours were no different. The meetings gave you ideas of how other parents coped with the problems, along with sharing the frustration of not being successful. Sound confusing? It was if you thought you had an answer to cure addiction. If you are still confused, go to a meeting and you will partially understand. The emotions are real, but they are emotional responses only. The meetings are there for support, but offer very little solutions if you are not the addict. Sounds cruel, but reality, as they say, is a bitch!

The summer was closing and college was getting ready to start. We packed up the car and prepared for the freshman orientation. We had gone out and bought the things on the list that the college recommended, including a computer, which Mark had begun learning to use. There was the special bedding we had to buy because we had nothing for a single bed. There were the toiletries that had to have special cases. There were the laundry bags, iron, sewing kit, etc. We packed egg crates for his books and a desk that we had to assemble there. We had cartons of clothes. The trick was to get everything in the jeep and still have room to sit for the six-hour drive. It was a gratifying feat when completed, as every dad who sent a child off to college will attest to with pride. Once we got to the college, we had to unload the jeep and walk two flights of steps just to get everything up to his room. We had to get all of this stuff unpacked, and put away quickly, because we had to be on time for the president's welcome speech, as well as speeches from faculty advisors and other students. We hurried and made the meeting and did most of the unpacking. We even met a few of the boys on the floor. (None of who volunteered to help the old man carry the shit from the car!) The meetings were basically "Hey dude, where you from? That's cool." This was our future!

The orientation was boring and lasted about two hours. The good part was that the weather was great and we had time to just sit out and watch 'college life.' We felt pretty good and were hoping this new influence would work. The library was close, as were the tutors. With everything in place, we could start to sleep at night knowing that Mark was in a dorm room in college with kids somewhat interested in getting an education. The first night we got home after six more hours of driving met with a phone call saying he missed his girlfriend. We should have told him to use his right hand and he would stop missing her, but we said we would buy him a round trip ticket to come home the first weekend. The deal was $49 each way so we thought that was cheap enough to keep him in a good frame of mind. The phone bills were getting high because he called home every night, like we lived next door. He came home the first weekend and this became his ritual for the first three weeks. Cindy asked him how he was doing and he said fine. We believed him, which was another mistake. If you get nothing out of this book, remember these words "It's not what you expect, it's what you inspect!" These words are borrowed from a close friend and they are prophetic!

After eight weeks, he said he couldn't handle being away and he withdrew from college. Cindy and I lost all of our tuition money, which was more than $10,000. He withdrew under the category "passing," which meant he could go back. We now had to go up and repack everything and find a place for everything of which we wanted nothing; but if he went back, would need the same stuff all over again. We went through our ritual of going up in a very depressed mood knowing he was coming home with no direction.

He was now home, eighteen years old, with no particular skill. He got a job pumping gas. His hours were terrible and he got the job because he was a warm body. He also got the job because another one of his friends told him about it. The only skill he developed was learning how to fix flat tires and plug them when necessary. He had strange hours and would be called in randomly if they were busy or he would be told to clock out if they were not busy. This was the type of job that either gave a person incentive to better himself or go through life with little self-esteem. The boss and manager treated him like shit and that bothered Mark. He was friendly with all the kids who worked there part time and they all hated the manager. The manager was about 35 years old, with the constant odor of alcohol on his breath.

We were sitting at home one evening and a police officer knocked on our door and asked for Mark, who was not home at the time. We asked why they wanted to see him and he explained that he wanted to talk to Mark and his friend, who worked at the gas station on the shift the night before. I said that when he came home, we would take him to the station. Mark came home about 10:00 p.m., and Cindy told him about the visit we had. He said that he would go over and talk to the police. He came back home about an hour later and told us why he was being questioned. Someone had put the residue battery acid, which was powdery, into the coffee creamer at the service station. It was mixed in so it was not distinguishable. The night manager drank some coffee using the creamer and became violently ill. The police thought that the two employees from the night before were responsible. Mark vehemently denied having anything to do with it and said he had no idea who did the prank. The night manager was not seriously or permanently affected, but would prefer never to relive that night, the testing at the hospital, or the pain that was endured. The police questioned the kids again and I also questioned Mark. The results were that he was completely innocent. The issue was dropped, but the two boys were fired because whatever occurred was on their shift and they should have been responsible. Cindy was considering speaking with the owner to discuss that it was not fair to fire the kids. Instead, she backed away because there were already too many problems that we were dealing with. About six months later, Mark told Cindy that he and his friends did take the acid and mix it with coffee creamer. She just stored the information and let it drop.

Mark spent the next few days hanging around the house with us, and as typical parents, we were harping on him to get a job. It was during these lounging days that we realized why we were happy when he was away in school. The phones were forever ringing and he was always running in and out, and again not showing up where and when he was supposed to. He was very depressed from dropping out of school and not working. He was depressed, but not making an effort to resolve the problem. He was afraid to face a new job or even a new job interview. The only thing that always seemed to show up were girls because he was unpredictable and the youth of today seems to find that exciting.

Mark was out most nights and whatever he said he would be back was insignificant because time didn't seem to matter to him. Also, it appeared that the day started at noon and ended somewhere before daybreak. One evening, Cindy was sitting home waiting for the latest adventure to start because Mark had missed a job interview earlier in the day. Nothing happened that night and he didn't show up at home. About 10:00 a.m., she got a phone call from the police department in the city. They said that they would like us to come down to the hospital. We asked what was wrong. The police said there was a problem with Mark and we should come down right away. We asked if he was all right. They wouldn't give us an answer. The drive to the hospital took forty-five minutes, but it seemed like hours. We discussed the possibility that he may be dead, or he may have been high and got into a bad accident, or he got into a bad fight and was really messed up with internal injuries, or he overdosed and was in serious mental incapacity. We immediately thought again that we didn't want another child who was like Ritchie, in a coma-like state forever. We said that if he was messed up, we would tell the doctors to let him die. We drove, talked, and tried to be rational about all of the possibilities. We got to the emergency room and were taken in right away. They put us in a room with no windows and only three chairs. We looked at each other and thought that something real serious happened and it wasn't good. We waited about five minutes and three staff members came into the room and closed the door. The staff all remained standing. We looked at each other and knew Mark was dead. We figured that the two staff were there to handle us when we broke down after the doctor told us the bad news.

"Your son jumped off the Walnut Street Bridge last night and it is a hundred-foot drop," the doctor said

"Is he alive," I asked.

"Yes," he said.

He said when he was brought in, he didn't have any identification on him, so the doctor asked Cindy if she could describe his tattoos.

"What tattoos?" Cindy asked.

The doctor told us about the one that was across most of his back, in the shape of a half moon and the one on his shoulder with his initials.

We were now confused and upset, but realized that it was our son, and we still didn't know how badly he was hurt. Our minds thought alike and we were now thinking broken neck and bedridden. That would not have been unreasonable. We were scared. We asked if we could see him and the doctor said we had to wait about fifteen minutes because the other doctors were still in with him. The three left and said that someone would come in and get us when we could go see him. Our thoughts again started with the assumptions that he tried to kill himself or someone threw him over the bridge. We realized that we heard nothing about his car, which was an 8-year old Dodge Charger we had bought for him two weeks earlier. (Yes, I did finally get my own way on some economic sense and bought a junker.) That thought passed quickly and our thoughts again were with his physical condition, which was still unknown to us. We kept looking at our watches, waiting. Fifteen minutes went by and we went out to the nurses. We told them we were waiting to see him, but the nurse told us to go back into the room and they would get us shortly. We were wondering if he was in a cast from head to toe, or just bandaged everywhere. How many stitches do you think he could have gotten?

After another fifteen minutes, a nurse came in and told us to follow her, which we did. We went into the emergency room, and they opened a curtain. Mark was lying in bed, slightly bruised on his face, and looking achy all over, but otherwise in good condition. The doctor told us Mark had three broken ribs, a punctured lung and various bruises, but was otherwise in good condition. He also said this was the first survivor that he was aware of who had gone off of that bridge. I asked how he survived and was told that aside from luck, the evening before, it had rained and there was about 6 inches of water, which broke his fall. He missed all of the rocks that were typical of the bottom terrain or maybe he hit the rocks with his ribs, which caused that breakage. The nurse said they got about a dozen jumpers per year and this was the first survivor that she had seen. I questioned Mark to see what happened and he said he was high, annoyed, and standing on the bridge wall when a passerby saw him, approached him and told him not to jump. He remembered that the guy was annoying, so he jumped. It occurred late at night, so Mark had no idea what he was jumping into.

After he jumped, the passerby, who no one knew, called police who came to the rescue. The bridge floor was not accessible from the adjacent ground. A crane was called in to lower the rescue workers to the ground. They attached a stretcher to the crane's wire rope to lift him out. He was not able to move by himself so the rescuers worked through the watery mud and rock formations. Traffic was tied up for hours during the rescue. Police on the scene told us that there was a car that looked like the one we described at the entry to the roadway about ½ block from the bridge. We said we would check it when we left the hospital.

We continued to talk to Mark to get all of the details. He said that he was bored and just didn't care, but he didn't want to kill himself. He was frustrated and took it out on his car, which we weren't sure what he meant. He said it was stupid and he wanted to go home. We asked the doctor what the release situation was and he said that the psychiatrist had to determine if he was a threat to himself. If he wasn't, they would release him in three days and he would have to stay in bed at home for two or three more days. All three of us spoke to the shrink who then said she felt that he was not in danger of harming himself. I must be really stupid, but I would have believed that after someone jumped from a bridge, he was quite capable of wanting to harm himself. I don't believe that 24 hours after an episode like that, the victim was not into fantasyland about his wonderful future. Well, it was obvious that I don't have medical training because my opinion certainly was different from the experts. At the final moment of our leaving, Mark told the doctor that he felt fine and would feel more comfortable at home rather than wait the required time in the hospital. To this, the doctor said he could go home with us. How many years of medical training did this genius have?

The hospital packed up his torn clothes that were cut off of him and we left the emergency room together. I guess they gave you the clothes back to tease you about the money that was wasted on what they cut off of his body. Mark very carefully maneuvered himself into the car as if he were 100 years old instead of eighteen. Every move he made evoked verbal and facial pain. Now that he was captive in the car and in pain, I laid into his stupidity of action and wondered if he was just testing his own endurance. I told him about his future potential and called him every name in the book. I accomplished nothing! His pain overcame my dramatic lecture. We stopped at the bridge to see where he went off, to locate his car, and to see what happened. As we looked down, it was a miracle that he wasn't killed by the fall. I sarcastically asked him if he would like to try again as the pain this time would really test him. He looked up and said it wasn't funny.

"Then why did you do it?" Obviously that was a redundant question.

We located the car or what was left of it. It was a good thing that I vented my anger a few minutes earlier because I was livid. The car looked like it was through a demolition derby and came in last! Every window was totally smashed. The roof was mostly caved in; the doors looked as if many hammers hit them, and the inside would have looked better if someone had poured on gasoline and lit it.

However, at this point, we wanted to get him home because he was in major pain. We didn't know who we could call about the car because mechanically, it couldn't be driven and it was only insured for liability. Well, one thing at a time. We got him home and he found his way by crawling to his bed and asking to be left alone with no more lectures, just sleep. We honored that wish because there was nothing else to discuss. I got the car towed to a salvage yard and asked what they would give us for the car. The owner was not stupid and knew he had us over the proverbial barrel and offered us $250 which we accepted. Prior to the damage, it would have been worth about $4,000. Another nice loss!

We figured that we had two or three days to decide what we

were going to do with Mark. He was not capable of being on his own and had very little concept of reality such as paying for bills, food, clothing, etc. We didn't really want to do another useless rehab center but he couldn't function on his own without screwing up somehow.

We learned about a program that was being used in the prison systems. The program was brainwave training. It gave immediate feedback to the user of the right responses for your brain. The patient had electrodes attached to his head and earphones that stimulated the response. The idea was phenomenal and the results had a proven track record. The procedure was to spend an hour per day for 35 sessions that were consecutive. This meant that Cindy had to drive about an hour each day, one way, sit outside the room, and wait. The hour session was monitored by a trained therapist and was controlled. Mark decided that it was worth a try. He figured that it would take seven weeks. Insurance would pay about half the cost and we had to pay the balance as performed. The key to this program was not to miss a single session. It had been about three weeks since his bridge episode so everyone figured that he would hang in for this program. Wrong!

Cindy was always very honest with Mark and told him Friday that the program would be starting on Monday. He took off on Sunday and did not come home for dinner. We knew exactly what happened and were trying to decide what to do. Mark panicked because the program was new to him and he always had a fear of something new. It was Sunday night. Should we call the program director now since he did an analysis to prepare the program for Mark and seemed to have a strong understanding of the situation, or do we wait and see if he called in the middle of the night to pick him up somewhere. We called his girlfriend to see if she had any idea of his whereabouts, she told us that he was with her, and he told her he was heading home.

Monday afternoon Mark called home and asked Cindy to pick him up in the projects. I went down with her to get him and he was typical of most druggies in that he was apologetic and unhappy with himself. He came home and Cindy called the program director, who said Mark could start Tuesday, which he did. Cindy was back to her routine of driving Mark to all of the sessions. After the first five weeks, Cindy was out of time and was needed at work. We asked the therapist about getting him a car at this point and he said it should be fine. We bought an old Chevy for $1,000 and it ran fine.

Mark and Cindy went twenty six times to the program. We really could not tell if it had any effect, but we learned to go to the program to the end unless there were obvious flaws. On the 27th visit, or should I say scheduled visit, Mark didn't show up at home. Cindy called the program and the director seemed concerned because Mark was so far into the training. They said to call them as soon as we heard anything. We didn't hear a word for three days and were getting concerned. We decided to drive down to the drug district to see if we could locate him. We did this for the next three days with no success.

My work at the office was suffering because I was tied up hunting for Mark or trying to keep Cindy's head and my head together. There was tremendous pressure because we knew he had no money and he had to do something drastic to survive, but we didn't know what. We checked police stations and hospitals. We watched the news at night to see what crimes were committed because we figured that we might be able to guess if they were his work. We thought of the crimes because he loved to read about gangsters, especially Al Capone, who he idolized. My thoughts revolved around whether he was straight or high. I felt that if he were high, even the little old ladies and their handbags were not safe.

On the 8th day, Cindy and Mark's girlfriend were riding in the drug district and they spotted Mark's car with four "be bopping" teenage druggies driving the car with the radio blasting. Cindy, in her infinite wisdom, forced them to the side of the road. Any one of them could have caused great harm to Cindy or Mark's girlfriend. The teenagers got out of the car with a rather tough demeanor because Cindy was on their turf. She said that was her son's car and what were they doing driving it? They said they bought the car from someone they described and it was Mark. The problem was Cindy was not totally stupid, just a little. The title was in Cindy's name. We kept wondering why we were so stupid and why we kept buying him cars! We came to the conclusion that we were hoping Mark would straighten out; but it was still the chicken or the egg routine, which came first? We were realistic that we were not going to save any money and everything we made was not only going into Mark, but also indirectly into drugs and drug seller's pockets. Cindy talked to the four guys and negotiated a deal. She said the boys didn't have the title, but she would give it to them after they showed her where Mark was. They thought they got this dumb old lady to give up the car so they told her to follow them to Mark. The girls followed them deeper into the side streets of drugville. Fortunately, these guys only saw the car title in their eyes. The car had been sold to them for $200. The only other problem was that the car was worth $1,000! The kids parked and said Mark was in a house a few feet away. The houses in this area were row homes with sixteen-foot fronts and mostly boarded up windows. Cats were freely roaming the streets and there were many vacant houses. That area was known for danger including frequent homicides. The kids walked right into the house. The door was wide open and drugs were just lying around. Young people were spaced out on broken down furniture that junkyards wouldn't take. Needles and crack vials were all over the floor. Both girls walked in and saw Mark in a corner. He was high as a kite. Cindy told him to get up, go outside, and get into her car. His girlfriend tried to talk to him, but he was doing his thing; he was still high and not coming down. The kids with the car were getting pissed because they wanted the title so they told him to leave. He didn't, so the four of them picked him up and put him in Cindy's car. He offered little resistance because he was out of it.

There were auto tag stores in that neighborhood that often

gave titles before they checked out the situation; they preferred not to know most things because they got very healthy fees for their auto tag work. The kids then followed Cindy, who was heading home. They were driving Mark's car. On the way home, from her cell phone, Cindy called the suburban police from our neighborhood to tell them what had happened and what was occurring. They said to continue home and they will take it from there. These city kids had no idea where they were, nor did Cindy believe that they were even out of the city before. The kids drove up to Cindy's home and two police cars sandwiched them in. The police asked Cindy to go into the house. About ten minutes later, the police said the kids told them they had bought the car for $200 and had the receipt to prove it, which they did. The police told Cindy that the kids would forget the whole thing if they could get back their money. She paid the $200. The police said that the kids would be dropped off at the bus station about three miles away with instructions not to come back to this community. The police did protect their community and we were grateful. No one could be sure if these kids would or would not come back, but if they did, they would be pissed at us! As for Mark, he just looked at this as another fuck-up.

After about a week, I anticipated what Cindy would say. Mark couldn't find any jobs that were within walking distance so shouldn't they take the financial risk and hope Mark believed what he said and could do it. At one point, I told Cindy that the old bike in the garage could be fixed up and he could go as much as five miles or more. I tried it just to show Cindy that it was no big deal. About one mile away, I thought I was having a heart attack because I was so tired; but I didn't want to give in to Cindy. The problem was the bike was broken and every pedal was like moving a ton of bricks! That ended that, and his driving was back into consideration, but with better rules. No one seemed to care.

Chapter Eleven

Two days later, while in the office, I wasn't feeling very well and drove myself to the hospital. I told them that I had chest pains. The emergency room hooked me up to monitor my heart. They called Cindy and told her to come down and that I appeared to be fine. Cindy walked into the emergency room and told me to stop stressing myself out. With that, Cindy looked at all of the monitors with the bleeping sounds and pulse lines. Cindy was sitting next to me on the bed and we were kidding with each other. There is a sense of security being in a hospital in case something happens. Cindy, with a twinkle in her eye, reached under the cover and started "messing around" in very sensitive spots on my body. The monitors started going crazy and the nurses darted into the room. What excuse does one make up at a time like that? "Sorry, but my wife wanted to see what a horny guy would do to the machine," or "there must be a problem with the machine when I moved." Either way, the smiles on their faces told me that the nurses knew exactly what happened! We went home that night and, well, let's say if the machines were hooked up, it would have blown their circuits!

The stress was from the situations that Mark put us in. I decided we needed some protection. I went out and bought a semiautomatic pistol. I drove to the parking lot of the shooting range, and went in for the first time. I told the guy behind the counter that I hadn't shot before but the attendant didn't pay much attention. That was probably because he didn't want to be bothered. I probably was crying out for him to help, but it didn't work that way. Besides, it wasn't macho to ask for help involving guns. I paid my fee and went into the range. I looked around and saw people standing in a specific area and they looked like they knew what to do. I found an open station and very carefully put the bullets on the front shelf. There were 100 in the box. I pulled out the clip from my new gun and very cautiously put six bullets into the clip. I was in a cold sweat. I checked three times that the lock was on. I pointed the gun toward the firing area, took the clip, and inserted it into the gun. I was very tense now because I had to take the lock off trying to keep the gun from accidentally firing. My hands were cold and clammy, but I was now ready to shoot. I decided not to take the lock off and practice aiming before I shot, which I did for about one minute. As they say in the movie, *Lion King*, "it is time." I took off the lock and aimed the gun toward the target on the string about ten yards away. I was afraid to pull the trigger because I didn't know if there was a kick or how the gun would feel. Should I grip it tighter so it won't fly out of my hands? My throat was dry. I looked and aimed and, yes, I fired – nothing happened. I was scared shitless. The gun jammed. I heard that semi automatics are dangerous if the gun jammed, but I didn't know if the bullet would explode or go off. Was it in the chamber? What do I do now? I could have hurt someone. I didn't know how to get the gun un-jammed. I sheepishly walked out to the same man at the counter who ignored me before and told him of my dilemma. He looked at me like I was the dumbest sonofabitch that he ever saw. At that point, he was right! The manager pulled the clip and removed the bullet that was in the chamber. The manager then did me a big favor. He asked me to leave and not come back until I had some training. I left and was too embarrassed to ask for my money back! I took his advice and signed up for a ten-hour class with Cindy. My thought was that if I'm not home, Cindy better know how to protect herself against intruders. Based on Mark's adventures, it was possible.

We started the course and the instructor taught us the parts of the guns and the type of bullets and what they could do. He explained when to and when not to use the gun. He told us to watch the laws of each state because it could be a bad situation if we were in a state that didn't recognize our license. It was a different world going from the adjacent classroom to the firing range. It was important to have the right-hand position as well as the proper balance and way to look at the site. We used the instructor's guns. He worked with each of us at the range on positioning and breathing. It was more complicated than we thought it would be, but we felt confident. We both passed and got their gun permits 100% legal. How many times have we said to ourselves that if someone were to invade our homes, we would have no problem shooting them? How many times have we thought that if we were fighting off the intruder, the gals could get the gun and be able to protect themselves? It was common for everyone to have these thoughts. In our case, the situations were getting as close as the thoughts, so we now had a comfort zone.

Cindy hated guns, but she understood it was a necessity. We were glad that we took the class together and then bought a revolver, which was the easiest gun to use. At the class, we learned that it could be more effective not to use the gun. Pepper spray had many more advantages because it disabled the attacker and if it were multiple attackers, the spray could take all of them out quickly and efficiently from ten to twenty feet. You just had to get it near them or on their clothing, which made it accessible to their face. You also did not need a license and there were no potential murder charges to face. It put the attackers down for a few minutes and the only things that they could do was rub their eyes and try to wash them out. We decided that I bought the right gun so I went back to the shop where I bought the semi automatic and asked for them to take it back, which they did. After all, after watching all of those western movies and seeing how the cowboys reloaded those revolvers, I knew that I could do that. We also learned that with a 38, you had better be close to who you were shooting. The gun was not as accurate as the spray! At the pistol range, twenty feet was a long way for a 38. We felt that from the top of the stairs at our home, it would do fine. We now had a gun and didn't get to fire one shot! At the class, guns were supplied.

We had the gun and the training, so what do we do with it now? Do we store it with or without bullets? Where do we hide it so Mark didn't find out we had it? If someone came in while we were asleep, if it wasn't loaded, what good was it? If it was under my pillow, what if I rolled over and hit the trigger because there was no safety? Should we leave it in the car? What if Mark found it? Should we leave the bullets in another place? Was it a good idea to get the gun in the first place? Those were the questions that we asked when the gun was first brought into our home. Things were starting to get out of hand because we were having concerns not only about Mark, but also outside people who may not play nicely. The process used for getting the previously mentioned gun was a unique experience for us. We went to the county seat for a gun permit and were told to take forms that they gave us to the police department in our community for approval first. They asked us what we wanted the permit for and we said safety. They approved the permit, we sent it in with $15, and we were legal for two years, which would then be the renewal time. Through this all, neither Cindy nor I liked guns and we were still afraid of them.

January and February were fairly calm. Mark spent a lot of time with Cindy and also his girlfriend. One of the neighbors owned a restaurant in center city and said that he could use Mark to prepare food and wash dishes. Mark always gave anyone who hired him a full day's work when he was there. He didn't look to hide out anywhere. That seemed like a great situation because Mark had to be in at 7:00 a.m. and that meant that he would probably be fairly tired by the end of the day. Mark was happy to work because sitting around the house was absolutely boring and he was storing energy and getting very cranky. It reminded me of when Cindy was pregnant and at home for the last two months, and again during Ritchie's first few months at home. She was used to being with people and then she was stuck at home with no one to converse with. The minute I walked through the door, she attacked me with the nonevents of her day. I came home to my refuge to get a few minutes of peace and quiet before getting into the hustle of crying baby and my refuge was gone. Cindy couldn't understand that I needed five minutes to wash up and take a deep breath.

This frustration of dead end work was what Mark was facing

at home and he couldn't cope with that feeling of being trapped. The restaurant job was going well for about three weeks. He was taking the train into town and being dropped off about three blocks from the restaurant. His job was to prepare the tuna fish and salad for the lunch crowd. Those items were always major sellers and the place used gallons of tuna. After the first week, I asked him if he wanted tuna for dinner and I'm lucky Mark didn't have a gun available. Even the smell started to make him nauseous. He said everything was fine and Cindy thought that he was learning a trade that he could always use.

Three weeks later, Thursday, March 19, he went to work. Cindy got a call at 8:00 a.m. asking why Mark wasn't in work. She said he left on time and should be there shortly. That was a wishful statement that should have ended with 'I hope.' As you can surmise, he never showed up. We had no idea where to look for him because he had no car and was not in the usual ten or fifteen drug places that we knew, since we immediately went to look for him. We just had to wait for him to contact us.

He went to work with sneakers and older clothes, but not a heavy winter coat. The temperatures were in the 30s and we figured he would call soon. Nothing happened for about four days. We then got a call from someone who went to high school with him and also knew us. He told us that he saw Mark in the underground train station in center city and Mark was crying and panhandling money. We drove downtown which was about thirty miles away and began walking the underground system with pictures of Mark. We were showing them to the security people and some of the homeless that lived there. We did this for two days with little success. There were people who said they saw him two days ago or a few hours ago, but we were unable to find him. The reason that he was remembered was because of his emotional state. It was obvious to the people that he was in trouble. I went through the homeless soup lines, but again had no luck. We saw parts of life, if you can call it that, we did not want to see. It made one think that with millions of dollars going into useless garbage that the government buys or finances, couldn't they make a concerted effort to help these people get their lives back in some form. Many lived in filth and physical pain. They trusted no one. At night, I went alone because I didn't want Cindy to be in a dangerous situation that could have occurred at any second. She drove the car above ground, while I walked the tunnels, and met me at pre-designated areas. I carried the gun in my jacket pocket as I walked over and past the sleeping homeless. I was out of my element. I thought that if they were cold and my jacket was appealing, I might have had a fight on my hands. It wouldn't have been because of the jacket, which was the oldest and rattiest that I had, but if they saw I was vulnerable, I feared that my safety was in jeopardy. I hated that feeling of helplessness.

During the day, friends of ours who were in town circulated Mark's picture. They got the same story about seeing him and that was days ago. On the seventh day, I talked to a train police officer that said he saw him about two hours earlier and that he put him on a train. Once he told me which one, I knew he was into the drug district again. Cindy and I drove there to no avail. We couldn't find him. Even the drug pushers knew our car and told us that they didn't see Mark.

The next day, my brother, Paul, came to the house. I told him what happened and he said to let Mark go and get on with our lives. I said that if he had cancer, would he try to help. Paul understood the analogy, but said it wasn't the same. I said that drugs were something that one couldn't understand unless you've been there. We explained that Mark didn't want to be a druggie, but an addiction was not easy to break. How many times had we tried dieting? How many times had we tried to stop smoking? How many times did we try to stop ... ?

Paul still didn't understand, but said he would go looking with me while Cindy stayed home in case he would call. If he called, he would not leave a message, so Cindy would have to coax him to talk. By this time, everyone was concerned about his safety. I drove to drug city with my brother. I said to Paul to go around the block one-way and I would go the other. There was a Dunkin' Donuts store on the corner and that seemed a logical place to start, since there was heat there and very often the homeless could get money near there and get a sugar fix. Also, the stores would throw away the old donuts and the indigents would grab a few before they were chased away. I got lucky. Paul spotted someone about twenty yards up the street and yelled his name. Mark turned around and started to walk toward him. Paul, who has seen Mark at least once a week for the past eighteen years, said that he didn't recognize him from close up or from the twenty yards away, but he had the walk of Mark. His expression was one Paul never saw and his walk was hunched over and he was shivering.

Just when Mark got to Paul, I turned the corner about ten yards away. Mark looked up and said he was sorry. I asked if he was ready to go home and he said he was. He got into the car and we called Cindy on the cell phone. I said to her that we had someone who wanted to talk to her. He got on the phone and spoke very softly with the sounds of tears in his voice. He was hurting from exposure and from hurting Cindy. He loved her and knew she devoted her life to him, and he wanted to make her happy, but his problems kept beating him. In the car, on the way home, he said that he couldn't move two of his fingers. We put the heat up in the car to try to get the blood circulating in his fingers and it seemed to work after about a half hour. The same thing was going on with three of his toes, but he didn't tell us until the next day.

He got home and again began to cry when he hugged Cindy. That was a two-way street. He asked if he could go take a shower and then eat. She said sure. He was in the shower about a half hour. He came down with a smile and ate an entire pizza that we had frozen. He then laid down on the sofa and slept twelve hours. We felt thankful that he was safe, but we knew he needed immediate help. During his sleep, Cindy called a number of rehab centers to see if any had openings. They always asked about insurance and usually we were covered for the thirty-day deal. We all knew it was temporary, but we needed the break and always had hope of the miracle place and program that would cure him.

The next day, the 28th of March, we found a place for him three hours away in upstate Pennsylvania that had a bed and was even willing to have a driver pick him up. We said yes to them for admission. Mark was in a precarious position because he knew something had to happen, but he didn't want to go away again, even though it was only a month. He had to agree to go and he was afraid that if he didn't, he would be in a fight with us because we would have felt that he didn't want to get straight. He also didn't want to leave his girlfriend. Before he left, Cindy had Mark sign over title to his car so that if there was a problem, it could be sold. We started putting titles in his name or just put liens on the titles. We were looking to avoid litigation should he have gotten into a problem. Everything that we did had to be scrutinized to see what could happen if there were more fuck ups. There was nothing spontaneous about our existence. Every night that he went out, we went to bed as early as possible because we knew there was a definite possibility of us getting a phone call at three or four in the morning to get up and go get him somewhere in the badlands or as they called it, 'down the way.' On the 29th, the driver came about noon and Mark was packed and ready to go. The driver just took a three-hour journey and was ready to make the return trip. We couldn't speak to Mark for 72 hours, so we had three restful nights' sleep. His girlfriend had concern, but they weren't 'future' serious, although they apparently were sexually compatible. Our biggest hope was that she didn't get pregnant. Cindy read one of Mark's letters to his girlfriend when she stopped over the house to speak to him one night when we were calling him at the rehab. The letters were really well written, which shouldn't surprise anyone because his writing always was deep, especially when he wrote poetry. One letter was as follows:

Mom and Dad,

Hi how are you? How are grandmom and grandpop? I am not feeling so hot emotionally toward others. I really miss home and I really miss my girlfriend Katie. I'm sorry for all of the heartache I have caused. I love both of you dearly. Today we did an outside event that was very challenging and difficult. I have been weightlifting and seeing results from it. This time is for real. I can feel it in my heart. I am really going to change my lifestyle. I have reached my low stand. It is an uphill battle from here. I really just need a change in attitude which I can see developing. I am more pissed at myself than ever and instead of self-pity, I'm going to do something. It will not be a halfway house or any other advice I received here but I feel the change inside. I want to ride the Harley and eventually my car and no longer be branded or scarred due to my past. I am not going to change and become a prep or a yuppie or anything I am not inside. I am honestly happy riding a bike (tattoos and all), and being involved with athletics – and being a man. I have found that I am a man but sometimes I fold and become a boy or a juvenile. I want to have a family with my beautiful girlfriend and I want her to feel as great as she is. No stupid attitude or definitely no idiotic drug will stand in my way. It's time that I really take a stand in my life for my benefit, which will also benefit the ones I love. (All of this I decided. I have not really had any counseling yet. This is me, not some sophisticated doctor talking). I have a whole life ahead of me, not like the 40-year old men I'm with. They do not understand me at all. We'll keep in touch and don't forget me.
I love you
Mark

I figured that we had until about the 27th of April to make decisions on what direction that we would push Mark. On the 21st, we got a call from the rehab and were told that he was coming home the next day because the insurance ran out. Every insurance policy is slightly different in that the amount of coverage per year or between visits varies and there can be lifetime limits. Who checks this type of treatment when one gets insurance? Unless you know or have known someone in this situation, there is no way to seriously consider these factors. It's like planning who in your family that is normal today is going to become a drug addict tomorrow. It is not your first thought. We had the problem of his arrival to consider and we were under time pressure. Did we go to work? What was his attitude aside from calling his girlfriend to get laid? Apparently that part of him had been very predictable. He told us of the atmosphere and the secluded setting, which he enjoyed.

He wrote to a few of the other people from the rehab and apparently got close to two or three people. One that he mentioned specifically was a girl, or younger woman who was twenty-two, and messed up because her boyfriend took advantage of her obedience. He had her high all the time and taking care of some of his friends. She was his servant and couldn't see what he was doing to her until she was a mess and not desirable any longer. Mark was always sensitive to pretty girls who had problems. He would talk to them for hours about philosophy and psychiatry. He was very analytical and also had street intellect. He always made friends easily. He became the leader of many of his group sessions and knew how to cut through the bullshit if someone was lying to the group or to themselves and he let them know it. The professional help in every institution stated that he was a challenge to them because he knew what direction they were going in private sessions. Cindy observed one session, with everyone's permission, and realized that Mark knew too much from all of the treatments and inside dialogue. He was playing to beat the shrinks rather than look to help himself. He did what he had to in order to gain privileges that were based on a system of achievement and merit. He came home and was waiting to decide what to do next. It was pathetic to see someone with no direction with only the knowledge of the drugs and drug culture. He was reading the want ads and there was very little that he was qualified to do. He interviewed a few jobs at veterinary hospitals because he liked animals and didn't have to satisfy many supervisors. He did not like being a peon and the gopher, but he wasn't qualified to do anything else. This went on for a little over a week.

We were at work and came home on May 5th. There was no note as to where he was. He disappeared again. We were pissed and frustrated. It was one of those times that you wanted to hurt him, but you wished he were with you. If he were with you, your fingers would be around his neck, trying to shake some sense into him. At this point, we were just trying to occupy our time, but our thoughts were totally on his safety. On the 9th, he called home and said "he let everybody who loved him down. Everything was going great, there was no reason to leave, and he didn't know why he did." He went on and on. He was again lost in his mind. His image of what his loved ones thought was warped. He forgot to care about himself. He also did not tell Cindy where he was.

We were upset because this was not the pattern that we were used to. He always showed remorse and folded into his mom's arms for security. She thought that he was going to hurt himself or just take off to get away from pressure because his thinking wasn't always rational. We notified the police and said that he and his car were missing. At 3:00 in the afternoon, the local police came over and sat at the kitchen table. The officer asked all types of questions that included Mark's past history and actions, as well as drug problems. That was a common question whenever there was a problem of any sort with kids fourteen to twenty-one. He stayed about twenty minutes and took all of the information as well as a picture of Mark. We tried to get a missing person report, but that was not easy. It was easier to get a stolen car report on the wire. About an hour after the police left, we got a call from Mark and he asked us to pick him up in one of the usual spots. We immediately called the police to say to cancel any action until we found out what was going on. They thanked Cindy for the call and dropped the issue unless she called them back.

It was now the 12th of the month and we were heading to

drug city to pick him up. On the way, we were calling Family Services to see if we could pick him up and take him to a help center. I had spoken to them before. They told me that since Mark called, there was no apparent danger to him and that it was not considered an emergency. If it were their kid, it would have been an emergency! This type of problem had no solution that was satisfactory, nor did it have a path to follow that moved toward a solution. I realized that we were on our own to make judgment calls on the situation and what path we wanted to try to get him to follow. We were emotionally involved, which made us intelligent enough to know that we shouldn't be involved, but we were. We knew that we did not control the situation and it could become volatile at any time. We also didn't know whether Mark was in any condition that would allow him to communicate sensibly, but we would soon find out.

We did know that he would be very depressed because he "lost" his car. We picked him up and realized that he "sold" the car, which he didn't have the legal right to do. Cindy called the state police and spoke to the captain about the situation. He told her that if she reported the car stolen, she would have a better chance of relief from liability should there be an accident involving the car. He also told Cindy, the lien holder of the car, that she would not be responsible for any loss that may occur. He then gave her the kicker that she didn't want to hear; if Mark stole the car, she must report that and press charges. That didn't sound exactly right, but they do this all day long so she pressed charges. That day, she got a parking ticket in the mail which said the car was in the area so we went to the courthouse and they verified the police report that it was stolen and dropped the ticket.

I then spoke to the police in our community and asked for their advice, which was a good move because they wanted to take action to better any situation, if possible. They were especially glad if it took little effort and they had good leads. The situation was if Mark was reported as a missing person, and a notice went out for the missing car, we could try to get a voluntary or involuntary commitment to the state mental hospital. The hospital said they were open 24-hours a day to accept anyone who was a danger to himself. I asked how they determined that and that answer was the most double-talk I had ever heard. I asked a simple question and was told about the rights that a person has prior to hurting himself or herself. The answer was that we were watching him because there was no other viable alterative. We took shifts watching him sleep, waiting for him to sober up and not take off right away after more drugs. He slept about fifteen hours. We didn't!

The stolen car report also had to go into the city district where the theft occurred. The police station was a haven for the down and out, as well as the druggies. What this meant was that the people actually lived in the hallway entry to the police station. They felt safe there because if they owed money to a dealer, the dealer wouldn't hurt him there. It was a horrible sight to see humans living for their next fix. At that stage, they were no different from untrained wild animals. The missing car, a 1979 Chevy Nova, was all but gone. I paid $400 for it. I didn't want to take any more chances on anything involving Mark selling the car or an accident, if he was high. He had a ticket come in for speeding from a neighboring township and it was legitimate. I had to decide if I should tell him he was on his own or do we pay the ticket and try to have the points not issued? How much shit can we let pile up on someone who had no responsibility or caring? If we let it go through the process, he would lose his license and have no shot of ever working because we had no public transportation within walking distance. On the other hand, were we just helping him make excuses for failure or were we enablers? We knew the only jobs that he could get were driving, working at a vet, cooking at a restaurant or maybe light construction. Even at that, the chance of him keeping the job was remote because he felt that he was above minimum wage work.

He was at a conflict because he saw his parents with college and graduate degrees and he never said it, but he felt inferior. It was now May 28th and Mark interviewed for a job at a local motor lodge. He was to work from 4:00 p.m. until 12:30 a.m., and he was to start the next day. We felt that this was a good start after all of the hours of our discussions. We tried to keep the lines of communication open for him. We praised him for having the initiative to get the job and he was telling us he would also like to get a job during the day to make the extra money to get a nice car. Cindy was waiting at home to drive Mark to work the first day and they were supposed to leave home at 3:45. Mark never came home.

In the meantime, Cindy had scheduled a hearing for his ticket after explaining to the officer the conditions and situation. The officer was extremely sensitive to the situation. The hearing was scheduled the next day. We postponed the hearing and were told that within the township politics, they removed the ticket from the files. They said that Cindy had enough problems with which to work. Mark came home late the next day and said he was proud of himself because he didn't do drugs and was out with his friends. Do we ream him for not going to the job, yell at him for leaving us hanging all night wondering where he was or do we compliment his new found sobriety? We felt that sobriety was the important thing so we went with that. What would Sigmund Freud have done? For every textbook question, there was a non-predictable response. We were getting nowhere and he was trying to stay straight. He wanted a job and was convincing as to his sincerity. He was doing everything that we asked and being the loving son that we wanted him to be. He was considerate around the house and washed the cars without our asking and found things to do, but he wanted to do something useful. We felt that he had his act together and we wanted to encourage him to continue. Cindy made deals that he would continue to go to NA (Narcotics Anonymous) meetings and work through problems that were being minimized.

It was the beginning of July and he was going to meetings and working cutting lawns for a contractor. He was our model son. We got a call from the contractor on July 11 saying that Mark went for lunch and never came back. Two days went by and we didn't hear anything. I was pissed at myself for being sucked in and I was pissed at the whole situation and dreading the anticipation of the next few days. Cindy was visibly upset because Mark was doing so well and he let himself down. It was the same old routine with the same result. We wanted so badly to believe and he meant every word that he said about being under control and going to make it. Crack was bad stuff and that was what he had been on. Crack was crack cocaine and was highly visible on the streets of most major cities. I don't know all of the ingredients, but it comes in capsules and can be smoked or snorted. There can be ingredients that can be deadly if a bad batch was put out and no one could guarantee where it came from or what was in it. If it was a bad batch, the manufacturer would not trash it. He would distribute it and not care about the end user who he didn't know. Why should the manufacturer lose money just because some druggies may die or become seriously ill?

We drove through the streets of the city and spent various hours looking. We had no luck. We learned that there were various places that were strategic to park where you could see three different roads that were heavily traveled during the cruises along the avenue. We were there three in the morning looking for a parked car and eight at night looking for cruising and three in the afternoon looking for anything, including our sanity.

On July 17th, we got Mark's call and he said that he was depressed and his car was smashed. He said that he didn't do drugs or alcohol and found someone who let him live with them for the six days he was gone. He had the car, but it could not be driven. We went to get him and then to go check out the car. It was in a garage and I called our friend who had a body shop to come and get it, which he did. He fixed the car in about a week and we paid for it, about $1,500. There was no police report and Mark couldn't or wouldn't give us enough details to report it to anyone. We had little choice but to fix it. We were trying to figure out why someone would let him stay with them. Was he letting them use his car? Was he getting drugs from them? Was there sex involved? We knew it wasn't quite right, but if he told us the truth about not doing drugs or alcohol, it was a big step. How far could we push him and how fragile was he. Usually, he would confide in Cindy and make her happy knowing that he was O.K. He would tease her when he was straight and tease her about the trash type of problems that he had. At least he talked about it and realized it so she thought that was good. He would always sit down with us when we wanted to discuss future problems or situations that he created, which were coming to the forefront. He was extremely intelligent and knew where our thoughts were going, but we all "didn't have the same train ticket when it came time to board the train." He was continuing to go to meetings every night with Cindy so she felt that he could have been on track with his program to get clean. He was spending most of his free time with his girlfriend and that meant fun time, but not productive time. He had a love of the worst rap music anyone had ever heard. From an adult's point of view, there was sex, extreme violence, ear shattering noise, and everything negative in that "music." We were waiting for him to grow out of it because we couldn't do anything except try to be positive.

July 25th, Mark was at his girlfriend's house and apparently had an argument with her. He also had been drinking a large amount of beer, which seemed to be the beverage of the day for all underage kids. She called Cindy to tell her that he was drunk and driving. She never called before to explain his actions, so she must have been concerned or he must have been really drunk! He went to the drug areas and we knew it. This time was different because he sold his car for $300 and we were on top of it. We contacted the police and wrote to the capital and the state department of transportation to report the car stolen. If anyone tried to get the title, it would show up as stolen. The police didn't care as they were starting to know us and they didn't want to be bothered with the dumb suburban couple that was always chasing their kid. Mark had phone contact with us and told us he slipped and did drugs. Once he started, he couldn't stop until he ran out of money or things to sell. The problem was that drugs and alcohol both stimulated the use of each other for an addict. He said that he could stay away from the drugs, but if he had a drink or two, he wanted the crack high. Once he had the high, which only lasted two or three minutes, he wanted another that was as good. The problem was that the first high was the best and the drive to get the same high back forced you to continue, but it was never, never, repeated.

The druggies didn't realize that and they continued to try to get high. They put the crack at one end, and their lips at the other. They light the crack and inhale the smoke. They burned the hell out of their lips because the holder usually got hot. They didn't feel the heat. The lips actually can and do blister. It is painful to see. We got goose bumps and chills looking at Mark's lips because they started to crack open as they healed.

When he called for Cindy to pick him up, he was sober and said he didn't do drugs within the last 24 hours. She spoke to him on the cell phone while in her car and realized that he was still high, but she don't know what from until he told her he had done some grass. When he got home and took his usual shower, Cindy talked and told him that they would speak further in the morning.

He got up and had breakfast the next day with both of us. He was very attentive and wanted to please us because of him blowing our faith in him. He had grown a beard that he liked, but it looked terrible. He looked like a kid who let the facial hair grow and forgot to trim it. Cindy knew with that look that he would never get a job so she said that if he was serious about moving forward, he would have to change his tough guy image and conform to society until he was wealthy enough to be independent and do what he pleased, and groom as he liked. She said that for us to take him seriously, he would have to shave off his beard and that would be a fast start to a change in image and attitude. He also should remove a few of his earrings and only wear one. He argued with her, telling her she was wrong and that his beard had nothing to do with the drugs or his attitude. She had no idea what he was thinking when he said he could get himself together without shaving the beard. It now became a symbol of him giving in, and it had become an image that he wanted.

We knew that we had to strip him somewhat in order to start over. We knew it would be tough for him to give in when we always encouraged him to be happy with himself and we never demanded any certain look. We spoke for about an hour and he said he had to think about it. We thought that was great because no matter what decision he made, it would have had some thought put into it. He came downstairs about two hours later with his beard shaved. He had a sheepish grin that tried to show how proud he was to listen, but also that he made the decision and it was not forced on him. I told him how disappointed we were with his past few days' actions, but we were happy that he made the decision to commit to a change even though it was not exactly what he wanted to do.

That was a tough decision for him, but with that, we began gently pushing and guiding him into what jobs to call and we started getting him up early in the morning. It was our feeling that if he got up early, he would get into a normal schedule and want to go to sleep at a reasonable time. I was going to work every day and Cindy was trying to work a few hours daily and spend the balance with Mark. I was working around schedules and trying to be accessible for the midnight runs, which we hoped would stop, but reality said it wouldn't.

Chapter Twelve

We brought him into the office to teach him about our real estate business, keep an eye on him, and to teach him how to deal with people. Dealing with people was already his strong point and he could sell anybody anything if he really wanted to. This was partially working, except we were feeling the pressure all of the time. Sometimes I took him with when I went out to solicit business.

At this point in our lives, I was in a family business with Cindy, which included sales, management, and consulting of real estate, which was now doing well. It also gave Mark and me a chance to communicate better with each other. Many of the drives that we took to see clients or property ended with tears of love and emotion by both of us. When he was in the office, if he went to the bathroom down the hall and took longer to come back, one of us was automatically going down to check to see if he was there. The thought would have been that he took off and we may catch him before he was out of reach. That was tension that detracted from the time dedicated to earning a living.

This pattern went on for about a month. He would spend days with us and nights with his girlfriend or go to an NA meeting. We felt that with that combination, there wasn't a lot of time to get into trouble. We were partially right. Note that we said that because we could have been partially wrong.

We kept asking him where his interest was and it seemed to be cars. He was always reading magazines about muscle cars and street rods. We thought that maybe a tech school that taught auto classes could give him something to do with his hands and a mechanic could always make a living. There were government grants, called Pell grants, which were easily accessed by the schools to encourage students to enroll. The school was only 30 minutes away and it was a full-day program. We enrolled him after a series of tests that basically said, "If you are breathing, you are accepted." One of the prerequisites was to buy a beautiful set of tools that could be used to fix almost anything, which cost about $700, which we did. Cindy drove him to school most of the time, but gave him some lead way by letting him drive a few times. The school was good and it had a lot of students that were not made for classroom academics. They mostly had the skills and backgrounds to tear apart cars. They were motor heads and they were good. Mark had some catching up to do, but he seemed to be learning all of the time. I read some of the homework. It was basically showing the functions of each major auto part and its relationship to each other. It explained how they functioned as one unit and if that was understood, troubleshooting would make a lot more sense. These students were good with their hands and had tremendous mechanical aptitude. He went there five days a week and when he wasn't there, Cindy generally had the balance of the day planned for him.

He was getting annoyed because he wanted free time and there wasn't any. Cindy thought free time for him was trouble time. One of Mark's friends, Danny, came over to the house and was talking to Cindy about having gone into the drug zones with Mark. Mark would drive and tell Danny to stay in the car because it was a bad neighborhood, and he friend looked "too white." Danny felt comfortable being with Mark He went along and consequently became part of a drug buy. He was not stupid, but also not fully aware of the situation he was in. He felt better when Mark got back to the car, because he told Mark that he felt like he was bait when they kept pointing at him and referring to him as "white bread."

On September 18th, Mark had another argument with his girlfriend and he came home at 2:30 a.m. We were awake and knew he had a problem because he closed the door hard. He came in, got undressed, and went into the bathroom. We could see this from our bed. His frustration was peaked by some rift with her, but we didn't know yet what it was about. We were conditioned at this point to sleep restfully, but with one ear and one eye open until he got home. Even though he was upset, we were able to quickly go into our full sleep because he was home. Fifteen minutes later, we heard the front door close. He left very quickly. By the time we got out of bed and walked over to the window, his car door had slammed and he had pulled out of the driveway. It was too late to catch up to him, wherever he went.

On the 20th, we heard from one of his friends that Mark

borrowed $35 from them for a motel. We knew it wasn't for a motel, but how far would $35 take him? We now had to wait to see what would turn up over the next 24 hours, because we figured that he would be out of money by then. We were right because he called the next day. Things were out of hand as he told us to pick him up because his car was stolen. We drove down to one of the worst drug districts in the city and met him on the corner. His clothes were like the worst of the homeless, once again, and he looked like hell. Cindy said she felt good that he felt so bad, because she was hoping that he would suffer and hit bottom. When he got into her car, she asked what happened to him and the car. He said a gun was put to his head and he was told to get out. It was then that he fell apart and did drugs and was lost for the few days. He was not aware that she knew about his borrowing the money for the "motel." He told her how scared he was and how he was worried about getting his car back. He was right in worrying about getting his car back, because if I got to it, Mark knew he wasn't getting it back for a while, which was why he lied. After we questioned him, we were able to get some of the truth.

When he left our house, he sold his radio from the car for $50. The radio was part of the upgrade when the car was bought months earlier. It was the type that could be removed when you left your car to prevent theft. Ironic, isn't it? We found out that he sold the car for $160. We found out who bought it by going through Mark's pockets and we found a receipt with a name and address. We went to their house with a uniformed police officer to recover it. The police asked to see all of the records and explained to the buyer what the buyer already knew. I agreed to give him his money back and he relinquished the car. I didn't know how much the car went for, but I would bet that it was less than the $160. It would have been anything when drugs were involved. It appeared that we were getting to be familiar faces in this part of town, and we were not the people the dealers wanted around there. We didn't fit and it made people buying drugs nervous, which was bad for the drug business. This was making Cindy feel uncomfortable, because life was cheap on the street. We were in nice cars, driving into areas that normal people would go way out of their way to avoid. On the 22nd, Mark went over to the high school to see his girlfriend, who was in her senior year. She appeared as immature as him, after we got to know her. She was mad at him for being mad at her, and she was mad that he didn't call her when he took off. The two of them were still boyfriend and girlfriend, and both being immature, caused a lot of petty arguing on both sides.

They would fight with each other for various reasons. Maybe one was talking to a friend of the opposite sex, or one of them smiled at someone looking hot, or maybe because they didn't wish to see the same movie. They stayed together with the usual fighting going on every other day. The relationship was convenient, probably not even infatuation. The sex was probably passé by now. Cindy assumed that from hearing one side of a telephone conversation that she wasn't supposed to hear.

At this point, he was out of jobs and killing time working with me at the real estate office, again. I didn't pay him because we were obviously concerned with where the money would go. One afternoon I took him to an area that was near the drug district because I had some appointments close to it that day. Mark asked if he could go to a store across the street to see what music tapes they had. It was a store that he had been in before. He was in there about ten minutes and then came back out to the car where I was waiting for him. As Mark crossed the street, he knew some of the people driving by who yelled his name. For once, we were both just observers in this area.

Things were status quo until the 18th of October when he had another fight with his girlfriend. This time we knew that she picked the fight and she knew exactly what buttons to push to make Mark explode. She told him to meet her and she had no intention of showing up. Cindy learned that when she called the girlfriend to see where he was. She told Cindy that she was getting even with him for something. He took off and you know where.

We kept giving him back the car because we were torn between him going crazy sitting around and not living a normal life. We were hoping that being clean for three weeks might have been the start of his trip back on the straight and narrow. That is the hope and optimism in all parents. Reality should have been to keep pushing for a nine-month rehab that was mandatory, but that couldn't be done unless the courts ordered it, or you convinced him to stay there and you paid upwards of $50,000, with no guarantees. You couldn't be sure he would stay if the going got tough. The ACLU had put the fear of God into all institutions when it came to an individual's rights. Everyone had stories about why something they wanted to do couldn't be accomplished because it violated a person's rights. The ACLU should have been in the other person's shoes when they used their power to prevent certain actions. The bottom line was that he was gone again. This time the car was in Cindy's name, rather than her as the first lien holder. From a mercenary point of view, we were concerned about losing everything that we had worked for.

The next day, the 19th, we realized that he wasn't coming right back. That evening, I went to our township police to report the car stolen. They said that they would not take the report at that time. There was a fee to put things on the wires and there was not enough time that had passed. They told me to write to the Department of Motor Vehicles in Harrisburg and advise them that if the car came across as being re-titled, it should read as stolen. They also noted that if anyone requested a duplicate title, they were probably going to forge the name and transfer it. Cindy then notified our insurance agent in order to cover us in case some other problems developed. We tried to cover our tails in a field that was foreign to us. What if someone got into an accident in the car, and someone was seriously hurt or killed? What happened if property was badly damaged? What were our responsibilities? What would our insurance cover or not cover? Did it matter if the car was reported stolen or not?

These sounded like simple questions, but in the heat of battle, there was not a good place to get an answer that one could count on. The insurance people didn't know the liability laws and the lawyers didn't know liability under these circumstances, especially since the circumstances had yet to be defined. We were never mentally prepared for the unknown and the unknown was what always took place in drug-related circumstances. The final results were usually predictable from the point of view that they would be negative, but the route to get there had a lot of flexibility. We did our preparation and now waited for the next move.

The police were right. On the 20th, at 9:30 a.m., he called and asked to be picked up at one of the "lesser" drug corners. We went down and parked at the corner. We saw someone who approached us from a distance, but we had to look twice. It was Mark. He was walking with a limp and looked bruised. He explained to us that he sold his Tommy Hilfinger clothes, his stereo speakers out of the car, and the roof of his car, which was detachable. After that, he sold his car for $200.

He told us that he did crack and alcohol. Mark was lost. He told us that he could get the car back, but the guy he sold it to wouldn't be back for about twelve hours when it was his "shift." We were told from Mark that we would have to bring the cash to the guy who had the car, and he would give us the keys.

This gave us time to talk to Mark who was sober and seemed slightly afraid of the whole situation. Mark told us that he would get the car back because he didn't want us to meet with these people because they were bad. He was concerned about our safety, and so was I! Mark discussed openly how bad he felt that we were stuck with him and he let us down. He saw no future in his position and just wanted to get out of our lives so we could enjoy ourselves. I said that maybe the military would be a good alternative because he was in good condition and needed discipline that the service could provide. Mark liked the idea and thought it would be macho and put him in top physical shape. We started to wonder if the military would want him. Why did we assume that they wanted rehab projects? We also discussed a long-term rehabilitation program to solve his problem first. Cindy planted some seeds into his head and we waited that evening to go get the car.

The actions of anticipating the "buyback of the car" described at the beginning of the book is where we will pick up the story. It was 1:30 in the morning and we had no battery. There was no way we wanted to leave the car there because it would have been stripped in a matter of hours. We didn't want to sleep in the car there because it was cold and too extremely dangerous. Cindy called AAA, which we became a member of for just this sort of situation. Cindy called and they said they would send someone within the hour. We waited until two and then called back. Someone at AAA said they would call someone else. We waited another two hours and a tow truck finally arrived. The driver said that he couldn't tow the car but he had chains if we wanted to tow it with our vehicle. We had no choice and said that we would. The driver said if he knew the location of where we were, he would not have come. He said that if we towed it about ten blocks out of the neighborhood, another truck would be waiting there to take the car to safety. He said that he would follow us. I spoke to Cindy and we coordinated how to give hand signals and safely get the car the ten blocks to the truck. The truck that could tow our car would not go into the neighborhood where we spent most of the night. The driver said that he feared for his truck and his life, and the money wasn't worth the risk to go into that area. We got to within a block of the scheduled meeting place and we spotted the truck parked under a street light and in front of a 24-hour gas station with a police car out front. I unhooked the chains, gave them back to the original savior, and went on with the second, who took the car to his garage about three miles away. I knew that we were going to get shafted by the tow truck operator for coming out in the middle of the night and he knew we were out of place. The tow truck operator loaded the car, and told us to follow him about three miles to his garage on one of the heavy drug avenues in the city. The sun was starting to come up and we were dirty and exhausted. We made arrangements to call the garage that afternoon so we could get a charged battery and the family could get some sleep.

At that point, we started for home as the sun was now lighting everything. We were so drained. We all went right to sleep from exhaustion and stress. When we woke up, it was about noon and our sleep schedules were thrown off so badly that we weren't sure if we wanted breakfast, lunch, or dinner. We called the garage and the operator charged us for the battery. He said AAA covered the rest. We spoke again to Mark that night to explain to him that the military was not interested in him if he was an addict. He had to get clean to be considered because they would ask if he had ever been hospitalized for drug or alcohol abuse. We told him this, and it gave him something to think about. It was still an option in his mind and he went to a recruiter to get information. He realized that the drug test wasn't given right away, so he would have some time to get clean which would have to be thirty days with marijuana, but less with crack. We believed that he did both on his last escapade.

For the next few days, things were peaceful. He was thinking about the military, and we didn't want to burst his bubble. We didn't discourage his plans by saying more than what was already discussed.

On the 20th of October, Cindy received two parking tickets in the mail. The tickets were from the city police for $200. I was furious because of the "constant shock" of problems. We just couldn't catch a stretch where everything went smooth for any extended period of time. We were very upset because he didn't tell us. Didn't kids understand that just because they forgot about certain actions that they were involved in, their actions had future affects? They didn't go away and the parents would eventually find out anyway. This was actually easy compared to the rest of the prior episodes so after the first five minutes, I relaxed, put things into perspective, and paid the fine to get it out of our minds with no one getting hurt.

We said that we better try to continue with some type of treatment so we went to a new shrink. This new doctor believed in medication and tegretal was his claim to fame. We went to him starting the first of November. Mark was still in auto mechanic school, but was falling behind due to missing so many days. We received notice from school that he failed the course. He didn't say it, but he hated failure even though he knew his actions would inevitably lead to failure. He was already starting the next course at the school and was going to have to repeat the past course. The courses were not contiguous and could be taken randomly. One course could have been transmissions and the next engines. Mark was frustrated and started looking for jobs. On December 2, he had a 4:00 p.m. interview at a local gas station. That would have allowed him to go to school and then get back in time for the interview. He had his car, which we sometimes felt good about because it gave us a better shot at finding him when he took off. If the car was located, we knew he would be somewhere in the area. That was probably one of the main reasons we kept him in cars – it was our security blanket.

Mark cut school that morning, which we found out by 11:00 a.m. That was not unusual since we knew he was afraid of the job interview. We found out that he went directly to the drug district when he left the house. It was 35 degrees and bitter cold. He went out of the house that morning dressed to work on the cars with the steel-toed leather boots and light flexible winter coat. He had $40 in his pocket and a few tools that were used for the cars. We decided to start looking for him at five, because we still had our business work to catch up on during the day. We drove around, stopped at a fast food restaurant to observe the traffic, and hoped to spot the car and him, but we had no luck. We kept looking. We were anxious to find him before he sold the car or got too depressed or too high. We found his car ½ block from one of the major dealing corners in the city. We pulled behind the car. It was empty. It was now 11:00 p.m. We sat in the car for about twenty minutes. The neighbors were watching us in our car and we were observing them. It was easy to see they were uneasy with us there. We listened to the sounds of the streets; distinctive code words were used that reminded us of old-time jungle films. Instead of the jungle drums, there were the screams of red, blue, or green. These words were code words yelled by lookouts to warn of the Police, and when to stop dealing and when it was good to start again when the Police were gone. There were other words, but we couldn't decipher the meanings. We figured the police were within a block when we saw the drugs being hidden under trashcans and in fake bricks in the walls.

Until now, we watched customers drive up and do the drug transactions from start to finish within twenty seconds. The entire neighborhood was transformed into a sea of people ranging in age from ten to about thirty years old. We didn't see any older people on the street, but you could occasionally some of them peer through the windows that lined the street. They would sometimes catch my eye. When that happened, you could almost read their lips saying, "What the fuck are you doing here?" We asked ourselves the same question and we always came up with the same answer; "you will do anything for your child if you love him."

Risking your life goes with the territory. Of course, that is not what you thought at the hospital when you were given the little bundle of seven pounds of joy, who you thought could do no wrong. You took him home, knowing he would be a major part of your life, and then he would grow up strong and healthy and go off to start his own family. What was happening to us, as we waited here in this drug-infested neighborhood, was never part of the plans we had for our son.

After a while, I stood outside the car; Cindy kept her hand on 911, with all the doors locked. She had specific instructions to drive off if there was any sign of trouble or violence. I stayed close to the car because I didn't want to initiate any conversations with the locals. I had no idea of who was carrying or if I could end up with a knife in my back.

After standing there for another twenty minutes, a guy about 6'2", 250 pounds walked up to me. I realized that I didn't scare this guy too much, since I was 5'6" and 170 pounds. He asked me what I wanted. I told him our son was a druggie and was somewhere around there. I told him that the car in front of ours was his mom's car and we wanted to get him home. We knew they wanted us out of there because we probably were in a spot that was causing the dealers to lose business. The guy went away and came back in about 10 minutes.

"He is in that house over there in front of the car. Don't tell anyone that I told you, but wait a few minutes and go in. If anyone knows I ratted, I'm in trouble," he said in a soft voice so no one could hear him. He turned and walked away.

Now I had a problem. Do I walk into that crack house or freeze my ass off standing and waiting for Mark to come out, if he was even in there? I got a little braver and began talking to a very young boy standing nearby, watching the whole situation unfold. I told him to stay away from drugs and he told me he would because his brother was killed because of drugs. I left that subject in a hurry and told him my son was probably in that house, motioning the spot. I went back to the side of the car and told Cindy that I didn't want to go in, although while we were there, at least fifteen people went in and out of the front door. Twenty minutes later, the guy who told me where Mark was, came over to me again. He must have known I was apprehensive about going in. He told me to follow him in, and for some strange reason, I did.

It was scary as hell. The four steps up to the front door seemed extremely steep as I did took each one very slowly. The door was half open so the guy just opened it the rest of the way. A tattered bed sheet that was attached to the ceiling was hanging down to keep out some of the cold. He walked through. I was a little slow following him and lost sight of him. I opened the sheet and took a few more steps in. There were two more sheets, which seemed to be partitions to smaller areas. I opened the sheet that was covering the area near the front window, which was the window from where our car could be seen. There was a broken sofa against the wall and either rags or a messed up rug covering part of the floor. Mark was sitting alone on the sofa, with a very spaced-out look on his face. He looked directly at or through me as though I didn't even exist. Mark was spaced, but seeing me did nothing to bring him back to reality. He remained passive and only somewhat 'there.' He didn't seem to me to be aware of much that was going on around him, but he did mumble that he knew we were outside for the past few hours. It was almost like he thought we would disappear if he didn't do anything, which, to him, probably seemed right and comfortable at the time. I spoke to him and asked him to come outside to see his mom, and I also wanted to get the hell out of that house. I was in someone's house, a crack house, unauthorized, with a lot of very stoned people, thinking at this point there was very little value placed on anyone's life in a place like this.

Mark was hesitant to see Cindy. I believe he never wanted to hurt her, and he realized that the condition he was in right now would do just that to the woman who has stood by him for so long. I convinced him to just go outside and talk to her so she would know that he was ok. He agreed with my request, and struggled to his feet to go out to the car where Cindy was waiting. Mark was not wearing a coat. He was wearing a long-sleeved flannel shirt, and I could see that he was cold. The whole process of getting him out to the car took about ten minutes. Once out there, I told him we should all go home now. Mark got angry, and said he staying right where he was, and that we should leave him alone. I thought it was best to kept quiet as he spoke to Cindy through the open car window, hoping she would have more luck in convincing him to get all of us the hell out of there. They spoke for about five minutes and Cindy was getting nowhere with him.

Mark said he was going back into the house, and I got angry. I told him I would physically put him into the car if I had to, but he said that I couldn't force him to go with them. We started getting loud and nasty with each other, and the next move would have been to have a fistfight with Mark, which was something I did not want to happen.

In the meantime, our presence was starting to gather a crowd of about 30 people, most of them Mark's age. I didn't know what they had in mind, but I was starting to feel like easy pray. The onlookers just made the whole situation that much more unpredictable. I was scared because I had no idea what was going to happen next. I was thinking, if this gets any more tense, I would need to change my underwear when I got back to my home, if I ever did. The more time went by, the more things deteriorated, and my gut feeling told me I had to think fast, and do something quick, to get us out of here and back to somewhere safe.

"These people don't want a sick druggie hanging around their neighborhood. Did they know that you are suicidal and on medication? They don't want a sick person to stay here," I yelled.

Now, I was at the mercy of the neighborhood. I didn't know if they would roll the three of us or just want me to put him in the car and leave.

Like some miracle, we heard people saying things like, "hey man, go on home" and "go with your mom and dad," and a few other words of encouragement to get him the hell out of there. They couldn't trust him after hearing what I just shouted.

Mark looked embarrassed and he looked at us. He lost face in front of everyone, and at that instant, he had nowhere to go. I guess he figured he now had no choice but to leave. He got into the passenger side of his car. He knew the routine. Cindy got out of our car and slide into the driver's seat next to Mark. Cindy drove his car and I followed. He always drove back home with her because he still had a slight fear of me.

We were home by about 2:00 a.m. His eyes were still bleary and we figured that he did twenty to thirty caps of crack cocaine. He was still high, but starting to come down. My guess was he also did other things because the caps don't keep you high for a long period of time.

We couldn't decide what to do so we told him to go to sleep. He still had school the next day and we had to go to work. We couldn't leave him home and we had nowhere else to put him while we again tried to figure out a new plan the next day.

Cindy drove him to school, after school, picked him up, and brought him to the office. He was not in a good mood. He was tired, depressed and seemed to be dragging.

"What the fuck is there to live for? I can't go out without fucking up and you guys don't trust me to do anything," he said in a disgusted voice.

He was actually right about some of the things he said, but he just could not seem to see into the future past one or two days. We noticed that his wrists had been cut pretty badly, but not down to the veins, thankfully. He had them wrapped and there was some dried blood left on his hands. Cindy asked what happened and he said that he cut his wrists. I said that it was a pretty stupid thing to do and he agreed. Everyone brushed it off because he appeared to be getting into tattoos and body mutilation. But inside, I knew that he just made another feeble attempt at suicide, trying to find some magic answer to his problems.

The days and nights were the same as we tried to make things predictable and easy. He was driven to school by one of us, picked up, and brought to the office to answer phones until we closed at about 5:00 p.m. We felt a tiny bit of control, since we at least knew where he was. Conversations with Mark went nowhere and it wasn't that he wasn't trying. He just seemed totally was lost. Sometimes the words were right, but the eyes were blank and the mouth was just moving, saying the things he thought we wanted to hear, things that would please us.

This pattern went on for a week, but on December 18th, he took off from school and we weren't sure where he went. I was thinking he wouldn't go back to that house in North Philadelphia where we found him last week. Everyone's mood was destroyed. Cindy thought she had gained at least some control over Mark's actions. Since Christmas was

133

coming, she thought that he would be good for the holidays to try to get back some of our respect and trust, as well as to get his Christmas presents. Drugs defy logic!

There was occasional times when we thought that things were missing, but weren't sure. We would go to pawn shops in the drug district to find watches or the gold chain that was sometimes gone. After a while, some pawn shops knew our faces and realized that they were not going to make any money off of us and most told Mark that he was not welcome to pawn stuff there anymore. This happened over the next two years on a monthly basis. The process was to go in with a pawn slip that Mark would leave in his room, or discover something missing and go to one of seven shops that would have been convenient to him. We probably lost about half of the pawned merchandise, which consisted of anything from a guitar to jewelry. The pawnshops were legal fences that knew exactly what was stolen and what was legitimate. These guys were pros. Most were good at legal thievery, but they had the law on their sides to do just enough to keep out of trouble. They are controlled by the State Banking Commission and have to get thumbprints from people giving them goods. They must get photo I.D. and also must give police a description of merchandise they bring in.

Cindy always bought great gifts for Mark for the holidays. She bought him the after shaves that I couldn't afford. She also bought Mark all the designer labels of clothing including Tommy, Nautica and Polo that I thought was ridiculous; everyone knows the label and insignia cost as much as the entire shirt. Of course, the sneakers totally blew my mind. When I shopped for shoes, I looked for Florsheims, because I splurged on my feet. They usually started somewhere around $100, but they always fit my tender feet very well. When we looked to buy ourselves sneakers, a beautiful brand-name pair could be had for $50. I almost died of heart failure when I read the price on the two pairs of sneakers that Cindy usually bought him at Christmas. They ran more than $100 a pair. And I was told that they ran much more for designer styles!

I must be a typical guy, because I hated going shopping with Cindy. Not going, I wasn't aware of the prices she paid for these things for Mark. Looking back, I'm probably glad she lied to me about some of the prices she paid for merchandise that didn't have the tickets on them. The Christmas morning ritual was presents all over the floor around the tree, and pictures being taken when the "good" presents were opened. It was always a happy time that no one ever missed. Cindy's parents would come over in the morning and spend the better part of the day; her father always wanted to leave while her mother watched with tearful joy as Mark was having a great time getting the things he wanted.

For some reason, Mark was always excited and didn't expect to get what he wanted. Most times, the items were costly, but affordable and accessible to us, but Mark never had the faith that he would get them. Maybe he thought Santa Claus had a way to know if he was a good boy!

It was as if he was lost and couldn't get out of his own way. He tried to do what everyone else did, but he picked and choose, and picking just the negative actions because it was easier. It was easier to fail doing something negative because there was little effort needed. We wondered if the drugs conveyed a negative message to Mark. We kept telling him not to take drugs, yet we gave him other medications, including anti-depressants. We were giving him conflicting views. "Take our drugs and not yours. Ours will put you into reality, and yours will give you a great feeling initially, but yours are not good for you."

We were never sure how that message got conveyed to individuals like Mark who were having reality problems. How many times did one hear that someone didn't take their Prozac and was having a rough day? Guess what that meant. The asshole knew he needed it, but didn't want to take it. The reasons included the fact that they wanted to be normal like everyone else, not an artificially induced personality. Sounds like a 21st century remedy that does not entirely get the message across.

After the holidays, Mark sold his new coat and sneakers on a new escapade. Instead of acting like an adult, he looked like a thirteen-year old kid running home to mom, ashamed of himself and afraid to look up at mom and dad because of his actions. This was similar to a family pet that was full of fun, and having a great time while the family was out shopping. It was as if the mom left two big steaks on the counter to defrost for a big family dinner, and when she returned home, the steaks were missing. Fido was slinking along the kitchen wall with his head down and his eyes catching a glimpse of hers with an expression of guilt, fear and apology. The tail would be wagging only at the end and only sporadically; waiting and encouraging her to say "it's okay, boy, we should have put the steaks where you couldn't climb up to get them."

It usually happened that you got pissed for the moment or you sat back in disbelief and laughed at the dog. Mark had the same sheepish look and there was nothing we could say to make it better. He knew what he had done. Try and put yourself in the position of the parents and try to logically say words that would be beneficial to Mark. Put yourself in Mark's position. What could he say that would have any meaning that would be relevant? Sometimes the expression "actions speak louder than words" has a very significant meaning.

Chapter Thirteen

The holidays were not very exciting; we were under pressure, constantly waiting for Mark's next disappearing act. He never gave us any warning signs, so we were waiting in anticipation, which was a very stressful way to live. I guess this existence could be equated to a game of Russian roulette; you know the trigger will be pulled, but you don't know if it is an empty chamber.

It was hard to keep everything normal around Mark. When he was straight it was OK, but trying to adjust to his Dr.

Jeckyl and Mr. Hyde personality was too tension-filled.

He typically would spend the day at school and then tell you his future plans, based on the days work, and he would tell you what he thought he could do and you listen with optimism. We felt that by working with his hands and getting satisfaction was a great start. He was learning how to fix cars and understood the functions of the transmissions and differences in the engines and what made them function and malfunction. He could always get work with that knowledge and be respectable to himself. He spoke to us throughout the holiday about getting back to school and how he knew he needed an education to do anything in life. That was what every parent wanted to hear. We were all on the same course and we felt that if he overcame his drug habit, it was all achievable. We were optimistic because here was a young man with an I.Q. level of 130. When we looked at the situation, we knew he was capable of doing anything he set out to do, if only the drugs didn't take over his life.

New Years Eve was here and Cindy and I did the same thing every year. We had three or four couples; the same ones each year come to the house. We ordered out for Chinese food, watched one or two movies, and took a break to watch the ball drop at midnight. It was always enjoyable because everyone cared for each other. Once in a while, someone would bring the hats and noisemakers, but that wasn't our style. We would usually call it a night about 1:00 a.m. The only thing Cindy waited for was for was Mark's call at midnight to say he was fine. He did that this year and Cindy said she felt that the year started out the right way. We kept telling him that he would have more fun drinking ginger ale rather than getting sloshed and not remembering what happened. It sounded good, but we knew he would do what he wanted. He told us that he was at a party at a friend's house and he was staying there all night and would not be driving at all. After our friends left our home around one o'clock, we drove over to Mark's friend's house to see if his car was there. The roads were empty and the house was about ½ hour away in a private setting. The car was there and we felt better. We went home and since both their minds were clear, went to bed and brought in the New Year with a "bang."

The holiday ended and on the 6th of January, and Mark informed us that he was dropping out of the tech school and wanted to go back to school in Boston. He said that he didn't fit in the tech school because he never worked with the cars and found it too difficult to understand. He also said all of the other students had worked on their cars for years and understood everything so much easier. He felt that he could go back to college and do well. He dropped out and there was nothing we could do to convince him to finish out the term. He had a Pell grant, which was wasted, and we had a set of tools from Sears that would have allowed me to work on my car and fix anything on it except that I hardly knew what a wrench was. (Did I spell wrench correctly?)

Since Mark dropped out of college, and didn't flunk out, he was permitted to return for the next semester. Had he flunked out, he would have had to reapply. His advisor was a nice older woman who was very fond of Mark. She called Cindy many times after Mark left to see if there was more she could do to help, but there wasn't.

Cindy called the school and told them that Mark was returning. They told her that there was dorm space so he would have to live on campus. That was great news for us as we gathered all of his belongings and drove to Boston. We put everything in my Jeep; three people, clothes, refrigerator, television, and the ever-present trunk. The courses that he took were assigned to him and were supposed to be geared to be realistically easy so that if he put forth the effort, he should be able to adjust and adapt to the "rigors of college life." The college also had advisors that were excellent. Mark was assigned to the same elderly teacher who cared about him. She saw Mark's level of intelligence and enjoyed discussions with him about philosophy. We were not sure what feelings to have because we were generally optimistic, rather than realistic. We communicated with Mark for most of the semester and he kept advising us that things were going well. We were happy as pigs in ... Oh well, ignorance was bliss and we were very ignorant. We probably had some of the most peaceful nights we had in years. Sex was good and we could plan a week in advance to do things with friends. Did I mention that sex was good? As a parent, the sex drive with the same partner was often times driven by the attitude of the children (like were they good or were they asleep?) It seemed that the word "drive," had different meanings and values to the teenagers and the parents, and wheels were the only meaning to most teens.

Mark was returning home March 12, for his spring break. As stupid adults in fantasyland tend to do when tweaked with some positive results, Cindy looked to reward him. As was the typical, "what does he want?" question arose, the answer was fairly obvious. I fought and put forth convincing, logical arguments that a used car would be ideal with the promise of a new car upon graduation from college. It was a reward, but also it was more of an incentive. If you were his age, and your parents made an offer like that, you would even go through the summer school session to get the car. It all made sense so obviously, I lost and a brand-new Amigo was sitting in the garage waiting for him. Mark was using the family car to come home and bring his clothes. When he got home, we were so excited for his anticipated pleasure; we had him go out to the garage and presented him the car keys. He thanked us profusely and then presented us with a $232 speeding ticket from Connecticut and a $20 parking ticket from school. Hummmm, sounds like a pretty good deal! As parents, we tend to make wonderful deals like this. Does being parents mean that from the delivery room to home, you get brain dead?

We felt that his being home was not a good idea, so Cindy planned to take him on a vacation so he wouldn't start up with the same crowd that he was with before. Our idea was that it was the people that you associated with that determined many of your actions We were hoping that taking him away would avoid some associations, especially when they found out Mark was back from school.

Cindy took him to the airport as a surprise to go to Cancun with her for a few days. When she got there, she was told that the airport was closed due to the major snowstorm that was in progress. They came home and waited. Cindy still wanted to get him out of the area so he would not associate with his old friends. There was no sign of the weather letting up so Mark went locally to see one of his friends who happened to be female. We knew that she liked him, but we thought as a friend. We also thought that she would be matured since she had a two-year-old child. We were wrong. She had Mark (and I mean had) at her house and Mark came back and said she hadn't changed and he "felt fine." They used to shake hands and now the greeting for the teens was all too often "how are you and let's fuck."

Maybe it was too easy or maybe the girls were looking for father figures since so many came from broken homes. Maybe it was too acceptable by the peer groups. Maybe it just felt good! It seemed to me that girls had a quest to not end up the last of her friends to become pregnant.

All these changes in behavior didn't mean that it didn't happen when we were younger, but it was more private except when one girl told her friends to try the same guy, so she they could compare notes. We had our fun in the 60s, but for the most part, it was more private. By the way, the only ones who didn't keep it private were the girls who usually were out every night by "popular demand." They were not the girls who usually were sitting next to you looking out the car window if your friends passed by. When you had this "popular" girl in your car, you shoved her head under the dash so you weren't seen with her, but that was another story. All of the actions that we took as kids are still going on except that now, it is the publicity and attention that surround it that is so much different.

Anyway, Cindy and Mark were snowed in and not able to leave, so Cindy called the travel agent and said to get them on the first available plane to any island so Mark could be out of the area and out of his environment. The 12th was still not available to leave. The tension in our home was escalating. The 13th and 14th were the same story. On the 15th, the weather broke and they were able to fly out. We didn't say much to him about why we were pushing him to be away, but I think he understood. Cindy and Mark were off to Nassau. They were on a hotel/air package so all they needed were meals and a place to sit in the sun. The hotel was a beautiful 20-story building in the middle of the high-end tourist area. What Cindy didn't realize or even think about was the drug situation there. While they were sitting by the pool, Mark was approached a number of times by the natives of the island and offered weed. He turned it down each time, but Cindy was sitting next to him not really understanding what was going on until he told her. Then Cindy started watching and was overwhelmed by the actions and activity that she saw. We, as adults, who read the papers, always pictured the islands as peaceful and tranquil. I guess that is true, but we now know why! Mark had a fear about the stories of Americans off the mainland getting stiff jail time and poor treatment when caught with drugs. Cindy was pretty pleased because of the openness of Mark during the trip. The real reason of Mark's candor was fear of the unknown, which was a good reason to stay straight. Whatever the reason, it was a good feeling for him to be straight or sober at the time.

They came home on January 20 with wonderful tans and really pleasant attitudes. That night Mark went to a party with his friend, Mike. He never came home that night. When we woke up in the morning, it was the same sinking feeling. Give up on him or play the same bullshit game of getting in the car and trying to find him before he got into some kind of trouble. We were caught between decisions. We were so annoyed that we hoped he got hurt to keep him in one place. That was really a sick thought, but desperation clouds one's thinking! He truly was our only son, even though Ritchie was still technically alive, and if there was a ray of hope, we had to take it. There was a philosophy that maybe he would grow out of it, so we had to keep him alive and progressing in some manner. Also, we still had to work to make a living while this was going on. My thoughts were at the point of thinking that working was only to pay for cars! It would have been nice if we were like Ozzie and Harriett, but working was a necessity for mortgages and food. By the way, for the younger people, Ozzie was the husband and father who was always at home in a lovely suburban home on the television series by the same name in the 1950s and 60s. No one ever found out if he worked to support his beautiful suburban home, two kids in college, and a great lifestyle.

That morning, I went to work and Cindy went to look for Mark. She took her father with her because two could see better than one, and it was safer to have two adults driving through those miserable drug streets. Also, Cindy would have been vulnerable to any lowlife druggie or rapist. It was not a good feeling for me going to work knowing that my wife was in the line of fire, but necessity was the reason. Cindy found him within an hour of her search on one of the streets, just hanging out with the rest of the teenage drug bums. They were sitting on the steps of a vacant row house. He saw her and came over to the car. He was pissed that she was there, but that was the typical attitude in that area. No one was ever sure why the kids were pissed, but they all had an attitude. Cindy knew why Mark was pissed even though Mark didn't know; his clothes were something that most people would have thrown away and not even used for rags. He traded or sold a $60 designer shirt, a $50 pair of jeans, and $100 Nike sneakers. I'd be pissed too! In return, we assumed that he received five or six crack vials. After the first trade, the addict tended to get really taken. He was in too much desire of the drug to be rational. I used the word desire because that's what it was. Crack was chasing the rainbow and never reaching it. Crack vials looked like capsules that were typical of over the counter drugs that were used for headaches. The empty vials were highly visible in the streets where drugs were found. The vials contained a substance that was sniffed and smoked. In old abandoned or vacant cars on the streets, you tended to see a lot of the cheap ballpoint pen holders that were half melted, which made great cheap pipes for crack. Of course you burnt the hell out of your lips and sometimes your fingers, but at that point, who cared?

Mark was basically sober when he came over to the car and got in. He never looked back or said goodbye to his street chums. Nobody cared! The relationships when drugs and money were involved were too shallow to describe. Again, he didn't know what to say or even if it was worth trying to explain something to her that he didn't understand himself. I guess you could compare it to dry heaves or seasickness at its worst ebb. The guilt continued to grow inside and he was afraid of not answering the one basic question that everyone on and off drugs asked: WHY?

It was at this time that Cindy asked him about the car. She found out that it was in a repair shop in the city with the radio missing, a speaker missing, and a very bad clutch. His beeper was also missing. She called the auto agency and had them tow the car back to the dealership because she knew we would only get ripped off a little bit that way. This put us in another dilemma; Spring Break was over and the car was ready in two days to be picked up from service at the dealership. Mark came home and did the usual shower for an hour to escape and get clean. He slept in that afternoon and through the night. He was beat mentally and physically. I said that he must straighten out and do it for himself and he should concentrate on school. We felt that it sounded good and may work on a day-to-day basis while we had time to breathe. Mark said he was with one of his old friends and was getting help on a paper that was due. Cindy had no choice but to hope it was for real because we didn't want to disrupt his mental state by asking what, when, where, and how for all the points of are you OK? Are you in trouble? Are you bullshitting us again? But he never called when he said he would, and he never showed up that day. We were back in the hunt. He obviously didn't sober enough to not want to be high again.

It was now the 22nd of March and he was not coming home.

I went to the six or seven drug areas that we knew he frequented in hopes of catching him before he overdosed or got more depressed after the highs we knew he would be on. The entire cruise took about four to five hours going from place to place looking for a sign of him. There was no one to ask because "nobody knew nothin."

We stayed home that night waiting for the phone to ring. For the first time, we started to actually consider the possibility of cutting him loose. We talked about it, but Cindy couldn't do it. Although I thought I wanted to, I was torn. We would watch TV and pretend that we knew what the show was about. Each of us was trying to avoid talking about the same depressing stuff that we knew was going on in each of our minds. Was he hurt, alive, outside in the cold, or in some crack house? We waited and every time the phone would ring, Cindy would have to answer it because Mark would hang up on me because he didn't want to get dumped on and in his mind, Cindy was easy and I was tough. When the phone rang, our eyes would look as if we were reading each other's every thought, which we were. When friends would call, we would make small talk and hang up because the conversations were going right through our heads. We tried to stick close to home the next day, so we planned that I would go to work late and come home early; Cindy could go in and get some paperwork done when I was home waiting by the phone. We always tried to be current because of the scheduled non-schedule. There was one hang up on the 23rd and Cindy tried to lure or actually beg for a response from the receiver. It didn't work.

That night we again stayed home to wait. The 24th was the same, except we went out in the morning to try again to find him. There was no trace of him. We were usually up each night, all night, except for a few catnaps to keep us going, because we were helpless to do anything else. Our eyes looked twenty years older than they should have, and we were beginning to show the wear and tear this lifestyle was causing us. Sometimes, when we would pick him up, he had bruises on him that were obviously received in a fight. You could see the black and blue around the eyes or the cuts on the fists. There were times when the lip was cut open and it wasn't always from the crack.

On March 25th, we went to our local suburban police station to file a missing person report. The detective suspected a major problem because there had been activity from other kids from our same suburb picked up in the drug zone. We mapped out Mark's haunts that we were aware of, and drew a map for the detective, which he requested. He went down to the city and met with narcotics officers in that unit. They said there was no information that they received after contacting some of their snitches. They did have snitches who were treated easier, because if they didn't have these people, the police would never be able to get information as quickly as they did. As disorganized as it appeared, the information network was very solid and deep. The detective was convinced that Mark was somewhere on the streets, and not dead, not yet anyway. We kept the home front vigil, and put in the slow time waiting. That was our only place for contact with Mark, and we knew that if and when he called, he would be crying for help immediately. If we missed the call for help, we didn't know when the next call would come. On the 29th, he called Cindy and said that he "fucked up" again, and was in center city at the house of a high school friend. His friend had gotten his act together and was now in college. He had his own apartment in a 3-story brownstone (townhouse). This was the same friend who Mark met in a rehabilitation center when he was doing the 30-day wonder program, the friend who was kicked out of his house and we took in to help get started. This was the same friend who we told could stay with us, but needed a job within a week to begin being responsible. This was the friend that we found out was doing crack and heroin in our downstairs recreation room with Mark every night and sitting at our kitchen table sharing food at dinnertime.

Cindy went down and picked Mark up. She always was concerned that by the time that she would get to where he was, he would change his mind and not be there. But when

Cindy got there, she picked him up. In the meantime, I called the shrink, who said to get him back to the school.

I still don't know the logic of the brilliant medical mind that gave us that advice, but when one is in an emotional state, one tended to listen to the experts. Understand that this college was six hours away and the only way to get him there was to drive or pay $500 for a 45-minute plane ride that would not guarantee him getting to the campus. Cindy left the house a 4:00 p.m. and drove him back to Boston. She stopped for dinner along the way and figured it would be a great time to be alone with him to try to get into his head. She got him there at 11 p.m.

After he was situated, she said she was going to grab a motel room for the night and drive home in the morning. I thought it would be a good idea so I could finally get in a good day's work. I went to bed about 10:00 p.m. to get a restful sleep because I knew Mark was back at school, and Cindy was going to get some sleep at a near-by motel.

At 3:30 a.m., I awoke to someone sliding under the covers with me. I was thinking, hopefully, it was not a burglar for many reasons! I figured it couldn't be Cindy, so who could it be? No neighbor had a key. It couldn't be someone totally violent or his or her technique stunk.

"Hi dear," whispered Cindy.

I was now totally awake, but not disappointed. I asked her how she got home and was everything OK. She said that she wasn't tired and after she dropped Mark, she started to drive home figuring that she would stop at a motel when she tired. She never got tired and made it home doing 80 mph in four hours with no traffic. I was annoyed that she drove that distance without a break, but it was over, so why hammer her since she was home safe.

She said Mark was very depressed when she left him, but it was for his best interest and for ours. We were again in the "hope" stage of his being in an atmosphere of other kids in his 19 year old category. These were the ones trying to cope with reality, get by in school, and get a degree while trying to have a good time. Neat trick if it could be pulled off. We kept thinking that he would realize that he keeps knocking himself down when he constantly has the opportunity to start over. Not only was he failing, but also he was getting hurt both physically and mentally.

Mark stayed in the Boston area and survived the semester as far as we knew. He came home May 14 and was apparently fine. We didn't have any problems, were at ease, and didn't change our attitudes at all. On May 22, we noticed that there was inexpensive jewelry missing from our open jewelry box. We didn't keep much accessible, but it was gone. Mark denied that he took it, which was a ridiculous statement since he was the only other person in the house. He was gone again that night and we actually found him driving his car on the street in the drug zone. I pulled up next to him and said pull over. He was high and we could see from our car that his eyes were glassy and he was out of it. He started to accelerate. We were on a 3-lane neighborhood highway in the lower economic section of the city. Mark went through a red light and we cautiously did the same. He went through two more and didn't even glance at cross street traffic. Our car was faster than his so we had more of a chance to be slightly careful. Hell, how careful could you be going 70 mph in a 35-mile zone? As we were driving, one girl, about 15 years old, being cool, stood in the middle of the street in an "I dare you to hit me position." She was in the middle of the path of both cars. My horn was blasting to attract attention and hopefully the alert police to help us, but also to warn anybody who heard it. This girl didn't realize the situation and she froze. I saw the whites of her eyes when we brushed by her. Our car was swerving side to side because we were both cutting between cars at major-league speeds. Mark said later he had no idea why he didn't stop, but he was caught up on getting away, and we were hell bent that he wouldn't!

He pulled to an inside lane figuring he would lose us. When he didn't, he suddenly pulled off the road onto a side street. Somehow, we made the turn without getting hit by the car we cut in front of. Cindy kept her eyes on him and we tore down the street still having him in sight. He did a 90-degree turn into an ally and went down to the end. We pulled into the ally after him and saw the sign saying "no outlet." We cautiously pulled down the middle of the drive not knowing exactly what Mark was going to do. He could make a U-turn and come head-on toward us, or he could just give up and end this whole car-chase episode. There were kids playing in the driveway. He had already attracted attention with his high-speed entry that scattered some of the kids. The noise had brought out some of the parents to see what was happening.

Mark decided to give it up. He got out of his car as we pulled to a stop directly in front of him. I tended to get into the habit of having some foresight when Mark left the vehicle. Mark got out and just stayed by the car. He then spoke directly to me and said that I once told him that I would give him $20 and give up on him when he asked. He again reminded me of that and said he didn't want to go home. He said that he didn't deserve to go home. He begged me to give him the $20 and go away. At that point, he would have traded his life for the $20 and two vials of crack. I said "no," and told him to look at his mother. Cindy said she never gave up on him, so how could he give up on himself. He was too high to reason with. He turned and started to walk down the drive. I grabbed him by the shoulder and said that he wasn't leaving and he was getting into the car. Cindy had checked his car while the confrontation was taking place and quietly nodded to me that she had the keys. We argued in the driveway for a few more minutes, and reluctantly, Mark surrendered to our demands to get into our car. His head was off somewhere else, and he lost his energy. If he listened to me, it would give him a few minutes of peace, so he got into the car.

He laid down the next day in the den with no emotion. He didn't want or need another lecture and he was pissed at everyone and looked like he was ready to explode. Some young guy came to our door and said that Mark had his stereo speakers and he wanted them back. Not knowing who this guy was, I told Mark to get up, and go outside to resolve this issue. He refused and put me in a position where I couldn't resolve anything. I wouldn't let this guy into our home, and I was between the inside talking to Mark and outside trying to straighten out another of Mark's messes. Mark looked like he was getting agitated, but so was I. We started yelling at each other from a distance of about 20 feet across the room. Mark was lying on the couch and I was still at the doorway. I told him to get his ass up to help me straighten out this situation.

"Go fuck yourself," was Mark's reply.

I picked up the nearest thing to me, which was an empty glass soda bottle and threw it at him with all of my strength. It missed his head and bounced off of the sofa and onto the rug in front of him.

With that, Mark picked up the bottle and fired it back at me, but he also missed the target. However, he did hit my prized possession -- the 46-inch large screen, color television. The bottle put a gigantic hole through the middle of the screen.

"Get the hell out," I screamed. With this, he got up and left.

Chapter Fourteen

Things were so bad now, I thought I would kill him, or Mark would kill me. I went outside and told the guy with the stereo speaker problem to just leave and call later, but I added that I doubted that Mark had any speakers left in his possession. Cindy remained quiet because I guess she realized there was not much she could do to smooth over the situation until everything calmed down. Mark made his way to center city and slept at his friend's house. Cindy was upset, but calm. She knew that frustration was the better part of logic and we better get Mark away again. On May 24th, Cindy drove Mark to Boston to help him get a room and a job for the summer. She checked into a motel with him while they looked for a room. Boston was a college town and housing was expensive and hard to find. She called home every night to complain about the problems finding a space, but she was persistent and knew she had to do something. Cindy went from real estate brokers to owners to rent signs for four days, and at night she went to the mall or to the movies. She found a furnished basement unit that was available for four months. She gratefully took it; the rent was about $600 a month plus utilities. The place was a dump, but there was shopping and transportation within one block. The unit was down three steps and the entry was from the street. There was a living room, which then went into the kitchen and a small bedroom behind that. There were ants around the kitchen area from dried food scraps that were left there for months. The appliances were old and barely working. That would not make much difference, because Mark wouldn't and couldn't cook anyway. It was a place to exist. Mark got a job delivering pizzas that was one-block away from the apartment.

One evening while at the movies with Cindy, Mark met one of the girls he was friendly with during the year. She was with two of her girlfriends. They were going to the late show and Cindy and Mark were coming out from seeing the 8:00 p.m. movie. Mark seemed to like one of the girls. He said she looked like a model – she was 5'7" tall with long hair. He spoke to her alone for a few minutes and then left the girls and retuned to the apartment with Cindy.

Cindy bought him a bed so he could stay in the apartment. She ordered a phone installed, and got him calling cards so the long distance bills would be only slightly outrageous. She took care of the logistics for leases, utilities, etc. Cindy told Mark that he was totally on his own. He had to be responsible for himself, and had to work for his own spending money, which he did for about two weeks.

Cindy came home on the 30th. She said she was emotionally drained. She spent six days with him, nurturing him, giving everything she could to try and make him understand how important a child was to a parent and what being a family meant.

She needed a few days to recover and get back her emotional

strength. I gave her no support and said it was time for him to make it or not make it. There were a lot of thoughts that we both had while they were in Boston. When Cindy and I were together we never discussed the situation, but we had been there before.

Cindy again felt very good for the next week as she had phone conversations with Mark daily and nightly. Naturally, the calls were collect, so buying him the phone cards made no sense at all.

The following weekend he came home and picked up his car, the Amigo. He was pleasant and appeared as if he were truly happy. He was anxious to be home to get some of the things he felt he needed, like a television and certain kitchen supplies. Before he left, I checked out the car and did some of the typical maintenance like oil and lube. I really liked that car because it was high off the ground and felt relatively heavy. It was also economical and had a great look with the top off.

Mark returned to Boston, and continued calling home at least once a day. That satisfied us for a while. We didn't mind the collect calls because we felt that we were his support and we wanted to be sure we were able to be reached at all times. Also, it was just human nature to want to be able to deal with the things you couldn't see or know as easily as you could with the things that were done directly under your nose. He told us that he was working and really enjoyed living alone. Roughly interpreted, that meant that he was carefree, with no aggravation and no one to tell him what to do. It meant that he was screwing his ass off and doing nothing. He was sleeping all day and partying at night. Cindy knew that because he never answered the phone when she tried to reach him during normal hours.

We were learning various techniques to try to regulate his money. We would send him checks almost every day for $10 or $15 for food and entertainment. We were not going to put big dollars in his hands. We set it up with the real estate firm for us to pay the rent. The utilities were in his name, but he was supposed to send Cindy the bills in the stamped envelopes that she left for him. She set up his phone so that his credit card allowed him to call only home or our office. This prevented him selling time off the card. He had to control his use of the car or get gas money for transporting people. Cindy couldn't control that. The major problem that we eventually faced was the parking tickets. Actually, they were not all his fault. Boston got a majority of their revenue from parking tickets. He could not get a permit to park on the streets because he was not a permanent Boston resident. Therefore, after the initial 2, 3, or four-hour limits, he would get a $15 ticket. He tried to get a permit, but they said no. Cindy told him to park in an area where the car was safe and permits were not needed. Obviously, she was not aware of his hearing problem when he had to be inconvenienced. After the first 45 days, Cindy had about 30 tickets. They were everywhere: home, in the mail, in his glove box, on the floor, in his apartment, and almost anywhere you could think of that was within tossing range. We knew this because we went up to his place for a weekend in July to check on him. He actually looked good and the apartment, although filthy, was quite cool. When we walked in, he hugged and kissed Cindy and he did the same to me. That made the trip worthwhile for me. We did the parent thing and took him food shopping, which he appreciated. He actually thanked us and told us how much he enjoyed being on his own. We were there for two days and although it was fine, we were ready to leave and let him continue getting his act together. It was not too comfortable for his style with us being there. If he got too comfortable, we would be fighting. We went to local restaurants and tried to be low-key. There were no problems, but part of the time was actually enjoyable because we didn't have the fear of him taking off. We went home and felt good thinking that he had grown out of the drug dependency. Maybe being on his own woke him up to the reality of working, washing clothes, cooking, cleaning, and all of the duties associated with living. We knew that in September, he would be going back to school in the Boston area and he was feeling good about it.

Cindy and I took a trip to Disney World in August to get away and celebrate our newfound freedom. I worked until 4:30 in the afternoon and Cindy packed everything. We left the house at 6:00 p.m. We drove south more than 1,000 miles, and to save time, did it overnight and arrived in Disney by 10:00 a.m. the next morning. The time spent alone in the car was great. We took turns driving. The drive was pleasant because, for some reason, we felt no pressure about Mark getting into trouble. We were like kids in a candy store, playing at the parks and going swimming and eating really nice dinners, sometimes with the Disney characters, and just plain having fun. After the week, reality set in again, and we knew that there was work to get done at the office and then the trip to Boston to move Mark from his apartment into the dorm and register for classes.

That was one of the few times over the past five years that we could plan anything over a week in advance. Even at home, when friends wanted to go out, they would try to plan a week or two in advance and we would just say that we would see that night if everything was OK. The feeling of no pressure that we constantly lived under was almost indescribable.

On September 7th, we went to Boston to help make the move. It was raining hard and it was a dreary type day. We felt that with our car and the Amigo, it would take one or two trips to get everything moved to his dorm, which was 30 minutes away from the apartment. We were going to pack on the 7th and move on the 8th. When we got to Boston, Mark told us that his windshield was broken, so I found a place about a mile away that would do the job in one day for $310. We had no choice and had to get the work started on the car because we were on a schedule to get him moved. It wasn't the point of being taken for more money, although we certainly were, but every time we turned around, there was another problem the was unexpected. I thought we had enough trouble just keeping up with the expected problems.

We were upset because there was a makeshift top on the amigo and the insides were soaked. Mark said the top was stolen. What could we do? We ignored that problem this day. We said that we would go to his school with him and register on the 7th, which we did. The apartment was a mess so Cindy and I went to a local motel and made plans to meet Mark at his apartment at 10:00 the next morning to finish packing and move. One of his friends appeared to be staying at the apartment, but we weren't really sure and didn't care. We just wanted to get the move over and get him situated back in school.

There were many signs of female residents at his apartment also, including female undergarments lying around, but again, we did not worry about small things. If anything, I thought the action in the apartment could keep him nearby. On the morning of the 8th, we got to the apartment at 10:00 a.m., as we had planned. His friend was there and let us in. Mark was not there and it appeared that he did not sleep there that night. We looked at each other, but didn't say a word. We didn't have to say anything. There was not much to do except start packing, which we did. Cindy, Mark's friend and I packed up everything and loaded our car, which was the only one available. We were all hot, sweaty, and tired. The weather was still rainy and we were soaked from the humidity, also. We were worried because of Mark was a no-show. Packing the car was strenuous because of the basement steps and the weather. The mood we were in did not help the situation, either.

We waited at the apartment until 3:30 in the afternoon and Mark still did not return. The check in at school was at noon. We were sitting with our thumbs. We called the police to see if there were any accidents or anything they knew.

Cindy and I were now at each other's throat. Was he hurt? He wouldn't screw us up at a time like this, would he? Where do we go now? Do we go to school and assume that he is there, or back to the motel where he can reach us, or stay at the empty apartment? There is no way for him to get to us because the phones are off. We decided to go to the motel and sit by the phone. Then I went back to the apartment and then to the school, while Cindy stayed in the motel room. Each of the places was ½ hour away from each other. Mark was not to be found. Cindy called home to advise her parents that we decided to stay over and visit in Boston. Yes, we lied to them! Don't many adult children lie to their elderly parents to protect them from distressing news at times?

At 9:00 p.m., Mark called the motel. He said that he got into a fight with his girlfriend. (his girlfriend was the girl that he met four months earlier at the movie with Cindy.) After the fight, he got drunk and woke up at 3:30 p.m., and couldn't find us when he went back to the apartment. Of course, we did leave a note on the door.

We left the motel and went back to his apartment where he was sitting outside. He got into the car and said he was sorry. I was furious and wanted to smack him to get rid of the frustration that had built up over the entire day. I was upset with him because we were the ones who had to pack his entire apartment and then load the car in the pouring rain. We were too old and out of shape to do this kind of thing. We drove him to a restaurant, next to the local bowling alley where we all ate, but I could have eaten dog food by that time and it would not have mattered. By the way, the dinner did not taste like anything to be consumed by humans, but it did fill our stomachs. The dinner table was quiet and everyone was just anxious to get out and away from each other, but we were trapped. We finished dinner and went back to the room. There were major decisions to make. We decided to take the direct approach because there was enough bullshit that had already passed between us. We told Mark that we didn't wish to hear any more stories because if he did the right thing, there would be no more problems. We laid it out very simply by saying that it was our way or the highway. We said to take three courses and do well, absolutely no cutting classes, and cause no problems. We talked until about 2:00 a.m. Cindy and I were like zombies. We were ready to give in to anything if we could have peace. We woke up about nine in the morning, and after breakfast, went to school to check Mark into the dorm, which we were still permitted to do. Everything there went smoothly and typical of the kids getting back to campus with the blankets on the lawns, guys tossing the football, and parents walking around reminiscing about their college days. We were here before! You could overhear the same garbage about how lucky the kids were who were coming to this beautiful campus. Yes, it was beautiful, but the kids were past psych 1. We were situated with Mark in his room and we left campus to go directly home at 1:20 in the afternoon. It took six hours of a very boring drive. The pressure was again off in our minds, but the immediate thought was the obvious: Do either of us think he is going to make it this time? Most parents have asked that question at least 20 times over the course of their kids growing up. It may have pertained to school, dance, drugs, alcohol, sports, or some mundane or redundant subject, but it was asked. In my younger days, pulling the car over and getting a BJ would finish off that kind of mental relief. As one gets older, and it takes longer to calm down, I would have settled for an O.J. There has to be some type of reward when the day is done.

We were home getting organized, but our minds had scattered thoughts that all pertained to Mark. He should have been in class now, but was he? Was he out playing with his girlfriend, who we didn't really know, but we knew he was spending a lot of time with her. Was he taking school seriously now? He had his car at school so that meant he had freedom. Could he handle the freedom? We just wanted to know that when he got off the phone most nights, it was simply a good bye and all was well.

We all dreamed of having two kids who were wonderful, respectful, and loving; Right! We read that it did happen in some families, but it seemed as if it was never in the cards for us. All of our work was tied to Mark, but what about our other son? He was still in the same state, doing nothing and going nowhere. The visits to him were less frequent, because they were way too upsetting to Cindy. He was so pathetic to watch, because of the seizures and his general condition of probable pain, but no one could be sure.

On the 16th, we received two more tickets in the mail totaling $500 addressed to Mark. The tickets were for speeding. When we asked Mark about them on the phone, he said the cop said not to pay them because he was out of state. Sure, like we just fell off the turnip truck! The ticket was for doing 70 in a 30-mile zone. We did not even bother looking at the second ticket. He said not to pay that and we didn't. We figured that the worst thing that could happen was his license would get suspended. We have bailed him out of trouble so many times, so it was time to make him sweat. He was made aware of the entire situation and said that it was fine.

On the 20th, we got a phone call from Mark and he said to us that he had a small problem. He had driven to Brooklyn, N.Y., and drove into a guardrail near one of the bridges. The car was in a repair shop and had $275 worth of damage. Mark explained to us that while he was stuck in Brooklyn, he was sitting in the park near the garage and was mugged at 3:00 a.m. in the morning. If you have any intelligence at all, you have just said to yourself, "why was he in the park at 3:00 a.m.?" We haven't figured that out. Cindy went to New York to check out the car and see what was really happening. I stayed home and went to work. Cindy found out that the car had $1,100 additional damage to the frame, but it could be straightened out. Now let's recap:

He fucked up moving out of the apartment.

He fucked up on the school registration.

He got speeding tickets.

He left school to go to New York where he screwed up the car and it cost more than $1,100 to fix.

He got mugged in the park.

He missed two classes while he was stuck in Brooklyn, when he was supposed to be in Boston.

He had no money in his pocket.

That's not bad for a little more than one week. I'd say that things were going better!

We took trips to Boston two or three more times to satisfy ourselves that Mark was in school. We spent time with him and some with his girlfriend. Our son continued to educate the brain below his waist. When we reached Mark at the dorm about two weeks after the semester started, he told us that he had a little problem with security. At this point, what kind of problem would anyone expect with security except maybe a parking ticket on campus. Mark proceeded to tell me that the guys were hanging out in the dorm eating pizza when some guy with an attitude came in and started messing up some of the guys. Mark grabbed a hammer and smacked the guy over the head and knocked him out. Mark never hesitated to do what he had to in a fight and generally had no remorse for violence with his peer group. The police were called in and Mark was reprimanded, but no charges were filed because the guy was wanted by the police and was trespassing. Mark lucked out this time, but he became quickly known on campus, for better or worse. I figured it was an ego boost in his mind; he said that people he didn't know were now saying hello to him and acknowledging his presence.

As parents, we were always the last to know the real truth. We knew that Mark was seeing a lot of his new girlfriend, Brenda, in Boston, but we didn't really know that they were spending most of their time together. When Cindy would call the dorm, she spoke to Brenda when he was out. This also occurred when he was in his apartment in Boston. We knew that Brenda lived in one of the small surrounding towns and was close to his school, and we figured it was just one of those one-night stands that took a few extra nights. It appeared to us that it could have been a high school girl that wanted to say that she was running around with a college guy. It could have been any of those things, but it wasn't.

Chapter Fifteen

On October 12, just about a month after school started, Mark advised us that Brenda was pregnant. That was not the news that we wanted to hear. We were hoping to hear that school was fine and he was a changed boy/man, but that occurred only in the movies. Cindy and I were really stupid because we were shocked. We kept him stocked with condoms, or so we thought. This was a dilemma because we were basically logical. Obviously, the brilliant question that we asked each other next was, "what happened?"

We started asking Mark some questions that we needed answers for, such as:

Is she going to have an abortion?

Does she want to have a baby at 17 years of age?

Who is going to support the baby?

How stupid could you be?

Are you staying in school?

Do you know what it takes to support a baby?

Where are you going to live?

What does her family think of all of this?

How stupid could you be?

How can you handle a baby when you can't handle yourself?

What are you doing the next six months?

How stupid could you be?

What do you want us to do?

Are you going to talk her into adoption by a capable married couple?

Do you want us to tell your grandparents? (Both sets were still alive.)

And then we had the internal thoughts that we asked each other that included more questions such as:

What are we supposed to do?

Is he still on drugs?

Is this his way out of school?

What can he do since drugs ruined so many of his jobs?

We should go meet her parents, shouldn't we?

We are paying all of Mark's support for his car, his spending money, etc. Should that continue?

How did we get into this?

How fucking stupid could he be?

We only had questions, lots of questions, because there were no answers that we could think of. If you were stressed out over a long-term drug problem with your son, wouldn't it be logical that if he knocked up some girl you barely knew, that you, as a parent, should not be happy? This was not a good scene and we knew it, but like almost all the things Mark did, was out of our control. We had too many choices to make that included the possibility of losing a son, who we dearly loved, but truly had been tremendous pain in the ass. He was caring and loving when straight, but drugs were a major part of his life on an average of five days a month. He was a binger and that was very dangerous to everyone, because he screwed up his mental and physical systems in great fluctuations. This is equated to a dieter who goes up and down in weight every month or two. After a while, the body couldn't take it. We could accept the situation and just wait to see what happened. That was like an ostrich burying his head in the ground assuming that since he didn't see anything, no one could see him. We knew what was going to happen. This was now something that we knew was wrong because of the situation, but in the back of our minds, we grasped to the hope that it could turn him around.

The best thing that we could do was to go up to the school and evaluate the situation, because without seeing everything and knowing the players, we were stereotyping and that was not good. Our minds were playing games on us and that, although natural, was really dumb. The situation was there and our perception was not based on fact. We went to visit him in school. After all, it could be reasonable, right?

We phoned ahead to various motels and had no luck of finding a room. Cindy asked Mark to find out if there was a local motel in the area so we could be close by. We were there for one reason and the less travel time, the better. We were told that one of Brenda's aunts had a connection at a motel that was only 15 minutes away, so we were able to get a room booked there. We figured that we would be there one night. We'll drive up early one morning and drive home the following night. We could make arrangements at home for the dogs to be fed and everything else was covered.

We left home at 4:00 a.m. to beat any New York City traffic, and figured that we could still get a full day with Mark. We knew we would be beat that night, so it would be an early dinner and a visit with Mark and Brenda and then to bed. Mark told us to go directly to Brenda's home which was 10 minutes from school and he gave us directions. We arrived at her house at 10:30 a.m. As we drove through the small town, we saw something that we were not used to seeing; a community with a small-town square. The town looked like it had economic problems because the storefronts were shabby looking and they covered one block on each side of the main road. The area was clean, but old and slightly dingy. We passed a McDonald's that appeared to be one of the originals and on the other side of town was a Dunkin' Donuts. The donut place was expected for two reasons: a police station was across the street, and the corporate headquarters for this national company was in the next town of Braintree. Brenda's house was about nine blocks from the square. We pulled up and parked in front. The house was a cottage-style structure with two small bedrooms on the first level with a living room, kitchen, and bath. It was neat, but neglected and needed major repairs. The clapboard siding was very old and showed signs of wear that could have been painted or really should have been replaced with siding.

We went up the five steps in front of the house and were greeted at the door by an older woman who we assumed to be Brenda's grandmother. We were told earlier that she owned the home and also worked in a nearby variety store. Cindy and I walked in and introduced ourselves and she said that she was expecting us. She was very cordial and invited us to have coffee at the kitchen table. We made a little small talk for about five minutes with the usual traffic was fine and we had no trouble finding the place, etc. Mark was not to be found at first glance. We looked at each other because our eyes started to tear and burn. The entire home was filled with smoke from cigarettes. Cindy's eyes were more sensitive than mine and she actually had to walk outside. I had a cup of coffee, which was already brewed and was joined by the grandmother. She told us that Mark and Brenda were sleeping in the other room. We asked her to wake him since it was now 11 a.m., and we were anxious to speak to him. Cindy realized that the kids were in the same bedroom as Brenda's brother who was the same age as Mark, who was now 20. That just didn't give Cindy a happy healthy feeling.

Mark came out of the room, dressed in cut off baggy sweat pants and nothing else, and he gave me a hug and gave Cindy a big hug and kiss. He then picked Cindy up as a parent cradles a child, which he always liked to do, to "play." As was mentioned before, they had a special relationship. Cindy told him to put her down, and gave him a big hug again. He sat down with us and asked how the drive up was and how we were doing. He asked about the dogs and said that he missed them. Cindy asked where Brenda was and he said she was still sleeping. We thought it seemed strange that Mark was sleeping at this time of the morning, here, but we would find out why soon enough. We were also on edge trying to figure out the pregnancy situation.

We asked him how he felt about the situation with Brenda. He said he was really happy about her being pregnant. He said that this child would be his bloodline. He felt like it was his creation and that Brenda was feeling the same way. With that said to us, we knew that we were walking on thin ice trying to logic all of the consequences of having a baby. At the next instant, Mark dropped another bombshell on us. He told us that he dropped out of school and was living at the grandmother's home. I asked where all of the stuff from school was like the TV and the furniture. He gave me names of people and places where everything was. That answered a few other questions and created a few more. We were actually stunned because we really had no idea of the questions to ask. Each question led to 10 more that had logic to us, but made no sense to someone with no foresight or ambition. It was like a child seeking instant gratification, except this was a very serious matter.

We lost all of his tuition because we only had three weeks to withdraw and get a portion back. We also kissed goodbye any of the possessions that we bought him for the apartment and the dorm. At that point, the physical possessions were the least of our problems. We were without words and just shaking our heads. It was probably one of the very few times that we were speechless. Cindy was always optimistic and loving in any situation, but she had an additional dilemma. She knew that I was ready to explode, but there was no target. Explode at who? What would I accomplish except get everyone agitated and alienate myself from the situation. That probably would have been the smartest thing to do, but unfortunately, unrealistic. I took a walk around the block and let Cindy remain to get a lay of the land. The land did not look so good. I asked Cindy to fill me in and break it to me very gently. We could read each other's thoughts so we knew this was going to be an easy communication between us.

We also knew that this was going to take a while because Cindy said that it was more complicated than we figured. I asked her to please start somewhere. I apologize to all of the women, but that was one of my dumber statements because with no direction and a messy situation, it was almost predictable that Cindy would lose me in her babbling in the first five sentences. I was wrong because I was lost in the first two sentences and after getting it clear, I understood why. I learned that Brenda was an 11th grade dropout who enjoyed sleeping until noon every day. We found out that the reason that she was living at her grandmothers was because her parents lost custodial rights to her and her brother many years earlier when she was two. We learned that her mother was a heroin addict and was in jail about ½ of each of the past six years and had rarely lived with her father. As it turned out, her parents were never married. Her father, Joe, was an alcoholic and a druggie who was able to only sporadically hold down jobs. The brother appeared to be slightly wild and liked his beer. He was also awaiting trial for dealing drugs in a school zone. The house had two bedrooms, one bath, and three teenagers. The brother, who was 19 years old, slept with the grandmother until very recently. The grandmother supported the entire house working part-time at $7 per-hour and received a small pension from previous jobs. Her husband had passed away many years ago, and her life was her grandchildren that she basically raised, and her other daughter who also spent some time behind prison bars. This was a wonderful thing for Mark to bring us into!

Now that we were aware of the situation, it was time to start to address the issues. We asked what thoughts the grandmother had of the pregnancy. She was not pleased that it happened, but said that the kids would have to grow up and take care of the baby. I did not bring abortion into the picture because it was none of my business. We then met Brenda's mother, who came into the room as we were talking at the kitchen table. She appeared to have looked young and alive at one time, but you could see the effects of the drugs on her. She sat at the table with us and started to talk to me, but would lose her train of thought and dose off. That was characteristic of heroin addicts.

She said she was excited about the baby, We spoke to Brenda, who started telling us about all of her friends who had babies and none of them were married. This pregnancy was a real accomplishment for her. There was a major disaster in the making, but we had no idea what it was. Mark said that he was working with Brenda's brother and planned to stay in the house and see what would happen. I wanted to ring his neck and say, "you ass hole, I'll tell you what's happening; you knocked up this kid who has no ambition, you ruined you education and chance for a future, you now have the responsibility of a child and you can't even take care of yourself." Had I said what I was thinking and really wanted to say, Cindy would have been aggravated and I'd be fighting with her and not be able to handle this wonderful situation we now found ourselves thrown into.

It was 5 o'clock and we wanted to eat before we began getting ulcers. "Let's go to town and have a relaxing dinner," I suggested to everyone. Mark and Brenda came along, but the others said they did not want to come along. Good, I was thinking, because this would be a good chance to be alone with the two geniuses.

We went to a nice Irish pub near Fanuel Hall and ordered Irish stew, which I had to admit was wonderful. I had a beer that I desperately needed and made sure I knew the server's name in case I wanted another quickly. I was getting in the grove of understanding that sometimes alcohol could relax you. There was a guitar player softly singing some Gaelic tunes, but all I knew was I was getting increasingly mellow with each note and swallow. Cindy asked questions about the future and there were responses that told us that the kids had no clue about what day tomorrow was. She continued to ask questions, which I had to simplify for the kids each time she asked. We felt like we were spoon-feeding a fledgling. We came to a reality that there wasn't a damn thing we could say or do that would help this situation; a situation these kids thought was just wonderful. With that, I had a great dessert and pushed the situation out of my mind for the time being. We walked around town and just chilled out and took things easy that night.

We dropped the kids off back at the house and went to the motel. We got back to the room, grabbed a can of soda from the soda machine, sat on the bed, and looked at each other. We said we had to try to evaluate our position and see if we were crazy or just getting old. We talked for about 30 seconds and realized that we were going to have to support a new family or give up our son. That may sound drastic, but it was reality. Mark told us that they were going to live in the grandmother's house and she could help take care of the baby. I asked how she could since she still worked and needed the money. The only car they had was the one we bought for Mark. We asked where the food was coming from and Mark said the grandmother was buying it, but he could only eat certain things and he wasn't allowed to drink more than one glass of milk per day. We saw this going far! The next day we drove back to the house and said goodbye to all, and then we got the hell out of there. We saw our son, who already had drug problems, being put into a situation that sounded good to him, but was foreign to his upbringing. He was lost and without money, except the $100 we just gave him, to hold him over until his next paycheck. The money satisfied my conscience, and got us on our way absolutely knowing that we accomplished nothing, and will face more problems in the immediate future. It was a very long drive home, and as we were driving away from the scene, we could rationally begin to discuss everything. We agreed to play it by ear, for the time being, because we were totally stumped as how to rectify this whole situation.

It was not something that we could anticipate or rationalize. It was something that we had definite opinions on and could not conceive anything else but the right moral and ethical actions. If you were married, this would have been a topic that could cause an argument between you and your spouse. At the very least, there would be conflict on the monetary support issue as to if, when, why, and how much issue. We were as drained as ever because of the frustration and the situation being totally out of our control. We returned home and said that we will talk to him on the phone to give support if he needs it. After all, he had his problems and he appeared to be focused away from drugs. Wrong again. Since Brenda now knew us, she opened up when we called and told us that Mark was out doing drugs when he wasn't with her. Wonderful! Now we were back in full swing over 300 miles away and the problems were growing deeper. We had to work, so there was not a possibility that we could devote our time going back and forth every other day. We said for him to fend for himself and talk to us when he wished.

That lasted for about two days when we got a credit card bill for over $300 and cash advances. We called and he told us that he just took Brenda out for dinner for her birthday and spent $35. I hit the roof.

"How the fuck can you spend $35 of our money when you just maxed your credit card and are overdrawn at the bank?" I yelled at him.

I was livid because Mark said, "we just didn't understand."

166

We could not believe that Mark would be that irresponsible to spend money on a fancy dinner and not have money to buy milk or help in the house or get out of some debt. Why didn't he realize that his mom and dad worked for a living and were helping him, which meant that he should appreciate it? Yea, right!

Have you given your kids something that you felt you went way beyond the call of duty to do and they treated it as if it was totally expected? That was total frustration and disappointment. We told Mark that we were not giving him any more money since he had a job and a place to live. We were only helping him at school because we wanted him to study and concentrate on doing well. Our every waking moment was consumed with thoughts of Mark. He was not really capable of making well thought-out decisions because of the drugs. There was a baby on the way and these idiots knew that they both smoked, Mark did drugs, and Brenda drank. Mark was screwing up every time he turned around. When he was home and in the house, he was warm, caring, and lovable, but he wasn't home and Cindy's thoughts were long distance. That was when we realized that our minds could play tricks on us. We started to think of all of the things that he could be into and we were too far away so we couldn't help. Was he drugged out in some crack house? Was he selling his body for drugs? Would he overdose? Would he get into a fight with a cop and get shot? Was he selling dope? What was he doing, because we knew from past history that he wouldn't hold a job? We were at ease that he wasn't home, but tense because we knew his actions. It was a no-win situation. He could get no help from anyone in Boston, because from the looks of everyone up there, they couldn't even help themselves.

We spoke to Mark on November 3 and listened to the same bullshit of how he was going to change. I guess he really meant it when he said it, but short-term actions take a back-seat to intentions when everyone was drinking and smoking dope and Mark was with them. Once he started, there was no return until he awoke after passing out or the money was gone and he sobered. We just went about our business at home and tried to keep rolling.

Cindy woke up the morning of the 5th and noticed that one of our dogs, the longhaired dachshund, was having an unusually hard time breathing. Normally, she sneezed, coughed, and then would be fine for a while. She was 10 years old and overweight; like us. We took her to the vet who said there were a lot of tests that could be done on her. We said that he did a lot of tests prior and the results said that there was nothing to do and she was healthy other than the coughing. Her teeth were shot and she was laboring when she walked. She had the best personality of anyone in our household and she was Mark's first love. He got her as a puppy and he picked her out. Even in his worst times, she would comfort him and would get through to him when Cindy couldn't. Cindy was given a lot of choices by the vet, which basically was to continue with more tests or put her down. The dog was so sweet that we felt that we could not let her suffer. We made a decision to put her down rather than go through more shots and tests. The vet said he felt we should keep testing because she could go a few more years. We figured that the vet wanted money for more vacations! He asked us if we wanted to stay with her for a few minutes to say goodbye, which we did. It was not pretty. Her big brown eyes were focused on us as she always had total trust in us. We were with her about 5 minutes and we told the vet to come in and give her the shot. He asked me to hold her and I said it wouldn't be necessary if we were petting her head. The vet accepted that and proceeded to give her the shot. Tears were streaming from both of us because we knew the next 30 seconds were her final. The dog slowly closed her eyes as we continued to pet her head and body. She was out of pain. The vet told us she was dead. We gave her a final pet and a goodbye and left her on the table. We felt good that she didn't suffer and that she felt comfortable with us by her side until the end. We got into the car and began the short drive home. Tears were still flowing from both of us. We had another dog at home that was the same age, equally dependant, and best friends with the dog that we just put to sleep.

We entered the house and were greeted by the little dog and then he started looking for his friend. He was starting to get upset because for the past ten years, they were together playing and sleeping together. Cindy tried to comfort him, but he kept looking for her. He calmed down and Cindy picked him up to give him some security, but it almost seemed like he knew she wasn't coming back. It seemed like the mourning period had unofficially begun. Cindy took up one of the dog's dishes because each one had their own. More tears came with every action that she took. The favorite spot that she laid in was empty. We didn't realize what a major role she played in the household. It seemed like we now were spending extra time with our other dog. I wasn't sure if the dog needed it or we did.

We did not tell Mark that we put his dog to sleep. We were obviously concerned about his reaction and felt that there would be a better time to tell him than over the phone.

At the same time, Cindy's mom, who was diagnosed with a form of leukemia, was beginning to get worse. We again did not tell Mark for the same reasons. She had been getting blood transfusions every month for about 2 years because her body was not making red blood cells. Her liver was not functioning well. She was always great after receiving a transfusion, but, like a car, would run out of gas almost like clockwork each month. She would go into the hospital as an out patient in the morning, take two units and be home by 5 p.m. Cindy and I would always go to the hospital to relieve Cindy's father so he could go get some lunch or just walk around for a bit. We knew that Cindy's mom would be extremely pleasant throughout the hospital visit and would be more concerned about everyone other than herself. She would always pull Cindy aside and get as much information on Mark as she could, because we believed she loved him more than anyone else in her life. She got so much joy from talking to him and he was extremely affectionate with her.

This last trip to the hospital was the most difficult because she needed three units of blood to get her back to the temporary acceptable levels. That was not a good sign. We did not tell Mark anything about the transfusion situation. Cindy's father was taking care of her when she was home in the evening, but she went out with her friends most days or she would sit in on a card game with the 'girls' up to the last three weeks. She was in her mid 70s but she appeared to be so young-at-heart for her age

All of these stressful activities took place within a 48-hour period and we were frazzled and waiting for some relief, but we had no idea from where. We woke up on the 7th of November and got a phone call that Mark was picked up by the police for traffic violations that were not paid. He also had spent 8 hours in the local jail in Boston. He was to go on trial in three days and he faced the possibility of spending 30 days in jail. Brenda borrowed money from different members of her family to bail him out. The entire bail was $500 and she had to beg for the money because there was not money to be had in the houses of these family members. An additional $125 was needed to get the car out of the impound lot.

Things were getting ugly again; we had our hands full and not nearly enough time to do all the chores and still earn a living. We wired the $500 to give back to the family and be under no further obligations. We got a call the next day from Mark that he was in Boston, had a flat tire, had no money, and no bank card. At the same time, Brenda called us and figured that we should know that Mark never showed up at home the night before. We told her that he was at a certain corner, we were wiring $125 for the tire, and he was out of gas with no money. We understood that he was screwing up, but there was nothing we could do, short of dropping him out of our lives.

Mark got the car, went to the bank, and pulled another $200 out on an advance. I called the bank and asked how he could do that and the teller said they allow it as a general policy. It was a general policy to allow overdrafts at the bank? We could now understand why banks and credit card companies had so many deadbeats. After I accused them of having no brains, I slapped myself once across the mouth and realized that these bank tellers almost made me look as stupid as them and I almost came down to their level. Stress can make one do dumb things. Speaking of dumb, we were feeling that we were the King and Queen of dumb after buying all of the excuses and buying all of the stories from Mark!

Everything done from here on in was done out of the panic mode; it was emotion, rather than logic that spurred along the events. It was now the 12th of November and Mark still didn't get his car that we had sent the money for. Brenda told Cindy that it was $85 for the car and Mark had lied to us when he told us it was $125. We knew he was lying, but at that point, just get the car! He didn't get the car and also never went home. Cindy spoke to him that night and he said the towing agency was closed when he got there. He decided to stay with a friend of his that he met at the pizza shop near his old apartment. His friend was a young lady who he spent a number of evenings with when he had his apartment. We never met her, but she apparently had no problem keeping Mark happy for short periods of time. He went back to the police station to clean up a few more warrants that were out on him and found out that on Veteran's Day, nothing was open. He had no clue. If you asked 100 high school kids what Veteran's Day was, I guarantee more than half would have no idea. Isn't this a wonderful future to look forward to as far as education is concerned?

The 13th of November came and he called home. We said to him that his dog died last week. He was down on himself and the dog thing was the final straw. The idea of school was again on his mind because he knew that without an education, it was tough to move ahead with his life in a positive way and have any hope of building a future. He was having conflicts because he knew what was best, but was not able to achieve it for many reasons, including the drugs.

His conflicts were much tougher than ours, and ours were enough. With the drugs, it was like cigarettes. "Sure I stopped smoking and it was easy, if fact, I stopped more than

40 different times!'

With his next phone call, he said that he wanted to come home and try to get his life together. He also said that he wanted our help to organize his life. The last thing he said was that his car was rear-ended! I decided to ignore the last part with the exception of asking if it could be driven, which he said it could. We said to come home and we would discuss everything.

We asked Cindy's father not to trade her mom's car, which she was not able to drive anymore based on her condition. It was worth the same as Mark's, but was in much better condition. He agreed to do this. Her car was a four-year-old Cadillac that was in mint condition. I said that it wasn't a smart thing to do to give him a car like that, but I was outvoted and maybe the logic was right. The car was beautiful, but not worth much because the big ones don't really hold their value, which was true. We looked at Mark's car, which was newer, but not near the quality of the Cadillac. We also figured that the baby would be safer in a larger car. We checked the value of both and they were about equal. The logic was there, but common sense wasn't. We figured that since it was his grandmother's and he loved her so much, he would take care of it. He had it for about two weeks and was doing pretty well.

Mark wanted to come in to see Cindy's mom. He came in with Brenda. That was a surprise to us, since he said nothing about it. It was fine, because we were back on our turf, not the Boston turf, and it was a much easier feeling. When he walked in through the door, we saw our son with six earrings and very baggy pants that looked like two people could fit into them with him. We said that he didn't look like someone trying to straighten out his life. With that, I went out to the driveway to see the car. The gas tank was on empty and blinking. There was a huge dent in the side and the steering wheel looked like someone tried to break it. I was absolutely furious that Mark wasn't as annoyed as I was about the condition of the car. This was not a normal accident or a break in where the intention was to steal something. This

172

was just wasted damage, whatever that may be. We just kept shaking our heads, realizing that Mark wasn't apologetic or even giving us the benefit of the doubt by at least trying to show some remorse. Mark told us that it was hit in a McDonald's parking lot. This statement pissed us off more because we knew that he was lying. Another redundant question was, "Who did he think was going to fix all of this?"

He came to see his grandmother and that was good for her. While he was home, we didn't speak about much of anything, and two days later, he went back to Boston.

We next heard from Brenda on the 20th when she called to tell us that Mark had called her and then took off somewhere giving her the impression that he was leaving the area. On the 22nd, he called us at 8:00 a.m. and told Cindy the following story: the car was emptied out, he got into a fight, he was in New Hampshire, he filed a police report, and said he had a problem, but the problem was not drugs. That may sound crazy, but since it wasn't drugs, we were relieved. He said he went with this guy named Tom, who nobody knew, and they were doing a bit of drinking, and the fight happened. We didn't ask any other questions because we didn't want any more lies. Mark said that he depended on Cindy, on whom he did, and he was straight now, but needed money to get home. She wired him $50 and said to call her when he got back. We decided that he should come back to our house to make some decisions, but we didn't know what questions and subjects he had to make decisions on!

In the meantime, we were thinking that we must set him up with a priest, Alcohol Anonymous or a strong social worker. When we hit on the third choice, you know we were desperate. Most, not all, social workers could care less about another druggie going through the bullshit of the ups-and-downs of a drug habit. We knew he needed help because in his last conversation, he was crying uncontrollably and admitting he was in need of help. He kept saying mom was his only ally and he needed her help.

We waited and waited and he never came home or called.

We made our calls to find him and places to take him when and if we found him. We did find a few hospitals that would consider him as a patient and support groups and social service organizations that gave advice. There was a problem; there was no Mark to follow through with some of the advice that was received with hours of making calls. We didn't realize all of the groups out there and also didn't realize that they were hardened to all of the excuses that could be given. After all of the prior episodes, each additional experience allowed us to get more detail of alternatives with deeper questions like, "we've done that, what's after that?" Was there a tough love for older kids?

On the November 23, he called home at 9:30 a.m. Our emotions were such that we wanted to tell him to fuck off or go play with someone else, but we knew he was sick, not a bad person. Cindy asked the same basic questions expected, such as "where are you" and "are you O.K.?" On the other end of the phone, we got the news that he was in trouble again and he got into another fight with the wrong people. He said that he had $20 and Brenda said she had $50. Towing on the car and storage was $60. Naturally, we asked the typical question of how the car got impounded again, but were sidetracked in the heat of discussion.

He said he wanted to come home for Thanksgiving, but had no gas money. He needed $50 for gas, which Cindy wired him. We were angry at his continued lack of responsibility, but Cindy's mom thrived when she saw him, so why not give her some happiness. She was getting weaker and the trips for transfusions were getting more frequent. If you have never wired money, which we hadn't before this year, it was a real treat. It was legal loan sharking because of the astronomical fees Western Union charges. Western Union should be one of the highest profit margin companies on the stock exchange based on these ridiculous rates.

On the 24th, Mark called first thing in the morning to say he wasn't coming home because he wanted to stay a week, but Brenda only wanted to stay one day. He also told Cindy that he was in another car accident. We decided that we better find what really was going on, so we called the police in Boston. We were on the phone from 9:00 a.m. until noon. We determined that there was little that we could do long distance. Things had gotten worse and Cindy's mom was not able to get any more transfusions and was growing weaker by the day. She was in the hospital and Cindy was dreading the worst. The doctors advised her that there was nothing that they could do and it was a matter of time. Cindy's mom had her mind in tact and asked if she could go home to die. Cindy decided to bring her home with her, because we could handle the situation better than Cindy's father, and our home had more activity. Cindy's father disagreed, saying he wanted to keep his wife in the hospital. He cursed Cindy up and down the hallway at the hospital, making a scene that was disturbing to the other patients. Cindy felt that if her mom was going to die, and had voiced her desire not to die in the hospital, Cindy could make that happen. However, her mom's first choice was to die at home. Since Cindy's father wouldn't allow that, Cindy set up a hospital bed in our den and gave her all of the conveniences that we could. At dinnertime, she was able, with help, to come in and sit at the table, but she ate very little. She had lost ½ of her weight and was always pale. She always had a smile and questioned everyone about the kids and their activities. She never did complain or do anything that she felt would inconvenience anyone. When things got worse, the flowing week, we set up a baby monitor and a porta-potty, and Hospice was coming in more frequently.

We helped her out of bed and into the potty. I yelled at her one night because she didn't want to disturb our sleeping so she tried to get to the potty herself. She fell and was unable to do anything. She called for help and we ran downstairs to assist and all we could do was to pick her up off the floor and clean a few bruises. It was frustrating because we tried to make her last days or weeks as comfortable as possible, but she still was more concerned about everyone other than herself. It was difficult and Mark came home December 15, at Cindy's request, to be with his grandmom. Her mom knew the end was coming because Cindy finally gave in and started giving her morphine for her pain. Her mom knew what it was and requested it at various times knowing it would also speed up the end. The first time we gave it to her was traumatic because we knew that was the final march to death. Brenda was with Mark when he came in and grandmom was happy to see him. Brenda was getting very heavy. She was eating everything in sight and smoking constantly. Cindy's mom was trying to live to see the baby, but she knew she was fighting a losing battle.

She died on the 18th of December. The morning of her death, she whispered to Cindy to take the kids to the store and buy a dress for Brenda and a baby present. She wanted to be a part of the newborn child in her own way. We reluctantly went, but spoke about her the whole time. It was difficult to go out shopping, even though that was her request, her last request. Cindy's father was with her at her bedside when she died. She just went to sleep. He called us on the cell phone to tell Cindy that he thought that she died. We raced home to be at her side. It took us fifteen minutes to get there. I picked up her hand and felt her skin. She was still warm, but dead.

The funeral plans were set months ago and she was scheduled for the burial two days later. The days between death and the funeral were typical of any death. There was a lot of remembering and tears and smiles of the good times. The difference here was how Mark handled things. We suggested that Mark write her a letter and put it in her casket to explain his feelings. This was not Mark's style, but we said it would help him feel better and let him know that part of his feelings would always be near her. It appeared that a lot of people tended to put things in the caskets prior to burial that were part of the life of the deceased. It appeared to do wonders for Mark in terms of closure.

We made a copy of the letter because it told a lot of the past and insight into it. The letter was as follows:

Dear Grandmom,

I hope you can hear me and I hope you are happier in heaven. I want you to know I love you and I am sorry for all that I have put you through. If I could erase or do over the past, a lot would be different. I will never forgive myself for yelling at you when I was little to when I would disappear for weeks and end up in trouble. I am sorry that I embarrassed you and grandpop. I know I am nothing that everyone hoped for. Sometimes I get mad and frustrated with grandpop but from now on I am going to look at him as someone who took care of and gave my favorite person all she wanted or needed. I respect him for that and I hope that I can be as good a provider. I love you with all my heart grandmom, and I won't or never could forget you as long as I live, you're always #1. I'll talk to you and keep you posted about the baby and I hope you there now like you always were, you were probably the only person that never was totally disgusted with me and I never felt awkward in front of you. I love you and always will. I'll see you. I hope in a long time but I want you to know that although I didn't always show it, I never took your love for granted. God please take care of my grandmom. She is probably the best person to ever walk the earth. She never was mean. She never cheated anyone and she was pleasant and kept a warm smile while she was in more pain than I know I can imagine. So please take care of her and take what you want from me. I love you grandmom, now and forever, Love, Mark

Chapter Sixteen

On the 22nd of December, Mark went back to Boston. There was nothing to do here. The car was fixed by a friend of mine and it was back to being almost new. We realized that Mark missed the court date that was on the 21st, but no one cared at that point, including Mark. He had no idea what to do to make money, how to act, or really what each day was going to bring. He called Cindy on the 25th and said he was very lonely during the holidays without Cindy and that he really missed his grandmother. He probably called home about six times that day. No matter how screwed up someone is, they always tend to go home for safety, even if safety was questionable.

He stayed in Boston over the New Year and we were getting the typical phone calls of not finding a job, being out of money, missing home, and all of the comments that any parent would get from their kid in college or even just out of the house. We were home and trying to shift our daily gears into our own lives instead of being dominated by the actions of Mark, which were normally disastrous. This was a major decision for us because this spontaneous panic and quick action had become our life. It was not a good feeling knowing that an erratic young man who couldn't plan two hours in advance for himself was, without realizing it, making plans for us through his actions. We were coping and slowly trying to let him loose.

The two weeks of the New Year came and we were fine and assumed that Mark found a temporary niche. We were wrong again, because on January 10, Mark was arrested for more outstanding warrants. This was getting ridiculous so I called Boston City Hall and was given the run around again. We decided that the newspapers should hear about the treatment that a visitor got when he was in town for a number of months. We wrote a lengthy detailed letter expressing the unfairness of the tickets and that permits should be given to people who were temporary residents of the community. Our letter was the last thing that we saw on the topic. Again, those in power blew us off. The fine now was $25 bail and $85 to get the car out of the impound lot. I asked Mark how he was going to repay us since he still had no job. That question was like waiting for a response from the newspaper. He was a beaten kid and he created it all. He blamed the world for his bad luck. He didn't buy my story that he was doing it to himself. We were our own victims and so was he! How could we get off of this path?

He got the car when we wired him the money. He came home as he said that he would. When he came home, he was with Brenda's brother who was doing the same as Mark, nothing. The car now needed a power steering pump, whatever that was, so I had it done. Mark stayed at our home with her brother for a week and just screwed around. The weather was cold so some days they went to the pond, put on ice skates and shot the hockey pucks back and forth the same as two kids would play catch in our day. Other days, they slept until noon and went out partying until two or three in the morning. I couldn't tell them what time to be in because they never listened or would only make excuses. That may sound like a cop out, but it was a reality. Our choices were to be constantly fighting with him, or realize that he had lived alone for the better part of a year so it was now even more difficult to control his actions. Also, I had to consider the feelings of Cindy, since it was a joint decision. It was fairly peaceful, but frustrating seeing a seemingly healthy young man wasting his life. The frustration for me was just trying to keep my mouth shut.

Mark went back to Boston on the 18th of January, although he said he wasn't really sure he wanted to go back. He left depressed and confused because our attitude was slightly more independent from what he was used to. When he got back to Boston, he called home and said he decided to go to Florida. He had a former girlfriend who moved there, my parents lived there, and Cindy had close relatives that lived there. We suggested that he seriously consider where he would live and what he would do for a living. Also, with the baby coming, how did Brenda feel about it? Up until this point, not once has the question of marriage ever come up. I was starting to understand that marriage to one generation does not mean the same to each generation. I'm also starting to understand that having a baby is more like a prize, not necessarily a responsible, thought-out act. None of this whole crew that we were now dealing with understood the duties of a mother and the responsibilities of a father. They didn't seem to realize that they had to sacrifice some things to do what was best for the child.

The crazy television shows that publicized the teenage mom who said that 'just because I have a baby and live with my parents, that doesn't mean I can't go out every night to have fun.' Those shows that everyone makes fun of are real. The babies being neglected are real. The mental attitudes of these kids are real. The fathers who make the sperm injections could care less if the girls get pregnant.

Cindy and I again did nothing because the entire scenario was beyond our understanding and to try to reason with the people involved was ridiculous. We were coming into the field with such diverse backgrounds that it appeared to be totally different cultures even though we all seemed to speak the same language.

Time went by and there were the usual problems with the police in Boston. That was going to be on going, and that became very obvious to us. Definitions of what was best for a child appeared to vary, and saving for the baby, and credit card fraud all have different meanings and values to these young kids, as the kids started using the easy to get credit cards. Maybe Cindy's thoughts of "the baby comes first" mentality, and plans for the baby's future were not as important to the kids as they used to be for the once removed parents. Maybe in today's world of credit, and the "protect the consumer" philosophies, the right thing to do was not important. It has become way to easy to rip off credit card companies and stores for a few hundred dollars. Either don't pay at all, or just write bad checks. Most stores don't have the time to chase down a small amount of money, and would rather write it off than go through the legal system. Maybe debtors' prison wasn't such a bad idea to bring back some morals. If you don't know what debtor's prison is, again ask someone with gray hair. Was this the way Brenda figured she would clothe the child?

It was now the end of March and time for Cindy and me to get away. We went south and said it was time to escape for a week. While we were away, Mark came home for the weekend. We made the mistake of leaving our phone number and he reached us. The old joke about moving while the kids were away and not leaving a forwarding address was beginning to sound good. Since we knew he was coming home, Cindy left $100 for food and gas to drive back to Boston. As it turned out, he came in with another couple. That was not expected, but should have been. He called Cindy the second day and said that he was out of money. This seemed strange to Cindy since we were away and he was home and he spent more money than we did. We found out that he took Cindy's sports car out of the garage and went to the drug district, by himself, leaving the three other strangers in our home, and he bought crack. The police in the city also stopped him because he looked suspicious driving the sports car in a drug neighborhood being at a young age. They let him go, as there were no problems except that he borrowed Cindy's father's credit card to pay for a broken window in his car. Cindy's father called and Cindy said for him to call the window repair shop and confirm the situation, which he did. Unfortunately, adults are not always as smart as they should be because when the police stopped Mark, he had 15 cartons of cigarettes in the trunk, but that was no crime. The crime was that he charged the cigarettes to the credit card and then traded them for crack. The credit card company called Cindy's father since the purchase appeared out of line, but it was too late to do anything except for Cindy to get furious across a long distance phone line. This meant nothing to Mark, except frustration for Cindy who had to explain to her father not worry about it. We did not want to try to explain to him what happened and all of the why's. We were living it once, and did not want to live it twice. Besides, her father already had a big fight with Mark about the credit card. There was irony about the situation; Mark had to get back to Boston and had no money. We were still away and her father certainly was not getting involved. We were up in the air, but figured we were away and didn't want any more aggravation, so we called a neighbor and asked them to give Mark $100 when the car was packed with the four people and they were ready to leave so we could come home to peace. That may have been another cop out, but it kept sanity and allowed a thought process rather than emotional responses. We needed some time alone because of the death of Cindy's mother and the situation with Mark. Everyone seemed to describe life as a game that had certain rules. I believed that they were right. In this case, they had one other factor. We were playing the game of life and added the additional game of "Beat the Clock" because of the pregnancy. Again, ask that same gray-haired person if the game doesn't ring a bell with you.

With all of the bullshit going on, there was still Mark's court appearance in Boston. I felt that if he handled everything himself, instead of only having to pay a fine, he could end up on death row! I called an attorney in Boston and explained the situation. I told him that we did not want Mark to know that we hired him. We told him to tell Mark that he was assigned to the case from the city and proceed as if Mark was handling the situation by himself. I sent a retainer of $1,000, with the understanding that the money would be the retainer and the entire fee, which was agreeable. It appeared that Mark broke three appointments and treated the whole court appearance as if it was just a walk to the park and he didn't feel like walking.

I was kept up to date about the non-actions, but was relieved to know that the situation was being handled professionally and would not get out of hand without us knowing about it. The kids were not moving forward and Mark was getting dumber and more illogical each time he went on a binge and got cracked up. He was getting tougher to talk to and he just had no insight at all.

Mark called us at the office to tell us that there was an accident and Brenda was driving our car and was hit by a truck in the snow. We asked all of the obvious questions and found out that Brenda and the unborn baby were fine. The driver of a truck, which was double the size of the car, saw her condition and couldn't ask enough how she was. The accident happened at an intersection near the mall in Boston. Both vehicles were going slow, and it was the slippery road that caused them both not to stop. The truck had no damage and our vehicle had the front destroyed, including the frame, but it still could be driven. The concerned truck driver's next stop was his attorney who settled the case against Cindy for $100,000 from our insurance company, who proceeded to cancel us, even though we found out later it was a bogus claim. Brenda's father knew the other driver and said the guy did this all the time with the same attorney. He also saw him lifting huge boxes a week after the accident.

On the 25th of March, Cindy got a phone call from Brenda. She called Cindy at the office at 10:00 a.m. and told her that Mark had not come home the night before. Brenda said that when he left, he was spaced out. Cindy and I left Philadelphia at 1:30 p.m. and headed for Boston. I tried to complete some business before leaving for an unscheduled 7-hour drive. We also were hoping that we would get a phone call that he showed up. No such luck. We arrived in Boston at eight o'clock and immediately filed a stolen car report. At 1:30 a.m. Mark came walking into Brenda's house. He gave us a story that he traded the use of the car to five guys in exchange for drugs. We went back to the police station to report the car found. Mark was emotionally spent and was in tears. He told us again that he needed help, a lot of help. I looked at the car, which was a maroon caddy, and it had heavy damage to the front and both sides. At this point, I seriously considered going into the body shop business and living off Mark! It was getting insane because you don't report damage to the insurance company unless it is high; they tend to cancel or raise your rates past reality. One company already canceled us when they paid another bogus claim and we had no say in it, so we were very cautious and kept paying to repair cars. We told Mark that we couldn't help him and that he had to help himself. We said that if he wanted help, NA (Narcotics Anonymous) was a place to start. He said he would, but he didn't. We left that day to come home because we still had our obligations, like making a living and paying bills. Mark remained in Boston to try to work out his problems. This time, I took the car home.

Three days later, we received a phone call that Mark was arrested for getting into a fight with a patron in a local restaurant. He was put in jail and remained there for about five hours until bail was posted. Bail was $150 and Brenda's family, who had to again pool funds to get the cash, put it up. I never knew what triggered the fight with the customer, but if Mark was coming down from drugs, he could be very touchy and downright mean! He had no fear of fighting with anyone, regardless of size or their fighting ability. He could handle himself pretty well for a suburban street fighter, but we didn't know if he knew street fighting well enough to survive long term. He always had either knives or baseball bats in the car so we knew he was not avoiding trouble. Whenever we were in his car and saw a bat or knife, we would remove it and tell him to avoid this type of confrontation. I had enough bats to start a baseball team! My guess was that the guy he got into the fight with just looked at him wrong. I didn't care because Mark was out of jail and I wasn't sure of anything and didn't question his next move.

The next day, we got a speeding ticket in the mail from New Jersey for $77. We paid it because it seemed like a bargain compared to the rest of the bills, and we just tried to keep things simple. Two days later, we got another speeding ticket in the mail from the same place for $47. Again we paid it. We were going to nail him, but why fight over something that he will say was not his fault and then have the authorities complicate matters by adding interest and penalties over more insignificant bullshit. We were again, or I should say still, on the edge of our seats because we kept waiting for something new that always seemed to pop up and needed our attention.

The next day, there was a call from the Boston court that told him that he needed $50 the next day or he would get picked up and go to jail again. It was so difficult to work long distance trying to decipher the truth and work finances without being hands on. In fact, it was impossible and as we found out, disastrous. Mark spoke to Cindy and she was told that he had no money for food, let alone funds for court. He couldn't get a job without a car and he had no car. I had no sympathy, but we did have to address some of the issues because he was getting more screwed up and losing any self-esteem that he had left. We were advised that Brenda's grandmother, who was supporting the house, refused to keep feeding Mark who was living there and not contributing anything. Her grandmother was working hard in a retail store to make ends meet and Brenda, Mark, Brenda's brother, and Brenda's mother were sponging off of her. She was timid and good-hearted and allowed it to happen for a while and now she had enough, especially since Mark was not family. Mark stole food from the refrigerator when no one was around and took what he could from the dry food shelf. We were undecided about what action to take because we were dealing with our "adult" son. This was also getting rough because Brenda was due within three weeks, and the father figure was not visible for responsibility. We sent $500 to the grandmother and told her to use the money for food, hoping that Mark would get some benefit from the money.

The next day, we had to send $400 to the Boston County Adult Probation Department or Mark would have been picked up again. I started losing track of the reasons for which he was getting arrested. We knew that most traffic violations in Boston were treated very seriously because a large portion of their revenue was derived from traffic related tickets. We just kept things flowing as best we could, hoping that Mark would grow out of his problems and realize the responsibility that being a father was.

On April 19, 9:30 a.m., we got a call from Brenda; she was going to the hospital. She said her contractions were every two minutes. Cindy told her that we were leaving Philadelphia right away. We left an hour later, but when we reached the bridge area of the George Washington Bridge, we got stuck in a traffic jam. If you ever have been to New York City, you know traffic jams were the norm. We had seen people leave their cars in the middle of a five or six lane road, walk to a store off the road, get a soda, and come back to their car, which was still surrounded by the same cars that hadn't moved an inch. Traffic police "controlling" traffic usually caused those traffic jams. The cars could remain for an hour or more. All of this without an accident! While we were sitting in traffic, we got a call from Brenda that it was a false alarm. I figured that it was going to happen any time so we decided to continue to Boston. We pulled up to her grandmother's house at 4:30 in the afternoon, said hello to everyone and then just "chilled out" with a cold drink. Cindy was a little uptight because we knew that Brenda had no transportation to the hospital. No one in the family, including the aunt down the street, had a car. She would have had to call a cab or the police when she needed to get to the hospital. Either way, it was not an ideal situation.

Mark was at the house, waiting for us and he greeted us politely. He acted very glad to see us, especially Cindy. That was a strange position for him to be in; sober. Also, at the house was Brenda's mother, who we had met once before, but we weren't sure if she was in jail for shoplifting or stoned out of her mind on heroin. It actually appeared that she was straight for the first time in a while.

That night, we stayed in the grandmother's house and slept on the floor in the living room. We wanted to be there in case Brenda had to go to the hospital. Everyone went to sleep by about midnight. It was a miserable night and our backs were killing us. The marks of the crumpled rug were imprinted on our backs. That was not a romantic night for us. The hardest thing about me that night was the floor!

About 2:00 a.m., Brenda walked into the living room and said it was time to go to the hospital. Everyone got up very quickly, grabbed the suitcase, and got into the car. The car now had a very "big" Brenda, Mark, Cindy, Brenda's mom, and me. I was driving, getting directions to the hospital from Brenda. There was no traffic on the road and the hospital was about 20 minutes away. With no traffic, we figured that we could make it safely in 10 minutes. We were moving nicely and stopping at every light, then going through it when there were no cars. Things were going great until we saw flashing lights in the rear view mirror. That got my heart pumping because I had to make a quick decision. Did I wait for the cops to slowly approach the car or did I run over to them and hope that they were not trigger-happy? The neighborhood we were in was not great and the car was packed with people. I decided to run over to their car with my hands up yelling "pregnant lady." They saw I wasn't a kid and quickly moved to our car, looked in, and said go ahead, which I did. We got to the hospital emergency room and the staff took Brenda right in. We stayed in the waiting room, the cafeteria, the hallways, and anywhere we could. Mark was with Brenda in a room where the staff kept checking her and the three of us were trying to also catch some Z's on couches. The hospital and Brenda decided on a midwife to do the delivery months earlier and she was with Brenda. Everyone was extremely tired and couldn't wait to close their eyes for a restful sleep. Brenda's mother seemed to be very edgy, which made me a little nervous. We were not used to socialization with a heroin addict. We were more used to chasing one down! We should have felt comfortable with her based on our son's lifestyle. We were afraid to leave Cindy's handbag anywhere and even I was concerned that if I fell asleep, she could reach into my pockets for money. Were we too paranoid? The baby was not going to happen that night. We reviewed the situation at the hospital and realized that they were treating Brenda as a welfare case, which, in fact, she was. The nurses were controlling everything, and seemed to be doing everything fine, but we were used to dealing directly with doctors. The hospital was cold and not in a great neighborhood, so I left the car in the emergency lot for safety.

At 11:46 a.m. the next morning, Brenda and Mark's son, Michael, was born. He weighed 7 pounds, 15.25 ounces. He was 20.5 inches long and appeared to be in excellent health. Mark watched everything and cut the cord. Knowing our son, we felt that the old joke about getting someone more qualified to cut the cord would have been very appropriate! We were all extremely happy since this was our first grandchild and Mark had been involved in his birth. We were hoping that this was the beginning of a new and responsible parenting situation for Mark. He was really excited and was talking about the future. Everyone went back and forth to the hospital for the next two days and then we brought the car, with some of her relatives, to the hospital to take everyone back to the grandmother's home.

On the way home, Brenda said she didn't want to go home yet and said to take her and the baby to the mall. That seemed stupid and irresponsible to me, but Cindy and I were not being decision makers in this new family. We stayed at the mall about an hour when they decided that it was time to continue home, which we did. It was chaotic at the house with everyone holding the baby. It was obvious that Cindy and I were the outcasts, so we kept our distance. This was the kid's time, not ours. The family planned a party that night to celebrate; they got a ½ keg of beer, pretzels and potato chips. What a party!

Joe, Brenda's father, stopped over the house with his girlfriend. He had been a passerby in Brenda's life and appeared sometimes to share in chosen activities. That evening, he fought with Brenda's brother. This was one of the few times over the past years that Joe had come to see Brenda twice in one week; the hospital and her house. He was too into his fun to worry about his kids. The first night home, Brenda said she was going out and asked everyone to watch the baby? That was never a problem with all of the family there. Why would a mother leave her child to go out the first night home? Oh well, a new generation and new ideals! We stayed one more day and then went back home to work. The day we left, we found a hiding place and put $100 above the window and into the lining of an old curtain. We were trying to plan ahead and have money there in case of an emergency rather than get a panic call to wire money. That showed you the confidence level that was built up with this situation.

The only thing that the hospital did after the birth was to circumcise the baby. They botched up the job. Probably an intern was doing his first, so their attitude probably was 'why not do it on this welfare kid.' It was a shame because it took a long time to heal and it was not shaped right so that the penis was not easy to keep clean. Besides, it was not something that a man wanted to worry about the rest of his life!

For the next few days, Cindy spoke to Mark a few times a day and felt that the kids were trying to get things going in the right direction. Mark said he was looking for work, but reality set in because he couldn't get any type of job other than minimum wage. He was getting depressed. He also was getting uncomfortable in the grandmother's house because he felt that he was being treated as a bum, which would be understandable. Everyone would want to know why a new father was not working and what was he doing all day? We were even thinking the same thing. Mark had a conflict because he was raised in a certain way and now the rules and standards were different. They were easier, but not what he now felt that he wanted for his child.

Cindy and I talked about the possibility of offering to bring them back to Philadelphia to live because we knew that Mark could get a job and the physical atmosphere would be better. The premises in Boston devastated us because the house was filled with smoke all the time. Everyone smoked cigarettes all the time, and when visitors came, they also smoked. Whenever we left Boston, our clothes were saturated with smoke and had to be washed. We didn't want Michael to have to inhale that poison. Was it typical for grandparents to put their two cents into a situation that was not their decision?

We also were faced with Mark coming home and again being a real problem 24 hours a day. We also were very selfish wanting to be a part of our grandson's life, which we wouldn't be if he stayed in Boston. We knew that he would get a better education with our influence. We also knew that to graduate high school was a momentous occasion for Brenda's family. We knew that Brenda had no chance at continuing or finishing her education if she stayed there, nor would her parenting skills ever improve living in the environment in which she was raised. We wanted her to be independent with Mark, but she had no background to fall back on.

The questions and answers were fast and furious between us. Did we or didn't we want to step in and take over? It would be a major commitment, and of course it would tie us down again. We were now free to do things. The dogs were dead and the kid was gone. Wasn't that the real honeymoon that everyone dreamed of? Well, it was obvious that Cindy had strong feelings that she wanted to help the baby and I was ok with that, if she was happy. Now it was going back to Psych 1 to figure out how to make that happen, while setting the tone for everyone to be comfortable with the decision.

We decided that the reasons they needed our help were obvious, but just had to be pointed out to the kids. We also knew that the family in Boston would oppose the move. It involved strategy and planning; there was not room for mistakes, and we couldn't piss the kids off by being take-over grandparents, even though neither of the new parents had a clue as to the reality of life. Mark was in and out of the drug scene and Brenda was a high school dropout who knew the welfare system well and learned it from her immediate family. Her aunt was on it. Her mother was on it. Her father was on it. Her brother was on It. There was no other way for her to know how to live differently. Even if she did work at a minimum wage job, she would make less than she would get by just staying on welfare! Fortunately, there are major changes in the works for the welfare system, but the veteran users would still find a way to beat it. Now we had to figure the right strategy to make the move. We also had to teach Brenda some pride and dignity so it could be passed on to her son. One of the biggest flaws we saw in Brenda was that she was an incessant liar. She lied to avoid any conflict that she was involved in. If she took a beer and it was the last one, and someone would ask her if she took it, her immediate response was "no," even if the can was in front of her! She would blame someone else. The reason I use the beer example is because I knew how important the issue of the last beer in the refrigerator was to that family.

Cindy spoke to both of them on the phone about two weeks

after Michael was born. She said how much extra expense was being put on the grandmother, how Mark could get a job here, and how the baby could have his own room, and how the schools were better here, etc. It worked because they were frustrated with the lack of room and lack of privacy up there. Two weeks later, we moved them back to our house. We packed up our bike trailer and moved the crib and toys, as well as most of Mark and Brenda's clothes. Mark got a job with a friend of mine who knew of the drug problems and he said Mark was a good worker, and he would keep Mark out of situations where he knew drugs would likely be. He had Mark working seven days a week doing landscaping at $7.00 an hour. That was more money than Mark had made in a long time and it was good because he was physically tired when the day was over.

Brenda was going along with the situation because she never said much in public, although when they were alone in their room, it was usually like the third world war. She always had an uncomfortable feeling knowing it wasn't her home and she had to follow the rules of Cindy's home. There were very few rules, except Cindy wanted to keep things in an orderly way. The rules included picking up her own clothes, not eating in the bedrooms, not smoking in the house, and helping out when she could. Cindy was also very intent on keeping the phone bills at a reasonable level because we were paying for them. Cindy said that Brenda could call home three times a week for 10 minutes after 7:00 at night because the rate would be less. Brenda was getting pressure from home to bring the baby back. It was a very difficult situation for her because she was now tied to Mark's friends and his transportation system. At this time, Mark didn't have a car and was walking to many places or his friends would pick him up. Brenda had to go wherever he went and she was anxious to go because she was stuck in the house when he went to work. The only thing that she could do was take Michael for a stroll. That was not bad because there was a park two blocks away and a small shopping center three blocks away. Brenda was used to walking because the bus stop was three blocks from her house in Boston. She was not used to being stuck and not going out with her girlfriends.

Mark had a number of "friends" that were from varied backgrounds. He had his druggie friends that he had met in various rehabilitation centers, and he had a group of friends that were local. The local friends said they loved to be with him because of his always spontaneous and humorous actions, which were usually off the wall. The local group was a mix of guys and girls; the drug group was whoever showed up at any certain location he would meet who came to buy or do drugs. There was a third group that was in and out of his life who were his friends from school. These guys were somewhat messed up, but they had some direction and they seemed to waiting for themselves to grow up. They were rebellious to some parental authority, but generally knew their limitations prior to getting into major trouble. Most of the people at these levels had their own cars and were working in some capacity.

He met the drug group on his binges and occasionally he would take someone from the other groups into that environment because he needed a ride to buy drugs. It was probably exciting to the suburban boys to be in the drug areas with someone they thought could keep them safe. However, most of them, even the ones who tried drugs, had no clue about the amount of Mark's usage. Most nights, the local kids would hang out at our home, either downstairs in the recreation room, or in the family room. Occasionally, they would sit in the kitchen and talk with Cindy or me. For some reason, the kids felt comfortable with us because we tended to listen and not judge, too much. Brenda was having a problem relating to the group, but to this day, we never knew why.

In general, none of the kids were going to go for further education, although it was always talked about. The one common denominator that I found was that the words "I'm gonna...," which didn't mean a lot. Each group was different and each tended to call Mark almost daily to do something. He was tired after work and always wanted to lie down after his shower. When he came home, he would always hold Michael, raise him into the air, and make high-pitched noises that the baby would react to. Brenda always wanted to do something with him because she waited all day for him to get home. Since both of them were so young, and so immature, they seemed to have a lot of conflicts about wants and needs. We did our best to stay out of the conflicts, and give them their privacy.

It was about three weeks since Mark had been on one of his binges; he was trying to be responsible. He had saved $500 toward a car and seemed on his way to getting on with his life, again. It was now May and the weather was starting to get nice. Mark was very short tempered because he was not used to working for a long-term goal, which was a car. He was getting tired of depending on everyone, even to get to the store. He was always happy when he came home from work to be with his new son, but he still seemed very much on edge. He was very short-tempered with Brenda, who tended to keep demanding more from him. She was polite with us, but different with Mark in private. If anyone has lived with adult relatives in the same house, you know that there was no house big enough for complete privacy. Cindy would hear comments like "you are still a druggie" from Brenda, and "you just don't care about anything except going out" from Mark. They seemed to be on two different wavelengths. Things were getting so bad between them that Brenda asked her father to come down to take her home. He was more than happy to do that because he got to see his grandson. He was trying to conveniently make up all of his past which included: drugs, alcohol, losing custody of his two children to the maternal grandmother, never having a place for his children to have a stable childhood, separating from the mother and possibly being a cause of her mother's drug use, never having enough money for anyone except himself, and not keeping a steady job. He was like someone trying to reform, but it was always "what I am gonna do" rather than any accomplishments. Brenda was torn because she wanted to have a real family and a father for Michael.

She was confused because when her father came down, she said that she changed her mind and wanted to stay. Her thoughts were emotional and selfish, rather than well thought out.

We were moving in a million different directions. We were trying to take care of the baby, talk to Brenda's father to explain the entire tense situation between the kids, give some guidance to Brenda, while trying to maneuver the situation to get our own selfish wants satisfied, by staying close to the baby. We were pushing for Brenda to go to work, even part time, but Brenda had no conception of why she would work when she could more easily apply to welfare. Her father knew the welfare game and since he was "reformed," he kept telling her that she should work and not get into the game that she was raised around. That was hard for a very young girl, who was already a mom, to try and understand.

The baby was only a month old and Brenda was dressing him like a little girl would dress a doll. He was getting a lot of love from all around; Mark's friends were coming over all the time and making a big fuss over their son. Their friends knew that everyone was usually home because the baby needed sleep. Cindy was asked to baby sit often and for short periods of time. Cindy was like any new grandmother who had a convenient opportunity to spend time with her grandchild; she loved it. When the weekend was over, Brenda's father, Joe, went home and said he would be back in two weeks to see how things were going. Yeh, like he was the new sheriff in town!

It was an interesting time because Cindy's father, two generations up, was in a very awkward situation. He couldn't understand why Mark was doing drugs and wouldn't stop. He didn't understand why Cindy cared about her grandchild because the kids weren't married. Cindy's father kept using the word " bastard." He kept telling Cindy to forget the kid and get on with her life, but he kept forgetting that the "kid" situation was her life. His understanding and compassion did not endear him to the immediate family. To make matters worse, he kept telling Cindy that I was going to cheat on her.

It was about that time that all parties involved decided that Cindy's father was old and we should treat him with respect, but not the respect that says we needed to listen much to him. We give him only pleasant information and very non-intense details of good things. It was basically a philosophy of " why get involved in more shit if it was unnecessary?" It seemed to work because we had our hands full with running a business, keeping track of Mark and his problems, knowing that we now had a financial responsibility for a new, if dysfunctional family, and it was all a new experience for us; or was it? At the same time, Cindy's father was getting all of the ailments that a spoiled old man who just lost his wife would get. Cindy had to be the runner to his house and be his new companion to try to help him through his loneliness. He was very nasty and bitter, and at the same time, he was helpless, as he never prepared anything more than peanut butter and jelly for himself. It was a pathetic situation for him to face and for us to watch.

If there are any men reading this, you must be wondering what happened to our sex lives. There wasn't a lot of time and there certainly were many circumstances that took the drive away. I will not go into detail, but I now knew what was universally known as a "quickie." I'll quote Cindy's father about what to do if you had the urge to make love. "Find a window, raise the window, pull out your 'love maker' and put it on the windowsill, and slam the window shut!" Her father assured me that this little exercise would immediately cause my "urges" to disappear. I felt that I just might take matters into my own hands before finding a need for that window. The ironic part for Cindy's father was that he didn't need to use a window to satisfy any urges he may have had. Women swarmed to secure men who had just lost their wives. They did it for money, companionship, money, maternal instincts, money, etc. Did I mention money?

Anyway, it was the middle of May, and we decided that Mark had been diligently working on his problems and we looked for a car for him at the local used car lot. Mark found an 8-year old car, a supped-up Toyota that had 50,000 miles;

some bodywork was needed, but it appeared to run well. We bought it on the 18th for $4,200; things were going well. The kids were out one afternoon with the baby safely buckled into his car seat, and life seemed to be relatively peaceful. Everyone got what they wanted. Mark had been straight for more than two months, setting a new record. Life was good, right?

Joe came back to Philadelphia on the 29th of May and Joe and Brenda decided to go back to Brenda's house in Boston for a few days to visit the family and show off the baby. There was no reason for her not to go because she had no work obligations here. Brenda was anxious to go because her grandmother would baby-sit the baby and Brenda could go out and party. She did what Cindy asked and called her when she got to Boston to let Cindy know that everything was fine and they arrived safely. On May 31, Mark took off about midnight for places unknown. We were very concerned because he was doing good, and seemed to find some responsibility with his son. Did he just go out to visit friends, something people his age always did? Did he go out to cheat on Brenda? Did he lose his grip on staying clean and go out and do drugs? The answer, we figured, was most likely, the latter. It was now 5:00 a.m. and we had some decisions to make.

Should we call Brenda and tell her to stay in Boston? Would the car be sold for drugs? Should we go out looking for him? Should we just wash our hands of everything, knowing that if he did do drugs, he'll be calling home in a day or two for us to bail him out again?

The past comes to mind with the "what if's." Maybe we screwed up by not dumping him four years ago; maybe we should finally give up on him, but now, there is a baby. Maybe we were too easy.

We were lucky this time because the choice was thrown at us. Brenda and Joe came back that morning and we all went out 'through the streets of Philadelphia.' We did not do it in "Springstein" style, although many of the areas were the same. We were out day and night. We had the cell phones on with call forwarding from the house, in case he called. It seemed weird to me that her father was almost enjoying the adventure late at night. He liked going into these areas. During the evening, we found out that he and Mark had been down to this area together doing drugs during one of Joe's prior visits! This was turning into a class act! It was scary because we saw drug deals going down everywhere, and the noises that were heard between midnight and three or four were unique. Dogs barking set the stage followed by intermittent sounds of bottles breaking against walls, tires squealing, and occasional police sirens. When you would see someone walking, there were always the thoughts of the kind of weapon he had and what did he want? You always hoped that he would be on the other side of the street so that you wouldn't have to acknowledge him. We called off the search about 3:00 a.m. the second night. I went to work the next day and Brenda and Cindy went looking again. Joe went home. Activity never started in drug areas until lunchtime. Everyone went to sleep somewhere; in cars, local houses, or to homes in the suburbs. We figured we had an idea where Mark was because of conversations the day earlier with some of the druggies on the street! The next day, about 2:00 p.m., we spotted his car parked on a side street where half the homes were boarded up. The front two windows were smashed and one of the tires was flat. That could have happened in a busted drug deal, or Mark just pissed off the wrong people. We looked inside the car and found Mark was sleeping. The radio was gone; Mark sold it for drugs. He was coming off his high and back into reality. He was teed off. I told Mark to get plastic and put it over the broken windows so the inside wouldn't get wet, and Cindy told him to vacuum out the glass. I blew my cool and called Mark every name in the book. It almost came to blows, but I stopped and realized that I was talking to someone not all there. Mark did his usual routine of coming home and taking a very long shower to possibly symbolically clean off his past few days, as well as the grime from the areas he was in.

When he completed his shower, he played with the baby

until the baby fell asleep, and then he sat down at the kitchen table to eat and talk; it was two hours later. He seemed normal, but embarrassed for his actions. He became our normal son at that time. We could talk and even joke about his stupidity. He was open about his actions and answered questions when we asked. We wanted to know where he was for two days. He told us that he met a guy who wanted to go to Wildwood, New Jersey, and he needed a ride. He and the guy got high on the way down there. There was action in that area because it was a young town at the seashore, especially on weekends. Mark said he got into a fight with the guy and left him there with no way home. He said that the guy was a heavyweight in the neighborhood and that he said if saw Mark again, he would kill him!

Mark was exhausted, but we wouldn't let him go to sleep until we knew everything. We wanted to know in order to find out his new patterns in case of more screw-ups. We let him go to sleep and then he had to deal with Brenda, who had nowhere to go on the issue. She was glad he was back and was fairly unemotional about the whole thing because she dealt with this in her family for years. Brenda sat through our interrogation of Mark and just listened.

The next day, Cindy said Mark had to go to a rehabilitation center. Brenda was upset, but knew there was no choice. We made calls to all of the centers and found one with a bed and a need for insurance money for another 30-day program. Mark went in and the usual procedure was isolation and detox for a week and then, depending on progress, visitation and privileges. Mark knew this game, and we did too. It was a relief for him to be there, locked in at night, and we were able to sleep. That same day, Brenda went to the county to apply for welfare. She qualified based on Michael. Too many able-bodied people, including her, could work for the money that they received. Why couldn't her job be to police the street that she lived on, or a park, or something that gave her a responsibility? There shouldn't have been free money if a service could be performed to make that person a little more responsible and proud of something.

Every Sunday was visiting day at the rehab. Brenda, Cindy, the baby and I would go at visiting hours. Mark said hello to us, kissed and hugged both of us, and wanted to spend the rest of the time with Brenda and the baby, Michael. It was beautiful to see his eyes light up at his son's presence. The center started to give Mark medication to calm his mood swings. The drug of choice of that center was Lithium. We said that whatever would work was worth a try, but parents had no say in the treatment anyway. Brenda was anxious for him to get out because she was lonely. She was bottled up in the house with the baby and didn't develop a closeness with Cindy. That was expected because we were not sure of our relationship with her. When someone saw us together, we introduced them as our grandson and his mother? Should have we said our son's girlfriend, maybe our daughter-in-law? We didn't have enough of a relationship to even try to identify it. It was subtle pressure for everyone and I didn't want to broach the subject. That was not a very mature approach, but when "walking on eggs," logic was not always clear. We didn't know if Michael was staying or leaving, or if Brenda was staying or leaving. If they left, Cindy would not be going to Boston very often. She was not sure that she would be very welcome. Why would the Boston family want us when they had no relationship with us; we were not even close to Brenda. I made sure my opinion basically remained my opinion. We knew Brenda didn't want Mark to go to the rehabilitation center because she missed him. She didn't have the insight to try to see the long-term problem.

Chapter Seventeen

While he was in the center, I sold the car for $500. The windows, tires, non-radio, body damage, etc. were sold "as is." We were glad to get it out of our driveway. We didn't want it there when he got back. The problem was that Brenda was using the car and starting to enjoy the area, which was working well to keep her home. We figured the more she liked it here, the better off the baby would be and then Mark would have an easier time getting adjusted without her nagging him when he got home from work. It was very difficult to rationalize with irrational people and situations, but rational people still tried. On second thought, was that statement even rational?

On June 22, we received a call from the rehabilitation center. It was bad news; Mark left the rehabilitation center with a patient, Lauren, after a rough meeting. He left at 2:00 in the afternoon and the center called us at five. We realized that there was no way for us to know where he was because he was with someone we didn't know and the entire area this new individual covered was completely unknown to us. We waited three days to hear from Mark, but no word came.

We figured that since Mark still hadn't turned up, and three days had passed, it was getting close to his calling home for help.

The next day, Mark called home at 6:30 in the morning. He said that he was coming home. We knew that he could get diverted at times like this. We asked where he was and told him that we would be there in ½ hour and he should wait there. We went to the northwest suburbs of Philadelphia and found him where he said he would be, near a gas station. We looked at him and something wasn't quite right. He was pale and normally his complexion was darker. He told us he got into a fight with a member of the Pagans, a notoriously rough biker club. His hands were swollen and one looked broken. It was swelled to almost double its normal size. He told us that his ribs hurt and that a few of his teeth were loose. Cindy noticed the ring she bought for him was missing. We didn't know whether to teach him a lesson or try to help him. Mark was in pain. Should we take him to the hospital? He was lying to us about the ring because it would never make it over his swollen fingers so we knew that he sold or pawned it. Also, if he were in a fight with a Pagan, he would not have been left in this good a condition. Therefore, we had no real idea of where he was for the last three days.

We tried to find out why he left the center and didn't work out his problems there. That was brilliant on our part because every drug addict and alcoholic would love this answer. He said that when he was out, he went to meetings two days and drank; the third day, he smoked some dope. Smoking dope meant that he had no idea what he was smoking or where it originated or if it was bad! It wasn't hard to see he was out of control for much of the three-day spree, but he was with people who conveniently wanted to be sober, a combination that never met with success.

We felt we were in the same position as hundreds of times before except this was a new theater and a few new players. We were wrong again! He was involved in having stolen a car or one that was conveniently borrowed. The law said it made a difference when they nailed you because charges were different.

The story that we eventually got was when they left the center, Lauren and Mark went to Mark's sponsor's house. A sponsor is a person who is in recovery, and still involved with the program. The sponsor takes on the responsibility of a newcomer who had been clean a shorter period of time and acts as a mentor to that person. Sponsors are available 24 hours a day, 7 days a week, to help their "project" stay straight.

Mark said they were at the sponsor's house and they decided to go somewhere. They took the sponsor's car and left. Mark's clothes at the sponsor's house and Mark 'borrowed' the car, which the sponsor immediately reported to police. That was a real mastermind crime! I got a call from the police stating that they would arrest Mark if the car was not found. I asked Mark where the car was and he told me he didn't know because it ran out of gas and they left it somewhere on the street. I was still trying to figure out what happened over the past three days; I was told about leaving the center, drugs, alcohol, car theft, police, and arrests. We decided that we couldn't worry about that trivial stuff, so we sat back and let time go by for a few days. The police never called back and all of Mark's clothes had disappeared from the sponsor's house.

Every day was an adventure because we knew more stuff would hit the fan. He was again working daily doing landscaping, but everyone knew that it was strictly a place to try to make him feel important and it gave Cindy and me a chance to have some temporary relief.

On July 8, the family in Boston had scheduled a christening. "Mazel Tov!" Obviously, we were not Catholic, had very little idea of what a christening entailed, and had no say in the ceremony anyway. Brenda's family scheduled everything and we went back to Boston for the church service and party. The service was hypocritical, in my opinion, because no one in either family attended church unless it was a special occasion. At this time, we were told the name of the baby was Mark's choice, and the godparents were Brenda's choice. The godparents were a 17 year-old female cousin and Brenda's brother. We were just sitting along the sidelines watching the play, but we were well aware that not much logic was used in most of the decisions pertaining to this entire situation. The cousin just had an abortion and had no clue about the meaning of life, and the brother had a successful drug dealing business.

The ceremony went well, we guessed, because it ended without violence and everyone kissed. It was kind of neat to watch without being in the spotlight. My job, which I chose to accept, was to videotape the ceremony. After the ceremony, everyone was invited back to the grandmother's house to celebrate. The house was small, with only two rooms available, the living room and the kitchen. Brenda's family was fortunate because it was a beautiful day and most of the 40 people in attendance stayed in the backyard. There were potato chips and a quarter keg of beer that seemed to be the focal point and favorite meeting place for everyone from 18 to 24 years of age.

This was not our style, but it was fine. Many people brought gifts and there were some envelopes with money. Brenda was quick to open the gifts for her son and discovered there was about $200 in envelopes. She put them on the table beside the gifts. Everyone was having a nice time and they were proud of the moment. We were trying our best to be sociable and we were enjoying ourselves and thankful that it was just a visit. We didn't appear to have our noses up, but we had different standards of behavior when kids were around.

The party started about one o'clock and after two hours, things seemed to be fine, until Brenda started yelling. She was screaming that someone took the baby's money from the pile of gifts. Brenda immediately called to her mother, who was not there. Everyone knew at that point that her mother had taken the baby's money and went off to buy drugs. Brenda was furious and actually began hyperventilating. She didn't know what to say or do, because it was such a despicable act. The problem, of course, was that there was nothing that a drug addict wouldn't do to get the needed fix. As for Mark, he was trying to be good, but was standing very close to the beer. I kept watching him, and was relieved to see he did not indulge. That surprised me because it was so easy for Mark to grab a cup and have a quick drink. Alcohol was usually the kick-off to Mark's addiction episodes. The alcohol made drugs an easy transition because the individual was not thinking 100% and all the concentration to avoid drugs was broken. He stayed at the party, did well, and was proud of himself. Brenda had someone drive her to the bus stop to see if she could catch her mom, but it was too late. The party continued, but talk always went back to the same topic; how could Brenda's mother steal from a helpless infant, her own grandchild? Brenda's father came to the party late in the evening, which surprised no one because his relationship with that side of the family was never great; there was a mutual disrespect for each other. Joe brought his own six-pack to the party. After about twenty minutes, he got into a shouting match with his son because Joe thought his son drank one of his beers.

Everything continued for a few hours until the beer ran out. At that time, the younger people said their goodbyes and departed. Mark and Brenda said that they were going to a party, and Cindy and I just hung around with the rest of the "old folks." The family sat around and played cards, which was their typical end of get-together evenings. It was a friendly game, in which I was invited to play, but politely refused and gave some bogus excuse. If I played and won, someone would be pissed that I was too good to play. If I lost, I would be pissed. We just sat around and made small talk with the other relatives. Our heads were concerned with the kids being at a party and what if Mark decided to start drinking. Brenda had no control over what Mark did, and usually didn't have the foresight to try to prevent the known disaster of what was to come. The worry that night was unfounded as the kids returned home and Mark said that he felt great and he refused to drink at all. He said that he had ginger ale the whole evening, and that made us feel great because we knew beer was everywhere for the taking. However, things didn't stay so wonderful. That night, while everyone was at the grandmother's home, Mark did decide to have a beer. With the medications that he was on, and the mix of alcohol, he flipped out.

He kicked in a fence and said everyone was all over him, which they weren't, and Mark raged out the door and started walking down the street. Joe followed him out the door and told him to stop and talk things over. Mark was out of control and ready to fight anything in his way. Half way down the block, Mark passed an older woman who was friendly with Brenda's family and her kids were friends of Brenda's father. Mark told her to "get the fuck out of the way" and with that, her two kids, who were off duty police officers, grabbed Mark and they wrestled him to the ground. Brenda's father was right there and prevented Mark from getting stomped, but Mark was subdued and physically held in restraint while Joe tried to calm him down. I came down the street and saw what was happening, but couldn't do much because Mark was in the best position he could be in until he gained composure. After about 10 minutes, Mark calmed down and took a walk with Brenda's father. Mark tended to communicate with him, possibly because they drank and did drugs together. I went back to the house. All of this was a new experience for me. Mark was so out of control that there was no way I could have stopped him. Mark was like a wild bull reeking havoc on everything in sight. They came back into the house about an hour later and everything appeared fine. When I got back to the house, Cindy was talking to the grandmother, who told Cindy some things that we didn't know. She told Cindy that Mark had thrown Brenda down the stairs when she was pregnant, and they continually had fistfights. Brenda was very uncomfortable, as she weighed more than 200 pounds near the end of her pregnancy. Cindy was shocked and asked why the grandmother permitted such behavior in her home. The grandmother said it was none of her business and it was both of their faults.

The balance of the short stay was fine and we told Mark how great it was with him working and trying to save, and taking responsibility for the baby. We felt that by building his confidence, we could help him keep all the positives in his life in focus. We were striving to turn a disaster into something more reasonable.

We came home from Boston and Mark was going to his meetings, mostly with Cindy, because no one trusted him alone. At that time, we suspected that Brenda knew much more about his drug activity than we were lead to believe. We could see he was getting restless and he stopped working. It was tense in the house for the next two weeks. Every night, Cindy went to meetings with Mark. She found out that Brenda didn't hesitate to lie to us to avoid any confrontation where she may have screwed up. By Cindy going to the meetings, it avoided putting Brenda in a bad position. Some meetings were AA (Alcoholics Anonymous), and some were NA (Narcotics Anonymous). They were all based on the same 12-step program. Anyone who hasn't been to a meeting should go to understand what the addict and the support people live with each day. Some of the rooms we went into were horribly smoke-filled, while others were church meeting rooms. These meetings are everywhere at all hours of the day and night, and there are books available that give locations and times to make it easy for someone to attend a meeting, even if they were away from home. Addicts are supposed to attend meetings every day, sometimes twice a day. Being an addict dominates one's life and the lives of everyone around them.

On August 1, Mark got a job at a beautiful, suburban kennel. This was a class place that would pick up your dog, set aside play time and do everything a people spa would do. The price was hefty, but the amenities were well worth the cost. Mark always loved dogs so it was a natural for him. He had previously worked at two different vets, but was always pensive placing the deceased dogs into the incinerator, especially when they came out of cold storage. At this place, his job was to walk the dogs and clean cages. He enjoyed that because there was no pressure and his co-workers were all young girls his age. He always got along well with the opposite sex. He especially liked playing with the Rottweilers. He took the job, but told them that he was going away for a week with his family shortly, to which they agreed.

Joe liked to come down to visit, especially in the summer because we had a pool. We had put a swimming pool in the backyard years earlier since we always spent a lot of time at home and loved the atmosphere of the pool. At this time, Joe had no job and no money. It seemed strange to me to have a grown man descend upon you and be your best buddy while he relaxed in your pool. My mentality would have been to get a job! What did I know? Joe just came and went over the next few weeks. Mark appeared happy with his job and saw a future. Cindy was getting used to saying that everything was nice including his 'cage cleaning' future. Things were again going well; Cindy was driving Mark to work every day and picking him up.

On August 7th, Brenda flew back home to Boston with the baby. She was going to leave Mike with her grandmother and come back here so the four of us could go to Florida to see the mouse. Before we left, Mark said that he wanted a new car and he called around to see if he could get a loan. I told him that if he could get the loan, we would help by putting up the down payment. I figured that there was no way he could get a loan on a car when he just started a $7 per hour job, and there was no job history.

We went with Mark and saw that it was an extremely nice car. It had some size and most of the safety features that one looked for. It appeared to be a bargain compared to other cars of similar price, which was about $15,000.

On the 11th, he got his loan from a large, local bank and he bought a new car, a Sonata, whatever that was. What we forgot was that years ago, we had borrowed money in Mark's name to give him credit and paid it off in a few months. We were trying to set him up to be independent and it backfired because now he was given a car loan. We told the dealer that we were going away and would pick it up when we came back. This was great because Cindy wouldn't have to chauffeur Mark to and from work, and we were handing back some responsibility to Mark to control his own life. I was thinking maybe it didn't backfire because he loved the car, loved his job, loved his baby, and we were seeing roses for the first time in a long time.

On the 12th of August, we all drove to Florida. The drive down took 18 hours, because we got hung up in traffic in Washington, D.C. I decided, while in traffic, that since we moved about 1 mile in the past half hour, we would pull over and eat dinner since it was about 6:00 p.m. That was the worst time to go through our nation's capital; cars were everywhere and there was no break in sight. We were just glad to be in an area with no problems except normal traffic jams. We ate for about an hour and then got back on the road. Traffic got a little better, but it was the wrong time to start out again. We would have preferred to drive the car to a deserted island, with no way back for about six months to sort out everyone's head, but that's what dreams were made of.

Cindy and I did all of the driving because we didn't feel

comfortable with Mark's mental attitude if he flipped out or with Brenda's driving, based on her accident record. We would not be at ease with Mark at the wheel and us sleeping. Cindy and I took turns sleeping and driving and got there about 7:00 a.m. the next morning. There was not much to do at that time in the morning. What we wanted were showers and to change our clothes, but the rooms were not available yet. We chilled around the pool for a few hours until our rooms were ready.

We stayed together most of the time, except when we went to the parks. Cindy told the kids where and when to meet us for meals. They had keys to get back to the room and there was ample transportation provided to get anywhere on the grounds. They had freedom and we felt that the kids were safe. Mark tended to be bored with many of the rides except the thrill rides. Brenda was doing whatever Mark wanted to do, but she wanted to see everything that she could that was entertaining, not educational. We ate together most nights and generally spent a lot of time together. Without the drugs, it was like being a normal family with a lot of joking and kidding around. Mark's sense of humor was dry and goofy, and he was a lot of fun to be around. Everyone swam and did some sun bathing, as well as nighttime activities. The kids stayed out until about 1:00 a.m. almost every night because they fell in love with the nightclubs and the music. It was great to see them exhausted from clean fun. The only thing that was obvious was that Mark was very short-tempered with Brenda. Cindy and I were used to this by now, and we thought it best to mind our own business.

We were due home on August 20th, and Brenda arranged for Joe to drop off Michael the day before. My parents were staying over at our house and they would baby-sit and have a chance to spend time with Michael. It was a plan that worked well because we certainly didn't want to continue up to Boston and then drive back to Philadelphia after all of the driving. It was nice to return home and have the whole family together, but I was worried because the fighting between Mark and Brenda was getting to be constant.

When we got home, we went over to the car dealer and signed all of the papers and Mark got his new car.

On August 27th, the kids had a major blowout. Brenda asked me to put her on the next train, which was at midnight. I suggested that she wait until morning but she was acting on emotion rather than logic. She said that "we didn't understand" and she had to leave. If you are in your 50s, that phrase is something you will tell your elders and the next generation will tell you. It's like laughing at the elderly when they talk about sex. They have been there and many are still there.

Anyway, we drove her and the baby to the train and when we got there, she changed her mind. She now said she wanted to stay, but I felt that this was not a good situation and convinced her to go home and think rationally about her next move, and give thought to what was best for the baby. We had mixed feelings about the situation, but anyone involved would. We knew that Mark loved the baby, but did he know what a father's love for a son should be? Was he capable of giving Mike the right atmosphere so he could develop into a normal healthy young man? Right now, he wasn't capable of guaranteeing that he would be sober tomorrow. Brenda hasn't learned anything about taking care of the baby and put most of it on Cindy. By being back at her home, maybe she would learn by necessity, or her grandmother would do it all for her like Cindy did it at our home.

This trip home lasted three days. She was on a train coming back to our home with the baby. Over those three days, our phone bill was more than $150. It was very annoying because these were two kids with a baby and they had no idea of responsibility. If they went somewhere, the baby would go. It didn't matter if it was three in the morning. This was typical of young people with no training on what responsibility was, let alone what a baby meant. We were stuck because we couldn't make either of them understand what was expected of them. We knew the baby would suffer somewhere down the road, being dragged around at all hours of the night. His resistance was getting low and he was starting to get sick more often. This still didn't prevent the kids from taking him and going.

We were still not warm to Brenda, who was an unemotional and ungrateful teenager, who had no one to get advice from nor did she even know to ask. She was like a new project, because for her to live in our middle class lifestyle, she would have to learn. That was not a word that she wanted to hear. In some conversations that were overheard, not purposely, it was like being back in high school hearing about Jimmy taking out Sissy who was supposed to be with Bobby, but they got into a fight when Suzie said something about Bill's car! There was no logic when it came to teenage bullshit and gossip. I was thinking that she should be doing things like figuring out how to take care of the baby with no job, no money and I meant NO MONEY, no car and no real future. Dumb me! She jumped onto the welfare roles. She shared Mark's car and continued to be a teenage mom. She wanted to go dancing and to the under age 21 nightclubs. Mark would go anywhere. Guess who was home with the baby? Cindy pushed for us to watch the baby after the "new parents" said they would not stay in. When Cindy tried to reason with Brenda, saying Brenda should look for a job, even a part-time one, and then maybe go out just on the weekends, Brenda resisted and said no. She said she was going to get her G.E.D (High School Diploma Equivalent). We thought that would be a great idea. The problem with great ideas by young people was that they didn't realize that they had to work at the ideas in order to make them happen.

Mark started to see another shrink because we said that he was not opening up with us and he was becoming extremely angry and losing his temper. We figured that it couldn't hurt and maybe something good would come out of it. We again got permission from Mark, before he started treatment, to be allowed to get information from his psychologist. When desperation set in, you started to look for experts in fields where you may have knowledge, but your views and thoughts were prejudicial. We were advised that he might have frontal lobal rage.

At this point, Brenda decided life would be easier if she, Mark and the baby were living by themselves. She went out and looked for an apartment. Reality set in when she realized it would take over $1,000 to be put up for one month rent and security. Of course, that was the moment that Cindy mentioned utilities, phone, food, cleaning supplies, etc. Cindy figured reality should be reality. Naturally, the $500 per month rent certainly did not put them into a penthouse. Brenda was frustrated so she went home to Boston with the baby for a visit.

Things were going along for a day or two and the weekend came. It was September 1st and Mark went out to a club. We didn't know exactly where Mark was, but we just knew any club was not good news. As the story went, he had a little beer, did drugs, and then Mark called home to tell us that his car was stolen. It was 1:00 a.m. and we were wondering where Mark was, and how did his car get stolen? He walked into the house about an hour later telling us he called a friend and got a ride.

We had questions that needed answers. Was his car really stolen? Did he sell it? What happened? We knew that this was going to be another 'fun' night. I called the insurance company and the police. The police told Cindy to come down to the station and fill out a report, which Cindy did with Mark. The police took the report while Cindy listened. Cindy told me that it didn't sound right. The story went something like this: "I was driving this guy I met home and along the way, he saw two of his friends and he asked me to stop so he could talk to them. I stopped and we got out of the car to have a cigarette. They told me that they wanted to show me something so I walked over to where they told me. The car was left running because I had the radio on. When I walked over to where they directed me, they jumped into the car and took off."

We may have been from a generation that was once removed from the rap scene, but we didn't think that we were that gullible. We were confused as to what to do because Mark made his statement to the police and was totally depressed about not having his car. We certainly believe that he lied to the police. Mark didn't even consider the status of the loan or anything else. We didn't want him more depressed, so we just said that he was safe and the insurance would cover the car so we should all get on with life. I wanted to ask Mark if he thought that we were that stupid, or was he stupid enough to think that we would believe such a preposterous story knowing that he sold the car for drugs. I figured he got scared, so he made up a story hoping that he could save face, and we would believe the bad guys took advantage of our poor, innocent son. I guessed that the young generation didn't realize that we did the same things, but to a lesser degree when we were younger. Also, he needed to understand it took years to learn how to lie efficiently to parents! Anyway, we went home and relaxed that night -- for a few hours anyway.

About 3:00 a.m. the phone rang. The police said they found the car along with the guys who stole it. They said the thieves were in custody and that we should get someone to tow the car quickly because it was in a bad neighborhood. I asked if they could keep a cop in the area for a short time and we would have a tow truck come by. I asked if there was much damage, but they said it didn't appear to be. We figured that since it was a new car, we better take it back to the dealer to check it out and I made those arrangements. We called a friend of mine who said that he could be there in 20 minutes, and I thanked him. After about 30 minutes, we got a call from my tow truck friend who said that he was at the address that the police gave us, but there was no car there. I figured that I marked down the wrong address, so Cindy called the police station to get the correct one. When she got the address, it was the same as before. We called the tow truck driver, who said he would look around the block, but he could not find it. Now we were at a loss in trying to figure out what to do next. We figured to do nothing since the insurance company was notified. Ten minutes later Cindy got a phone call from the same police district. They said they had some news for us. She figured that they found the car or it was towed and there was some mix-up in the police station.

The officer told her that the guys who stole the car, who were in custody, were released and went back to the car and stole it again. This time they did some major damage to it. She said that she would get the tow truck again, if they would keep a police car at the scene until it got there, which they promised they would do. They also told her the car looked bad and that she should notify the insurance company to just how bad it was.

We now were wondering if the tires were gone, or maybe some windows broken, or even if it could it be driven? The next day, we all drove over to the yard where it was towed. The car was covered with a tarp. I thought that this was not a good sign. One of the lot men took off the tarp and all three of us gasped in disbelief. The car looked like it was in a demolition derby and lost. Every window was gone, the roof was smashed down to the seats, the tires were flat and obviously slashed, the seats were cut from one end to the other, every inch of the body was dented, the steering wheel was gone and the steering column was nowhere to be found. The engine was hammered with something like a sledgehammer, and in general, anything not mentioned probably was gone. The only thing that was recognizable was the original color.

It was not a pleasant ride home for Mark. We did feel bad for him, but what the heck -- Cindy and I still had our cars! With every experience, we hoped that the kids learned, but they didn't until they were ready. We figured he lied to cover up whatever happened, but we didn't care because his attitude that night was 'this was going to end fine' which was a nice change. Mark was home and we could get a night's sleep.

Brenda had gone home again and was being torn between both places. Her family wanted her to stay so they could play with the baby, but she loved Mark and wanted to be here with him. It was now September 2, and Mark felt that he had beat the drugs. He felt good mentally, but he knew that he had a constant urge to run.

Cindy was aware of his feelings because he told her how he felt. It made it easier for us to monitor him and get an idea of how closely we had to watch him. There were many days when Mark felt lousy and everyone knew the reason; he needed drugs. We kept encouraging him to stay clean. We told him to look into a mirror of himself and told him how proud he should to be clean. He was doing it for his son and for him. He was going to meetings every night with Cindy and actually planning which ones to go to. He was starting to take pride in staying clean and getting his 30-day pin. He was starting to talk about getting a sponsor again. It was a good time for him. It was something that he wanted to do for himself.

On September 9th, Brenda flew in and we met her at the airport with Mark. The first thing Mark did was yell at her for flying in without so much as a dime in her pocket. He proceeded to tell her how irresponsible it was to travel with the baby and not have any money. He was right, but we didn't say a word. Cindy and I wouldn't leave the house without money, or at least the credit card, but again, we are a different generation. At this point, Mark was still working at the kennel and things were good. He had some money in his pocket and wanted to be the one responsible for his son.

On the 10th, Mark came home at noon from the kennel and was driving the company van. He told Cindy that he had to go to center city to drop off two dogs. She thought that it was great that he got a promotion and they trusted him enough to take the van. He had lunch at home and went to finish his job. I went to pick him up at work that night at six, which was his regular quitting time, and was told that they haven't seen him since he left that morning and they haven't seen the van. Fear was in my heart. What happened to the dogs? Did he drop them off? Where was he and did he sell the van? What do we say to his employer? The girls at the kennel were covering up for him with the boss and I could see that the way they spoke to me. I was headed home, but I told the girls that if Mark called, or came back, they should call me. I also checked to see if the dogs were delivered and they were. The only thing that made sense was that Mark wouldn't hurt a dog; he did deliver them safely. We waited at home for the phone to ring. It didn't. We went to look for him that night in the drug-dealing zone, but had no success. We were out riding around from 11:00 p.m. until after 2:00 a.m.

We knew it was time to wait again and Brenda felt that it was time for her to leave. I drove her and the baby to the airport for an 8:30 a.m. flight. Cindy stayed home to wait for the phone call. After dropping them off, I decided to hit the streets again to find him since the drug area was between home and the airport. I got lucky and found him within 10 minutes. Whenever we did find him, he was usually listless and accommodating. He told me that he did Angel dust and crack. He said that he lent out the van and slept in an abandoned car. His eyes were still glassy. I called Cindy on the cell phone and told her we were coming home. Once home, everyone decided that he couldn't do it on his own and Cindy immediately set up another rehabilitation center. This one sounded good because they discussed the normal 28-day treatment and then a six- to nine-month program in the southwest part of the country. Mark was anxious to start the program and put the very recent past behind him. Brenda came back a week later. Brenda was anxious for him to get to a rehab, but she was not anxious for him to go away for six months. She was afraid to be alone and she was upset about her future, meaning the next few months. Everyone went to the new rehabilitation center in Valley Green and was very impressed because the facility seemed to have a certain control over their clients. They accepted Mark on the spot because they had a bed and it was business to fill it as long as he had insurance left. He entered on September 12th and we were relieved to go home and get a night's sleep. Cindy checked his beeper for any strange phone numbers and called the police to give them the approximate location of the van as told to us by Mark. We also advised the police that Mark was in the drug rehabilitation center. Cindy spoke to him almost every night, although his calls were directed for Brenda. When men are away, they tended to think (or should I say fantasize) when they talked to their mates. Mark was no different. He was better and more loving when on the phone with Brenda than when they were physically together. We visited him on each weekend with Brenda and the baby.

One weekend, a friend of mine, who had extensive experience with drugs came along. He was hoping to connect with Mark, but it was futile. Visiting hours were usually from about two to four o'clock in the afternoon, which didn't interfere with his meals or his meetings. He seemed to adjust well, but we were getting vibes that the facility was getting ready to give him the boot. The administrator called me on the 22nd and told me that his insurance ran out. I asked him what that meant to me. He said they could not keep him. I asked if his treatment was completed. It seemed that when they admitted him, they saw he had insurance, but they neglected to see how much was left. The insurance companies allowed a certain amount of institutionalized time with most plans. The time was measured by allowance per 12-month period and /or an amount for your lifetime. It amazed me to find that an individual's mental health could be treated for a specified time by an individual trained for years in the health field, but the patient's release was determined by a business person who may or may not have had any health training. They didn't have not any thought of the patient's well being. After seeing five rehabilitation centers, the professionals that ran them, and the actual results of the patient's well being, our regulators must be the dumbest individuals on this earth.

If you reviewed statistics regarding repeat drug users and other problems being treated, you wonder if the center's purpose was to try to cure or gear them to be ready to come back for the fall semester! Their rate of success was under 10%. If you were doing almost anything in this world from heart surgery to playing sports to ANYTHING, at 10%, you would be fired or you wouldn't be allowed to do it. This whole rehab thing was a money game and the patients lost. We were called almost every day to come and get Mark to take him home, but I wasn't "available" so the rehab was stuck with him. On the 28th, the administrator called and told me that Mark had an argument with his roommate and because Mark was disruptive, he had to leave.

They told us that it wasn't his fault, but his behavior was unacceptable. TRANSLATION: roommate still had insurance! We were forced to go get him and that eliminated any thought of him going out west to continue treatment, which Mark was still encouraged to do. The center said they would help with the transfer and they got jobs for people. Mark didn't want to leave Brenda or the baby.

As parents, we realized we only had so much control over his life. It was frustrating, but we had no choice and brought him home. For the next week, he went to meetings every night.

<u>Chapter Eighteen</u>

On October 4, we got a call from the police in some township that we never heard of. An officer identified himself and explained that he had warrants for Mark's arrest. Mark had two choices: he could turn himself in or they could come down to get him. I agreed that he would turn himself in the next day, which was when we could drive him to the police station. He was up for stolen car charges. We went to see the district attorney with Mark. The D.A. said that he wanted to talk to Mark alone. This made us feel uncomfortable, but at that point, what could be done that couldn't be undone. We found out that the D.A. was sympathetic to Mark's situation and really didn't want to nail him, but unless Mark went to a plea of being mentally unstable, he could end up with some jail time. That was more bullshit we didn't need now. Mark was trying and he was facing problems head on. The problem was that the van from the animal kennel was never recovered. The good part was that the van was old and had little value. But the vet was putting on the pressure; the kennel developed a reputation and the owner was determined to show any worker not to mess around with his business. He was right, except he didn't know that it was mental problems and drugs, rather than a wise-guy attitude. Mark was handling the situation well and realized that all of this was from actions that took place before he "got straight."

We told Mark things would continue to crop up from his past and he had to handle them. He agreed and seemed to be doing fine. We decided that we should get an attorney because Mark didn't have a great sense of reality when it came to the respect of a courtroom. Also, his mind was not as good as before, because of all the drugs he did. We told the attorney everything and said that if he could make a deal with the judge for a long-term mandatory rehabilitation, Mark would plead guilty. Otherwise, we could not see him going to jail to sit and do nothing to help himself. He needed help, not punishment. The judge said "no" and said that in this system, he would have to go to jail and then be evaluated; if they saw a problem, they could commute the jail time to a mandatory, recommended rehabilitation center. I suggested that the judge look at Mark's history, which we documented. We felt that if Mark were in a long-term program, he would have a chance at making it. If the court ordered it, there was no way he could leave. It seemed like a winning combination for everyone.

Another concern we had was that if Mark went to jail, he would pick up the excitement of the convicts and learn some of the tricks of their trade. It would be easy to do, and we were sure that it would have been glamorized in Mark's mind. Since the judge wouldn't or couldn't make that deal, we had to tell our attorney to get him off, which was not difficult based on the advice of the D.A. At court, the manager of the kennel came right over to Mark and gave him a big hug and kiss. Obviously, he didn't alienate her.

He was doing so well over the next 30 days that Cindy said she was having more and more confidence in him. The day after court, Cindy said that she wanted to get him another car. I hit the roof and said that he has gone through 11 cars and I wasn't investing in another one until he showed more responsibility. As the true man of the house, Cindy won and we compromised; she would only spend $2,000 at the auction. This auction was only for dealers and unless you were a dealer, you couldn't gain admittance. Normally, you could buy these cars for 60% of what they would sell for on the retail market, so they could be used for a year and then resold and you wouldn't lose a dime. I arranged for Cindy to go with a friend of mine, who was a dealer, and she got in as one of his drivers. The dealers all have to take drivers if they buy the cars. I was out working and didn't care what car Cindy got, because there was not much risk and my friend knew what to look for in case the car was hit or had some covered up a problem. I called home from my cell phone about 5:00 p.m. to let Cindy know that I was on my way home. She told me she bought a car, and I would see it when I got home. I didn't give it a second thought because in his mind, I knew the risk going in, and if Mark blew $2,000, I could handle it. It was also better than fighting with Cindy over an issue for which there was no answer. I pulled into the driveway, but didn't see any car. I came into the house and was given a greeting like the President of the United States had just walked in. I knew there was a problem since it was usually a "how was your day?" Cindy asked if I was hungry and told me dinner was ready. She said to sit down and eat. Mark and Brenda were very attentive and I was getting nervous.

I said that I would like to see the car that was bought. She said that she had to explain something after I saw the car. I agreed to hear her explanation. She told me the car was in the garage. I opened the garage door and couldn't believe my eyes. I was speechless and numb for at least 30 seconds. "What the fuck did you do?" I said.

I realized that I was getting out of control so I said, "I'll be back in twenty minutes." I started to walk around the block mumbling to myself. I continued around the block and returned home twenty minutes later. I didn't go inside because I was furious and still out of control. Cindy came out alone and said that I had to listen. She said that my friend looked at all of the cars in our price range and didn't feel comfortable with any of them. I listened. She said it was getting late and this car came on the block and it was beautiful. I listened. She said Mark fell in love with the car. I listened. I then asked if she was through and she said she was.

I asked what kind of car it was. She told me it was a 1992 BMW sport model, with a white exterior and a black convertible top with white leather seats inside.

I asked her if she had any idea what she went to the auction to buy. This car was nicer than any car I had ever owned, and was bought for $20,000! I asked where the keys were and proceeded to take them, hold them, look at them like the car would change, and I just bit my tongue because I had the keys and Mark wasn't getting his hands on them!

I was livid at the stupidity of Cindy, but then I should have known better than to let a mother pick something for her child. She would only pick the best. I said that she was wiping out our savings, which we were going through quickly anyway, but that was ridiculous.

That night, Mark got a phone call from a candy manufacturer and retailer in the neighborhood. They told him that he got the job that he applied for, which was working the stockroom. That was good because he didn't need a car to get to work. This went on until October 26th, three weeks from his last episode. That was the day that Cindy told Mark and Brenda that they could take the BMW out for a ride. The instructions were to stay in the suburbs and enjoy a nice ride. Mark went down to the drug district and told Brenda to stay in the car, which she did. He sold his watch and some jewelry that he stole from our home and got back into the car. He then went to a gas station, called home, and said that he would be home in 15 minutes. They both got out of the car to catch a cigarette and he put some gas into the car. Somehow, he tricked Brenda into going into the store to get more cigarettes. When she went in, he drove off leaving her there. She called home and told Cindy what happened; we were furious and seeing double!

Brenda admitted to us that Mark told her that if she didn't say anything to Cindy and me about buying drugs, Mark would buy her new sneakers, which he did. Brenda was mad because he drove away with the new sneakers in the trunk and she knew that she would never get them back because they would be traded for drugs. Cindy picked her up at the gas station, and proceeded to try to find Mark. She stopped police cars in the area, advised them of the situation, and gave them our phone number. There weren't many cars in that neighborhood that looked like this one, being driven by a young kid. Cindy for him from 9:00 p.m. until 2:00 a.m., but had no luck.

The police tried to convince her to leave the area because the police said that they could not guarantee her safety. She came home and went to sleep. At 4 a.m., we got a call from the police and they said that they had Mark and the car. We typically took our small can of gas with us. We went to where they said he was and it was a small one-way street with boarded houses on one side and a vacant lot on the other. The lot was full of bricks, glass and old tires. There could have been some bodies under the rubble, also. I pulled up and saw the police car in front of the BMW. The officers got out to identify themselves. It was very dark and scary, but we were getting used to this familiar routine. We thanked the police for calling us, and offered them a few dollars for coffee. They declined, saying they understood our concerns; they were sympathetic to the situation because they also had families. After the cordialities, they said they would get Mark out of their squad car. They walked him back in handcuffs. Cindy identified him and the police asked him if he would behave if they took off the cuffs. He appeared beaten and submissive after sitting in cuffs in the back of the police car for over an hour. The cuffs came off and he just stood there looking dejected. He was also shoeless and walking around in the cold in socks. The car was out of gas which was why it was located on that back street. The reason he was shoeless was he sold his shoes for drugs. I put the gas in the car, and drove it home. Mark stayed home the next morning, which began as we got home with the sun rising. He was exhausted and couldn't go to work, anyway.

The car sat in the garage for the next week without the engine even being turned on. I told Cindy that we were selling the car, but she said to wait because she may want it for herself or else she would sell her car. That made sense to me because it was a beautiful car. She took it out over the next week to take Mark to his meetings. I changed my mind and said the car was going to be sold. Cindy didn't argue with me, and we put it up for sale.

Brenda decided that she was going back home after Mark left her at that gas station. I told her that was probably a good idea and best for her and the baby. She left the next day and Mark told Cindy that he didn't miss her at all, but really missed seeing his son.

On October 28th, Mark was back at work at the candy factory. The boss appeared to be happy with his work. Mark still gave 100% when he did work. He was attracted to one of the female workers in the retail department and he brought her home the next night while we were out. When we came home, Mark and this girl were leaving his bedroom, puting their clothes back on. We just looked at each other; we had worse problems than this and just went on with our business. That romance only lasted a few days. This situation was no big deal for Mark; he always was in bed with someone since he was 13 years old. It would have, and should have, been a sign to push him into not having sex and locking him in his room for ten years, but that was hindsight and rediculus.

Mark used to play ice hockey, and at thirteen years of age, he and his team were invited to an all-expense paid trip to Russia and Sweden to play five games, where they could interact with the players from the other teams. He decided that he wanted to give up hockey and not do the once in a lifetime trip. His brains were below his waist and that was not a good sign. We tried to explain all of the reasons not to quit and all about sexual protection, but it was difficult to speak to a face when you knew the brain below the belt was not listening. We bought him protection, lots of it, and we believe he actually used some on a few occasions. It made us feel better, as we were looking to get any positives that we could.

On top of all of the other problems, we didn't need anyone else getting knocked up by him. We didn't care that he was running around on Brenda, as long as he was straight and drug-free for a while. The strong bond that exists between some couples was never there between the two of them; both cheated on each other whenever the opportunity presented itself.

He was doing so well that Mark's boss promoted him to drive and deliver to the other stores. Unfortunately, we didn't know this. On November 2, while Mark was making a delivery to one of the stores in the delivery van, he freaked out and took off. No one was aware of it until Cindy called work to say she was picking him up and found out that he was gone with the van. I went to find him. I knew that the van had the company name on it so it would be easier to spot than most of the other vehicles. I got lucky. Within 15 minutes after I hit the first area, I saw him driving toward me on a one-way street. I waited until he was within easy stopping distance and pulled my car into Mark's path. He could have pulled the van close to the corner and escaped, because there was enough room to squeeze the van through, but he stopped and got out. I sarcastically mentioned the room he had to get away, but inside I wanted to do more to him than be sarcastic. I immediately took the keys, and I backed my car out of the street. I tried to talk to him to tell him how disappointed we were in his actions. I kept my temper, trying to stay rational. We spoke for about 10 minutes and Mark said he was disgusted with himself. I told him that I was calling Cindy and asking her to get a ride down there so that we could get the van back to the factory. I didn't want to go through another court hearing if it could be avoided.

While we were waiting for Cindy to show up, Mark begged

me to give him $10 and leave him alone and he would be out of our lives forever. He was still coming down, but he was serious. I asked him what his plans would be if I gave him the money. He looked at me and said he would kill himself. My next thought and reply was "it was a selfish thing to do." "Don't you care about your son or us?" That was a dumb question on my part because Mark couldn't think in those terms. How do you, as a parent, try to make this state of affairs any better? This was a difficult situation, and Mark had no concept of the magnitude of loss that his death would cause all of us.

Cindy was on her way, and I knew she felt the same relief I was feeling because we found him so quickly. We were fortunate that it was early enough in the evening, making it easier to get our neighbor to drive Cindy to this drug-infested area to meet us. When Cindy arrived, there was the usual crying and hugging, which was probably a big relief for Mark. We decided that I would take the van back and leave it in the parking lot. I would put the keys in the mail slot with a note saying Mark wouldn't be in the next day and that the owner should call us as soon as possible.

The van was dropped off at 9 p.m., but there was no one there. The van was old and had some damage, but I had to assume it was in better shape prior to Mark's leaving with it earlier in the day. I couldn't lock the back door. There were still some boxes in the back that I assumed he didn't deliver to the other stores.

While I was driving back alone to the store, I was thinking about Mark. I didn't know where he saw his life, where he saw his future. I didn't know what was important to him besides the drugs, of course. I was depressed by the fact Mark felt he wanted to die. Didn't he know how much we loved him, and wanted him to get past this dark period in his life and move to a better, brighter future? We knew he could do this, if he could only get past the dependency on the drugs. He now had a son, a son that needed him. I was frustrated and sadden by the way things weren't progressing, and something needed to be done before it was too late.

When I got home, we both wanted to talk to Mark about what he did again today. This time, he decided to open up about his feelings. We listened and tried to understand his feelings. He told us that he hated himself and hated what he did. He was tired of people looking at him strangely, people talking about him like he was a freak, people watching what they said in front of them, and he hated his life. We stayed up for a while discussing philosophy and what life was about. We talked about how he could make his life whatever he wanted it to be. We talked and talked, but we had no idea what progress or impression we made on him. It was late so we went to sleep, telling him things would be brighter in the morning.

In the morning, I spoke to the owner of the candy factory and explained everything. He said he understood, and told me not to worry. He said he would not take any legal action against Mark because our family had enough problems already. He wished us good luck. We graciously thanked him and took a major sigh of relief. It was a great feeling to have a new weight removed from our chest before it damaged our internal organs.

Mark then got a call from Brenda saying that she was coming back that afternoon. He said he wanted to see Michael, so he was happy about the news. We picked Brenda and the baby up at the train station and brought them back. Cindy explained what happened the day before, and told Brenda how important it was for us to keep him under close supervision for the next few days. One reason was his mental state, and the other reason was his intense need for drugs. Anytime someone was came down from a binge, they needed to detox, meaning they needed to completely sober up to help reduce the intense need for the drug that was always on their mind and their body. She said she understood, but she didn't come here to baby-sit Mark, so she just nodded and walked away. The next morning things seemed back to normal. Mark was ashamed to face me, but he was comfortable enough to realize that this was his home and he could relax. It was a Saturday and we were resting at home because Cindy and I had a formal party to attend that night. Mark and Brenda said that they wanted to go to South Street in Philadelphia. South Street generally was very "in" or "hip," depending on your reference. The police were at every corner and the action was non-stop. There were tattoo parlors to fine restaurants to head shops to fine art shops. We knew the kid's preferences, which was why we suggested they not go. We stressed that it was no place for a baby. The kids said they were going and we said we would have no part of it because Mark should still be watched at home until the detox period was over. The kids said that they were going and taking the baby. Again, Cindy pleaded for them not to go, but both of them insisted and we were not in a position to fight with them over their own decisions. We were concerned that it was very cold and the health of the baby was not being considered. It was 2:30 p.m. and the kids said that they were leaving and taking the train. Cindy said she was not driving them to the train. She did everything that she could to discourage that trip. The kids walked about a mile and took the train, which put them about six blocks from their destination. We went to our dinner affair and hoped that they would be fine the balance of the evening.

At 9:00 p.m., Cindy received a page from Boston while we were finishing dessert. It was a call from hell! Cindy called Boston and was told that Brenda was on the corner of 6th and South streets, and she had not seen Mark or the baby in hours. Cindy told them that we could be there in 15 minutes, which we were. We raced through the streets and arrived at the corner to see Brenda talking to three police officers. She was in the most panicked state that we had ever seen her. As we pulled up to the corner, we spotted an illegal space in front of Brenda and the police, which we took. The streets were mobbed with people. There were police at every corner to insure the safety of all the tourists. There were occasional gangs that went through the area and grabbed gold chains or pocketbooks. It was chilly and the circumstances made it worse.

As soon as we pulled up, Brenda ran over to our car and

started babbling. I calmed her down and spoke with her and the main officer. We quickly learned that the worst might have happened. She was telling the police that Mark kidnapped the baby. The police said that Mark was the father and obviously had permission to take the baby. I pulled the officer aside and explained that Mark was a drug addict and was in a fragile state based on the previous evening. The officer told me that unless the child was in physical danger, there was nothing that they could do. I told him that there was a distinct possibility that the baby was in danger because of Mark's state of mind when he was on drugs. We knew he was on drugs by this time because of the circumstances. The story that we got from Brenda was that the three of them went into town and the kids decided to get more tattoos. Before they went in to get the tattoos, they went into a bar and had a few drinks. Brenda was under age and Mark should not have been drinking; it always led to drugs and more problems. We didn't even want to think of the baby inside a bar, let alone Brenda, who was underage. I didn't want to think of what would happen if Brenda were arrested inside a bar for underage drinking with the baby on her lap.

Brenda said they both had a few drinks to deaden the pain from the anticipated tattoos. They went in, and Mark had his done first. Mark's tattoo read R.I.P., and it had his grandmother's initials underneath. He loved her so much that it was his way of keeping her with him.

Brenda was next and Mark told her that while she was getting her tattoo, he was going to the head shop next door with the baby and he would be right back. She was waiting for him for over an hour and then she started to look in all of the stores in the area. With each store that she went into, she was feeling more panicked. When we got to her, her mental state was understandable. The baby had not eaten since noon, and had never been cared for alone by Mark. I told the officer that it was time to panic. He bought my story and a full hunt began. Within 10 minutes, there had to be 20 police, both in uniform and plainclothes, working the streets under the direction of the sergeant who was on duty, and my new best friend at this point. They had a picture of Mark and were methodically checking stores, streets, and the housing projects, which were four blocks away. Cindy, Brenda and I were escorted to the police substation to wait. There was nothing that we could do. Two hours went by and there was no word. Brenda was making promises to herself including, " if the baby came home safe, she would never..." That sounded good, but it was emotional talk from a panicked mother. Brenda called Boston to keep them advised because they had been in a panic after her phone calls. They said they wanted to fly down to kill Mark. I told Brenda that, at this point in time, if they came down and started that nonsense, "I would blow their fucking heads off." I explained to Brenda that Mark was obviously sick, and that was not the important thing right now. That seemed to quiet her because she knew that I didn't make idle threats.

We were sitting, waiting, and listening as the officers reported back. There was no luck for 2 ½ hours. They told the three of us that we had to go to the detective's division at another precinct. They told us that the police would drive us there while they continued the search. We were in the car about five minutes when another officer stopped our police car and said that he thought they found Mark, but they were still on the street and couldn't make a positive I.D. The police car continued on to the other station where detectives got all of the details from Brenda. They told her that she was irresponsible and that they would consider taking the child away from her. She panicked some more and told them what a good mother she was and they asked how in her right mind could she leave a baby alone with an addict who was obviously high? Was the tattoo that important to take that risk? It was beyond her understanding to have that type of foresight. They told her that she should evaluate her priorities and that they didn't want to see her again. We were pushed out of the line of questioning. The police treated us with respect, but didn't want us to say anything. The police did an unbelievable job from start to finish from handling and finding Mark and the baby to hopefully scaring some sense into Brenda.

The officer came back and said that they were sure it was Mark that they picked up and they were back at the substation. They said the baby appeared fine. They drove the three of us back and it was a very strange scene. The rooms were large and open with cold tile floors. There were a few offices around the perimeter and a few desks scattered around the room. When we walked in, Mark was in a chair along the wall and he was glassy eyed, but coherent. The baby was at the other end of the room in his coach, next to an officer at a metal desk. Brenda darted over to the baby with all emotions flowing. We followed closely, asked Mark how he was doing, and then checked on the baby. The baby was fine, which was what the detectives told us at the police station. Mark was sitting in a stretched-out awkward position with his head down.

I asked the officers where they found him and they said at the projects, which was the last place he should have been with the baby. They said that they thought he was getting ready to sell the baby's coat off his back to get drugs. All of his other possessions that were in the coach were gone. I confronted Mark about selling his son's jacket and Mark said that he would never do it. A young woman in the projects said he offered to sell the jacket to her, and she was the one who notified the police. They picked him up within five minutes from that point. The officers at the substation told Brenda that she better get her life together or they would call in the department of human services to see if she was a fit mother. Brenda started to protest, but I told her to shut up and listen because these officers are the ones who prevented a potential disaster. She shut up and listened through her tears.

We all left the station about midnight and no arrests were made because there was actually no crime committed. We got into my car and Brenda didn't want Mark anywhere near the baby. She was shaking so badly that it was difficult for her to hold Mike. Mike was safe in the car now and it hit her that she could have lost her child. She was talking to Mark by the time we got home. They stayed up and talked until 5 a.m. We had no idea what they talked about, but a decision was made during their all-night talk. She made arrangements to fly home at 2:30 that day. I was driving her to the airport, while Cindy was talking to Mark. I parked the car and walked her to the terminal. I carried the baby coach and she carried her luggage. I gave her a hug and said to take care of the baby and forget Mark and have a nice life. I asked her to call us, to let us know how she and Mike were doing. I cried the entire way home because this looked like it was over and we may never see Mike again. I could certainly understand that Cindy and I were "guilt by association," and her family needed someone to blame. Mike was about five months old and totally innocent.

When I got home, Mark was terribly depressed. He loved Mike, but he couldn't be the normal dad that he pictured. He moped around for two days. He didn't know what to do with himself. He told Cindy that he wanted to "blow his head off." Later that evening, he said that he was going to the bar up the street, but he wasn't going to drink. At that point, we felt that he had to go over and not drink if that's what he wanted to do. He had to make it by himself. At 9 p.m., he called to say he was coming home to change because he met a woman at the bar and he was going to "play" with her.

He asked me to drive him back to the bar at 10. He told me that the woman was 34 years old and was from a neighboring town. At that point, we were also depressed. Mark told us that he would be late, but knew he had to be up for work. We had him working with us at the office so we could earn a living, and we still could baby sit Mark for a while.

Mark never came home. He called the answering machine at home and left a message that he loved Cindy. Two days later, he called her at 1 a.m. from inside a bus terminal in the middle of Camden, N.J. Normally, this situation would be suicidal for a young, white suburban boy. This terminal, like many others, had its share of resident derelicts. We got there and I walked in with both hands in my pockets to give the 'creatures of the unknown' a fear factor as to what I was holding. I knew that I couldn't take my revolver into New Jersey because there are extremely strict rules for out-of-state people carrying guns. The hands in the pocket attitude was meant to be a 'leave me alone look.' It was getting to the point that I kept a lousy set of clothes available just to go to places to pick up Mark. When I walked into the terminal, I saw Mark walking toward me. He looked like hell. His clothes were straight out of the trash. He had different shoes on each foot and dirt all over his face. He had no jewelry or anything that matched. Actually, he fit in well for his surroundings. We met and I asked how he felt and Mark said "not so good." I asked what happened and he began to explain as we walked to the car. Cindy got nauseous at first sight, but quickly got it together.

We all wanted to get the hell out of there because we were in the badlands and the people may not have been friendly at that time of night. As we listened to him, our minds were thinking very bad thoughts. Mark was telling us a horror story, and the more he spoke, the worse it got.

"Dad, I was with this lady and we took a ride. I never saw her again. I woke up in bed wearing just my underwear in this project apartment with a bunch of derelicts all around. My underwear was all bloody. They gave me these clothes, but it was a day and a half that I don't know what happened. My ass hurt badly and it was bleeding. There were empty bottles all around the area but I don't remember anything."

He didn't know where he was and he said that his body hurt. I said that we should take him to the hospital. Mark said no and that probably was because he was afraid or ashamed. I was thinking the worst. Was he raped and by who or what? I was thinking about AIDS, too. We took him home because he said he refused to go to the hospital. He tried to sit in the car, but he was unable to because of the pain. He had to lie on his stomach.

We again suggested that he get checked out at the hospital, but again it was an absolute no. We couldn't get the ugly picture out of our minds of what could have happened when he was passed out. It was something that parents could need

231

counseling to get over.

Chapter Nineteen

For the next two weeks, Mark was working in the office with Cindy. He would occasionally go with me on sales calls and he seemed to enjoy it. He was diligent and was proud of himself because I gave him full responsibility to handle the in-coming calls and direct them to the proper people. He was back at AA meetings and home every night. He always had a lot of his friends over at night and sometimes they would go out together. This group was a little younger than Mark, but generally were very nice and did not do drugs. They were more into beer, except for Mark. They all knew that Mark had a problem and made sure he did soft drinks when he was with them. They often went to under 21 clubs, where they met younger girls and listened to great bands, but there were no alcohol problems. They liked Mark to go because he always ended up with a group of girls and that made it easy for them to meet women. Whenever Brenda was back in Boston, they insisted on Mark going with them.

After another week, Mark started to feel comfortable at work and the meetings. He was the good son again. Mark would anticipate things at home and try to help doing certain physical things. Cindy praised everything that Mark did because he seemed to thrive on it. Over the past two weeks, Brenda and Mark were speaking on the telephone almost every night. They still seemed to respect each other better from a distance. They both had a great love for the baby and both wanted to be together. She was somewhat lost back home because she saw everyone doing nothing with their lives. She saw action here and people trying to move ahead. She started to go back to get her GED, but her commitment wasn't sound enough and she failed to complete any of the courses.

Mark was getting to feel good about himself and his friends, but he felt that he needed a car. He found a 1981 Monte Carlo for $900. He earned some of the money working in the office, and Cindy loaned him the balance for tags and insurance (just liability). I drove the car and it was a great running car. I took it to the store and it rode as well as my newer car. Three days later, Mark took the car to the drug area. I didn't go to look for him. I figured that Mark had to call us. Of course, we waited by the phone and slept whenever we could whether it was morning, afternoon, or evening as we weren't sure what schedule we would be running over the next 24 hours. We were getting to the end of our tolerance levels and it was difficult. We were physically and emotionally drained. Cindy cried during any conversation that we had about anything, as her thoughts were of Mark.

The next day, we changed our minds and said that we were going to go look for him. It was 8:30 in the morning, and we went driving around one of the drug areas we knew he frequented. It always came down to guesswork in figuring out which area to look for him. Each area was more than five square blocks and each area was a minimum of one mile from each other.

We got a page and Cindy answered it. It was Mark. He was calling from the police station, which was five minutes away from our current location. She told him to stay there. We got to him and he was standing in the foyer of the station. We had been there before. It was cold, old, and dirty. Vagrants were again sleeping on the floor and everyone just walked around them. That was a safe place for them to sleep and be out of the cold. Mark walked out to the car with me and got into the back seat. There was nothing said between us because it had all been said many times before. Mark said he put up his car for collateral to get $30 worth of drugs. He said I could get the car back at midnight from the dealer on one of the corners if I paid the money he owed. I told Mark that the reason we were looking for him was because he had a 10:30 a.m. court date in the suburbs to face charges on the stolen delivery van from the animal hospital. Mark said that he didn't want to go and that he needed a shower. He was right about needing a shower, but he was going to the hearing because our attorney was meeting us at the courthouse to represent Mark. We drove directly to the courthouse and walked into the waiting room with about 15 minutes to spare. We told the attorney what happened and the attorney told Mark to keep his mouth shut until he was told to answer. The attorney went into another room, came back five minutes later, and told us that the case had to be rescheduled. Even though Mark had problems, he had no record yet. We thanked the attorney and told him to let us know when our next meeting would be, and we went home. I tried to take a nap between work, but it was difficult.

We knew that we had to go back to the dealers that night to get the car back. We did not look forward to walking back into the lion's den again. We parked the car a block away from where we could catch up to the dealer, who was on his corner. I was once again armed with my revolver and Cindy had the pepper gas. Mark was in the back seat. He still didn't know that we had the gun as it would have disappeared and possibly have been used in a way detrimental to someone's good health. It may also have seen the pawnshop! We were there about 20 minutes early. We parked where we could see if anyone was coming at us. We were getting good at this whole routine. The dealers spotted us instantly. They saw us from the moment we pulled up to the curb.

I stared at everything that moved and was hoping that no one would come our way. We were getting experienced, but were still way out of our league. We waited and kept trying to slump down so we wouldn't be obvious. Three guys started walking toward the car. It took them about thirty seconds to walk from where I first saw them to our car. It was a very long thirty seconds. They were big, rough shaven, and walked with attitudes. They looked like everyone else in the streets, but they looked extra ferocious to me. As they walked up, Cindy told Mark to keep his mouth shut, no matter what they said. I felt that Mark might try to get us out of danger by trying to talk to the dealers in their street talk.

They got to the car and I rolled my window halfway down, in case they tried to grab the keys or me. The truth was that they could have blown us away and the window being half down would not have made a significant difference! I told them the story. One of the guys did the talking while the other two peered into the car. The 'talker' said to wait here and they would be right back. We did what we were told. This was getting to be a bad pattern and I didn't choose the game or the rules. There was a feeling of deja vu, and the feeling got worse each time, not better. We were pushing our luck and we didn't want to be there. Now, while the dealers were gone, the thoughts of death, theft, and fear always ran through our minds. The gastric system also seemed to know the situation! All three of us talked in the car realizing that the dealers scoped out the situation and knew that we were extremely vulnerable. I had no leverage and was obviously in their territory. Five minutes went by and there was no action. After about ten minutes, the talker came over and said to drive over to a spot he pointed out in the middle of the block that I had been watching because of all of the activity. The middle of the block put us in a no-escape zone. We knew that their weapons made ours look like toys. We also knew that Mark could be a loose cannon if put in the right circumstances and it was getting tense, at least to Cindy and me. I had no choice, so we drove up and immediately the guy who took Mark's car as collateral walked to my side and put his head within an inch of the glass. There were at least six other members of their group within ten steps of the car. It was now about 1:30 a.m. He said to give him $100 and he'd give me the keys to the car. I told him that I thought the price was $30, and I had the money in my hand to show them. The dealer again said that it was $100. I said these thirty dollars was all that I had. I purposely had three tens in my hand and nothing else that could be seen unless they took the car apart. The discussion went back and forth for about 10 minutes, and I could see they were getting nervous. The reason they were getting nervous was because my car was in the way of other customers waiting to buy drugs.

Fortunately, he realized that I was right when I said if he took the $30, we would leave and he could continue doing business and make a lot more money with no more hassles from us. They all agreed and he said for me to give him the money. I said that we would trade at the same time. I put my hand out slowly and he put the keys into my other hand while he took the money. We knew how Bill Murray felt in "Groundhog Day" as everything was happening again!

I felt good because I had the keys. I felt we had beaten them on their on turf and showed Mark how to be tough with brains, not brawn. Even in these circumstances, I was still trying to teach Mark a lesson. I showed him that thinking and using one's head would win every time. The exchange was made and we were ready to go. I asked him where the car was and then realized that we weren't home free. He told us that the car was four blocks away and it was on a small one-car street. He said to me "don't come back or you won't leave healthy!" We went to that street and there was no car! We decided that our lives were worth more than the $900 car so we decided to just go home. We got right to bed and figured whatever we did next, we must get some sleep. Cindy went on with her day's activities and I went into work, my ass dragging, my eyes heavy, and my attitude lousy. I got home about three in the afternoon and collapsed on the sofa for about two hours when Cindy said that dinner was ready. We were tired, but felt that we had to keep going until we were totally exhausted because Mark was going to Florida for a week to visit one of his girlfriends who moved down there, and we could rest when he was away.

Mark announced to us before we went to bed that he was going out with one of his friends and would be home early because he knew that he had an flight in the morning. Cindy and Mark had to leave by 7 a.m. for the airport, which was 45 minutes away. Mark left that evening about 8 p.m., and we went right to bed. We figured or hoped that he would be in about one or so. We didn't care about anything at this point but a warm, comfortable bed!

At 12:30 a.m., we got a call from Mark to pick him up in a

rough neighborhood about 40 minutes away. We always told him that no matter what time it is, call us if you are in trouble and we will pick you up. Sometimes we wanted to take those words back!

We got there and he was waiting for us. We all got home at 2 a.m. and climbed into our bed to finish that restful sleep. The alarms went off and Cindy got up and dressed to get him out and away for our "vacation" at home. That was one plane that we didn't want him to miss. The events that took place over the past 48 hours took their toll and drained most of our energy. Cindy got to the airport on time and told him to enjoy himself. As the plane took off, it was such a great feeling to not have to worry for the next seven days and nights.

The next week was wonderful in the sense of getting a full eight hours of sleep and not be on edge waiting for the door to slam, or a phone call in the middle of the night. We got collect phone calls from Florida and Mark would tell us that he was having a great time and that he saw relatives of Cindy, who took him and his "girlfriend" out to dinner. He may have been lying to us, but it didn't matter because we didn't know better and he was there and we were here! Cindy and I got to know each other again, which was great because it allowed us to remind ourselves why we wanted to spend the rest of our lives together.

The week flew by and we picked up Mark at the airport December 12. He was glad to see us and we were actually glad to see him and anxious to see if there was any real change in his approach to life. When he saw us, he picked up Cindy like she was a little kid running to see dad after work, and gave her a big hug and kiss. He shook my hand and gave me a hug with the other. I jokingly checked my pockets to see what Mark took with that hug. It was a true gesture that was heartfelt. It felt like a normal family who was glad to be together and was totally at ease with each other.

We got into the car for the ride home and Mark was telling us about the trip and how he was able to relax in the sun and go out every night to neat places. He told us how much he enjoyed seeing Cindy's relatives and how nice they were. He said they even gave him $20 to go out one night. For the next few days, Mark told us where he would be and he was out looking for jobs because he was ready to get on with his life. It sounded great to hear, but there was both doubt and hope, which was a difficult combination to handle. We felt that the Florida trip may have been a turnaround for his attitude. Sometimes it was difficult for a "kid" to grow up until he got out on his own. At this point, we were thinking maybe we should have joined the Optimist's Club.

On the 20th of December, Cindy got a call from a national jewelry store chain in the local mall saying that Mark had opened a charge account and bought a $500 gold chain. We knew that this was the start of more problems. Mark came home that night, had the chain, and was so proud that he bought it himself and that he had the credit to do it. Mark didn't realize that we established credit for him over the past two years by borrowing in his name for small purchases and then paying them off very quickly. We were not smart enough to foresee the future and realize that he had no conception of credit or interest rates or the ability to pay back a loan. The reality was that not many young people had that knowledge or perception until they were in over their heads. Apparently, that was why the collection business had been a strong growth business. When I asked him how he was going to pay off the jewelry, he said that he was going to be working and it would be no problem. The next day we got a call at 10:30 a.m. He told Cindy that he sold the jewelry and was "lost." Cindy drove down to pick him up because I had to work. She got home with him and he was in a major depression.

When they got home, Mark asked her to take him to a NA meeting, which Cindy did. That was the 28th of December. The next day, Mark went to a shrink from the Medical Assistance referral agency. He was starting to get nervous and uptight about every move he was making. He had no car, but he still had credit because there was not even one payment that was missed, or made, for that matter. On the

31st, we said that since none of the rehabs have worked, he should try acupuncture. We figured that since it was non-invasive and we had nothing to lose, it was an ideal ray of hope. Cindy took him to a local center for treatment. It appeared that the spirit was involved with these types of treatments. There was a feeling of the cleansing of the body. The thought of needles going into one's body that way didn't sound half as bad as a druggie injecting one needle into his or her arm. It almost sounded celestial! That was one heck of a way to prepare for the New Year's Eve festivities.

Speaking of New Year's Eve, our tradition was to be with the same three couples. We would have a nice local dinner, or bring it into one of the homes. We would watch a handpicked movie (that usually was liked only by the hand picker), and then turn the TV on to watch the festivities. We would enjoy a glass of fake champagne, give each other kisses, wish each other a happy and healthy New Year, and go home about 1 a.m. Sound boring? Not to us. We wouldn't trade it for any other type evening. Each New Year's Eve, we were wondering if Mark was O.K. because we knew that if he started drinking, problems would worsen at a fast pace within the following two hours. That New Year's Eve was a good one because he came home about five in the morning and told us that he didn't drink and he had a good time.

On January 3rd, Mark applied to another bank for a car loan. Within one hour, he got a call that he was approved for $5,000! I couldn't believe it. Was this a great country that we lived in where someone on drugs with no job history and no job could get money within one hour of application? It made one think that we should get away from all of those burdensome legal papers and go back to the trusting handshake that our country was based upon. Yeh, right!

He went out and bought a Toyota that had a little steering wheel and little chrome wheels. It was all black and ran well. It was the type car that every police car would go after. Even the steering wheel was unique; it was the size of a go-kart's steering wheel. I drove it once and thought that an accident was coming as every move was accentuated with each small movement of the wheel. It cost $3,500, but it was what he wanted and Mark also realized that he couldn't make the payments on a new car.

On January 7th, the attorney called us about Mark's court date for the stolen work van. He said that he still didn't have any results. Mark left at 6 p.m. to go out and we left at seven to go to a car show that involved a weekend stay. We told Mark that we would call him at ten in the morning and we wanted him to be home to answer the phone. We made the call as scheduled, but there was no answer. That now caused us concern since we were five hours away. On the other hand, there was nothing we could do by being there. We stayed at the show and had a great weekend; although we were aware that Mark probably had done some damage somewhere.

Mark was starting to miss the baby, but he was weighing the burden of having Brenda along for the ride. We got home the afternoon of the 9th and noticed that Mark had not been home. Every parent knows when their child had been in the house when they were away. There were so many tell-tale signs that blast the parents as soon as they enter the house. Although kids carefully cover their tracks, it is with the obvious flair and softness as a herd of elephants.

That evening, Mark called home to tell us that he was in Scumville at the police station. He sold his car, jacket, clothes and shoes. He asked if we would pick him up. Again, he was very apologetic. He had a meekness today that was not him. We both took the thirty-minute drive because I didn't want Cindy driving down there herself. We got to the station and he was sitting inside with old pants being held up with rope and a shirt that even our fathers wouldn't wear. He was wearing socks, but no shoes. He looked like a bum. The station hallway smelled like a bus station men's room. If you had a full stomach, this could empty it. There were four other "bums" sitting on the floor, just getting out of the elements. There was bulletproof glass for the window and locked doors in three directions. The whole place was cold.

Mark got into the car. Cindy cried and Mark felt worse

because he loved her so much and she stood by him through everything. He could talk to her and confide in her. He was usually good for the two or three weeks after a binge, and then get the urge to take off and do drugs again. When he was straight, he would try to help when asked and he would come into the office to help and maybe learn the business. He would feel a great deal of pride answering the phones and realizing that he was talking to people who were successful adults. It also put pressure on me because I was always concerned what Mark's attitude would be. He was dealing with people who were a key element of our livelihood.

That night, I got a call from a guy who said he had the car and would give it back for $200. I asked Mark how much he owed the guy for the car and how did that guy get the home phone number? The guy again told me that it was $200. Cindy checked the title and the paperwork for the car, which she had and found that Cindy did get her name on as holding the lien, so the guy couldn't easily sell the car. This now became an easy exchange. I told him to meet me at a neutral shopping center with the car and I would give him the $200. In reality, I figured that one could say that we indirectly paid for Mark's drugs! We met the guy and exchanged money for the car and it almost seemed like a normal business deal to me. It went smoothly and was done in broad daylight.

On the other hand, we were concerned that our home phone number was now out there. It didn't take a genius to find out home addresses and we didn't know what problems or enemies Mark had made out on the streets. Generally, we were told that the drug pushers tended to stay in their own area because they had a fear of the suburbs and suburban courts, when it came to their treatment. We were getting concerned about our safety at night or when we were asleep, which were not always at the same time.

Two days later, Mark was getting itchy to take off again and we saw it. We told him he should see a doctor immediately. He agreed and we went to a doctor from one of the rehab centers and explained the situation. The doctor prescribed a pill called Antibuse. This drug was strange. If alcohol were taken with this drug, the person would get violently ill. This was good because many times when Mark went on his missions, he would start out with an innocent beer. Mark knew that the drugs were potent and he knew that the mixing of alcohol with the Antibuse would be pure hell. He was good for the next five days. He came home every night and told us that he drank ginger ale. He was still hanging with the local kids, which was good.

We felt that this group of young men was a good influence, but Mark still had his wild side. The guys and girls loved him because he was still cool, had a good body, was funny, and was very carefree. He would sometimes have the guys being jealous because the girls flocked to him. They always did. He was so casual; he was always drawing the people around him. He went out with one of the guys to meet the others at someone's house, and he told us he would be back in about an hour. Then, they were all coming to sit out back at our house. The kids tended to hang at our house because we had a screen house near the swimming pool. It was convenient and, as we found out later, a safe place to drink beer with no hassles because they couldn't be seen. A few of the group came over and were waiting for about 10 minutes. They told Cindy that Mark should have been there by now. We waited another 15 minutes and then one of the other guys came to the door and knocked.

He was visibly upset. He said that there was a car accident and Mark and one of their friends were on their way to the hospital. He said that he had no idea how serious it was, but there were ambulances all around. He told Cindy which hospital to go to so we rushed over there to the emergency room.

The attendants told Cindy that the ambulance had not yet arrived. We felt this was not good because they had plenty of time to get them out of the car and drive about 10 minutes. Our thoughts were that it was a bad accident and the kids couldn't be easily moved or they would have transported them by now. We kept looking out the emergency room door, watching for the vehicles to arrive.

242

About 15 minutes went by and then we saw an ambulance pull in without the sirens or lights. Our hearts sank because we figured it was so bad that he was dead or they would have been rushing to get him to surgery. The ambulance backed into their slot and the attendants opened the doors. We could only see through the hospital doors. The attendants were in no hurry. Cindy was trying to see what color blanket was on him. We knew that if it was red, he was dead. The blanket was not red and she saw his eyes as they wheeled him past where we were standing. He was awake, but his face was very bloodied. He saw Cindy and gave her a very weak smile, and a wink, to reassure her that he was ok. They took him into a private room and said the doctor would be out to let everyone know what was going on as soon as possible.

We felt relieved to know that he was alive. As we waited for over 1½ hours, his friends kept arriving. There were over seven in the waiting room with us. The last one to come in was the one who was in the car with him. He had a few cuts, but was fine. His parents came in with him. He said that he didn't need any treatment.

We asked him what happened. He said that another car cut Mark off at the stoplight, so Mark had to angle his car to avoid being hit. When that happened, he lost control and went into a traffic light pole. The accident happened about five blocks from our home. Everyone was talking; waiting to hear from the doctors on Mark's condition, but the time seemed to drag on.

Finally, after what seemed like hours, the doctor came out and told us Mark had bruised ribs and glass embedded into many parts of his skin. He said that they will work themselves out and he would be very sore for a few days. His face was all red, cut and puffy. It appeared that he would scab up over his entire face and both arms. We went in to see him and then I came out to assure his friends that all was OK, and we would be taking him home that night. His friends said they would see him in the morning. We thanked them for their concern and the friends left. It appeared that there was no alcohol involved and it was just unfortunate that it happened. The police did not issue any tickets.

The next day, we went to the tow yard about a mile from our home to see the car. The owner of the lot told us he wanted money to store the car for a week in advance. That pissed me off because the car was taken there without our permission and it would have been closer to take it right to our home. The yard operator was nasty and treated us like dirt. I told him that I wanted the car out of there and would pay him for one-day storage because he was being such an idiot. I also told him that he had our car without the owner's permission and that he should call the police if he had a problem. At that time, I didn't need some ass hole trying to steal an extra $100 from me for storage. The car was obviously totaled. The roof was cut away and there wasn't a place on the car that was without damage. Mark must have swerved and hit more than one pole. All of the glass was shattered. He was lucky to be alive! We then went to the scene of the accident. The pole appeared to be bent almost in half and there were two other signs next to the traffic light that were obviously hit. That convinced everyone that Mark was very lucky.

In the meantime, he was calling and receiving calls from Brenda. They always spoke about Mike and his growing up. On January 21st, Brenda and Mike came back to our house for a prolonged "visit." Mark and Brenda wanted to be together, but they still would fight and argue about either drugs or going out. Mark and Brenda got along much of the time, but they were two kids who had a kid. They would want to go out and take the baby. The problem was that they would take the baby to the wrong places. It wasn't where babies learn to play or associate with other kids. It was to places the two adult children wanted to go. Time was not a factor, as they didn't understand that babies needed schedules and the comfort of their own setting. Babies needed a comfort zone for security. While she was in Philadelphia, Mark was uptight, but happy that Mike was with him. Mark would always hold the baby and play with him. He loved to hold him over his head and have Mike look down on him. It appeared that things were going in a positive direction. Brenda was home taking care of Mike, but was bored because she said she had nothing to do. Cindy let Brenda use her car if she wasn't using it in order to let her go to the mall or the park, both of which were within two miles of home.

Chapter Twenty

By the 31st of January, the pattern seemed to be working. Mark would come into the office or go out with me to solicit business. Both of us were getting to know each other and the family bond appeared to be strengthening. That morning, Cindy had to go to school for continuing education and I was going to the office early. Mark was to be in at 9 a.m. At the office, I was working and told my secretary that Mark was coming in to answer the phones to free her up to do other work. It was 10:30 and Mark walked into the office. I got on his case about work and responsibility, especially, with a baby at home. I lectured him about learning the business and the importance of schedules. I believed that Mark got tired of the lectures or he had a hard time sleeping through them with his eyes open. Mark went home at noon.

He told Cindy that he was taking Brenda and the baby to the mall for the afternoon. We felt that as long as Mark was out of trouble and doing something constructive, it was fine. He was home, upstairs, with Brenda when we arrived home about 4:30 p.m. Cindy was making dinner and Mark came down stairs about five minutes after Brenda. He announced to us that he was going out now. I said to wait for dinner and Mark started mumbling something. Brenda was sitting at the table and whispered to me that he was high right now. I told him to go upstairs and we would be right there. I quickly spoke to Brenda to see what was going on.

She told us that Mark went out that morning and bought drugs. After he bought them, he went to the office, which was why he was late. When they came home from the mall,

Mark was upstairs in his room with her and the baby and was doing crack. As was the usual case with crack, he used it all and now wanted more to try to get the first high, which he wouldn't achieve. When we heard what Brenda told us, we were angry and anxious at the same time, but we didn't have a lot of time to react.

We immediately went to up to his room. Cindy went in to talk to him. He started pacing as he spoke to her. He would appear calm, then snap, and then calm down again, all within five seconds. He was like a caged animal. Cindy was the best one to try and calm him down. I stayed at the top of the stairs to prevent Mark from going downstairs and out for more drugs.

Brenda stood off to the side at the top of the stairs. Cindy kept telling Mark to sit down and think about what was happening, but he was ready to explode. I knew that we were heading for a showdown within minutes unless she could talk to him. Mark was totally out of his mind. Cindy was talking to him for about five minutes and asking him to please sit and talk to her. She told him that there was no way we were letting him go out of the house to get more drugs. He was infuriated. He said that he had to go to the bathroom. Cindy let him go. We were drained, but hoped the bathroom trip would calm him down. We knew that there were no drugs left or he would never have come downstairs in the first place.

Mark came out of the bathroom with a crazed look in his eyes and passed his room where Cindy was waiting for him and he proceeded to face me at the top of the stairs. His room was next to the stairs so he surprised me by passing his room. At the instant he got to the top of the stairs, Brenda yelled, "look out", as Mark swung his arm from waist level. Everything was a blur! I felt penetration into my chest and I just rolled around, still standing, but holding the rail with one hand. Mark ran past me on the stairs and ran out the front door at the bottom of the stairs. I was wearing a white shirt and blood was coming through the shirt. Brenda lifted her hand and one of her fingers was cut. The adrenalin was flowing. Cindy was screaming something, but no one remembered what or to whom. When Mark hit the bottom of the stairs, I regained my composure and ran after him. Mark went outside and part way down the street. I followed him, at a slower pace, and Cindy and Brenda also were outside trying to keep up with me. The baby was in the house asleep in his crib. When I approached Mark, he slipped around me and ran past Cindy and Brenda and into the house. He locked the door as we approached. We used Cindy's key to get in and as we got in, Mark took off into the garage and out that door. He then jumped into Cindy's car and drove off.

I grabbed my keys from my back pocket, raced into my car, and took off after him. My chest was dripping blood, but there was no pain. Mark raced down the street in Cindy's car at about 60 miles an hour. I kept up to him and tried to turn on my cell phone. Mark was going through stop signs and traffic lights. I thought that Mark saw me in the mirror. I was running the same traffic lights and stop signs to keep up to him. We were up to speeds of more than 80 mph on back roads. I called 911 on my cell phone, got the police in the neighboring township, and told them I was following Mark at high speeds in their township and needed help. They told me to call my own township police and they proceeded to give me that phone number. I begged them to patch me into them and they refused. In the meantime, Cindy called our police department and when I called them from the car, they were waiting for my call. They stayed patched in and told me to stop the pursuit. I told them that I wouldn't stop until they picked up the pursuit because it was dangerous. The police followed my conversation and had the other police department ready to pick up the chase. I was scared because there was a lot of traffic and Mark knew that I was right behind him. As we approached a traffic light, Mark got boxed in because he was in the right lane and there was traffic in the left lane preventing him from going left. When he stopped, I pulled up close behind him and at that instant, four police cars rolled up around the stopped cars and the police, with guns drawn, approached Cindy's car on foot. As they carefully walked up to the car, Mark hit the gas, turned onto the lawn on the right, and flew past the light. The police were now in the chase as they ran back to their cars and took off after him. I was on the phone the entire time with a police officer from my township. The officer told me to stay there and he would have an ambulance there in a few minutes. I told the officer that I was fine and would be back at the house in ten minutes. I pulled up into the driveway. The police were there, and an ambulance crew was there. I told them that I was fine and wanted to know if they caught Mark.

They told me that they caught Mark about a mile down the road from where he was cornered and he did hit a police cruiser in the side, which stopped him from driving further. The officer told us that Mark would be in the township jail for a day or two, and then to County jail. At that point, the officer said that he wanted me to go to the hospital. The medical team was standing by listening the whole time, waiting to see if I was in trouble because they saw my shirt and the flow of blood. They were anticipating either shock or something worse. I told the police that I didn't need the ambulance and they gave me a paper relieving them of liability for not going with them. The officer convinced Cindy that I should go to the hospital, based on the location of the wound. By that time, I was feeling a little tired because of the action. My neighbor drove me to the hospital with Brenda. Cindy stayed at home with the baby. We pulled up to the emergency room and I told Brenda to go and get stitches because she was cut when Mark swung the scissors at me. As soon as we walked into the door, a team of doctors and nurses grabbed me and had me in X-ray within seconds. There was a nurse with me at all times. Cindy took the baby, went to get the car that Mark took, and was going to meet me at the hospital. She had no idea of the actions at the hospital. My tests came back and didn't show damage to my organs, but the doctors said it could have damaged the heart or liver based on the location of the stab wound. They said that I had to stay overnight and they would have someone with me around the clock because there was no way that they could tell how far the wound went into my chest. I found out that a surgical team was made ready and an operating room was available should it have been needed. Cindy came in and saw me lying in a bed. She looked very pale because she thought that she was picking me up to go home. I assured her that there was no problem, as my body did not feel any different. She told me she found out that Mark was in jail in our township and he had no idea of what had happened. She also let me know that I was stabbed with a scissors that had a 5-inch blade. The problem was that it was difficult, if not impossible, to ascertain how deep the wound went.

When I was in the hospital bed, I realized that there was nothing to do but think; I thought! Some of the things that popped into my mind were why didn't Brenda tell us that Mark was doing drugs in his room? If the kids knew that their friend was doing something wrong, shouldn't they have told someone who could help if they couldn't? Was it loyalty or stupidity that allowed their friend to drive drunk or do drugs?

I wasn't sure if I was annoyed at Brenda for not telling us or happy that she finally did so we wouldn't let him out. I was feeling bad that she got cut. She was given a butterfly band-aid, but no stitches were needed. We had mixed emotions about everything that went on, and we were more sensitive to many of the problems that we already faced and knew we were going to face more in the future. We wondered when it would all end and we could live in peace. I remained in the hospital overnight and the doctors released me in the morning.

I kept in touch with the police to see how Mark was making out. We purposely did not go to see him as we were hoping that this would make an impression. The police said that he was depressed because he figured that he could have killed his father. There was nothing that we could do about it except leave him in jail to think. He was charged on two counts of aggravated assault. The police told me that if we left him in, which could be a good idea, be sure to get him out before he went into general population at the county level. After two days, Mark was sent to county jail, but not into general population. They usually waited about a week before the prisoners were sent to general. We didn't go to the prison, but Brenda did. She said he asked about us and said that he was sorry. I didn't take his phone calls from prison because I wanted him to realize that life was good if you were straight and lousy if you were not. It was very tough to leave him in jail because, despite all we went through, we worried about his safety. Who would be the big guy's "next girlfriend?" Would he be sleeping with murderers and other hardened criminals? Would this teach him a lesson or would he get a criminal education? It was a tough decision, but it was agreed that we had to do it.

Six days later, we got a call from the police that Mark was going into general population that afternoon. We drove up to the county seat and put up bail money to get him out of prison. We went in to see him, first as visitors. It was awful. Cindy and I, middle class suburban law-abiding citizens, were searched when we entered the facility. The atmosphere was cold and chilling. The closing of doors, metal doors, echoed through the air. It was like a television drama; it made the hair on your arms stand up! We walked in the direction that we were told. The halls were long with off-white painted blocks on each side of us. We saw a heavy steel, drab green door ahead. We waited outside until someone pushed a button to let us enter. We were getting claustrophobic going down hallways just to face another green door. I actually flinched from freight twice as the doors closed behind us with loud clanks. It made us think of the concentration camps where the people were treated like animals and they did everything they were told to avoid being hurt. The sounds of prison take all of the humanity out of a person. You are absolutely not in control of your minute-to-minute destiny. I would be scared to go to the bathroom because of the vulnerability. We were afraid to make eye contact with any of the prisoners that we saw through the different windows.

After walking through the maze of hallways, we got to the pod that Mark was in. We felt like we were part of the Skinner rat experiment. We were in a room where we could see a good portion of the area, including some of the bunks. A thick wall of unbreakable glass surrounded us. We saw Mark walk toward us in a very regimented way as though he was told when to take each step. He had to use a telephone next to him and across from us. Mark had tears in his eyes when he saw us. We purposely had the baby with us and Mark touched him through the glass since there was no direct contact. When he saw the baby, he said to the prisoner next to him that Mike was his kid. He was so proud of Mike, but didn't know how to show it over the long haul. He knew the touching and hugging and kissing, but not the security of keeping the family together. Cindy told him that we were going to bail him out and that he would be leaving in a few minutes to come home. His face brightened as if he found a million dollars. He kept asking if "we meant now, like right now." When he was sure, he ran over to his bunk and gathered his belongings.

The release procedure took about an hour. When he walked out the door, the first thing he did was stretch. One thinks that was appropriate since he had a caged-in feeling throughout the facility. He thanked us for getting him out, but he was at a loss and fumbling for the words to say to me. He kept asking me if I was OK. After trying to make him sweat to make it sink in, I said to him that I was and that I had a new hole in my chest that will heal. I also said that I hoped he understood what could have easily happened if the wound were ½ inch in either direction. The doctors said that was all the lead way I had and that luck was on our side that he didn't puncture a major organ. The hole was between the heart and the liver.

We all went home and tried to start fresh without harping on what happened. The whole ride home and in the house, Mark kept checking on me. His imagination and the mystery of the stabbing played havoc with his mind and he was obviously thinking the worst. I laid down some rules about hours and phone calls coming in. We told him no calls after 11 p.m. Other kids were used to calling at 3 in the morning, not even considering if anyone in the house was sleeping. We now told them we wanted them in during the week by 11 p.m., if there was work the next day. How long would those rules hold up? We didn't have a clue.

It was now February 5th, and it had not been a great year so far. We did a lot of babysitting and were glad to have the opportunity to work with the baby, although Mike was probably too young to understand much of anything. It would have been nice to be a grandparent, but necessity required that help was needed if we wanted to see regularity in the baby's schedule. It was now at the point where Mark and Brenda would decide where they wanted to go, and the baby would be dragged along, even if it was not in his best interests. They just thought it was their child and they could do what they wanted. Actually, they were right!

We again saw Mark restless. In our society, even if the parents know something is wrong and try to tell the courts, the courts don't listen as the judge did in the prior stolen vehicle case. In the troubled times faced in the schools today, especially with violence, which is blamed partially on the parents, how can the parent tell authorities to help? The authorities refused to listen to us! On the other hand, what if Mark went on a wild shooting spree at a school, wouldn't there be an outcry for our heads because we should have known? Where is the right answer?

We knew that jail was not going to help Mark. We also knew being out on the street wouldn't either. Mark needed the long-term facility to get him on track. It appeared that most drug addicts needed that over the long term, but again, it was not available. We learned that Mark's type of crime was slightly more than a nuisance to the courts. If an attorney were there to fight any of these cases, there was always a question of misunderstanding of the time to return the vehicle, or some other trumped up excuse to get off.

That last court date seemed to give Mark a sense of reality. He started asking questions about becoming an attorney. I tried to answer them as well as I could, but Mark was thinking that he could practice law while he went to school. Based on some attorney's actions, he probably could have done better! Mark had no sense of timing. He had no concept of how hard he would have to work, and how much blood and sweat it would take to achieve such a goal – this type of approach was never a strategy of his. If he couldn't do it quickly, he would become frustrated. He needed instant gratification. We guessed that we all could sleep safer knowing that he didn't want to be a brain surgeon!

Chapter Twenty-one

Whatever his thoughts, Mark was acting differently since the last hearing. He tended to stay home more and seemed to spend almost all of his spare time with Mike. Of course, that was until it was time to change a diaper. He came into the office and worked a good part of the day and he was actually starting to think about business. It took about a week for him to realize that law was out of the question. He actually started to talk about opening a sandwich shop in one of the drug areas. I asked him why there and he told me that there was a need for one and he could help feed some of the homeless that helped him while he was on the street in the past. I asked him to make a business proposal for how he would do it and the size of the place that he needed. He gave me back a five-page plan that actually made sense. He had learned about business in our office and by being out on the street with me. He learned about the real people and what can happen to anyone based on his own experiences, which we didn't discount.

Mark was growing, but in strange ways. He was half adult, but his mind was not as good as it was in prior years due to the drugs. He would talk about the future now, which he never really did before. The sandwich shop was a driving force behind his trying to plan for the future. The plan for the sandwich shop was to earn enough money from the paying customers to help feed the poor. He would keep it open all night and put a lot of meat on the rolls. He would have it lit up like a Christmas tree so it would be a safe place to be at any hour. He even picked out the spot to put the store. I looked at the spot and said that Mark should have been a missionary based on the location. He was right in one aspect; it would do business if he could get out of there safely. He did give a lot of thought to many of the aspects of the business.

Mark was always talking about Mike and how he wanted to be perceived as a father. He was starting to get on Brenda to do something with herself. She had originally dropped out of high school and enjoyed sleeping late and watching television, but only spoke of the GED. Mike would be left in bed until about 11 a.m., if Brenda could stay there too. Both Mark and Brenda were getting frustrated because neither could understand what a relationship was all about. Cindy and I didn't mind supporting Mark, Brenda, and Mike, as long as things were going good. We knew there were some relationship problems, because the kids were always yelling at each other in their room. They didn't talk much to each other, but they liked the same music and lifestyle, which included late nights and late mornings. The only thing that ever bothered Cindy was their sloppiness. If a glass was half full, and one of them was done drinking, the glass was left on the counter. If food left a ring on the counter, which usually got hard and sticky, no one bothered taking a sponge to wipe it. There was little consideration by them, unless it was requested. This was frustrating to both Cindy and I because neither one of them valued our possessions. The kids did not work hard to get theirs. What happened to all of the training and manners we taught him? When he became a teenager, he either picked up the habits of his friends or just became instantly brain dead!

These young parents in our home were young teenagers in mentality, but physically, they were adults. They were never open to suggestions or ideas. They always knew that Cindy

and I were the old generation and " just didn't understand."
Understand or not, people couldn't stay together fighting all
of the time the way the kids did.

On March 3rd, Cindy was at work and got a call that Brenda
and the baby were leaving immediately. Another fight
between Mark and Brenda was obvious. Her family in
Boston said to put her on a plane and they would send me a
check for the amount of the plane ticket. I knew a last
minute-flight was going to cost a lot of money, yet I paid for
it anyway. Also, I was charged an additional $90 for a baby
coach! As for being reimbursed, I'm still waiting for the
check.

I drove her to the airport while Mark was with Cindy trying
to resolve some other problems. On our way to the airport,
the car became a confessional. It started out as me saying
that it was better for her and the baby not to be in an
atmosphere where all the fighting was taking place. I said we
would talk after everything settled down. The conversation
turned to Mark and his drug habit, which seemed to be the
problem that Brenda saw in the relationship. She was
familiar to the problems that drugs can cause in families.
Her mother had been in and out of jail for the past 10 years
due to drugs. It caused her mother to commit various crimes
to feed the habit. Her dad, Joe, was now a recovering drug
addict and alcoholic. He got his life together by meeting the
right girl and wanting to straighten out. He didn't miss a
meeting and now was beginning to value his body. He
slipped occasionally, but appeared to come back and be
straight. He came a long way and was an example to Brenda,
although he still was not an angel based on his doing drugs
with Mark. She saw what went on and was starting to realize
it was not going to get better, despite the fact they loved each
other. She continued on, telling me Mark never went to the
NA meetings when they were supposed to be attending.
Instead, Mark was taking her to drug city where he was
doing weed and angel dust.

When I heard that, I was thinking to myself that we had a
little communication problem. Why didn't she try to stop

255

him? Why did she go with him? Why was I asking questions to myself that were not going to have intelligent or meaningful answers? I dropped her off at the airport and kissed Mike goodbye.

I didn't go into the airport because the emotions were starting to be drawn from deep inside. I always showed strength to her and I didn't want her to see me emotional. I also knew that she had a fear factor when dealing with me, and that fear sort of kept her in line. Brenda never listened to anyone and I was the only person who sometimes got through. When I got home, I casually asked Mark about what I learned on my drive, and he denied all of the "confession" from Brenda.

Cindy was upstairs when I arrived home. I went up, her eyes were red, and she was drained. It was obvious that it was taking a toll on her because the trash basket was full of tissues. She already missed the baby. He was 300 miles away with no real ties to us. Mark was missing the baby, but knew what happened was inevitable. Mark knew that they would talk and discuss things, but didn't know how quickly. Three hours later, Mark and Brenda were on the phone talking to each other like nothing happened. Cindy was upset because she had gotten used to the baby being part of our immediate life. She looked at the pictures of Mike that were all over the house and she kept dripping tears. Mark would see her, give her a big hug, and tell her that it would be fine. He had a way to calm her. Mark was still her baby and she was so proud of him, no matter what. She always said that her other child, who was so severely disabled, made the problems with Mark easy to handle because Mark could at least communicate. He always meant well, but his unsupervised actions usually caused, at the least, a minor disaster.

That night, Mark told us that he was going out. Of course we were concerned and scared to death that he was also emotionally spent and would tie one on as his escape. We told him of our feelings and told him that it would be a great test for him to handle this tough situation and start to grow up. He didn't come home that night and we decided that we had to find him since we were going away the next day. We went to the usual areas and had a very positive attitude that we would find him. We pulled down a small side street and saw his car. It was parked tight between two other cars. As we pulled up, we saw he was the front seat of the car and there was a neighborhood girl in the passenger seat. Her head was bobbing in and out of sight and we assumed we knew what she was doing to him. We pulled up directly next to him and blocked the street and his car. The girl lifted her head and seemed confused to see these old people next to the car. Mark obviously told her who we were and probably told her to take off because she opened the passenger door and left.

We had it planned that Cindy would get in and Mark would drive out of the immediate neighborhood. Cindy got into the car and I backed up to be in position to follow them. This was the worst of the neighborhoods and Cindy didn't immediately realize that Mark was high. He started to pull out of the space. He was not sharp. He hit the car in front and then backed into the car in back. He did that twice and then I saw a bunch of guys running and yelling in Spanish. They were not happy and I was scared. Mark pushed the car in front with a crash. He then started to pull out. The crowd was at the car as he was pulling out. They didn't realize that I was there with Mark. As Mark pulled away, they were trying to grab at the car, but they just missed as Mark got lucky. As Mark pulled away, I heard the crowd yell to get their cars and get him. With that, I started to follow Mark, but very slowly because I wanted to keep the street blocked so they couldn't follow him. That was touchy and I was trying not to make it too obvious. Cindy and I knew where to meet up, so the first priority was to not get killed by these people in the next ten minutes! I blocked the street successfully and met up with Mark and Cindy about eight blocks away. We wanted to get out of there because we still were in a dangerous position in the wrong neighborhood.

"Let's get out of here NOW" I yelled to Cindy as I drove up to the car.

Cindy said she couldn't because they were out of gas.
"Oh shit!"
I quickly pulled out our gas can, emptied it, and threw it into the back of the car. I told Cindy to drive Mark's car, and get the hell out of there as quick as possible. I would follow her from a little distance to be sure the guys chasing them did not follow them. They got about two miles away and pulled into a gas station to fill up. Two miles from where the incident happened was the same as being in another city, so it was safe.

Mark told Cindy that he felt good and that there was no reason to worry because he had his act together. The words sounded right and very familiar, but he didn't have us sold. He was quick to change based on the situation, especially if drugs or girls were involved.

There was the other problem that we had; we had planned to go away to Florida for Bike Week in Daytona Beach. One of the few pleasures that Cindy and I developed was riding motorcycles on the weekends and meeting a lot of interesting people. There were ten of us going to Daytona and we were concerned about being away with Mark and how he would act. Mark knew how to ride a motorcycle and had his license, but he was a speeder. He handled the bike well, but I felt his speed would be dangerous so we always had Mark ride between Cindy and me. We were committed to go on the trip, so there was no real choice except to go and worry either there or here.

There were five cars and trailers that were loaded and we would caravan straight through for the 18-hour ride. We were all mature adults going to a big party that had ½ million motorcycles in a 20-mile area. There were vendors from all over the world for every item you could think of. The town's streets were busy with bikes and activities and everybody had a great time every year. The food and entertainment were everywhere, including female coleslaw wrestling, pig roasts, bike shows, etc. We just had no feel if Mark was going to be depressed or go with the flow. We got the answer very quickly. He was great with all of our friends on the ride down and in the restaurants. He probably got the feeling that things would be alive when one of the guys in the caravan held up a sign that read, "show us your tits!"

Although many people in the group were professionals, everyone was made of the same leather at biker events. There seemed to be a philosophy of fun and respect among all bikers in both large and small groups. We pulled into Daytona and checked into a motel where we had reservations. The motel was a three-story catwalk on the beach with a large parking lot. Most of the motels were geared for trailers of some nature since Daytona was known for racing.

It took about an hour to unload all of the bikes. Mark helped with the muscle work unloading bikes from the three trailers that our group had. It made life easier since he was the youngest and probably the strongest. He went upstairs to use the phone after the last bike was unloaded. He then told Cindy that his girlfriend, Linda, from Miami, was coming up to stay with him for a good part of the trip. It was a girl that we knew from home and she was very nice. She knew how to party, but she knew the limits. She was very respectful and was always on time when she would meet up with us. She arrived about six hours later and was like family. Linda had been on other trips with us before. After some of the usual amenities, the two of them went to some of the events and would split for hours or until the group met up with them. The only thing that she said to me was that she felt out of place. I asked why and realized that with all of the people EVERYWHERE, Linda and Mark were the only ones not in black or leather; in fact, they were the only two wearing red and yellow Hilfinger clothes!

During the stay, they tended to spend more time with the group each day because it was fun. Mark was fine with everyone for the next four days. Everyone had a great time and was very busy all the time. Linda went home after three days because she had to be at work. She hugged and kissed everyone and thanked us for a great time and she was gone. Mark stayed with the group and just relaxed.

One morning, when we were getting ready to go out for a ride, we were on the third floor balcony. Mark was leaning against the balcony facing in. He started to lean back and kept leaning until he was almost horizontal and easily could have fallen over the rail. One of the guys quickly pushed down on his legs and that pushed him to a standing position. I saw this from a few feet away. Mark said that he was in full control, which everyone who saw the incident questioned. He would have fallen three stories onto the parking lot or a car. He may have just gotten a thrill or he may not have cared. It was hard to put anyone in his shoes to have his feelings at any given time.

If anyone could have been in his shoes, that would have been the best way to try to understand, but why? What difference should it make how he felt since everyone was trying to make him feel the right way. Maybe we were just hoping that he would follow the actions and thoughts of the "normal" guys. The entire trip worked out great and everyone had developed a warmer feeling about each other.

Mark was talking about the future. He said that he was through with drugs and he was starting to feel good about himself, again. He hadn't done drugs in about three weeks and a lot of the atmosphere he was used to was away from him. He said he would like to stay in Florida. He liked the tan and the good feeling he had. He developed a very strong relationship with one of the guys, John, who was heavy into the musical band Metallica. The group could shatter your eardrums if you were not weaned on that type of music. Mark and John listened to music at night and seemed to develop a genuine friendship. John seemed especially attached to Mark because he reminded John of his own son, who had passed away about five years earlier in a freak accident. John's son would have been about Mark's age, 21, and seemed to have many of his interests and attitudes. It was neat to watch this bond forming. The pair had known and enjoyed each other's company when John and his wife were with Cindy and I on many prior social occasions. John, as well as most of our friends, was aware of the activities that were going on over the past few years in our household with Mark. It was something that was not secretive because it was too obvious. Mark hated the fact that everyone knew what was going on, but friends who were true friends could be very supportive, even if they hadn't been in our shoes.

We were open with Mark about that issue because it was now a part of his life. Mark knew that he would always be an addict and that there would always be meetings to go to. He had seen many of the people at the meetings he attended who had been sober and lost it only to have begun again. It was not a great thought for a 21-year old to be labeled for the rest of his life, but drugs and their effects were a reality.

Everyone hated to see the trip end, but it did. The drive home took about 16 hours. It took less time because we didn't caravan. Cindy and I were tired, so Mark drove a good portion of the way. Since we were exhausted and knew Mark was a good driver when he was straight, we were able to sleep. Mark didn't help with the drive down because we weren't comfortable not knowing if he was high or not, or depressed or not. He drove about six or seven hours and that made the trip home easier. The difficult part was waking up to his music on the radio. When we were awake, it was great to speak with him because he was making sense for the first time in years. His attitude reflected all of the ways he used to maneuver the shrinks in the rehabilitation centers. We joked about some of the stuff he did to get brownie points and get exactly what he wanted. Mark told us about some of the people that helped him when he was out as well as some of his scary experiences. He opened up as though it was his confession. He was happy that Brenda and Mike were away because he needed time to straighten himself out. He said that he did miss Mike, but it was best this way for a while. He was right because he actually didn't know what a relationship was. That was not unusual because today, many young adults, as well as older ones, don't know what goes into making a strong relationship.

We arrived home safely on the 16th of March and were feeling great. We asked Mark to help us unload the bikes and unpack the car. He not only helped, he basically did it with very little help from us and he did it the right way by taking care of things rather than the usual rough 'let's get it done' attitude. That was one of the better night sleeps that we were going to have. Mark made a few phone calls and basically spent the evening with us reminiscing about the trip. He said it was great that he had freedom with the adults as well as our company, when he wanted it. He called all of his friends and told them how cool it was with all of the neat bikes and the bikers, who were nice guys. This was the happiest he had been in a long time. He had no real worries and felt like he could continue being a responsible adult.

It was the 17th and we were back at work. Mark was looking at other job situations in the newspaper. He made lists and was systematically calling for jobs. He still liked the idea of working with animals, but also thought that a supermarket could work for him because he knew the workers eventually made money. There were a few markets in the area so he wouldn't need a car. He was thinking that he could start to save. He also realized that if he worked for something, it would mean more to him and he would get self-satisfaction. He was thinking that Mike would have a father that he could respect. He actually was excited to see us when he got home so that he could tell us his ideas and plans.

The 19th of March, Cindy and I went to a show at one of the local convention centers. It was a craft show that was for three days, but we went for the evening to observe and look around, enjoy the vendors, and probably buy some items that we didn't need. Mark told us that he was going out that night, but he would be in early, about 9 p.m., because he had calls to make for the jobs early the next morning. We were out late that night, but we called home at nine, then 10, then 11, then midnight. We realized that our problems started again because there was no answer on the phone. We got home about 2 a.m., and were very uneasy. Mark was gone again and we were thinking that we were back to square one. We were so up from his attitude of the previous three weeks, but we should have known better. We tried to perceive what was in our best interests and what we would like to happen. In fishing, they call it baiting the hook. Mark didn't mean to suck us in, but that was the nature of addicts, and Mark believed he was fine.

Each day we waited for the usual call to come and get him, but it didn't come. It was three days and we were busy at work making up for lost time so our days went by rather quickly until we had time to think after work. When that happened, time stood still. There was absolutely nothing we could do to take our minds off of the situation. Our thoughts would travel from one scenario to another. There were some very ugly thoughts. What made it worse was that we that we had just spent that great week getting to know him again in a wonderful atmosphere, with very little pressure.

On the evening of the 22nd, Mark called and asked to be picked up. He was near the same police station where the bums slept on the floor in the heavy drug areas. Cindy went down by herself so that Mark and I would not get into a conflict. She picked him up and brought him home about 8 p.m. He was completely depressed. He was disappointed in himself. He told us that he had to pick himself up, go to the meetings, and believe in himself. We told him how proud we were of him being straight for the last three weeks and how we felt that he was turning it around and that this was just a setback, but there was no further harm done. We lied by telling him that because we knew that he was trying so hard, there was still a little bit of trust that was built up. We didn't spend too much time with him that night because we felt that I would start to lecture him again and he knew what I would say, so why say it and get blown off or politely listened to. The thing he wanted most was a shower and sleep. I was not happy with him or the timing since we were all so upbeat.

We held off eating dinner since we knew the routine. After he was home for about ½ hour and had his shower, Cindy called for him to come to dinner. He said that he wasn't hungry, but Cindy insisted. Mark said that he was into writing and he wanted to skip dinner and write. He was a great writer and he was able to express his feelings through short paragraphs and sometimes poetry. We insisted that he come down for dinner and said that he could write after he ate. He wouldn't disobey at those times, so he reluctantly came down. He ate like a horse. The meal consisted of his favorites including a steak, mashed potatoes, and brussel sprouts. He looked exhausted and said he was going up. I said very little to him at dinner because it was said before and I was pissed every time I looked at him. We felt that a good night sleep would help him think better and more rational the next day.

We went to the office the next morning early because Cindy wanted to come home by noon to be with Mark. Mark was still sleeping when we left for the office. We were extremely busy and figured that Mark would sleep until about noon. Instead, he called the office at 10:30 a.m. He said that he was going to shower, go over to the local supermarket, and fill out an application for a job. This was typical except today he seemed more motivated by getting up early. He always called Cindy when he woke up. He had security by doing that with her. Cindy told me what he said about going for a job and doing it on his own. She knew I was happy about that, but reserved based on Mark's past actions. We were both excited that he had some motivation and it was on his own. He had a certain excitement in his voice.

Mark called back to the office five minutes later, but was not real attentive when Cindy was asking him about his plans for the rest of the day. He answered very slowly and then kept quiet. He told Cindy that he had to go and then he hung up. Cindy called back again and he answered, then dropped the phone, talked and told Cindy that everything was fine and he was going for the job. He said that he called Brenda in Boston and everything was great. Mark called the office again after another five minutes and said he was fine, but getting tired. That sounded OK, but Cindy said she wanted to go home to be sure. The next call into the office was from Brenda in Boston who said that Mark called her and sounded strange. She said that he told her to take care of Mike and never let the baby forget him. She said that he was crying over the phone and then he hung up on her. Cindy called Mark after that call and again he said everything was fine and he said he felt great, but again, he kept dropping the phone. That was strange, even for Mark.

Cindy quickly drove home because she said she was just not feeling good about her conversation. She walked into the house from the garage. She yelled for Mark. There was no response. She knew he was still home because the garage door was open.

Chapter Twenty-two

She had a bad feeling as she walked into the den off the garage. She saw Mark lying naked on the rug with his arms and legs awkwardly under him. She ran to him, bent over and saw that he was not breathing. She didn't notice anything except there was a lot of blood on him and on the floor around him. She quickly called 911 and within 15 seconds, a neighbor arrived. He was a volunteer firefighter, who was driving by our home and got the call on the radio. As soon as he walked in and leaned over, he knew what Cindy already knew. He turned to her and said, "I'm sorry,"

Cindy immediately called me at the office, crying, telling me to come home because she thought Mark was dead. I ran out of the office and yelled for my secretary to call for an ambulance to go to my home as the office door closed behind me. I ran down the hall and got to the elevators. It came instantly and I was down and in the car within two minutes. I got home within 10 minutes. As I ran up the lawn, the neighbor from the fire company, who was the first to arrive, looked at me and said, "I'm sorry." Cindy was on the front porch with another neighbor, her eyes filled with tears.

I ran past her into the house. Mark was still on the floor in a fetal position. Cindy followed me in and just hugged me. There was already a flurry of activity. The police were there and more detectives showed up within ten minutes. There were more than ten officers in and out of the house. I saw him lying there, but couldn't believe he was dead. I stood over him about a minute and then went out to Cindy, who was with a neighbor on the font porch.

She and I came back in and stood over Mark, sensing finality, but again, not believing it. We were both in a daze. We looked at each other with tears in our eyes.

The police asked neighbors to please stay out of the house. The police were upstairs as well as downstairs. They didn't know if there was a murder committed because you don't have 21-year-old men dying every day in our township. For the next five minutes, I was inside, out front, out back, and looking at Mark through each pass. The police told Cindy not to go upstairs because it was a mess.

Word of tragedy spread very quickly. Friends who saw police cars in front of our home were usually nearby to see, and in this case, console. My only emotion, as his father, was shock. It felt as if I was outside reality, although the empty feeling deep inside my stomach was real. I wanted the time to stand still, but it didn't.

The police were moving around with plastic gloves and investigative tools. The neighbors were gathering outside while the Cindy and I were just going through the motions, in a state of limbo. After about 15 minutes, we started to gain a sense of reality and looked to each other for strength. We looked at Mark, who was being ignored while all of this activity was going on around them. I went out to see a few of the neighbors who were trying to console me. They seemed more upset than we were because I guess it was something we didn't believe actually happened. I'd look at Mark laying there, waiting for him to open his eyes. I started to notice what everyone else had already seen. Mark's arm was sliced from the wrist to the shoulder on the inside of both arms. He had dried blood over his face and mouth. He obviously was bleeding and wiped his face with his blood soaked hands. There was some blood on the rug, but not puddles. Cindy and I were numb. The last twenty-one years were finalized into this scene; police going through our home, cars everywhere, but not much emotion on our part because we were in denial and shock.

Just then, a police officer came down the stairs carrying a razor blade that was the type used to open cardboard containers. It was red from dried blood. We looked closely at Mark's arms and it was obvious that he sliced up his arms with that razor. His skin was wide open about ½ inch wide and there was no blood left in his body. It looked as if he made sure that even if someone came in, there would be nothing anyone could do to prevent his actions. Although the police told us that it was a mess upstairs, I knew Cindy would want to see everything for herself. The police were firm in their recommendation that we not to go upstairs, but we were with him through his actions for the past twenty-one years; we were used to seeing everything.

As we walked up the stairs, we could see blood all over the beige rugs and the papered walls going up the stairs. When we reached the top of the stairs and looked left, we saw heavy blood next to and on our bed. It was splattered all over our rugs, over the entire hallway up to six feet high on the walls, in Mark's room on his light gray rug, and in the room where a Jacuzzi was located, which was where Mark sliced up his arms in warm water. The tub was still full of water and the water was red, not bright, but a thick darker red.

We looked at all the signs and began to visualize his actions. He filled the tub with warm water and got inside. He then sliced his arms, and waited. Warm water would help the blood leave his body quicker. We figured he got tired of waiting in the tub, so he got out, walked into his room, turned around and went into our bedroom. He picked up the phone and probably called Cindy, dropped the phone a few times, which was when Cindy knew something was wrong. He walked down the stairs struggling to keep on his feet and dragging his arms along the wall going down the stairs, and collapsing in the den where Cindy found him. The police assumed that after his blood drained, he had a heart attack.

We came back downstairs and asked the police what to do. We had no clue what the next step was, but we knew something had to be done. We needed help.

The police were wonderful. They were trying to protect us and yet, many of the police had never seen a bloody trail like this and they were having a hard time, as well. They said that when the officer felt the drain in the bathtub, the razor was there. The officers told us that the coroner's office had to take the body. Cindy immediately asked if they could skip the autopsy as the thought of him being cut up any more sickened both of us. The officers said that they would see what they could do.

We wanted to keep a part of Mark, but knew his body was leaving our home for the last time. We knew that we could only see his physical body a few more times and we wanted to stretch that time, but we couldn't. We just kept looking at him. I just paced, with my eyes never leaving Mark. Friends would try to make eye contact with me from outside to try to help, but I was not receptive to anything except seeing my son. Cindy was sitting in the hallway with her head buried in her hands, but she would also keep looking up to see Mark.

His dignity was gone, as he lay naked with strangers walking around him. This was a child who, when sober, would not leave the house without checking the mirror to be sure every hair was in place and that he looked cool.

When the ambulance personnel came in, they asked us not to watch as they prepared to take Mark away. We had to watch; we had to see what they were going to do to our son. We stood there watching as they put him inside the black plastic bag, and watched as they zippered the bag closed. We gasped for air as it was closing because we knew that he couldn't breathe inside the plastic bag. Our minds were not all together at that instant.

When the coroner came for the body, it was an awful cold feeling, deep inside, because we knew he was now leaving forever. Two medical staff carried him out in the bag on a gurney; we stood there, powerless to do anything but watch as they took our child away.

Cindy told me to stop the medical people and get the gold bracelet from his wrist. I went outside and caught them before they got to the truck. We were standing in the driveway in front of the garage. I told them what I wanted, and they nodded. I unzipped the bag and reached in and held Mark's hand, the one with the bracelet. It was our last real touch. I felt like I was holding Mark's hand and I couldn't let go.

How could I keep my son? I took the bracelet off and gently placed his hand back into the bag and zipped it up. The finality of the situation was starting to set in. Neighbors were starting to gather closer to the house, not knowing what to do, but feeling the pain of the situation. They hugged and spoke sympathetically, but again, we heard nothing. We were numb. We went upstairs and found the clothes that he last wore. We went through the pockets and expected to find a note, but we didn't. To my surprise, we found a cheap piece of jewelry that Mark had bought six months earlier; it was a charm with the initial M on it, for Mike. He could have sold it a hundred times in his adventures, but he valued it so much that it never left him. I realized that it was special, but it meant more now that he was gone. Mike will eventually know the truth and will someday have that charm. I vowed to wear it until Mike was old enough to decide if he would like to wear it or save it. It would be a sign of his father's love for him.

The police stayed about ½ hour after the body was removed to be sure we would be OK. They suggested we go to a motel for the night because of the blood in our bed and the general condition of our home. That was not going to happen. They told us that Mark was being taken to the morgue. Cindy asked why they were taking him there and they said the law required it. She felt strongly about the autopsy and again asked if the body could be released so that we could bury him. They again said that they would try to speed up the report so he could be released.

I called the funeral director, a friend of mine, and alerted him of the situation. I told him we would call him a soon as Mark's body was released. We knew that we would have to make plans for the funeral as soon as the next day. Our ideas were always similar, but Cindy weighed the options more and discussed them while I made quicker decisions. But any decisions concerning the funeral would be made by both of us, as a team. The funeral director made life easier and guided us through the painful process, because it was not a normal progression for anyone to bury their child.

After the police cars left, there were no exterior signs of what had happened. A few hours later, while we were sitting at the kitchen table, one of Mark's friends walked in and asked where Mark was. "He is dead," I blurted out, not realizing what a shock this would be to this young man, since my mind was still numbed from all that had happened.

We had not realized that his friends didn't know what had happened. Death was something that was tough for young, immortal people to fathom. We made some calls to a few of our immediate friends and family, but we didn't know why. It was logical, but at that point, we didn't care about anything; there was no protocol to follow.

We knew it was going to be difficult for many of Mark's friends. What could we say to eighteen to twenty year olds about the death of one of their playmates? What should we say to them? I did notify three or four of his friends, although it was amazing how quickly the word spread on its own.

We stayed home that evening, mostly sitting at the kitchen table in view of the front door. We had no problem sleeping in the house because we raised Mark there and he was comfortable enough to end his life there, so why leave? It wouldn't make the pain any less and we've faced all the problems head on before, so we felt that this was no different. When the police were in and out of the house most of that day, we asked them if there was someone we could get right away to clean the walls and remove the rug. The officer in charge said that the clean-up group would have to be from an infectious disease control team because of the blood. The blood and the areas hit by the blood had to be disposed of in a certain way. There were only two such qualified groups in the area. The control team was encouraged by the police department to come out that evening. They arrived in suits that appeared to be from another planet. They had gloves, masks, and special bags with medical markings to show that special disposal was necessary. The team of four men worked fast and hard. They were sensitive to what happened only hours earlier. They tore up most of the rugs, ripped off wallpaper in most of the house because Mark bled on most of the walls. It appeared that Mark hit veins and arteries based on the location on the blood. In talking to the police, we figured that reviewing the path mentioned earlier and the entire situation, it took Mark 45 minutes from the time he made his cuts until the time that he died.

We tearfully went to bed about two a.m., but just laid there. We thought that when he wanted to write the note the previous evening and we wouldn't let him because it was dinnertime, he was going to write a suicide note. Looking back now, we feel certain that it was his plan.

We had comfort that he ended his life in the home he grew up in because he was comfortable there. We would have had a harder time if he were found in some dumpster in the middle of a drug area. We were trying to find closure, or at least a sense of continuation with his methods of life. He was not trying to hurt us by killing himself in our and his home. He did what seemed natural to him.

By lying in bed that night, our senses were dull, but our insight was sharp. Mark told both of us that he was so high on life the past three weeks that when he slipped, it was a long fall. He didn't have the time or energy to climb back from the bottom to the top. He knew how good he felt with a purpose in life and with dreams such as he recently had. The reality of where he was and what he had to do was too much. He knew we were always there to pick him up. We hoped that he would grow out of it, but addicts didn't grow out of it; they work out of it!

There would always be the thought of what would have been in the suicide note. It probably would have left a direct message for Mike; or maybe a chance to explain everything to Cindy; or … The police were successful in getting his body released quickly and the funeral director picked him up and brought him to the funeral home for preparation. We went to the funeral home the next morning to be with him again for a few minutes when we learned he was there.

The funeral was planned for three days later. We went to the funeral home with clothing for his burial. Cindy chose one of his favorite outfits that was very casual. She figured that he should be relaxed on his long journey. We planned to have an open casket, as he looked fine, except you could still see evidence on his lips of his crack smoking. They were slightly burned and chapped. He actually looked peacefully content. The funeral was divided into a mismatch of religious beliefs (Catholic, Jewish, and Quaker), but it was what Cindy and I wanted in order to try to make sense of the situation to all of the people, including and especially the young adults and his friends. We hoped that it could be a wake-up call that would do someone some good.

Brenda arrived the night before the funeral and stayed at our home. She was distraught and said she didn't have a clue that he was going to kill himself.

In the morning, the three of us arrived early at the funeral home, and visited with him in private, before the doors opened to his friends. The three of us stood over him and took pictures of him with each of us standing and bending over him. We left pictures of Mike with him in the casket. We wrote him a note telling him what we always told him; "We love you." We kissed him and cried.

We then had a 2-hour viewing that started at 9 a.m. This would allow some people to come and leave right away. Others had the opportunity to stay, if they wanted to.

After the viewing, people went out to their cars and Cindy, Brenda and I stayed and watched as the casket was closed. We were with him from birth to death, and we wanted to be with him at the end.

We drove to the cemetery in a procession. We asked that the burial at the cemetery be private because there were more than 300 people who came to say their last respects. Secretly, there were many who said to each other that now Cindy and

I could get on with our lives! Although it may have sounded heartless, we understood people who were concerned and cared for us said it.

There was only room for about thirty cars at the cemetery. We invited our close friends, and allowed many others who asked to be present.

Our friend, the funeral director, told us that we should use a limousine for the trip, but I said that we followed him his whole life and we were capable of the final trip. We were in our car following the vehicle with the casket and as they made a turn near the drug area, I commented to Cindy that Mark was probably in the casket yelling to take a right for his final hit. We laughed a sick laugh, but that was how we coped with many of those times.

At the cemetery, we chose not to have a religious leader. We felt that we could tell of our love for him from a letter that we composed the prior night. It said it all, but one could never really say it all to a 21-year-old child. I asked that one of our friends stand by me in case I couldn't get through the letter and that he read the balance if necessary. Cindy was not able to read the letter or do anything other than try to stay somewhat composed and teary eyed. I read slowly and, with short periods to get composure, read it in its entirety. It read as follows:

Dear Mark;

We guess this is your way to start over. You look restful and peaceful. We love you and we always will. You always said that your business was private so read the letters we put next to you. You gave us 21 years of love, excitement, trauma, fun and every feeling one can think of. We will always remember you as you, our son. This burial is only a symbol of your new life. You are here, next to your grandmom, so you have family with you. You will never be alone. Somehow, this doesn't seem right. Parents should bury parents, not their children. You were always older than your years and you lived many lifetimes in the short time you were on this earth. Your friends are all here, and yes, everyone really loved you. May God give you eternal rest and peace.

We love you.
Say hello to our dogs. We will see you later. Leave us a note
on the table where you are and don't forget to call us.
We love you,
Mom and Dad

We then felt that the 23rd psalm would be appropriate and I proceeded to lead everyone at the close of the service. About half way through, I forgot the words to a prayer that I had said a hundred times over and needed help to finish. At the conclusion, we felt that the Quaker way of opening the field to comments was a good feel. A few people made comments, but it was very unorthodox to mix all of those concepts and in this type of situation, everyone wanted familiarity, not creativity. We felt good and did what was comfortable to us. Everyone was invited back to our home for the balance of the day and there were trays of food to accommodate all that came. Mark's friends decided not to go to the cemetery. It seemed like it was good for them to remember him "above ground" in a quiet sleep. They came back to the house later that day to just be there. They had no idea what to say so they would make eye contact with us and that said it all.

There were many ways to look at this, and each way made sense depending on one's perception at that time. The hard parts to figure out were that twenty-one years of caring and building have turned totally to shit and were now a memory. Memories were the things that we were supposed to have from parents who died, not children. All of the building for the future was gone; there was no future. The future was now finite because children were the one's whom we built on to leave our "legacy." In our case, we were lucky because there was a grandchild, but who knew what could happen two generations down? All of the scraping of bruises, hugging, loving, training, little league, family dinners, etc. were gone. They were a memory. All of the aggravation was a memory.

Maybe it could have been looked at as his destiny. He was troubled. Mark loved us and knew that he was dragging us down and ruining our lives. That made him more depressed. He hated getting off his high to face himself, reality, and us. He said many times that he didn't want Mike to grow up with drugs and have a drug addict father. He had a conflict that he couldn't win and he knew it. Probably the love and care that Cindy gave him kept him alive an extra two, three or four years, but who really knew. You just had to believe whatever would help to get you by.

When Mark died, part of us died. It wasn't buried with him, but it was dead. You couldn't say what it was, but when you went to the supermarket and saw his favorite food that you always bought, you felt a penetrating effect and tears forming. When you looked at the pictures that you were saving, you asked yourself "why you were saving them?" Look at the dishes, bank accounts, cars, jewelry, and you ask the same question, why? Why were we saving those or what should we do next? What is the future or what was the past? Which would we be living in for the next few years, the past or the future?

Brenda went home right after the funeral. She had come in with her aunt and cousin; the three of them stayed at our house. They were going to attend the funeral, but the cousin got sick and threw up all over the rugs. It added more stress to the situation, but we brushed it aside, thinking at least their intentions were good. Brenda left Mike in Boston, which made sense because at eleven months old, a funeral was not a place for him to be.

People came to the house for about a week after the burial, and calls were received to check on us to see if we were coping with what happened. For a while, the calls were constant, but when the calls ended, we still were on the same page as before. People meant well, and it was good to have company so that we didn't bury ourselves in grief and pity. We tried to get to work at least part of the day as soon as possible. Whenever either of us was alone, we just did whatever activity we were involved in, and tears just ran down our faces. It could have been going to pick up milk or walking to get the mail or anything. Mark's friends made it a point to come over each night and sit around. We found comfort just knowing what the kids were doing.

I made it a point to bring up Mark's name so that they were all comfortable with his life and death. It was interesting because his friends would tell us things that we didn't know about some of Mark's activities. We laughed about it and inevitably, Cindy would have tears in her eyes and the guys were always quick to give her a hug. She needed it from the kids. We were told by friends not to go through pictures or clothes for a while until we got adjusted. Cindy did go through his clothes right away. She asked a few of his friends if they wanted any shirts, pants, or shoes, which some of them accepted.

I decided that we would keep a few pieces for Mike in case he felt that he wanted to eventually wear or have something from his dad. I was wearing the charm that Mark never sold. From the day of the funeral, I wore that charm around my neck. It was something that Mark cherished and some day, Mike probably will, too.

I tried to think of all the rehabs that Mark went to and came up with five. They did nothing for him except teach him the seriousness of life, death, and what reality was about. They taught him how to die, not make half-hearted attempts. They gave him choices to make. They did what they could do. They were real!

Cindy tried to think of all of the cars that he had, even for short periods of time, which she counted at thirteen. We tried to count the number of jobs he had and the schools that he attended. We gave up trying to figure out the number of times he went on drug binges. We couldn't count the clothes that were "lost" in the drug districts, except that we felt that we indirectly clothed the entire district. We knew that we did our best and gave him love, but it wasn't enough. We knew that he loved us, but I guess that wasn't enough, either.

After the first week, the house was empty and there was a quiet atmosphere. We were there for each other, but we each shared the loss and the pain differently. Cindy looked at everything and tears flowed while she continued her activities. I stayed close to give her support, but lost it every time I was alone in the car. There was nothing to do except start to talk to him as if he were next to me. You're not sure whether to look up or down when you do talk to him! You tell him that you understood that he had to do it and you were happy that he was at peace. You wondered if he would be able to talk to Mike and guide him down the path that he wanted to follow, but couldn't. Even today, when in the presence of anyone watching or discussing the Disney movie, Lion King, I choke and tear up when the monkey tells Simba that his father is with him. I actually try to avoid seeing that movie as it is too real and eventually, Mike will say that his father is with him. Every move that we made referred to Mark and we joked that he wanted us to have our freedom to do any activity that we were planning. We decided that we must get ourselves together, but we also felt that we were.

Each day, we got many phone calls and letters from friends and acquaintances from Mark, and each one was a very slow read. The mail was painful when the letters would be for him and would be offering him credit cards because that always and instantly had you dreaming of the future, and there wasn't one for Mark. Mail actually came for Mark more than five years after his death. Letters from friends, in the same position of losing a child, poured in. We knew many of these people for years and had no idea that they had buried a child. We saved some letters with the thought of responding, but the words could never come out. The feelings were so deep that we just absorbed them. It was a shame that those people couldn't realize how closely those letters were read and how much comfort they brought. Some letters just meant a lot because of the long-term relationships. Here are a few of those letters:

Dear Ed & Cindy,
I have just recently been told of Mark's death. I am so sorry that he chose that way to end his pain. Mark was a special person that I loved. I respected his enormous intelligence

and his humor, which was an innate gift. Every once in a while, he would reach through the seemingly impenetrable wall he had built around himself and I would see genuine sensitivity and love. I know that he knew of your unconditional love for him and he loved you both very much as well. I am sorry for your pain and sorrow. As anyone who knew him, he will remain in my heart, and I will miss him. Love, Jennie

Dear Ed & Cindy
My mother telephoned me last night and informed me about Mark; I am so sorry to hear of your loss. I only wish... I have to admit that I have never written a letter like this before, but after hanging up from my mother last night, I felt it had to be done. Since I went away to college, I really hadn't spoken to Mark too frequently, and because of this, the news of his death didn't fully affect me until I began to think about our childhood. Mark had been one of my best friends throughout Little League, Junior High, and Basketball leagues. When I began to think about all of those years and how truly great they were, I cried for a long time. I think back to all of the times we swam together and goofed off at baseball practice; these are memories that I have of Mark, the one's I will cherish forever. I'm sorry I couldn't be there. Take comfort in knowing that Mark is at peace.
Respectfully, Charles

Chapter Twenty-three

We were adjusting and looking toward the future. We decided to go to Boston about a month after the funeral and visit Mike for his first birthday. We took one of Mark's friends, Danny, with us. Danny knew Brenda's family and was spending time with Cindy over the past four weeks. Danny friend said that Mark changed his life and that he will always be there for Mike as Mark would have wanted him to. He knew that we talked openly about Mark and it was probably great therapy for him, also. We drove up and stayed in a motel about four miles from the grandmother's house. We tried to blend in and see Mike, who knew us, but there were a lot of distractions, which was fine, because he was in his new environment.

We stayed outside in the backyard as much as possible because of the smoke. The grandmother had promised us that there would be no smoking in the house because of Mike. Then they told Cindy that they had ashtrays that absorb the smoke. Then it was forgotten. The house was a smoke shop! This seemed to be typical of decisions that took place in that household.

I noticed that Brenda was never home. When we asked, we were told that she went out, Brenda's grandmother, the one who raised her, was taking care of Mike. When we went into the house, her grandmother had a cigarette in one hand and a can of beer in the other. We tried to ignore the surroundings and hoped Mike was getting lots of love and being taught right from wrong.

Instead, we found that he was being passed off to whoever wanted him. There was no schedule of meals or sleep. His life was basically revolving around whoever's schedule he was with. Cindy felt empty seeing his new lifestyle. He was not our child, and our suggestions were not welcome.

Besides, Brenda was telling everyone that she was the mother and she made all decisions herself. Unfortunately, she still had no basis to make any decisions. She allowed Mike to keep the bottle in his mouth throughout the night, although it was strongly suggested that it would rot his teeth. She refused to listen. By the time he was three, Mike's teeth had major root canal work, as well as total decay from the nipple and from milk lying in his mouth.

He was constantly hearing the words "fuck and shit" in everyday vocabulary. We left Boston and came home. We got very depressed and frustrated when we phoned there, so we didn't call often. Besides, Mike was still too young to speak with us.

Six weeks later, we went back to Boston to visit once again. We saw absolutely no progress in Mike's situation. We feared our grandchild's life was going to be wasted without any value systems, especially growing up in this mostly trashy situation. Our concerns were justified; Brenda was going nowhere and she wasn't even looking for a job. She was sleeping until noon every day. Mike was removed from her bed in the morning by her grandmother when he woke up crying. Brenda did not move or even stir when he was crying, right beside her.

Brenda's father, Joe, was on and off drugs again. Her brother was awaiting a hearing on selling drugs. Her mother was in jail again on heroin and theft charges. The good news was Brenda's aunt, who lived down the street, was out of jail. The bad news was, the aunt was buying Mike presents with stolen Toys R Us dollars. We found this information out from relatives of Joe's side of the family. These people also stayed clear of Brenda's relatives unless they were thrown together at a family function.

Brenda was always sleeping from boredom, and never tried to get a job. Even in high school, Brenda's grandmother would tell everyone that Brenda was in school, but she was sleeping. Education was not a priority. Most of Brenda's girlfriends were pregnant or already had kids. Also, in her family, just graduating high school was a major feat. No one ever even considered college as an option.

After visiting and seeing Mike's daily situation, Cindy and I decided to offer Brenda the opportunity to come back to live with us. She could get her GED, a job, and basically have the opportunity to give Mike a better life with a better education. We told her that she was young and should date, but should also keep in mind that her actions now reflected on both her and Mike. We explained that the rules of the house were liberal, but Mike had to be her first thought and concern. She agreed and came down. It was an easy transition for her. She already knew many people from the area because of the time she had been here with Mark.

About a month after she moved in, Cindy invited her and

Mike to go to Disney World. We were driving down there for a vacation. We already had the room, so it was no extra cost, since we were buying their food at home anyway. Also, it was nice to see Mike's face as the characters approached him. He was in awe, because each time he saw a character, it was his "first time." He wasn't afraid and actually enjoyed all of the action. Brenda appeared bored, and actually said that she did not want to be in EPCOT because "she was on vacation and didn't have to learn." Obviously, we knew that we were dealing with a genius! We enjoyed the rest, the swimming pools and all of the summer activities. Cindy and I enjoyed being with Mike, but Brenda was bored, saying she needed to be entertained, too. It was like having a big kid jealous of the younger child.

We arrived back home and began to assess the situation. Brenda was now nineteen years old and was starting her life over, with a wonderful baby boy. Brenda was able to drive one of our cars, when we weren't using it, so it would allow her to get a job and do something. We were babysitting every night for Mike. We were patient with Brenda, thinking she was getting acclimated, so our sitting was not a problem. We were also hoping that it would allow her to develop a better social life in this area. Cindy was treating her like our daughter. She felt it would improve Mike's life if his mother found stability. We agreed that she would enroll in school and go for her GED here, although we were told she dropped out of her GED classes in Boston. Maybe this area would be more convenient. She agreed to get a job during the day to get off of the welfare rolls, which she constantly told us she hated to be a part of. Because of Mark's death, Brenda was getting SSI (Social Security income) payments for Mike of $145 per month from the government. The money was to be used for the child's needs. However, Mike never saw a penny of that money; Brenda spent it on cigarettes, gas and clothes for herself. When that check came in, it was spent within 48 hours. Between SSI and welfare, she had no reason to work and no expenses except her own. Cindy paid for day care, which was $125 per week. Cindy drove him there every day because Brenda was sleeping. When Cindy tried to wake her, she would not get up and would mutter to leave her alone. Cindy would pick him up from school because Brenda was out with friends and couldn't make it back early enough to get him.

Brenda was advised that the rule for her was to have self-respect and use good moral judgments. Based on whoever's value system was used, that was a very difficult rule for her. She was used to sleeping with whomever and whenever, and the 'buddy system" around her did the same, so that was her accepted system of morals.

The reason Brenda's moral standards were concerning us was that we shared a bathroom with her. Although it is a delicate matter, it did make us squeamish to think the toilet seat might not be clean. It was not a comfortable situation, and those speculations were infringing on our minds and sanity.

Cindy noticed that Brenda was living on Ambesol, a painkiller. She questioned what was wrong and Brenda, who told her that she had a major toothache and part of one tooth had fallen out. We were sympathetic to this young girl who had no one to turn to, so we felt her future might be brighter if she still had her teeth. We contacted a friend of ours, who was a dentist, and asked for a favor. He took X-rays of her mouth and told us to sit down. I knew that was not a good sign. He told us that she had not been to a dentist in years and all of her teeth were decayed. He could save most of them, and even with our friendly discount, it would still cost $7,000. It was time to make a long-term decision because that was a ton of money. Cindy and I were working our asses off playing catch-up from all of the monetary losses from Mark.

We realized that Brenda was being treated as family and was going to be around for a long time. She was Mike's mother and the odds of her meeting a successful, future husband and father for Mike, decreased substantially if she had no teeth! We bit the bullet and told the dentist to go ahead. Brenda was happy. The work would be done in a few visits, but a lot of work would be done at each appointment. I told her we would help her to get her teeth back in shape, but that the follow up regular appointments and cost, would be her responsibility.

After not going back for any check ups, her teeth were hurting again. I told her about a local teaching hospital clinic that was free and also, good. The only problem was that she had to wait and it could take ½ a day to be seen, if she was not there early. She said that was fine and went there for an emergency visit because that could speed up the process. She never bothered to go back for any routine work and her teeth slowly began to decay again. It was difficult to watch because she was attractive, but based on her entire family's teeth, she was not going to look good very long. It also made me feel like a fool for wasting all of that money.

The next thing we did was review jobs with her. We told Brenda never to quit one job until another was found. We kept telling her that we were concerned about Mike and his schedule, lack of stability with eating, and different late night hours she was keeping with him. We looked at each other and realized she was referencing her childhood background, which was so foreign to how we thought things should be done. We figured she didn't even know how to plan a healthy daily schedule for Mike.

With Brenda's permission, Cindy took Mike to a well-known family pediatrician for a complete examination. We were all pleased because he was slightly above average in both height and weight. We felt good because we didn't want him seeing a clinic doctor if the private one was available. Brenda agreed with our thinking.

Brenda started a job in a local pizza chain as a waitress. I thought this job might be great for her for a few different reasons; she could do better than minimum wage, gain some social skills, possibly meet some people to begin a different circle of friends, and learn a trade. This all made good sense to me, at least philosophically. Brenda saw things a bit differently. She hated it. She told Cindy that she didn't like being a waitress because people were always telling her to do things like get them water or silverware or things like that. It didn't take us too long to figure out that this job was not going to be a "keeper."

Brenda was fired within two days. She said she forgot to show up at work. Cindy and I went away for a long weekend and got that news and more, when we got home. Brenda told us that she was bailing her new boyfriend out of jail for dealing drugs. We told her that was not the type of man that she should be looking for. Cindy was told, in a nice way, to mind her own business, which she did. Brenda was nineteen and Cindy and I were OLDER! Hell, what did we know? We didn't even know who the wildest rap artists were!

Brenda looked in the paper for another job, but was spending more time just enjoying her boyfriend, Carlos, who I was tolerating. He was polite, but even if I had patches over both my eyes, I could see his sleazy manner. I figured Brenda would wake up, not because we didn't like him, but more important, because all of her friends said this guy was no good. I checked on his record and found out that he was in trouble with the law as a juvenile, but his father had some pull and got it wiped off the record.

Brenda got another job. This time, it was cleaning new homes. This was good because she had no bosses around and she could work at her own pace using a checklist. She was able to do two homes a day and make as much as $100 per day. That lasted about two weeks. She decided she only wanted to work ½ days for $50. She started smoking in the new homes and mysterious burn marks showed up on the new carpets. The company also complained that the bathrooms were not cleaned properly. Brenda started calling out from work saying her babysitter didn't come in. That was untrue because Cindy was ALWAYS there. The real reason Brenda didn't go to work was she was too tired from her prior night of partying. Brenda was fired and never turned in the cleaning equipment that was supplied to her, like the vacuum cleaner. Judging from my experience with Brenda in our home, I would have bet that she had no idea how to even turn it on!

Two months later, Brenda wrote an application for a position as an aid in a day care center. The application was all lies, including the section about her high school graduation. Mike was allowed to attend free, but it was decided that since he was happy and doing well, why change him from his present center? Also, in the back of Cindy's mind, she knew that the job wouldn't last, so why disturb Mike's stability. The day care kept pushing her to supply proof of her high school degree. After about six weeks, they gave Brenda a choice of either leaving or producing the degree. Since there was no degree, she was history and back on the welfare roles. This did not bother her. Her partying was every night and the hours were later and later. Some nights, she didn't bother coming home and just called Cindy to tell her to take Mike to the day care.

Now, Mike was one year and nine months old, and Brenda was pregnant with Carlos' baby. We were undecided as what to do, tell her family or mind our own business? Our belief was that if you did something good or bad, confess or just don't do it in the first place. One week after she told us, we decided to tell her family in Boston. I was shocked by the response. We were told that this was her third pregnancy since Mike was born. She had one miscarriage in New York and one other abortion that was another child from Mark. She did not want Cindy to know about that one. Since Mark was dead, she didn't know how Cindy would feel about aborting the last child Mark would ever father. To this day, Brenda has no idea that we were aware of that abortion. Our feelings would have been to question how stupid she was to get knocked up again from Mark, who had nothing but problems. We would have told her that it was her business, but question if it was fair to Mike to raise a second fatherless child. Brenda honestly felt that abortion was a form of birth control, which technically, it was. Cindy had, in the past, taken her to the doctor for birth control pills and condoms. She had a tendency to forget to take the pills and told Cindy that her boyfriend did not like using condoms. We were told that Carlos had another child with a girl that he doesn't see, and that he was already a deadbeat dad. That child was the same age as Mike, and also was named Mike. This man was not a favorite of Cindy and me. Brenda seemed to care more for him than her she did for own son, and chose to be with Carlos every night. Carlos usually had some type of job and held it for three to six months. I knew how close Brenda was getting to this "man", so we reminded her that what she did outside of our home was her business, but we did not want any men in her bed for Mike to see.

If and when Brenda came home at night or very early in the morning, she would take Mike from his bed, usually wake him up, and put him in bed with her. We asked why she did that, and her response was that she wanted to spend time with him and she didn't like to sleep alone. I guessed there was a difference between time and quality time, but Brenda did not know the difference. It was getting obvious that once she felt independent, it was hard for her to take orders or advice, especially when she already knew everything! Independence was a very general word that was, and is, idolized by every teenager who came home from college after one semester. That word did not take into account family responsibility, financial independence, auto insurance, social responsibility, or most other responsibility except "me-ism."

Continuing on to the adventures of the loving and caring mother, Brenda took Mike to a friend's house. He banged into a table and came home with a puncture wound above his eye. He was fortunate that there was no major damage, but things could have been much worse. The cut was an inch from his eye. "You have to watch him at all times, he is a baby and has no idea what is dangerous," I said. I did try to resist the urge to state the obvious to her, but felt I needed to. The next night we went in to wake up Brenda and we found Carlos in her bed. I told her that it was not acceptable in our house. The reasoning was that her son should not see that type of morals from his mother. The fact was that she could go screw the 7th fleet outside of our home if that was her wishes! We knew that this sexual activity occurred when she slept at her boyfriend's house, and we knew that Mike saw much of this "activity" when he was with her. We had no control over her actions, but we did when she was under our roof.

The first rule for Cindy was to protect the child. She told Brenda that the episode with the male overnight guest will never happen again, and her boyfriend was not welcome in our home. I told him to leave. Brenda told us that if he left, she was leaving with Mike. With that, we had a very quick decision to make. If she left, Mike left. If we allowed her to threaten and blackmail us regarding Mike, we lost and Brenda would be unstoppable. We made a decision on the spot and said that it was Brenda's choice, but she should think about the ramifications of her actions. She couldn't think that far ahead and she packed in ten minutes and was gone.

Chapter Twenty-four

The effect of her walking out was devastating to both of us. We pictured Mike in the slums with no food and no parental care. We knew we had to make the decision we did. We weren't second-guessing ourselves, but we were thinking about the impact of our decision on the child. We were empty inside and each thought was worse than the one before. Brenda quickly moved in with Carlos. We found out that Carlos' father lived in the same one bedroom apartment. The more we learned, the worse it became. We came to the conclusion that Brenda felt more comfortable around alcohol, cigarettes, drugs, no educational pressures, no rules, and a freedom of nightlife. Mike was three and able to see things and ask questions, but her activities were not the norm for a child. We had to do something when we found out that drugs were a part of her life and could soon become a part of Mike's.

We were feeling Mike's pain. It was a realistic attitude that was learned through first-hand observation and interaction with Brenda. If someone handed Brenda a high school diploma, she would take it and proudly announce that she graduated. She would also expect presents and resent you if you didn't give her what she thought that you should. That was not a caring and mature individual. She called us back two days later to say that she was coming for the rest of her clothes. We asked about Mike and if she wanted his clothes? Her reply was "Oh yea, I'll take them too!"

This was the mother who now was going to be with her bedmate and take care of Mike? This was the person who couldn't hold a job, when every store had help wanted signs. This was the person who had to go out every night. This was the person who didn't give a damn about the welfare of her child. This was the person who was so in love that she told everyone that just because she was living with this guy, and had her child there, she was still going to go to the clubs at night. Cindy was told about Brenda's activities from many of her girlfriends, who knew that Mike was not being cared for, and that Carlos was a closet cocaine user.

With all of the information that we were given, we decided that we must get more verification. We investigated and found it all to be true. She was leaving Mike in homes where he knew no one and the main language spoken was Spanish, which Mike did not understand. This had to be giving Mike a real security problem, and it probably created a sense of fear, also.

Initially, Brenda said we could see Mike, but we had not seen him for about two weeks. She seemed to be making sure we couldn't. We were concerned about his safety; he had no crib and was, in some cases, being watched by known druggies!

Cindy went to the day care where we had Mike registered to see if Brenda continued to bring him there. The answer was sometimes she did, but always late. We assumed that meant the days a "babysitter" wasn't available, the day care would do. Cindy visited Mike at the day care for three days when Brenda was at a new job, although that was not the policy the day care encouraged. The people who worked there knew the situation, and closed their eyes for the fifteen or twenty minutes that Cindy. During those three days, Cindy noticed that Mike had different cuts and bruises to both eyes, and on his forehead. The bruise to the right side of his forehead was the size of a fist! The teachers noted the injuries, but were powerless. They could have been caused while he was playing with other kids. Cindy was told that Brenda had left strict orders with the day care that she was the mother, was independent, and was to be the only person to pick up her son. We were not permitted to pick him up anymore. She did make one exception. She gave permission for Carlos to pick him up. That was the boyfriend who recently was in jail on assault and drug charges! That was the boyfriend who was driving on a suspended license. The day care center was upset because they were used to us doing the picking up, the conferences, and the deliveries. The center also didn't want to become involved in a domestic situation. I found out that one reason they didn't wish to become involved was fear of Carlos, knowing that he had a history of violence, and they had their own families to protect.

A week later, a stranger knocked at the front door. I opened it and the man introduced himself as Sandy Minten, a private detective and former state trooper. I was impressed and he asked me if he could come in. I asked for and received ID. Sandy said he had questions that he wanted to ask us about Brenda. We were always very open with anyone and were at the point of not knowing if she did things to involve us, so the truth seemed the right place to be. Sandy pulled a check out of his briefcase for $2,000 that Brenda had endorsed. He asked Cindy if it was Brenda's signature, and Cindy said it was. Brenda's signature was a combination of writing and printing, so it was very easy to identify. He then asked if we had something with her signature so that he could see it for himself, which we did as Cindy showed him one of the notes that Brenda wrote.

Sandy saw that we were cooperating, so he told us the reason for his visit. He said Carlos was working for a television satellite company as an installer and he stole the check from a customer's checkbook while he was doing the installation. I asked what Brenda's involvement was. He said that she endorsed the check and put the money into her bank account. I asked what was going to happen. He stated that his client was a famous sport's celebrity in the Philadelphia area and he wasn't sure if his daughter was the thief or somehow involved in the theft.

Later, I asked one of Brenda's girlfriends, Tristen, about the incident. She told me that Carlos came into our home when we were out and bragged about the theft. He said since he didn't have a bank account, he told Brenda to put the check in hers, which she did. The next day, Brenda went to Victoria's Secret and spent more than $1,000 on things for herself.

I called the detective a week later to see what was happening and Sandy said that the case was airtight against Brenda and Carlos, but the client did not want to prosecute because he didn't want the publicity. It was also ascertained that his daughter was not involved in the theft. The money was not important to the celebrity. Brenda had no idea of how we became aware of the details of the check.

I asked Sandy if any of this information could be used in the custody situation and Sandy said that his client preferred to keep the situation confidential. I asked Sandy to talk to the client and appeal to him to help us save Mike's life and that appeal was ignored.

After ten days, Brenda called and said that she was sorry for what happened and she wanted to come back. We welcomed her to bring Mike back with her. We were afraid the past was going to be part of his future if nothing was done. We didn't know how long this would last, but Mike was temporarily safe.

Mike's daily schedule was not getting better. When Mike woke up screaming, Cindy took him out of bed, dressed him, fed him breakfast, packed his lunch and drove him to day care by 9 a.m. He spent the day there, where he was very happy, stimulated and learning. Cindy picked him up at 5 p.m., came home to prepare dinner for Brenda, Mike and me, and then did the dishes. Brenda would take Mike upstairs after dinner to give him a bath and put him to bed. She wouldn't read to him. She did let him watch Barney tapes while she talked on the phone. She put him in bed and got dressed to go out or let Cindy or me play with him while she then took a bath, got dressed, talked on the phone and went out. She spent little time with Mike, and certainly no quality time at all.

While Brenda lived with us, we gave her only a few responsibilities. One was to pay ONLY her long distance phone calls. At first we said she could call home to Boston every night at 10 p.m. (rates are lower then), and speak for ten minutes. However, she easily would run up bills of more than $200 per month on long distance only. We told her to either pay the bills or have the long distance shut off on her phone (she used our second phone line that we paid for). She did the same thing in Boston and the phone company shut off her grandmother's long distance service for non-payment. In Boston, she ran up a $900 bill in one month. She loved to talk on the phone. She made as many as 23 calls in one day to Boston. She was getting tired of paying for the long distance calls because we were very strict on her payment for those. She decided to try and beat the system. She called different people and used other people's numbers to charge the bills. The phone company caught her and charged her line with all of those third party calls. The phone company said that the calls were made from our lines, which they were, and we were responsible. We ended up paying for those bills, which were over $300.

As for food, she only made cereal, waffles, peanut butter and jelly sandwiches or hot dogs for Mike to eat, when she made anything. We were hoping she would feed him something more nutritious. Another problem was how she handled routine doctor visits. If Mike got a fever, she took him to the hospital emergency room. The hospital called Cindy and asked why Mike was brought in. Brenda had a doctor, but didn't call him. She also refused to pay the hospital bills.

That happened often.

We wanted her to get her degree. We sent her to school two nights a week for a cram course for her GED. School called us and asked, "Did she drop out?" She told me that she went to school every night. Obviously, she wasn't telling us the truth.

The lying was a major problem. She told a different story to every person. She told Cindy that she was going back to Boston on January 20. She told her father that she was staying with Carlos, who had a juvenile and an adult record for drug-related charges as well as assault. That was why we did not want Mike associating with him, especially since he was not reformed!

Brenda was uneducated, had no drive to get off welfare, spent the baby's welfare money on herself, and contributed nothing to benefit her child. If she did spend more than two hours with him on a weekend, she got totally frustrated and put him into bed, where he screamed until he fell asleep. She also drove her car without her glasses, which was very dangerous with her poor vision. She has had more than 10 car accidents in a three-year period. For obvious reasons, that was not a safe situation for Mike.

The next month, Brenda told us she was going back to Boston to live with her grandmother. We realized that the reason she was leaving was because she had a fight with Carlos, so Boston was her escape. We knew this was certainly not a healthy environment to raise a child. She came back a week later as she and Carlos made up. Brenda had very little self-esteem. She allowed her boyfriend to abuse her and she, in turn, would physically fight with him. At one point, he was hitting Brenda when Mike was in the room. Mike told us that he was kicking the boyfriend while he was "hitting mama." Brenda told Cindy that Mike put her pager into the toilet, but Mike told Cindy that the two of them had a fight and the boyfriend broke it on the floor.

One night prior to going out, Brenda was giving Mike his bath. The telephone rang and she left Mike alone in the tub to answer her phone in her bedroom. She did not return immediately. After her phone call ended, she came back and Mike was floating face down in the water. She quickly grabbed him and he started choking. Luckily, he did not lose consciousness, but he was scared. He clung to Cindy for a long time after the incident. The bathtub episode wasn't enough to keep Brenda home as she continued going out to clubs every night.

We knew that she was scheduled to sit for her GED test on January 19th and 20[th,] since that was scheduled prior to her leaving three weeks earlier. We also knew that she was scheduled to fly back to Boston after the exam for her grandmother's surprise 70th birthday party. She was scheduled to return on the 21st. I knew because we bought her the plane ticket months ago. We said that the exam was very important and so was the party, so it was our present to her to do both. She moved in with Carlos again the week before the exam. Since she moved out, we were not privy to her everyday schedule, so we weren't positive of what her plans were. It was funny, but those two words didn't seem to mix, plans and Brenda! We were able to find out the result the following week. Brenda exchanged her ticket so that she could leave for Boston on the 18th and return on the 22nd. She did not take the GED exam

We found out that Brenda was back in town on the 23rd. We still hadn't heard where Mike was and our concern heightened. We believed he might have gone to Boston with her, but that also had us stressed out. We spoke to Joe. We agreed that if he was at the grandmother's house, Brenda's mother might try to steal Mike and sell him for drugs.

While Brenda was gone with Mike, our minds raced. We envisioned all kinds of horrible things happening to him. We were thinking back to a time when Brenda was vacuuming the crumbs from an area where Mike ate. She purposely took the vacuum and put it on Mike's hand. The vacuum sucked in his little hand and ripped off the top layer of skin from his wrist to his fingers. It hurt him so badly that he wouldn't use his right hand for ten days, and he refused to let anyone near it. We tried to forget those things, but they came back to our minds when we got into the heat of battle, which was where we were about to embark. What bad judgment at the expense of the child! At this point, what could be said other than "that was stupid"? We kept quiet, and concentrated on nursing Mike out of his pain; the only thing that would have been accomplished if we confronted her was another major argument.

We were worried. We knew that we couldn't allow Mike's life to continue in jeopardy, so we had to do something. What was that something? Where did we start? Who did we call? What did we want? What questions didn't we know to ask? This was a good time for Cindy and I to review the situation and the players. We truly believed Mike was in danger and we needed to act on our assumptions to protect him.

We called social services, but they blew us off. They were too busy looking at more serious cases. We came to believe that family services were always playing catch up and never spending their energies trying to be preventive. Medically, everyone stressed preventive medicine, but when it came to children, it seemed to us that help only came after the harm had been done. We were thinking of the eccentric comedian Gallagher, picturing him making a statement like that and flipping his fingers through his hair wondering if someone could answer such a basic question? Most social service agencies were running into padded walls because of regulations and overworked scheduling. Please note that I did not say they worked those schedules, but just that they were scheduled. We were told of a social worker that made a scheduled emergency visit to a home because of reports of major abuse to a six-month-old baby. After making the appointment, the worker went to the house and looked into the crib only to find a healthy six-month old. End of story? NO! The abusers changed babies for the visit and to this day, the social agency hadn't a clue that there was an abused baby that should have been instantly removed. No one knows if that baby is alive today. This type of action was leading us to dead ends.

We called the politicians to get direction. We called the senator's office and were blown off with "call family services." We got the same from all of the politicians. We knew we had to do something so we called social services again and encountered the attitude that there were children being abused, so why bother the agency about a "potential problem." We called family services and received the same answers. Family services obviously never spoke to their own department or they would have been frustrated, also! We then called the police who rightfully said that there was no crime and they couldn't do anything.

We had no idea what to do next. I looked up support groups and there was one about an hour away. We spoke to a friend who was an attorney and were told that there were not really laws that were cut and dry about this sort of problem. We realized that everyone was burying his or her head. We knew there was a real problem and no one was doing anything to help us save Mike. We asked ourselves how many other caring grandparents faced this same problem. We found there were many and the numbers increased by as much as 10% nationally per year.

We looked at the many support groups listed in the newspapers, but none seemed to fit the bill that what we needed. There was one that discussed a father's fight for custody of his children, so we called them. They told me that our case had differences, but they did give us a referral to go to a place on the other side of the city called "Second Time Around Parents." The group was concerned with certain cases that involved grandparents and kids, so we made a contact. At the same time we were told from a neighbor to seek an attorney and she, being an attorney, knew of one with experience in this field. I thought that we were now in a good position because we were associated with a group, and had an attorney knowledgeable about protecting kids.

We met first with the attorney, who immediately told us that he never lost a case, and his retainer started at $5,000, which we felt was cheap to get Mike's safety. Boy, were we dumb and inexperienced!

The attorney filed for emergency custody, which got us into court within two days. It was a whirlwind. Brenda came to court with her father and a lawyer from Boston. Based on conversations we had with him at the breaks, we believed Brenda's lawyer was a very street-smart ambulance chaser. Our attorney was class and knowledge. The first thing that happened was Mike saw us and put his arms out to hug Cindy. Cindy asked Brenda if we could hold him and she impolitely said "no" and walked away! Our attorney commended us for our non-actions. We went into court and the other attorney said that he was not licensed in Pa and wanted the court's permission to represent Brenda. Our attorney said fine and the court welcomed him like a long-lost brother. When the hearing started, within ten minutes, the judge ripped our attorney a new asshole. The judge questioned his integrity on making our case an emergency and said he would still fit the case in during the day between his other cases since we inconvenienced everyone from Boston. Great, we're getting to pay our attorney a huge hourly rate while we waited for the judge to take us in between cases. We were in the courtroom three times prior to noon for a total of thirty minutes. We then went to lunch and came back at one. Each time that we went before the judge, we were losing more ground. This went on two more times in the afternoon and at 4 p.m., it was decided that we could continue tomorrow unless we could resolve everything. This changed the tide for us. In our conversations with the attorney during the break, he said he had to leave to get back to Boston because he had to go to a hockey game with his son that evening, so he had no plans on staying over.

Cindy took over the negotiations and told our attorney to keep quiet. Cindy was strong and demanding, which was not her usual attitude. She was flexing her muscles!

Brenda started with three days a month visitation for us, but by the time Cindy worked out the compromise, Brenda's attorney sold her out to get on the plane. We settled for ten days a month. In the meantime, Brenda figured that if she moved back to Boston, Cindy would be out of her life, so she moved back to Boston. She also was fighting with her boyfriend in Philadelphia, so that was her perfect opportunity. Everyone went back to the courtroom and put the agreement on record. In the meantime, we retained our attorney because if Brenda didn't honor the recorded compromise, she would be in breech and the court would correct this immediately, so we thought that an attorney was needed to do the legal paperwork.

It became a major expense for us to get anything because we were captive, inexperienced, and also frustrated. It would have made a good TV sitcom to review the logic used, but the case was over, so we thought. The courts were not too receptive to anyone except the lawyers and that was obvious by the way the judge spoke to me. When I was on the stand, Brenda's attorney, who blamed Mark's death on our parenting, berated me. Our attorney didn't object nor did the judge ask where he was going with his questions and comments. Also, I brought up the theft, deposit, and spending of a $2,000 check stolen by Carlos and cashed by Brenda. The judge asked where the copies of her deposits came from and then he disallowed them because Brenda didn't give permission for that information to be given out. Didn't the judge care about the rights and the welfare of a child?

We met with a few members and organizers of the "Second Time Around Parents" and realized all of the stress and trouble they already went through in this field that we didn't understand. All they wanted to do was to protect the children and so did we. Then the scenarios of "what if" started popping up. What if:

1. *Brenda got married and told us to get lost.*
2. *Brenda got nailed for drugs.*
3. *Brenda's boyfriend got violent with Mike.*
4. *Brenda got killed in a car crash.*
5. *Brenda physically abused Mike.*
6. *Brenda, with a history of joblessness, became homeless.*
7. *Brenda had Mike in a morality issue and taught him theft.*
8. *Brenda left him unsupervised or in immediate danger.*

What would happen to Mike? Who would he go with? His godparents were a 17-year-old cousin and the drug-dealing brother and that was not a comforting thought. We were very frustrated and still didn't know if there were any laws to protect the children. As we found out, there wasn't unless the child was battered.

We never felt this frustrated in our lives because there was no one to ask questions, no one to discuss the "what-if" situations with, no one to go to if rules were broken, and no one who was knowledgeable who could help us. We used the Internet and found the same results except for an organization in Michigan, which happened to be a state where this issue had always been in focus. We wrote to them and joined. We received a newsletter that had no application to our situation. I phoned the director, who referred us to a local woman, Diane. She was part of a national organization of grandparents who were trying for years to get legislation passed for many of the "what-if" situations. Diane also started a local support group for grandparents raising their grandchildren and people who were "lost" in our same situation.

Diane was raising her grandchild because she did get custody in a battle that took five years. It financially buried her, but she said it was worth every penny every time her grandson looks at her, and now, thanks her. I called AARP and was blown off with some more bureaucratic bullshit. Family service was not prepared to handle "before" crisis situations. Raising grandchildren groups were available, but they were only good if you already had custody your grandchildren.

We discussed the option of going to one of these support groups to try to find a tie in to our case, or just try to network.

We were more into activist situations, not support groups. We had gone to one support group as parents of Mark, and found that it was for people who couldn't get the help and understanding at home. It was for people to understand that they should not feel guilt and they couldn't control the addict. It was to advise people how not to be facilitators for the drug addict. It obviously helped many of the people, but we didn't feel it was for us. We did what we felt was comfortable and the right thing. We were able to talk to each other and resolve our concerns except the problem that there was no solution for Mike's future or Mark's past and we knew it. There was no guilt. There was no remorse. There was an empty feeling every time something came up where Mark was associated. That meant that there was still no solution to the original problem. How did we protect Mike? What was the relevant term that had been used in every article and discussion about the "best interests of the child?"

This situation went on for five months while the legal bills piled up. I fired the attorney and said we could do things ourselves. We were in contact with other people who quietly were fighting for children's rights. Cindy and I coordinated with one of the groups and started a five-county organization that grew to twenty-two counties. The purpose of the new organization was to not leave shocked grandparents and grandchildren in the same position as we were; not knowing who to turn to or what rights anyone had. The group set up attorneys in twenty-two counties and lay people in the same counties to screen the referrals so that wasted calls would not be made to lawyers giving their time pro bono. The organization was geared to function out of a local office with one full-time employee. She would fax the updated literature to both the lawyers and the lay people. We set up regional meetings to educate the attorneys on new laws, which the six original people worked on and had signed in the governor's office. The law allowed the judges lead way to consider the "best interests of the child."

It was amazing to us how many family attorneys had no knowledge of the new laws passed, that directly affected their practice. Fortunately, many of these attorneys came out to the workshops and learned as well as volunteered to be involved with the group and our function. I was pleased to see that this information helped them in their practices, also.

This work put us in the public eye. We were on TV, talk

radio, and mentioned in various newspaper articles geared toward helping keep kids safe and to prevent obviously dangerous situations.

At the point of our firing the attorney, I contacted the judge's office. The secretary said that I must have an attorney. I said we had one, and I fired him, and wanted answers that we, as taxpayers, were entitled to receive.

We were getting smarter as each day passed. We faxed a letter directly to the judge and threatened to expose the operation of his office and the treatment that we were receiving, unless we got answers. This put the judge in a precarious position that he got out of by having his clerk pacify us. We received a letter stating that there was a communication problem and that I was correct. Although an attorney was not a necessity, it could be a good idea. This sufficed temporarily, as we decided that publicity would help the organization's cause and in turn, our own personal cause.

We had newspaper and radio interviews. We had the group's literature distributed. A few of the founding members of the organization were involved in this cause years before us, and they gave us more ammunition for the press. We were on a roll with meetings and counseling phone calls. The six of us got together numerous times to plan the strategy for the organization, which inevitably would save many children from harm.

We had another bill moving forward, a bill that the members were trying to pass for eight years. It was finally coming to fruition and it was great publicity. The bill was on and off the table in congress so many times, it had scars all over it. Politicians didn't care about the elderly or the young because they didn't vote and they were not great fundraisers. The demographics of the case made it a tough to get a bill through.

It did eventually go through as part of a gay right's bill. The law, Grandparent's Custody Act, allowed for judges to give custody to grandparents if it were in the best interests of the child. Now this was a wonderful victory, but the judges in our county had no idea of the new law. Judges in other counties were educated on the new law and sensitive to the kids and their plight. Our county was still in the dark ages on these issues and didn't want to change. We were still in a dilemma! How do we educate intelligent judges about the purpose of these acts that were partially authored by our group? We went to other hearings for members of the organization and people needing our help and were starting to see some change, but it was a slow process. Judges, especially new ones, were safe leaving kids with the mother because they took no risk. The thought was " if the kid gets hurt with mom, she was a bad mom," but if the judge had the child with the grandparents, and the child got hurt, the judge would have to defend his actions on why he took a child from his mother. Win, win situation or lose, lose situation, depending upon one's viewpoint.

We saw kids that were physically hurt by mothers or dads and nothing happened to get the kids to safety. We counseled grandparents on child molestation cases and proof was obvious, but the courts didn't seem to want to take any action. It was easier to go through the motions of trying to enforce the law rather than doing it. It was frustrating because we were counseling at least 10 people a day by phone.

We were frustrated because we could see problems, give advice, but were, otherwise, unable to help. Other parents have experienced this same kind of frustrating situations over the years. We heard from parents who walked in on a daughter who had just been beaten by her boyfriend, while their grandchild was cowering in the corner. What could they do? If they took the child, without the permission of their daughter, they could be charged with kidnapping. A criminal charge could make their life miserable. They would never be allowed to see that child without supervision, when all they wanted to do was save the child they loved.

The members of the statewide organization we were working with had numerous meetings and conversations to determine the best way to achieve our goals. We were the least experienced of the six-person group, but since we were the newest, we brought new vitality seeking our goal. Unfortunately, this fact did not mean a thing. Did the lawyers know the bill? Did the judges know and understand the bill? Did the ordinary person thrown into the same situation as us have access to the bill? The answer was NO, NO, and NO! We went to township buildings, malls, churches, and anywhere that we could get a free meeting room. We set up seminars for attorneys and grandparents in similar situations and many who were lost for years chasing their tails. We met with everyone from related groups who could either transfer information or use us as a reference. We were now getting at least fifteen calls per day to give guidance. These problems and related situations were growing and help was needed. We wanted to set up the previously discussed office and a network of available help. We would hire a layperson that would receive some training, and hit the ground running. He or she would receive bulletins from the one main office, and pass on the information that was taking place elsewhere in the state. The plan was for everyone to network and learn from each other. We also had one or more attorneys in each county that was willing to give a half hour of their time, free, to determine if a case required the assistance of an attorney and if the case needed to go to court. Obviously the attorney would have the opportunity to offer his or her services. This gave him or her more reference in their field. The situation was a win for everyone, and most important, a quick response. The layperson also would have to make a decision if it was worth the referral to the attorney. If there were questions, or the layperson was in doubt, he or she would call the main office for guidance. At the office would be the salaried staff person, who was a member of the original group.

We took this plan to the original twenty-two counties. We were functional with attorneys and lay people, but we were still working from our home. The funding was coming from our savings and our own resources.

Although our purpose was noble, the funding was getting dry. We were helping a lot of people and some were asking if they could pay for postage or a few dollars for phone bills, but that would have cost more for accounting. We figured the total budget to run this program across the state, with a small office, phones, supplies, copier, fax, computer, and a one-person staff. The total operating budget for the year was $200,000. We felt that was cheap to save children's lives and to allow the grandparents an outlet to get help for either emergency or traumatic situations. The best way to do that was to hope that insurance and pharmaceutical companies would wish to fund such a noble cause. If not them, maybe banks would consider giving this program a gift for the communities across the state and any of the above were welcome to get whatever publicity that they felt would make their contribution worthwhile. Also, what a picture it could be to show the compassion that the sponsor helped create by having a child gain the security of grandma and grandpa. For these companies to spend this kind of money would be like a regular person taking a dime out of his or her pocket to buy a bum a cup of coffee. I personally went to twenty-five major corporations and still have the responses of those few who took the time to answer. The gist of what the companies wrote back was 'thank you for considering our company, but we are putting our resources into the technology of education for research.'

We felt the response that we received was a disgrace. These companies derived a major portion of their revenues from the elderly and the young. If they wished to be all encompassing, the middle-aged public was at some point going to be old, also. This was a crushing blow and basically crippled the operation. The lack of response to our plea forced us to go back to helping just the local referrals. There was a need for this plan that we envisioned. It could have worked on the same principle as before. Eventually, it would have worked better if the effort grandparents made to save their grandchildren, could have had statewide exposure, and eventually, nationwide access. The members of the group were asked to get down and dirty, and get rid of the red tape. Cindy set up a trip to pick up Mike in Boston where Brenda still was living. Cindy said that she was flying in to pick up Mike in at 8:45 a.m. on February 10, and her plan was to return to Philadelphia on a return flight at 9:30, 45 minutes after picking up Mike.

Cindy called Brenda's home and Brenda's mother answered, which sent butterflies through our stomachs. Because of her drugs and theft, as well as the court order that was supposed to stop her from living in the same house as Mike, we felt Mike was unprotected and in danger when he was in that house. Part of the court order was that her mother was not to be in the same house and definitely not without supervision on a visit. The court could do nothing since we couldn't prove that the mother was in Boston at the house. Once again, we were stuck and our hands were tied. Should we tell the judge? Tell him what? Proof was only what we physically had to show. Our words were insignificant. Should we hire a detective in Boston who proved that we were right and fly the detective down as a witness for the judge to say to Brenda, "Don't do that again?"

Brenda arrived at the airport at 9:20 a.m., just as the airplane doors of Cindy's return flight were closing. Cindy managed to get the doors open by pleading her case and returned, with Mike, to Philadelphia as planned.

Brenda's father told me that Brenda came down to Philly two days later, on the 12th, to be with Carlos. The same boyfriend she told everyone she had broken up with because, "He don't respect me!" She called and told Cindy that she was going to visit Mike on the 15th. She never showed up. On the 16th, Brenda called us to say the reason she didn't show up the day before was because she knew if she came over, Mike would cry because he missed her so much. Mike was at our home and having a great time; the 'crying' routine was another excuse for not coming. It would have been very nice to call the day of the visit, not the day after! We were used to not believing anything Brenda said, so we weren't surprised.

The 17th, Brenda stopped over with a girlfriend, Tristen, and stayed for five minutes. The next day, Mike was supposed to go back to Boston. We got a phone call in the morning that Brenda had no ride to the airport, so we volunteered to drive her since we didn't want Mike stuck in the cold somewhere. She called back about an hour later and said that Carlos was driving them. Translation: she had a fight with him and they made up so he will drive them. However, we knew he was driving with a suspended license and had no insurance. We would have made other arrangements, but we already knew Brenda would not obey any orders from anyone. The reason Brenda was taking Mike back to Boston was because Cindy and I had set it up with the court that transportation would be provided one way by each party. On the return flight, we had no say in the matter.

Chapter Twenty-five

We went to the airport the following month to pick up Mike. Brenda was coming in also, so we planned to give her a ride to Tristen's house. When we arrived at the airport, Brenda declined the ride, gave us Mike, and said Carlos was picking her up. She told Cindy that she had gotten a job as a nanny for $200 a week in Boston, which was hard to believe because in this day and age, most people checked out sitters pretty closely before entrusting someone with their children. We kept Mike for the week and during the Philadelphia stay, we made arrangements with Brenda for the following three months with adjustments for Easter and a few birthdays, but it was amiable to all. Brenda then told us that we would have to work out transportation differently on the next visit because she just got a job as a bank teller (that was a lie because she couldn't make change of a dollar without her fingers!), but we said "that's nice." We spoke to her the next week when we called to speak to Mike and were told Brenda got a new job as a 911 emergency operator. She had already established a pattern for switching jobs before she worked them. We then got a call from Joe telling me that the visitations were going to interfere with Mike's ice skating lessons, which never formally got started, but were supposed to. I told Joe to take it up with the courts.

Everything from our agenda was going as scheduled. On the next visitation when she came to Philadelphia, we got a call from Brenda from our local police station two days after Mike's arrival. She said that she was staying with Tristen while Mike was with us. Unfortunately, Carlos came into Tristen's house, pushed Brenda around, pulled a knife on her, and left her bruised. Brenda asked for and got a restraining order against Carlos to keep him away from her. When he left Tristen's house, he slashed two of Tristen's car tires. We were sympathetic, but that was not our problem! Our thought was how she could possibly put Mike into any situation with Carlos. It was at this time that she told Cindy that she was now going to medical training school to be a tech. She also told Cindy that her welfare was cut from $160 every two weeks to $102, but she could beat that by saying that her grandmother babysat and charged her for the service. So that was how to beat the welfare system!

The next month, we scheduled the normal visit. Cindy had plane tickets because we were taking Mike to Disney World. We called Brenda at seven the night before to confirm her meeting us at the airport. She said to call her back in five minutes. Cindy called back in five minutes and there was no answer. What happened? Our minds were racing because we knew something was up, but what? At 9:35 p.m., Cindy called again and reached the grandmother who said we were not getting Mike tomorrow. Cindy told her that we had the letter from Brenda saying everything was arranged and all of our plans were confirmed. I was pissed, depressed, and wanted to kill someone. How could people be that inconsiderate and irresponsible and deprive their child of a wonderful vacation?

We realized that we were at war. We could care less about the trip, but it was the thrill of seeing our grandson's face when he saw Mickey again. The first thing I did was call our fired attorney. By the way, being a family attorney could suck if he gives out his home number, which he did. He was furious at the situation so he went to the courthouse at 11 p.m., found a judge and had the emergency court order delivered to Boston an hour and a half later. You don't want to know the cost of that service. Note the choice of words because we got serviced! I believe the attorney jumped to our aid because he still felt that he could get more money from us for a long time, and he wanted to prove that he was worthwhile to keep around.

I picked up our copy of the order at midnight in a restaurant 45 minutes from home, because we wanted to take it with us when we flew to the Boston airport the next morning. We did not get much sleep that night. I spoke to the grandmother at 11 p.m. before picking up the order. She said we were seeing Mike too much, and Cindy said this timetable was to accommodate Brenda's schedules for prior birthdays. The phone call ended in a shouting match. Cindy said that we would have never known that they planned to screw up the reservations if she didn't call to confirm the time. We flew to Boston as scheduled and had all of Mike's clothes and his baby stroller. We waited and had her paged and waited some more. She never showed and half the airport knew of our situation by that time. The plane to Orlando was ready to leave and we were torn. We had no choice. We had all of our plans and reservations and could do nothing else because we were in Boston. We could have spent a week trying to find her, but what good would it have done if we had? Cindy was crying her eyes out and I was just there, stunned, livid, not believing that she would disobey a court order. We had the airport page her more than ten different times. The airline people saw everything. They felt sorry for us and moved our seats to first class. We kept looking over our shoulders until we couldn't see out of the plane. We had the hope that she would still bring him. We must have looked sad for the airline to bump us up to first class!

Nothing more happened and Brenda got away with another one. The following month she said she would bring him, but she wanted to see him every day. We had enough of her bullshit and said she could visit, but it was not going to be on her daily schedule. She said she would drop him off at 8 p.m. at our house because she was driving in from Boston. At 10:30 p.m., she arrived and said Carlos was in Boston for the weekend and he drove them here.

"Isn't this the same guy you have a restraining order against, the guy who held a knife to you?" asked Cindy.

Oh, well, being older, Cindy just doesn't understand!

Since we temporarily compromised at the emergency hearing, we were set for the newly scheduled regular court hearing about her care for Mike, but were up against the odds because she was the mother and Mike had not been hospitalized from abuse. Brenda called Cindy and said she was leaving early and going to Boston because she was not having a good time, which meant she had another fight with Carlos. Brenda called home and told her grandmother to wire funds so she could take the train back. Brenda picked up the money and then went back to the boyfriend's house to continue her stay with him, and enjoy 'making up.'

The visit lasted a week. She again went back home because her 17-year-old cousin was going to be living alone for the following six months. The cousin only lived a block from Brenda's grandmother's home, so it was a perfect place to hang out. Mike was being taken to all of the places Brenda was living, and many times, he had no place suitable to sleep. Why would Brenda stay one block from home? Why would the 17-year-old cousin, and Mike's godmother, be left alone all of a sudden? We figured this whole scenario offered a few hints.

The grandmother's phone bill for long distance was $1,300. The aunt would be gone six months, unless she got out for good behavior. The cousin had a fresh credit card. Was this heaven or what for Brenda and her cousin? Could this be a start of an audition for the Jerry Springer show?

Three weeks went by and we decided to visit Mike in Boston. Since we were now on speaking terms, and Brenda had control of Mike, Brenda said to stay at her aunt's place. That was not unusual since each time there were visits from the other side, housing normally was supplied and the visitors were always "good little boys and girls."

We got to her aunt's house in Boston and noticed a few things that were unique to us at first glance; the front door would not close and was broken beyond repair and there was the sound of water coming from the basement, which had water about two feet high. Since we were trying to mind our own business, we asked if we could shut the water off at the main valve as not to damage the foundation of the home. I also rigged up an adjustment for the front door that allowed it to look like it was locked. Cindy noticed that there was no food in the house and she inquired as to their present state of hunger. Also, they had the nicest German Shepard mix dog who appeared drained, but very friendly. Brenda advised Cindy that they were getting money the next day from somewhere and everything was great. I asked if we could take them out for a bite and they were in the car before I finished the sentence. We went to McDonald's, which was the only place to eat within ten minutes, and Cindy knew Mike would eat a cheeseburger. After eating, we stopped at the supermarket and picked up a few things to eat for the next week, as well as a fifty-pound bag of dog food. I asked when the dog ate last and they said, "yesterday, but she doesn't have to eat every day!" The AKC should be made aware of this new economy dog.

While we were there, Brenda's cousin was to go for her first day of work. The night before, I heard them come home at 4:30 a.m. She had to be at work by eight, 3 ½ hours later. Later that night, after her first day at her new job, Brenda's cousin got a call from her new employer telling her not to come back anymore. I couldn't resist and asked her what happened and she said that she fell asleep for three hours at work. It appeared that she didn't understand why she was told not to come back. She told everyone that she didn't like the job anyway. The night before, Mike was sleeping with Cindy and me so we could care less what the two girls did. In the middle of the night, Mike woke up screaming and in a cold sweat. It took Cindy over an hour to calm him down. It appeared that Brenda had put him into a daycare that was city-subsidized and apparently something happened that made Mike turn into the most frightened child that we had ever seen. He was screaming uncontrollably and that was not Mike! To this day, we never could tell what triggered it, but we believe that Brenda did not do her homework for this daycare.

We stayed for two nights and the same thing happened the following night. Mike held on to Cindy and wouldn't let go. It took about ½ hour the second night, but Cindy was ready and able to calm him easier. We pleaded with Brenda not to send him back and said we would pay for a good center if she promised to take him. I said that I would pay the center directly. That was a real dilemma since we knew that she would take him at her convenience, but what choice was there? Her lifestyle left something to be desired as the flow of boys in the house over the two-day period reminded me of the recruiting office where everyone knew why they were there. We guessed that everyone enlisted in the service that they were offering.

When we left Boston, we decided to push to have Mike and Brenda move back to Philadelphia, as we were convinced there was no future for Mike. We told Brenda that we would put him into a good daycare and work out some things that would allow her to get on with her life. We talked about a car for her to go for the GED and her meeting a nice guy. That GED kept coming up, but the discussions never were completed. I sat down with her and Joe, and discussed the rules that we insisted upon.

With the set of rules was the caveat about keeping her job, whichever it was. Going back in history we reviewed her work record over the past three-year period: house cleaning for six weeks; daycare for four weeks; dental office for two months; pizza restaurant for a week; three fast food chains for a total of ten weeks; health care facility for eight weeks, another healthcare facility one week; nanny for three weeks; roofing company for two days; hair washer for three weeks; pizza place for two days, and another restaurant chain for three months.

We decided that without her sleazebag boyfriend, who she said she again broke up with, maybe she would straighten out. We fixed her up with a guy who was divorced and had just opened his own mechanic shop. He was divorced, but naive, so we figured that she would take it easy on him. She went over to the shop to meet him to see if he was cute, which was how she judged a date. They went out and he liked her. She said he was too straight. I explained that he must be straight to run a business and have responsibility. That logic went nowhere!

She was into the hip-hop clothes and guys with their pants halfway off their butts. Were these the guys she was thinking her son should be around? As grandparents, we realized there was a distinct generation gap. Whatever we did, we were old and wrong! But were we? What did the courts say? When did the court become responsible to act in the best interests of the child? That last sentence could be the buzzwords of many lawsuits that will be coming to the courts over the next twenty years. There were minority advertisements on television ten years ago stressing the need for college education for Afro-Americans. The ads said, "A mind is a terrible thing to waste." What about a defenseless child being raised by someone who doesn't care about education or what is in the child's best interests over a lifetime? It is too late to start to educate someone at eighteen? Now is the best time to begin to control their destiny or the destiny of any young adult. Are the children totally defenseless or can someone help? Do poor, smart children want to go to bad schools, not get educated, not realize that some day he or she could escape from the slums? If a child wanted to get ahead, wouldn't it be a shame for that child to be held back by a mother who said she didn't have the time to invest in her child's future?

The entire life of a child is determined over their first sixteen years. That sounds like a lot considering that all of the psych books keep saying that the first five years of a child's life are the most important. Bullshit! The first 20% of a child's life pretty much determines the next 80%, and that is a scary

311

thought. Do you know how many very nice kids in the slums are not going to make it because of a parent who won't give the time to allow their child to move forward on their own? How many kids are given clothing in poor areas and the parent sells them for drugs, or even food?

At twenty-two years old, Brenda had five years with a child to straighten out and she didn't. No one could dictate to her and if they tried, she would put them in their place. Everything had to be handled with psychology to have her believe it was her idea, no matter what the situation. Problem was, most ideas needed to be put into some type of action, which meant planning. Did we just go full circle because no one in Brenda's position wanted to plan ahead? If it felt good now, do it! Come to think of it, we had that philosophy at Woodstock, but we did grow up.

It appeared that there was no start and no end. We were back to the same old problem. How did we save a child? Could we save Mike? Whose business was it about what activities a child should be involved in? Which generation's morals were we trying to impose? Have morals changed? These were some of the questions that we faced.

We had again major cause for concern. Brenda had a bad driving history. She was involved in accidents in Boston when Mark was alive that forced cancellation of our car insurance. She put dents on every side of every car she ever drove. When she was driving Carlos' car when he went to jail, she had two accidents in that three-month period. The old Nissan that we bought for her to get around was destroyed in nine months. The mirrors were off the doors; the bumper was held on by rope, the rear window would not go up, there were holes in every seat from cigarette burns, the engine was run without oil for a long period of time and the car could be heard from a block away. On top of all that, every panel of the car had dents. That was not a nice car and Brenda called it "a piece of shit." Of course it was now, but it was in great condition when it was bought. Cindy didn't feel safe with Mike in the car with Brenda driving. What solution could we come up with to try to keep him safe? We did try court and found that the mother was "God." We tried to set up a stable atmosphere and couldn't control any of it.

Mike was doing fine so we overlooked most of the disasters that Brenda was involved in from jobs, to smelling grass on her clothes (the smoking kind of grass), to running around with known drug abusers. We kept telling her to get a job, but all she would say was that she was "bored." Cindy said that she would be too, if all she did was sleep all day and not accomplish anything except talk on the phone about some guy she met in this club or that club. As this was happening, Mark's old friend, Linda, who had lived with us before and moved to New York to follow her "dream," asked about coming back to our home to live so she could finish college in the area. She had been on vacation with us many times that we considered her part of the family. Also, when she had stayed with us before, she had always been a big help around the house and she was also very pleasant. Mike was always happy when Linda was around because she played with him and showed him a lot of attention. That situation was making for a crowded house. We figured that since Brenda kept Mike in her bed anyway, it didn't matter because there was a spare bedroom. That worked out fine because Linda and Brenda were the same age, but they had different personalities. Linda was very neat and considerate, while Brenda was not. The girls would sometimes go out together to clubs for something to do, but that was for convenience. Eventually, Linda put a lock on her bedroom door to keep Brenda out when she wasn't there because Brenda would 'borrow' her clothes. She would wear them, and then put them back with the smell of her perfume. Everyone knew, but Brenda would always deny that she did it. After a while, I would just tell everyone that I borrowed the clothes to take the tension out of it. It was not fun! And I was the wrong size!

Mike was still being driven and picked up at school by Cindy. Brenda apologetically said that us "old folks" were right and she was getting her life together. Since she was in the car with Mike, and the car was getting dangerous for him to be in, Cindy decided to buy her a new car since she had worked for a month at a personal care home and seemed to enjoy it. Based on her driving performance, Cindy wanted a car with safety equipment. We decided that all of the reports on the VW Beetle were great; it had air bags and virtually every safety feature that could be found. I almost fainted when I saw the price of $20,000. I bought my old beige Beetle for $1,995! I had even put some stick-on flowers on it. Now we had to figure how to do this purchase because she already had cost us our insurance based on her accidents. I spoke to the dealer and said that the car would go into her name, but Cindy was to be the lien holder. If she got into more accidents, we would not be sued or get canceled again, but we had control so she couldn't sell the car. That seemed like a good solution, so more rules were made as part of deal for getting her started without debt for the car.

Here were the rules of the contract signed by Brenda in October:

1. No one was allowed to smoke in the car – NO ONE!

2. Must drive with glasses on – maximum safety since she had a strong prescription.

3. Must save enough money for emergencies – $300 to be set aside.

4. No excessive driving – using up life of car and remaining warranty. (A total of 250 miles per week maximum to keep one year warranty – She was driving 550 miles per week presently.)

5. NO ONE except Brenda, Cindy or I could drive the car.

6. North Philly is off limits – too much chance of another accident.

7. Need to show responsibility to yourself, Mike, job, bills, service schedule of car, etc., by having no more additional bills. If you can't pay for it, you don't need it and you don't buy it until you can pay cash for it.

8. Must practice driving defensively, not aggressively.

9. Since you are already done with Carlos, you are not to see Carlos again. No exception.

10. The car will be in your name, but there will be a lien on it and the Title will be pre-signed.
11. You must pay a minimum of $150 every two weeks to pay for auto insurance. This will be adjusted when the amount of insurance is known and will start with your next paycheck.
12 We will sell your old car and apply the proceeds to your insurance payment.
13 If you are out of work two weeks and can't make insurance payments, this contract will be considered broken by you.
14 You are not to deceive us in any way.
The above are all the terms of this contract and should you break any of these terms, possession of the car will be taken back and sold by Cindy, who will keep the money since we paid for the car.

The deal was great and Brenda thought it was wonderful. She also thought that the Beetle was her dream car and she was so proud to tell people what she was getting. I ordered the car, which was supposed to be delivered in two weeks. The quick delivery time was because everything on those cars was standard and there were few options. We ordered a red one, which stood out in the showroom. The car came in and it appeared that things were going well and Brenda was on her way. Mike was happy as he was always playing with his friends in the neighborhood.

We had scheduled another trip to Disney World and that was a family trip including Cindy, Brenda, Mike, Linda and me. Linda and Brenda, although close in age, didn't get along great. Both girls were experienced in life, but not worldly. Linda was enjoying family, while Brenda was enjoying partying. We drove to Disney World, which took seventeen hours because we drove straight through. We found that if we left about 6 p.m., Mike would sleep about twelve of the hours and it became an easy drive. Cindy felt it was easier mentally for her and I to do all of the driving. The sense of responsibility of knowing that one was not invincible could not always be relied upon when young adults were involved. It was a long trip and when sunrise occurred, we were usually around Jacksonville. At that point, all I wanted was a toothbrush and shower!

We checked into our room and did the usual stuff including unpacking, setting up sleeping quarters, making plans for the next few days, etc. As that was being done, anticipation of each activity was bringing different highs to each individual. Mike was anticipating swimming and going to see Mickey and "all his other buddies." Linda was excited to do everything, as was Cindy. Brenda was thinking about Pleasure Island and the nightlife and starting to get ready an hour before, and taking a nap so she could stay late as the clubs closed at 2 a.m. We decided that we would keep in touch with each other, but not force each other to go everywhere. We did decide that we would meet for dinners. Obviously, economics was a large part of that reasoning with the girls!

The entire time was wonderfully uneventful, but a few things just screamed out at all of us, except Brenda. When Cindy went to the parks, Mike always was bouncing and ready to go. Linda was there. I was taking continuing education courses for business that were planned for months, so I didn't meet up with everyone until dinner. Brenda didn't go to the parks. She slept in because of being out each night. It bothered everyone except Mike, who was too busy having fun. No one could understand how Brenda could not see the joy in Mike's eyes when he saw Mickey, or rode the amusements, or discovered new things and was so proud of himself.

The entire trip was like this as Linda divided her time, but Brenda partied. One night Brenda came in about 2 a.m., woke up Linda and said she was going back to some guy's room that she just met. She said she was going back to see him and his brother, but Linda said no to joining her. Brenda left to go back to their room alone. Maybe I was naive, but going back to a room with two guys from New York at 3 a.m., who just picked you up at a club, didn't appear to be a long lasting relationship in the making. My thoughts were that I hoped they used condoms. The entire trip was fine and I was able to meet for dinner each night and spend the last few days vacationing with everyone, well almost everyone!

When we got home, everything was pretty much the same except the relationship with Linda and Brenda seemed strained. It appeared that Brenda was jealous of Linda's freedom and activities. She wanted to party with her at the clubs, but Linda would only go with her occasionally. It was also strained because of Brenda's "borrowing" of Linda's clothes. I was not too concerned, as the girls would have to solve their own problems. If not, it was like two five-year-old kids fighting when the parents stepped in. Needless to say, the parents became enemies and the kids were best friends ten minutes later.

Brenda was still not spending much time with Mike, who was now four and one half years old, but he was busily involved with different activities that Cindy took him to. When he was not outside playing ball, he was on the computer playing educational games, or on his roller blades.

Brenda had another series of auto accidents including one where she cut out an elderly woman and Brenda had no insurance, and was taken to court. Brenda settled for paying $1,400 in monthly payments of $100, and two years later, had failed to make payment one! Ironically, she did to the attorneys what they did to her! She was putting more than 500 miles per week on the old car. That was supposed to stop when the new one came in. While we were waiting for the car, Brenda sprang another bombshell on us; she said that she thought she was pregnant again. She said that she didn't have any money for an abortion and could I loan her $600. I said I would, but she must pay it back.

I learned that the fee for abortions depended on how pregnant you were. We learned later that she was six months pregnant. We were in shock! How could she have an abortion at six months and not be devastated? Not only was she not devastated; she was out kicking a soccer ball with Mike within ten minutes after coming home! Cindy was upset, but with mixed feelings. Whose kid was it? We didn't want another child. Brenda couldn't take care of one, let alone two.

We had many emotions and feelings concerning Brenda. What was our responsibility to her; to Mike; and could the responsibility be separated?

We talked to Joe, since we didn't believe that Brenda had the sense to know that five abortions could screw up her body. Also, we were not supposed to know about all of the other abortions. Cindy was told that Brenda had to get back to the clinic for treatment of "things" that were not right. Joe basically told us that we should mind our own business, which we proceeded to do.

Brenda was not affectionate, nor was she nurturing. Cindy tried to keep her healthy for Mike's benefit, but Brenda resented that, even though dental hygiene in today's world was achievable. Mike never knew about the abortions. He was too young to even have any thoughts about the subject, unless Brenda was showing. Cindy had a feeling based on her size, but couldn't say anything. All her father wanted was to be left alone to his new lifestyle with his new bride. He didn't want to spend money on Brenda, nor did he want to be anything but a consultant to appease her when things were not going her way. Joe's new bride was very upset since neither Brenda nor Mike went to her wedding. Actually, Brenda's brother, who lived in the area, didn't bother going either.

Things were not getting better with Brenda. She knew that she had to stay with her job since the car and the job went hand in hand. She had problems because she was totally committed to Carlos. She couldn't make time to fit into Mike's schedule, get the privacy with her boyfriend and not be in a drug zone with Mike, which caused fights with us. That was a conflict for which there was no solution. Did I say no solution? Wrong, because there was a solution: lie!

And lie she did. She got the new car and went to the drug zone to see Carlos, her drug dealer and a thief. She told work she couldn't make it in most days. She dragged Mike to the drug zone by telling him she would take him for ice cream. She slept out most nights, and took Mike late to pre-school, since he was already over tired. All these things are what worked for her!

Things were getting tenuous since work was getting in her way. She was suspended without pay while an investigation of her for patient abuse was going on. That was a perfect time for her to quit. I kept asking what happened, but was told the personal care home didn't know what they were doing. So let's see how the world economy existed with all of Brenda's past problems in trying to hold on to a job. Did unemployment or welfare count as a job? It should have because she held that the longest by far!

The situation was fair with Mike, but deteriorating with Brenda. I kept trying to be logical with Brenda, telling her Mike would have a lot of respect for her if she got her GED, stayed at a job showing pride and security, and went out with people who had responsibility. He would feel safe and secure. We stressed that the past was over and the new rules for the car would put her on the right track. The truth was that she was brought up as a self-centered brat and that wasn't going to change, but her ethics could have been improved to help make her son responsible. We knew that Mike was only five at this point, but he was sucking up everything and he didn't forget. That could be a blessing or a curse!

Mike was seeing all aspects of life. I videotaped him and asked him questions to try to explain things that he should not have seen. This was good and bad. It made him relive the situations, but it also kept him into reality for the outside world. What no one, and I mean NO ONE, including shrinks, could guarantee, was the affect each incident could have on each individual child. We felt that Mike needed explanations about films showing a man "kissing a woman's pee pee." He needed explanations about seeing momma driving two guys all bloodied to the hospital. We thought that Mike should know police are to help but "cops are coming to get you" was not a good thing. We thought Mike should know that playing with an older kid with a knife was not good. We thought it was not good to have Mike bite and kick momma's boyfriend when Carlos hit momma. We thought that he should know that he didn't have to sleep in a bed where he saw rats. We thought he should know that all people didn't smoke a funny smelling pointy cigarette. It would have been wrong for him to draw his own conclusions.

When we were away for a few days, Brenda put Mike to bed and had eight people over at the house doing lines of coke on the kitchen table. Linda told them to leave, but was ridiculed and told it wasn't her house. That was not good. Linda had a problem of what to do. She could have called the police. If she did that, what would have happened? The police would bust the kids, alienate Brenda from the house and possibly force her to move out with Mike, and basically, ignite a bomb!

Instead, Linda chose to ignore it after being told to mind her own business. She saw them doing the coke and went upstairs to keep an eye on Mike in case any of the people approached him. Where did Mike fit into all of this? The answer was simple; he was along for the ride. We felt as if we had to allow Brenda to be free, so she would leave Mike at home with us; this way we would not have to worry about him when she was out for the night.

The whole scenario was wrong! Mike should have been with a mother who should have put his best interests first. She should have tried to be responsible. She should have realized that she was single with a child and she had responsibility. She should have given him extra security since there was only one parent. She should have...

As we were told for years, and our parents were told by their parents, " a leopard doesn't change his spots." We guess the church doesn't believe it, but the jails do as you look at how many repeat offenders there are. To bring it home, how many married people do you know that ONLY cheated once, even though they knew it was wrong?

Chapter Twenty-six

We wanted to be good grandparents who kept our mouths shut and enjoyed Mike. There were so many obvious harmful things going on that we had to use psychology in dealing with Brenda to protect him from her actions. It got to the point where we could care less about her or whether she got beat up by her boyfriend or got stabbed to death by him. We knew that she was doing some drugs, but hadn't really seen it, except for her doing grass in the driveway of our home. Sometimes her clothes would have the smell of marijuana. It always made us look like ass holes to accuse her because she would deny it. On the other hand, we only could tell her father and let him evaluate and take any action he chose. She only "respected" him when she needed money or wanted something. Brenda was very good at telling any story that made her look good and everyone else look bad. Joe, two years recovered from drugs and alcohol, with a tenth grade education, and who never owned anything of value in his life, was being played like a sucker. He kept telling me that all she did was lie to him. Joe still backed her all the time because he didn't want her to think that he didn't love her. I saw what was happening and told Joe that if her actions continued, he would have to make a decision to back Brenda or protect Mike. Joe acknowledged that, but was in denial. Was this what society called a dysfunctional family?

Mike was in daycare doing great and beaming every day as he told Cindy all about what he learned each day when she picked him up about 3 p.m.

The new car arrived. Brenda got the new contract again since we knew she had forgotten it and we went over it. One line that was put in was about not seeing Carlos. That was put in for two reasons: one, she told us that she broke up with him because "he don't respect me" and two, because we knew he was scum and his association with Mike would lead to physical harm when Mike got in the way. When we spent all of those dollars, and we made the deal in advance, we had a right to an opinion. The reason for the new car was safety. Mike now had air bags on the side of the car. This was for protection in case he was in the car for her next accident. At the time of receiving the car, Brenda was still working at the assisted living facility.

The first week she had the car, she told me, "a bunch of niggers threw pennies at her car while she was driving and scratched the trunk." The next week, she was driving along the road and she was run off the road into a ditch, but was able to pull the car up, and only scraped the bottom and part of the side.

Three weeks later, she pulled out of a driveway at a health club, went out the entrance and scraped the bottom of the car. Next, a ticket came in the mail and it was for Carlos driving the car without a license. Brenda went to the VW dealer and told them that when she went over a bridge and the bottom of the car got all scraped up; they should fix it for no charge since it was their fault! She also demanded that they do it right away since she had places to go! The auto dealer service people basically told her where to go and it "wasn't where the sun shines!"

Rules were being broken and thrown into our faces; mileage was double, jobs were not kept, bills were not paid, Mike wasn't being picked up, and essentially, EVERY rule was broken. Four months had gone by and I reminded her and gave her warning almost weekly.

I told Brenda that we were repossessing the car and were going to sell it. I said that she had no responsibility and we were not going to be a part of it. She called Joe and he in turn, called me, and said he was coming down to straighten Cindy and me out. He came down and told me that we caused all of her problems with the new car and it was our fault that Brenda was having all of the grief. We were told that we put too much pressure on Brenda so Joe and Brenda decided that we should take the car back immediately. I said that was fine since that decision was already made. Of course I went over the contract with Joe and Brenda, and she admitted to breaking every rule, but, according to her, there was a reason for each one to be broken. Joe asked why she didn't tell him about the contract, to which she said she forgot. Joe felt like an ass, but he always did when he was ready to pounce on me. Every time Brenda got mad, she would lie to Joe, who would always take her side, and then realize that he was lied to when Brenda, Joe, and I were face-to-face.

Brenda gave me the keys and I proceeded to put ads in the paper to sell the car. Brenda was totally annoyed with everyone, except herself, and told all of her friends how we "screwed her." We could live with that attitude because it was the first time she had something that she had to give back. She was spoiled and no one knew why. She cold-shouldered us for about a week, and then said that we were right in what we did. That was her way of saying, "fuck you."

She was seething and it was obvious because she was stuck in the house, unless one of her friends picked her up. When she was picked up, she stayed out as long as possible and sometimes for two or three days at a time. She would always say that she would be home for Mike, but when she went out with a suitcase, it didn't take a genius to figure out that she had other plans. The good part was that most of the time, she was not taking Mike. She knew that she could not get him to school the next day, which would annoy Cindy.

This whole atmosphere was not conducive to a strong relationship. We were getting to hate her. The same held true toward us from Brenda. I was taking a stronger role with Mike because she really wasn't around. I knew that Mike thrived on the positive male image. Mike was very responsive to me in every way. We told him what would happen each day, and it actually happened. He was so used to hearing what was "gonna" happen, but never did. He did learn how to try to play one against the other when he wanted something. In the crazy relationship with all of us, the only stabile thing that existed was that when any of the three adults said something, the other two backed it. That taught Mike that rules had to be followed and there was no way to try to con one or the other. It was at the point where Mike only asked Cindy and me questions and permissions, although we tried to have him ask Brenda whenever she was around.

The situation was turning into a conflict because we were forcing Brenda to be a mother, when she was home, and that was not a role she wanted. Brenda wanted to be a convenient mother. Mike started to play little League baseball so I pushed Brenda to go to the parent's meeting. She went with Cindy and Mike so that everyone got to know each other. Brenda volunteered to help the coach. She was given a schedule and told to be in the dugout for every game. She had yet to take him to a practice or to go to any games. The coach was furious because the little league organization was based on volunteering and each person was important for planning the activities with the kids. I coached in the league for years with Mark, but tried to stand back and let her assume the parental role. Instead, she didn't bring Mike to practice because she couldn't get back from "wherever" in time because of traffic, car breakdowns, delays at work, flat tires, or any excuse that popped into her head.

One day, out of frustration, I told Brenda that if Mike had an activity that day, she was not to take him away from home after school. Her answer was she wanted to be with Mike. However, the problem was she would pick Mike up after school, with Carlos' car, which she took while he was working. She would drive Mike more than 60 miles through city traffic to go back to Carlos' house. She didn't get Mike home until almost 11 p.m., if at all. Cindy was firm on keeping him home after school if he had an activity or obligation. Brenda reluctantly abided by that request. Mike would plead with her not to go. He didn't want to be in the car and drive all day. If Mike would protest, Brenda would take him to his room, scream at him, slam doors, and finally come back downstairs with him. Brenda would then say to him, "tell nanny and papa that you want to go." Mike would look up with tears in his eyes and mumble in a very soft voice, "I wanna go." This behavior was brainwashing and fear. Cindy was undecided as to what to do. It was wrong, but Mike was not her child, and we felt our hands were tied. Our main fear was that it was obvious that Mike was being hurt psychologically. He was starting to cling to Cindy for security, something that was not common in his behavior. He was usually very independent. We tried to work around the situation without causing a lot of friction. We managed to get Mike to his activities and I tried to help the coach out and pick up the slack.

The situation around the house was getting worse. Brenda was out and didn't sleep home for 55 out of the next 60 days. Mike stopped asking if she was coming home. She would stop in for an hour, shower or change or do something, but it was rare that she saw Mike. When she did, she would say, "I love you baby." Maybe she didn't realize that he was growing up! The few nights that she did come home, she kept saying that she was bored. Brenda would frequently call a taxicab and go to Carlos' house. That confused me because it was a $30 fare and she wasn't working; yet she called a cab to take her to his house at least three or four times. Another thing that had me baffled was that she went to the State Fair and stayed there for about seven hours. The prices at the fair were very high, yet she came back with everything she could buy. It had to cost her a minimum of $300 that day. We knew something was going on, but couldn't figure out what. We were worried that she was doing something immoral or illegal.

Coincidently, Cindy was going through her checkbook and noticed that her next check was missing. That afternoon, our bank called and said a person came in to cash a check that was 40 checks from where Cindy currently was in her checkbook, so the teller refused to cash that $400 check. Cindy then questioned the bank on the check she found missing. She was told that check, made out for $350, was cashed three days ago. The bank immediately credited the $350 since it was obviously stolen, and then put everyone on alert for checks in that account. We knew Brenda stole them, but without proof, we could not accuse her of being a thief. We also had no proof to accuse one of her friends who were in our home when we were out. Either way, a confrontation would just be a waste of our time. If we did confront her, Mike could suffer if she decided to move out. We asked the bank if they would prosecute if we found out who the thief was. They said "no," explaining that it wouldn't be economically feasible. I asked them if they believed it would happen to them again and they say it probably would. I was wondering why banks didn't set up a fund to prosecute in order to protect each other and the public. It was only logical that if these offenders got away with this type of behavior once, then they would just do it again. Why not show them that they can't steal and get away with it? Today, with all of the security, the bank surveillance camera photos are accessible and the proof is easy and obvious. Maybe I was being too logical, but if the bank wanted a great public relations move, why not tell all of their customers and shareholders that they cared and were protecting their customer's money. Why not tell them that their bank had foresight and wouldn't tolerate theft? By not prosecuting, wouldn't the crimes get more frequent? With more frequency, there was more risk of harm to tellers, customers, and even the thieves.

We had to say something because it was making us crazy to think that she stole from us and was smug enough to think she was getting away with it. We brought the subject up to Brenda, but didn't accuse her. She immediately denied she or her friends were anywhere near the checks. Where could we go from there? We knew she was involved, but without proof, what could we accomplish by accusations? Hopefully, by making her aware, she would avoid doing it again. Also, Cindy now hid her pocketbook at all times. That was one hell of a way to be in the privacy of our own home, but again, there didn't seem to be any other choice. What could we do? Protect our grandson or throw the thief out? Sigmund, what psychology would you use?

How do we get rid of the gnawing inside our stomachs every

time Brenda tried to lie about something else? I just wanted to tell her I knew she was lying, but instead I just said, "Oh, that's great." The only salvation of acting stupid was that Mike got a better influence every day. With such a gem for a mother, we felt that Mike had a better shot at life if we got him into a private day school.

There were at least six reasons that included:

1. Better education based on history.

2. Teachers can monitor better if he is having problems adjusting to one parent.

3. Odds are improved that delicate situations will be handled better with more caring teachers.

4. His learning habits will be improved drastically with other kids who "qualified" for admission.

5. If kids tease him about not having a father, it would likely be handled in a better way.

We spoke to Brenda and explained that it would be better for Mike in a great school with twelve students in a class. I explained that these kids tended to be more successful and could make average students better. She agreed because it was presented in such a way that she had no choice.

We didn't know where Mike would be week to week, so this gave him stability and a work ethic. We made applications for two schools, with Brenda's permission. She called her father who said that it wasn't a good idea because Mike wouldn't know what real life was being with these spoiled kids and if Joe had extra money, he wouldn't spend it on education at a private school. That was the 6th reason that was not listed!

Mike visited one school and was with the other kids playing at a table. The teacher called all of the kids over and Mike didn't go. The teacher called him again and he said to her "as soon as I clean up, I'll be right there." We taught Mike two specific lessons in life, which we hoped, would stay with him: try your best and don't give up, and always put things away before you tackle another activity so you know where your things are. The not giving up has stayed with him and he has gained a sense of pride. The school loved him and his attitude, but had no openings and put him on a waiting list in the top five out of forty-five. We checked out the other school, which was smaller and closer to home. Mike was warmly accepted there and the headmaster made us feel at home. The headmaster sat down with us (including Brenda) and commented that in all of his years, he never had the grandparents take that much interest. I explained the situation and Brenda backed way off knowing she was over her head and didn't understand half of the questions or comments. Unfortunately, the headmaster did not ask any hip-hop questions to bring Brenda into the conversation. Mike was very comfortable and it was obvious, when he asked if he could stay the rest of the day. We signed him up immediately as there was a waiting list there also, but the school wanted him and we wanted the school. It was a good feeling that Mike was going forward educationally, and he would have an advantage in his schooling even before he entered kindergarten.

There was a sense of relief to us that Brenda agreed to allow him to attend this school. This took some pressure off of us Our thoughts were that Mike would go to a big intercity school and get lost because no one cared about each child. Also, Brenda would not be there to help or stress the importance of Mike's education. Of course we were aware that Brenda could change her mind in an instant, so we paid the school in installments. We still knew that there was tension in the house, but we were actually adjusting to it. Every time we wanted to stop the bullshit, we thought of what was best for Mike.

A week later, Cindy checked her credit card bill and noticed withdrawals from three ATM machines. Cindy never used ATM machines. There were twenty-three withdrawals in a two-day period. Cindy called the credit card company to find out what happened and they said someone in their office gave out our pin number. I thought, were these people idiots? We tried to get the credit card company to resolve this problem. I called their security department, and they said I couldn't talk to the supervisor. I asked, "Who can I talk to if I couldn't get anywhere with security?" They told me to write a letter. I questioned who would read a letter since no one listened. That made them think and they responded with "that's our policy."

I was furious; they gave away our pin number, screwed up our credit, wouldn't talk to us, and I had more than $3,000 on the street that I was responsible for! I called the Corporation President. I was then able to talk to a supervisor. I said that someone, thanks to their security breach, stole money from me. The credit card company said that they would reimburse the account. I asked if they cared or would want to know who stole it. They said they didn't care because it would be cheaper to just pay me back. I didn't buy that logic. It must have been the little bit of Ralph Nader in me because I asked if the credit card company realized that this person would do it again to someone else, maybe even them! Still, no luck. I then said that it was not fair to the public, so I called the bank that was behind the credit card and told them the whole story. The bank said they would look into it. We found out the videotape in the cameras at convenience stores rewind every 24 hours. That meant unless a crime was caught in a 24-hour period, it was permanently erased! Therefore, it pays to hit an automated teller using false ID, but don't hold anyone up! The bank said to drop it since it was now their problem and because we were being reimbursed.

The frustration was building because we knew that Brenda was involved. When we approached her about what happened, she acted as shocked as we were. Yea, right! It didn't matter since we were scheduled to go on vacation as a 'family' to Las Vegas the following week. We felt that she would be good because she always wanted to go there. It was a free vacation (her Christmas present), and a chance for her to be with Mike in an atmosphere to promote a true mother/child bonding without a phone or distractions. Cindy and I had friends in Vegas and we said we would all get together. They told us they would be happy to baby-sit one night for Mike if we wanted to stay out late.

We stayed at the MGM, which was magnificent. We saw great shows and stayed at the pool during the day. Mike found lots of kids to play with. Only problem was Brenda because she constantly griped about being bored. She didn't spend any time with Mike except when they were captive in a theater, at a meal, or with our friends in town watching the laser show. Mike was having a ball; he loved seeing the desert and the different colors of the sand. Overall, we had a great time, despite hearing how bored Brenda was. One night we went to a show. We left Mike with our friends at the hotel and a hip-hop kid, including baggy pants and backward baseball cap, picked up Brenda. He picked her up in the three minutes it took from getting out of the show until we got to the car. When we got to the car, Brenda said that she would meet us back at the hotel later. Stupidly, we asked her if it was smart to go with this stranger while her son was waiting at the room.

"Bye," was all she said as she walked away.

We went back to the room where our friends had put Mike to sleep. They said they had a ball with him, and Mike told Cindy the next morning he wanted to go out with them again. Brenda showed up at the room about two hours later and said the guy was a bum. He was too young to buy her any drinks. We looked at Mike and at Brenda and asked ourselves, which one was smarter today and which one had enough common sense to handle responsibility at their level? Mike won!

I planned a surprise for Cindy. Since Vegas was a town known for weddings, I decided to renew our vows and surprise her. I told Brenda to go down to the game room with Mike and we would be right there. The game room was next to the wedding chapel. It was set for our friends to be in attendance with special Disney hats that had mouse ears; hers was a veil and mine was a top hat. When we got there, I said to Cindy that we should go to the chapel and look at the pictures on the wall. I glanced into the game room but no one was there. In the meantime, Cindy was talking to the girl in charge, telling her how stupid it was for people to come in there and spend a ton of money for this! What could Brenda do to screw this up when she didn't even know what was happening? Finally, our friends came in with the hats, joined by the Clergyman and the organist. Cindy realized what was going on, and she was slightly embarrassed.

Five minutes later, we saw Brenda in the hallway and asked where she was. She said she wanted to look in the stores. I should have known the game room for Mike was a second choice! After the ceremony, we took everyone out for dinner, watched the pirate show at the Mirage, and walked around all evening wearing the silly hats. Brenda, on the other hand, had an attitude throughout the evening.

We kept wondering why Brenda was moody and bored. We just assumed it was her youth and impatience. We returned home the following week and life was normal, except Brenda was out more than ever and spending money "like a drunken sailor." She was taking more $30 cab rides to Carlos' house. That was her business!

We decided it was time to get Cindy's jewelry, videotape it, and insure it. We were talking about it for a while and decided it was time. Cindy had received some of her mother's jewelry, which included jewelry from three generations back. The pieces were unique and extremely rare. Cindy had hid the box in our bedroom and was careful not to let anyone know where it was stored. I walked into the room, put down the video camera and pulled out the soft jewelry case. I emptied it on the bed; Cindy said to spread out the items so I could take clearer video shots. She looked at the jewelry on the bed and immediately asked where certain pieces were. I said that was all that was there. Her face turned white and she sat down on the bed in shock. Her great grandmother's rings, her grandmother's bracelets, her mother's diamond ring, the pearls and rings I bought her on her anniversary were all were gone. Our stomachs felt hollow. We looked all around the room, but knew the jewelry was gone. We rechecked the jewelry bags. I didn't know the things were missing because, well, I'm a guy!

After about twenty minutes, we gathered our composure and realized that Brenda stole them. We figured that was where she was getting all the money she was spending! We again had no proof and could not accuse her, but it made sense with her spending tons of money without having a job. Cindy inventoried the jewelry and wrote down each missing piece. There were 13 pieces, including my diamond ring that I only wore on very special occasions. I then called the police and asked them to come over when Brenda was not around. I told the police that we had suspicions of one of three people, and all associated with Brenda, had taken the jewelry. When the police came over, they asked for the list of items. They asked for a more detailed description, at which time Cindy drew pictures of them and described them well enough that the items were very identifiable. The police were very attentive, but the case could not be a priority to them. Bodily harm always took center stage, even though there was more than $100,000 in retail value taken. I decided that this was no different than when we were chasing down Mark. We knew the streets better than the suburban police and we knew about a dozen pawnshops that appeared to be the choice of young people. We went to about five of them and checked out the jewelry cases. The jewelry that Cindy had was far superior to the items in each store. We figured that the pawnshops had a better stash in the back room, so we leveled with them. One of the merchants told us that one officer in the city was assigned to all of the pawnshops and the officer had a relationship with all of the shops. I contacted her and told her the situation. I gave the local suburban police her number and they contacted her. As stated earlier, the State Banking Commission also directly regulated the pawnshops. This fact was a major break for us. We knew it had to be one of the remaining seven pawnshops. A friend of a friend owned two of the shops, so we called him and he checked his records and said it wasn't his places. That left five more. Before we could check those, we caught another break. The two police departments were able to coordinate Brenda's name and it came up on one of the pawnshop slips. The city police contacted the pawnshop and asked them about Brenda. The shop records showed that she was in on six different occasions in a five-week period; she sold jewelry on four and her friend sold jewelry on the other two while Brenda was with her. The owner bought the pieces rather than taking them for pawn. The reason was that the pawnshops could sell the pieces they bought, after holding them only five days. If they didn't buy the pieces, they were required to hold the pawned items 120 days.

I was thinking that a pawnshop owner should at least be a little suspicious of a young girl bringing in $100,000 worth of fine quality and antique jewelry over a five-week period. Knowing the clientele of most pawnshops in a drug area of the city, it should have thrown a caution flag to these people, which it probably did, which was why they bought the goods! Good business sense made the shop realize that if the merchandise were pawned, the police could have identified them and the pawnshop would not have been able to sell them for a huge profit.

After the connection was made, Cindy and I were told to go with our local police to identify three pieces that the pawnshop still had which hadn't made the five-day period yet. We were also told that if the items were ours, we would have to BUY them back for what the pawnshop paid for them. The old proverbial adding insult to injury! When we went, I had to direct the police to the pawnshop because the suburban police were not as acquainted with the area as I was. Cindy followed in her car. We drove toward the shop and as we kept going, the neighborhood kept looking worse. We parked near the subway tracks and the police made sure the car was locked and in an open area. We got to the front door and looked in. The store was well lit and large, but the door was locked and after you rang the bell, they would buzz you in. We walked into the shop, saw at least five people who were obvious employees, the detective identified himself, and the shop owner and his wife became very cooperative, as they were advised that they should be. We went to the back of the store and the owner and his wife were there. He said that he would go to the back and get the merchandise. Cindy looked at the envelope that the owner brought out. We were hoping it was our jewelry on the one hand, but hoped it wasn't because of the situation that Brenda would be in. It was ours! We bought back the three pieces for $3,000, which usually put a value of those items at ten times what the shop paid or $30,000. I was thinking I was in the wrong business!

We asked about the other items and the owner said that all of the others were sold and they had no idea who the buyers were. We can guarantee three things in life: death, taxes, and they knew the buyers! It was a sleazy business and the object was to get the most money from bums, addicts and desperate, vulnerable people. This shop did well!

The police detective asked for a copy of the receipts that were given to Brenda, and the receipts showed all of the necessary identification to identify Brenda as the person who sold the jewelry. We started talking to the owners and they remembered her for two reasons that stood out in their minds: first, she had a Boston accent, and second, she told the young boys who worked there to forget about her and the short skirt because there was no way the jewelry was hers and she may not be around long.

Two days later, the shop called and said they found two more pieces that we could buy back, which we gladly did. We also realized that two more pieces were missing, but the police said to forget about them as we probably have everything that we were going to get. Fifteen pieces stolen and five recovered was not bad considering everyone felt that all of them were lost. Even the police figured they were gone. Sometimes even bad experiences can be useful in one's life, referring to our knowledge of pawnshops.

Now we had the goods on Brenda, it was eating us alive to be in the same home as her, knowing she was going to be arrested. It took two days to get an arrest warrant. In the meantime, we had to prepare for the arrest and the situation with Mike. When she was arrested, would they let her out right away? I drew up papers to file for emergency custody.

I had an attorney friend who gave me the format to use. I wrote up the papers in one night that took me into the early hours of the next morning.

The papers were done, but how could we get them to take effect? I went to the courthouse and spoke to the clerks to see the procedure. It was complicated as the different departments had to collect money for filing and the petition had to be presented to a judge. It was complicated and that was why a lawyer was needed, but it was too late. We didn't want the same lawyer that we had before, so Cindy and I said we would do it on our own.

I was ready to go to the judge's chambers when she was arrested. The clerk advised me that I should present Brenda with the papers when she was arrested so the police would witness it. We also were told to ask if Brenda would give us custody by signing on the spot.

The police called and said they were coming over to arrest her. We said she wasn't home but we would call when she came back.

The anticipation was unbearable. We couldn't let Mike see his mother get arrested. We had to put him in an area where he was away from visually seeing the police cars. After two hours, she came home with a girlfriend, but said she was going out in a few minutes. I called and the police came over to arrest her. Mike was outside in the backyard swimming and had no idea the police were in the house. Brenda and her friend were in the yard finishing their cigarettes. I asked Brenda to come into the house. When she came in, they arrested her. I told her that we knew she stole the jewelry and we were taking care of Mike. Brenda denied knowing anything about jewelry.

At the station, when the police searched her pocketbook, which she insisted on taking, they found heroin and charged her with possession. As she went out the door in handcuffs, I gave her the papers and asked her about custody. She said to me to "go fuck yourself," and that we would never see Mike again when she got home. She figured that she would be out in minutes. She probably would have, had she not given the police so much trouble. She denied everything and wouldn't bend her story. After two hours of questioning at the police station, telling Brenda they had her prints, pawn shop receipts, and the shop owner identified her and her girlfriend, she confessed.

Chapter Twenty-seven

Now, I had to go to court to get the emergency temporary custody of Mike, because as soon as she got released, she was taking him to live in the drug zone and out of our lives forever. I quickly took the prepared emergency petition and went to the courthouse, but it was closed until the next day. We were in a panic. What could we do?

If the police released Brenda, Mike would become a tragedy. If we ran with him, we were breaking the law, although we were protecting Mike. If we stayed at home and Brenda got out, knocked on our door, we would have to give Mike up to her because he was her kid and she was entitled to take him. We had a real life problem. What should we do? Protect the child and maybe break the law? We have read about people running away to save children, and then they ended up in jail.

We figured that since Mike was technically with us by permission, Cindy could take him on a vacation, which she did. Cindy and I decided that we would not be in communication unless it was by cell phone and I didn't want to know where she was in case the police questioned me. I, on the other hand, had to be in court at the opening, and if I was not home, I was not a fugitive. We didn't know if Brenda would be in or out of jail because it depended on when she got arraigned, which was when the judge came in. I visited some friends' overnight and reviewed my petition, in case the judge would hear me. My concerns included not having a lawyer, or even if a judge would hear me, acting alone as an individual without being represented. I got to the courthouse at 7:30 a.m. and waited to see the clerk of the courts. She came in a half-hour later. Everything went great and she said she would see me. I explained everything, including what would happen to the child if this petition didn't go through. I gave her the following reasons for the judge to review to see if he would hear me:

EMERGENCY PETITION FOR CUSTODY

Reason for emergency custody hearing: Stability, safety, and the best interests of the child.

PER Domestic Relation, Title 23, #5313, we wish physical and legal custody until a full hearing can be set.

1. Ed and Cindy have taken a role equivalent to the father in Mike's upbringing. Mike witnessed and was involved in a fight when Carlos, Brenda's boyfriend, strangled her and Mike tried to protect her by kicking Carlos.

2. The drug and alcohol activity being witnessed by him is a slow death to the child that must be addressed before it is too late!

3. While this is being resolved, we propose that the mother, if not in jail, have unlimited visiting rights, but under the authority of Ed and Cindy; to not make any decisions that could put Mike in further danger. Since it is temporary, the child's safety is secure and IF the mother can turn it around, she can regain custody, the child is stable, and the mother can still be a part of his life if she chooses. Brenda will not be permitted to reside in our home anymore, since this is the third theft in one year from our home (police reports on all three, but on this one, an arrest was made).

4. IF this is not granted, Brenda will take every step possible to prevent Mike from ever seeing his grandparents, who have been the only stable force in his short lifetime.

5. On June 2nd, she was too drunk to take Mike to or from school so Cindy did it and made excuses for his mother and this is a very common occurrence that can be attested to.

6. She has done drugs, which Ed witnessed, and neglects, physically and mentally abuses Mike for her own pleasures.

7. She has often left him with known drug addicts to go out for social evenings. Her known associates are drug abusers and she has no problem putting him in that environment.

8. She has tried to brainwash him into saying that the kids in the suburbs are all "phony" and all of her friends are "real"(proof available).

9. She has had him where people have been badly beaten and bloodied and he has viewed them in drug areas (proof available). She has exposed him to AIDS through these processes.

10. At this point, since Mike has been with the grandparents more than 80% of the time, his safety was assured. The mother cannot and has not been able to stay alone with this child for any extended period of time without pawning him off to someone else. She loses her temper and gets violent and Mike becomes the recipient. When in our home, she uses the "pinch" method so no bruises can be seen.

11. He has the beginnings of psychological problems, which can be seen by his reactions to questions related to his mother who has ordered him not to say anything about her to us. He has the conflict in telling the truth, which the grandparents have taught him versus the continual lies of his mother. He is always looking for her approval and constantly gets frustrated by her neglect (as proved on video). He has no way to vent his anger and that is destroying him inside.

12. The grandparents are the sole support of Mike as well as support of his activities in the area and have done so for the past three plus years. This includes private school, camp, soccer, little league, etc. Brenda did not prepare as many as 20 out of about 200 lunches for Mike, who needs lunch prepared daily, during the entire school year.

13. Mother will be arrested for theft of approximately $100,000 in jewelry on June 9, based on evidence secured by detective M of the local police.

14. She has no visible means of support and Mike does not have any other relative other than grandparents in the area. Mike has resided with grandparents for four years of the five since his birth. The mother has mostly resided in the same

338

residence, but has slept away approximately 30% of the time, although it is about 80% the past three months.

15. Mike has been neglected almost since birth and the grandparents have been the "fixers" and stabilizers in his life (as recently published in newspapers and it has gotten worse).

16. The grandparents have assumed the father's role in his upbringing including 100% of his room and board and education, 70% of his clothing, 80% of his transportation, and his medical expenses after his mother neglected him. All of his vacations to non-family destinations were by his grandparents.

17. The reason for temporary custody is the unstable nature of the mother. She has ruined his teeth by not knowing or caring to learn about personal hygiene. As a result, he has had 6 teeth pulled, and she still won't have him brush his teeth. Consistent mental torture about how bad he is unless someone is listening. He lives with his head down after every browbeating from her. His mother smokes drugs (weed) in front of him and he admitted that he gets sick from it (proof available). He is scared to disobey his mother for fear of harm, he has been with her during drug buys, is in a home that is occupied by her boyfriend who has a history of weapons offenses and spent part of last year in jail for his temper when he pulled a knife on a coworker (County.) On June 4th, while with his mother, Mike was unsupervised in streets of North Philadelphia and was in an accident and had to receive six stitches in his hand and it still has not been determined if he will have nerve damage, although indications are positive for Mike.

18. His medical insurance from welfare has lapsed because of her lack of interest in filling out the forms. The grandparents wish to be able to get Mike medical treatment.

19. For over three years, Brenda has not been able to hold any job. She has had more than eight jobs that usually lass anywhere from two weeks to eight weeks. She has not worked in over five months and is very able-bodied.

20. She spends over 50% of her time in the North

339

Philadelphia area and provides no care for her son with stability, although the words are there. There are over eight bill collectors who call weekly due to her passing bad checks and owing money, which a credit report will verify. Since she lost her phone and used ours, we have the record of the callers. Due to her violent nature and unstable lifestyle, the grandparents fear for his life.

21. She will not obey the courts, as she does not value any agreement, including one made for her to protect Mike's safety when the grandparents purchased a car with seatbelts. She has a history of ignoring legal violations and snubbing the law.

22. Brenda has no conscience by stealing from the very people who fed her and her child, housed her at no cost, paid for her dental ($7,000) so the young girl could keep her teeth. She again let her teeth decay. We have provided all the amenities of a family home situation and asked her to get a job to give her a sense of pride for her and her son. She would not hesitate to inflict physical harm to Mike to achieve her desires.

23. This request is being made to protect Mike's life and limb. If our request is granted, Mike's stability remains in tact as his mother is rarely with him more than one to two hours per day, if that. He will be safe! That is what the law was meant to do by giving the judges the lead way to have insight into the best interests of the child!
Petitioners

The judge's clerk was a middle-aged woman who believed me and said, "Wait here." I waited the longest fifteen minutes of my life. She came back in with a smile and said that the judge would see me first. I asked what the judge was like and she said to just answer his questions short and to the point. I got to the courtroom and sat in the front row as instructed. My stomach had a feeling similar to when we found the jewelry missing. It felt horrible and I was shaking. The number of cases listed had to be in the thirties. I was scared for one of the few times in my life, not for me, but for

Mike. I was sitting in the front row and got a tap on my shoulder; it was the attorney that we fired years earlier. I said hello and turned around because I believe that I was praying, but I'm not sure if it was promises that I was making or prayers; either way, it was a new experience for me.

The judge came out and called me to the front desk. He said he read the emergency petition and then started asking me questions about Brenda's status (jail), what Mike was doing (camp), other relatives here (none), and a few more questions which were now a blur. He then stopped asking questions and just stared at the court and me. It seemed like hours and I definitely was shaking. He said that it was highly unusual for any decision to be made without the mother being present to speak for herself, but in this case, he gave us a thirty-day temporary custodial order and he said Brenda could challenge it anytime during that period.

When he said that, my body finally loosened up and I had a tingly feeling throughout my body. I was feeling so good, even though it was temporary, because someone in power actually valued Mike. I thanked the judge and it was obvious that my emotions were tears. I was told to wait and the order would be written up immediately. I got to the car quickly and called Cindy on the cell phone because I didn't know where she was. She started crying as soon as she heard and said, "Meet you at home!" It was happy crying.

We then realized that step one was over and we needed a real attorney who knew the law better than our quick reviews because we only had, at most, thirty days before custody was over. Brenda's father called that night to see what happened to Brenda and I told him. I said that she was involved with drugs when she was arrested. He called me a liar. Joe then told me that Brenda said no drugs were involved, because he asked her about it. She said there weren't any and there were no drug charges. The reality is unless the police identified the substance positively, they would not make the charge, so at that point, and there were no formal drug charges. Brenda figured that the police were stupid and didn't know what drugs she had in her purse.

Brenda was released that day after posting a $5,000 bail, obviously from the stolen jewelry. Her boyfriend Carlos called me and asked if she could pick up her clothes. I said she could, so we loaded her clothes into five plastic trash bags and put them out on the front lawn since we didn't want her in our home.

We said to call before she came. As we emptied the drawers in her room, we found a crack pipe. We turned it over to the police after wrapping it and not putting any more fingerprints on it. In our naive frame of mind, I thought that someone might have been interested in drugs or drug pipes in our home. We believed that we were lucky that the police didn't search the house, find the pipe, and arrest Cindy and me.

Cindy took Mike next door to play so he wouldn't see her come over to pick up her clothes and maybe say the wrong thing to Mike. Brenda came with Carlos and he started loading the trash bags into the car. Carlos came over to me and said Brenda did the wrong thing. He then proceeded to tell me how she stole money from him by taking money off his bureau or out of his pants pockets. He said it was only $10 or $20 at a time, but it was all of the time! I started to ask why Carlos put up with that and then stopped because there couldn't be any reasonable answer!

As Brenda was leaving, she said that she was not going to petition the courts now to get Mike back because she had some issues to deal with. Also, she was getting advice from her friends and family about the court system. These were the family who had all seen the inside of a jail cell. Their advice was that she should keep quiet and the courts will give her probation. I figured that we better find out about criminal court so we called the district attorney's office. The D.A. wanted to know what we wanted, so we explained the situation. We knew that there were now two cases; criminal and custody, and they could not be mixed. The D.A. said that Brenda could get off with probation, so I wrote him the letter that follows and faxed it to his office:

TO: D.A.

FROM: Ed & Cindy
RE: Docket # (Grand Larceny Receiving stolen merchandise, etc.)

Dear D.A.;
Sorry to hear you were under the weather yesterday, but Mary filled us in on the procedure. We understand that we have to wait for the notice for the sentencing hearing. We were concerned after seeing the earlier cases and the quick probation that the judges appeared to be handing out. That brought some questions into focus that said our judge must be given the ammunition to legitimately fulfill the guidelines that are set forth.

We have been extremely vocal and realize that you go through many cases and it is sometimes difficult, if not impossible, to point out differences that change intent, i.e. pawning jewelry instead of selling it shows a plan as the pawn shop can sell bought merchandise in five days and must hold pawned items 120 days. We could have recovered (bought back) the items if she pawned them, but she sold them!

We are concerned that there were no charges of possession of drugs (heroin) as that appears to be taken seriously, based on a case we saw that day. That must be part of this! She lied to this judge as she did to another judge, and that was on the transcript, of which we are requesting a copy (regarding the recovery of the jewelry). When asked if she was ever in trouble before, does a bench warrant qualify for trouble? Doesn't possession of heroin qualify as trouble? Does driving with a suspended license after being told not to by another judge qualify as trouble? Does possessing a counterfeit inspection sticker qualify as trouble? I assume lying under oath is not looked at real favorably with the courts. All of the above are verified in police records. We are trying to figure out how there could be a question of felony one! We are told that she is questioning our appraisal of the stolen merchandise. If she has no money for an appraisal, why is the value of the jewelry taken in doubt from

343

probably the most professional and recognizable jewelry appraiser in the city, if not the state.

I was under the impression that more than $100,000 is 9-16 months, not 6-14, based on my reviewing the book with guidelines. Please review that page as the judge certainly is depending on your research.

D.A., please understand that we are not upset with what is happening, but the system needs your strong input to work. After seeing results of crimes and their punishments, our first thought was to hit the media who have been following much of our case with the headline "How Much Time is Grand Larceny Worth in our County?" If you told me that if I stole $100,000 and could get six months in jail, IF CAUGHT and prosecuted, that comes out to $200,000 a year, which seems like a pretty good risk for criminal types. It would appear to be better to do this type crime than risk bank hold-ups or convenience store robberies for a few thousand dollars; we should let all the criminals know a better, less risky method to increase their incomes!

We would like to spend ten minutes with you, at your convenience, so that some specific questions could be answered for us and possibly fine tune the" wrong wording" that appears to be something that could change the entire intent of her actions.

This crime has changed our lives! My father-in-law now lives with us, and this crime put him into a position of not being able to handle life. After he heard of all of his wife and mother's jewelry being stolen, he could not live alone. This may have been what put him over the edge, but he goes to a psychiatrist who basically and in writing said he couldn't handle his affairs or function alone. We are now his caregivers. Cindy was devastated to lose what she valued as family heirlooms throughout her entire life. We know Brenda. She will lie, cheat, and do anything she can, even when caught, to self protect. She can act with big tears.

We have enclosed a preliminary copy of what we plan to read and give to the judge when we are permitted prior to sentencing. Please advise us when you would be able to

344

meet with us, even if it is after we get the hearing date.
Thank you, Cindy and Ed.

The D.A. returned our call within fifteen minutes of receiving the faxed letter and set up a meeting with us. In the meantime, we were spending thousands of dollars on the custody attorney's fees so that we would be set when the custody hearing came up. We tried to envision all the possible scenarios that could arise and figure how to counter them. Our attorney gave us good advice: stop! We stopped thinking for a while and still tried to monitor Brenda's movements. We told Brenda she could have visits with Mike, but I would be there. We weren't obligated to give any visits, but she was still his mother. She showed up four times in that month, out of a possible twenty. We called the attorney to see about extending the temporary custody. The attorney said it was automatic; she was wrong and I pushed her to review the order, which she did and it was the last day. She realized that it was time for quick action by her, not her staff. She was good and knew the ropes. Somehow, she got an audience with the judge that day and received an extension until Brenda petitioned the court. Mike again was able to stay in a safe, secure place he had called home for five years, even though we were all one hearing away from disaster. We both felt that we actually got an attorney that knew the laws and could read the players. We also realized that we had to know what was going on because you could not depend 100% on any attorney as they have many cases; if your file wasn't open, you were out of their thoughts.

Cindy was still keeping records and writing what happened every day, even when the other family made contact with Mike. We realized that we had to show Brenda's nomadic lifestyle to the judge or at least give the ammunition to our attorney when the time was right. We wrote about Brenda moving four times in three months, the lies she was telling everyone about jobs, money, bills, drugs, etc. As the old joke went, "she only lied when she opened her mouth."

We weren't comfortable doing nothing to protect Mike, but

we sat and waited. The courts set a date for the custody hearing while Brenda was awaiting trial for her criminal actions. We spent more than five hours with the attorney preparing for the case in her office the day before the trial. We came into her office two hours before the trial with three witnesses to attest to Brenda's lifestyle. The judge saw the situation when court convened and he said that he didn't wish to hear the case until after the criminal hearing. It was possible that Brenda could go to jail and he didn't wish to uproot Mike too many times; Mike again appeared to be safe at this point.

The judge said he would allow Brenda unsupervised visits on Sunday, Tuesday and Thursdays and Brenda could take him out. At that time, our attorney said it was dangerous for Mike because Brenda did not have a valid drivers license, was running with a felon who was violent, and was taking Mike to the felon's home in the drug district. The judge said his order stood, except Mike was not to be in Carlos' company, in his house, or for Brenda to transport Mike without a valid driver's license.

We knew that she would do all three restrictions, but we wouldn't be able to prove it and if we brought it to court, the judge would throw it out, as Brenda would deny all charges. We were livid that the law was being laughed at and Mike was put into dangerous situations. Brenda laughed at us when she picked up Mike. I felt that it would be nice for a truck to hit her for revenge!

We called several detective agencies to see how they could help. That was an experience. They charged as much as $200 per hour. I found a new one that only charged $35 per hour and was sympathetic to the case because the owner had small children of his own. He knew the profile of Brenda and her friends. We hired him. He followed Brenda one day when she picked Mike up and videotaped her actions. She took Mike to a large discount store in a rough neighborhood and Mike was wearing shorts and a tee shirt when he left home. Mike came out of the store wearing three shirts and a pair of long pants, all of which she started to peel off him in the car; theft and corrupting the morals of a child. Next she left him alone in the car with the car running and the door wide open for over five minutes; child endangerment. Then she blew through three red lights and could have caused major accidents. She went to Carlos' house in the drug zone and left Mike outside on the steps. After two hours, Carlos, Brenda and Mike got into his car and drove off. The detective followed, but was unable to keep up as Carlos also blew through the lights and the detective lost them. All of the above was on videotape to show the judge at the right time. The next hearing was scheduled for three weeks later. A week before the hearing, Brenda picked Mike up at home and drove off on a Tuesday at 5 p.m. It was cold and rainy. Cindy received a call from the local police about an hour later asking if we could pick Mike up about five blocks from our home. Cindy asked if anything was wrong, but the police dispatcher said to just pick him up. I drove over and parked the car next to a police car, which was parked next to Carlos' car. I "happily" observed that she screwed up again and it would be on the police record. I asked, as a concerned custodian for Mike, what happened and was told Brenda was driving with a counterfeit inspection sticker and there were three children observed playing in the car unrestrained. Also, her driver's license was under suspension. Also, the license plate did not match the registration on the car. Lastly, the driver's door was held together by rope and would not allow for escape should there have been an emergency.

As I walked over to the car, to my surprise, Carlos was in the back seat laying down or hiding. I was wet and dripping from standing in the rain. I looked up to the dark, wet sky and said to myself that there was a God. The police said they were leaving the car and taking Carlos, Brenda, and the other two kids to the station and the car could not be reclaimed until it had the proper ID. I asked if the records would show Mike at the scene with Carlos and the officer nodded it would. I asked Brenda if I could take the other two kids so they would be safe and dry; she blew me off.

347

On the prior visit, Brenda brought Mike to the door and said "Mike wants to know why he can't live with me so you tell him because if I do, it wouldn't be nice." Obviously, she tried to brainwash him in a short period of time, but she didn't even think about his feelings by opening up that topic. This was sweet revenge, but it was about Mike, but the revenge was good!

With that information and her actions, we felt that we were ready to go to the hearing. We had the police, the investigator, and two neighbors as witnesses. We went with another attorney at the same firm as ours was out of town. Brenda started telling the judge what a good mother she was and how she made a good living. The judge said that she could tell the court that later and he proceeded to ask why we were in court, since the judge said there would be no hearing until after her criminal trial. The reason we were was because the court had no idea what the last ruling was and they automatically scheduled the present hearing. As long as we were there, we asked that the court put her back on supervised visitation. The judge was hesitant until our attorney stood up and stated that with the recent events:

1- She disobeyed the court order.

2 - She drove with a suspended license.

3 - She took Mike to the drug zone to her boyfriend's house.

4 - She left him alone in a car in a parking lot for more than five minutes.

5 - She was with Mike and Carlos, together.

When the fifth item was stated, the judge asked for our attorney to sit down and he turned to Brenda. He looked directly at her and asked if the statements were true and Brenda said "no!" With that, the judge asked the attorney to bring up the officer, who was sworn in. The officer affirmed all that was said. The judge asked Brenda if the officer was lying and she said that it was mostly true. Our attorney then said that we had a video showing the rest to be true. The judge requested a projector, which took about ten minutes to get. When it came into the courtroom, the technician hadn't a clue how to run it so the clerk and everyone else were making suggestions until finally someone hit a right button. The investigator was called to the stand to describe what happened. As the tape was running, he was describing the five-minute view of Mike alone in the car. The entire courtroom was watching and saying nothing for five minutes. Everyone was waiting for something to happen, like Brenda coming back to the car! It was eerie watching the judge go from attentive to pensive to shaking his head in disbelief while watching a five year old child at the steering wheel and with the door wide open. We then watched the screen as Carlos and Brenda entered and exited Carlo's house, with Mike playing on the steps.

"Isn't that you, Carlos, and Mike in the video?" the judge asked Brenda.

"Yes, but I was next door so I really wasn't with him, and besides, I don't see why I can't be with Carlos because he is a nice guy," she answered.

"I'm going to tell you why you can't be with him, BECAUSE I SAID SO!" yelled the judge.

He told Brenda he felt it was not safe for Mike to have unsupervised visits with her, so he was reinstating the supervised visits. He also said all parties must get full psychological studies and guess who had to pay for them since she couldn't? The judge ordered Cindy and me to pay for hers, also!

This whole process was legal bullshit, in my opinion. This was our third appearance before this judge, and we had yet to have a scheduled custody hearing. However, fortunately for Mike, this hearing landed on the side of safety, but it would have taken an idiot to rule otherwise.

It was a great decision, but a problem developed for us. Brenda was a thief and a drug user, and she totally disgusted us. Because of the ruling, we had to let her into our home once again for these supervised visits. We had so many concerns about her behavior. Would she do drugs in the bathroom? Should we make her keep the bathroom door open when she peed? We have learned a hard lesson to never underestimate her actions.

In the following weeks, the appointments were made with the psychologist to do his testing, which cost $6,000. Cindy and I went to his office and took three hours worth of tests, including "do we like our moms and do we want to be fireman." This was preposterous, but necessary. He then came for a visit to our home and saw me playing soccer with Mike, which I always did. When we were showing him Mike's room, Mike was asked to throw his dirty clothes from the floor into the laundry chute, which he refused to do. With that attitude, the doctor saw Mike get disciplined and how our interaction was. Mike also played connect the dots with him. Cindy asked him if Brenda made the appointment and he said she made three, but never showed up for any; surprise!

Brenda was out of jail, maybe working and supposed to visit and call. She visited three times; once with another child about two years old, who she let unsupervised in our garden until I told her to watch the child she was supposedly sitting for. I was concerned because the child was shaky on his feet and kept falling near the cement walk.

Brenda made it very clear she hated my guts and displayed a very nasty attitude when given any supervision from me. I refused to take any more shit from her, and she fought back verbally. Half of my conversations with her consisted of, "not in front of Mike," but she didn't care.

The second time she came, she brought a puppy and told Mike it was his when he came to live with momma. She also told him that she was moving to a big house with a yard for him to play with his puppy. The puppy was very young, probably about six weeks old. Cindy and I just looked at each other when we saw the dog, which was a pit bull!

I told her that she should not bring the dog next time, because it could give Mike the feeling of losing something else. Also, Brenda was using her feet to play with the dog, and it was encouraging the dog to act wild. It also showed Mike the wrong way to treat an animal.

Brenda never really had much to say to Mike except, "Tell

momma you love her, hi baby, what did you do today, and momma has a good job (which was always something different)." That went on for about four months and then, Cindy and I were notified of the criminal trial date.

Brenda was supposed to show up for her criminal trial. Hell, she was the star of the show! The D.A. said that we didn't have to be there, but we wanted to be there to nail her butt and we didn't trust the D.A.'s office to really prosecute.

The worst thought to us was that Brenda believed that she would get Mike back as soon as the hearing ended. Brenda actually told everyone that she would not see any jail time.

In the meantime, Cindy continued to get calls and letters from bill collectors looking for Brenda. Once they saw that Cindy was cooperative with them, they opened up to what Brenda owed. Cindy assumed that these people got a percentage of what they collected, which is why they cooperated with us. Some of the calls that we got included car rentals, for which Brenda rented a car for a month and then just dropped it at their door. That bill was for $461. They said that they were going after her for payment. That generally won't happen, but she did have money from her job.

She was in town, but rarely made it over to see Mike. She still had not come over or called Mike. That gave us mixed emotions because Mike couldn't have her come in and out of his life at her whims. As far as we were concerned, Brenda was not an asset for him. She only loved him when it was convenient. She felt like she should have a son when the other girls talked about their babies.

We didn't understand why the courts took so long. The date was nine months past the arrest for theft. Was that a speedy trial? We were getting stressed because we were trying to protect Mike from her mental abuses. How could she say to him "I'll see you tomorrow" or "I love you" and never show up? How could Cindy allow or better yet, how could the courts allow a person to build a child's hope and then always let him down? Brenda never had Mike's best interests at heart and wasn't that what this was about?

Chapter Twenty-eight

The criminal trial hearing was set and since she pleaded guilty, there was supposed to be no problems. The hearing was only to confirm that she waived an arraignment and the judge could set a date for sentencing. We were told that we still should bring our expert witness to testify to the value of the stolen merchandise. I asked the D.A. to contact the expert and tell him that we would pay for his time. That day, I saw the appraiser at court at 9 a.m., which was the time for everyone to show up. The expert told us that he was served with a subpoena to show. We were somewhat embarrassed because that was like us not trusting him to come. The D.A.'s office sent it out and neglected to say that they would call if they needed him, but he didn't have to come. He was perturbed because of the lack of organization from their office and he was right, but we had to stay focused on the issues.

It turned out that the D.A. said that we could agree to let Brenda out on probation and she would pay restitution and report to a probation officer every two weeks. I asked if he was out of his mind. Why would a judge, who knew someone committed a major felony by stealing more than $100,000 in merchandise, tell him or her they don't have to go to jail? I was enraged. Probation certainly didn't seem like enough punishment to fit this crime.

I told the DA that if that happened, Brenda would have once again beaten the system, and this would allow her to laugh her way to more parties. She owed everyone money and would tell them to get off her back and she wouldn't pay! This was in no way a wonderful person who wanted to raise a child to be a responsible citizen. How could the courts not look at this person for what she was? At twenty-four years of age, her only changes in the past four years were for the worse. What did she have to offer to a child except instability, psychological damage, poor education, no positive role models, no morals, etc? We couldn't understand why the court couldn't see that this person should be incarcerated and hopefully be reformed. To leave her in the same mental state she was now in would be to give society a menace that would hurt many others. We convinced the D.A. that it was in all best interests to not make any deals or "blow out the case," which is what the courts liked to do. The D.A. told her counsel that no deals would be made. We were standing in the hallway at the courthouse. Brenda was shocked. When told news, she fired her counsel. Cindy and I just watched from a distance and the D.A. said that since she fired her counsel, who was court appointed, she had two days to hire another. We went home and waited for two days and then went back to court at 9 a.m. We waited and at 9:30 she was a no show. The court issued a bench warrant.

She showed up as we were leaving and her new attorney had the warrant lifted. The judge acknowledged that the new attorney did not have enough time to work the case, so he said they would go to trial in six weeks. Brenda still had not come to see Mike nor had she called him in over two months. The criminal case was scheduled. We set up a meeting with the D.A. and explained the entire situation, including all of her actions and non-actions with Mike. We were told that the case had a suggested sentencing of nine to sixteen months of jail time.

Brenda had no contact with us, but Joe kept informing us how well she was doing. We knew from others, and told him that she was strung out and totaling lying to him. It was something that she had done for the five years that we knew her.

The day of the hearing, we went to court and were ready for either the hearing or the definite agreement to plead guilty. We knew that she would be smart to plead guilty and go to the mercy of the court. She was unpredictable. We hoped that she would go for the hearing, at which time the judge would be annoyed since the proof was so airtight against her. The morning that the hearing began, she was a no show. No one knew why, but we guessed that she partied too much and couldn't get up.

The court ordered a bench warrant for her arrest. Generally that meant that when someone was stopped for a driving violation, it was probable the warrant would show. We asked what happened to the bail money and were told it was forfeited. Ok, what next? We were told that when she eventually got picked up for some type of violation, and the police checked her records, they would see that she had a bench warrant out for her. That was not good so we decided that the law worked faster when it got a boot in the ass. I called the Sheriff's office and told them where to find her, which was Carlos' house. It took about a month and the sheriff went there at 3 a.m. and knocked on the door; but no one answered. The officer said he was about to break down the door unless someone opened it. Carlos did, and Brenda was put in cuffs and taken to jail. She promptly received a new bail. Many times the courts let the people go. It amazed us that it was $5,000 bail at the original arrest, but when she failed to show up for her hearing, the bail was dropped to only $500. We could care less what they did because we were still concerned about Mike. Secretly, and not so secretly, we preferred that she be put away for the full-recommended time. Because she was issued a bench warrant, she was not in the court's favor.

Brenda's poor attitude never changed; she continued to lie to her father about working so many hours and being so diligent. We asked that our attorney get Brenda's work records to show that she lied about working, which was her stated reason she didn't come to see Mike. We were getting ready to catch her in more lies. There was a tense feeling because while all of this was going down, Mike was not aware of anything because he was busy with friends and many activities. He was gaining knowledge and thriving on learning. He once said that momma didn't visit any more and Cindy asked if that was ok; his answer was "yes." It was amazing that in those three months, Mike only mentioned Brenda's name once! Cindy asked if Mike if he wanted

Brenda to come more often, and he said "no." Cindy didn't push him any further as she was fine with those answers and didn't think it was worth her time to discuss it.

Everyone was happy that Brenda didn't call or visit, except she did show up one week later on Christmas morning. It wasn't much of a visit; she fell asleep on the sofa for two hours. The heroin probably was doing to her what it did to her mother. It was possible that if she never called or visited, she would not be part of Mike's life. I truly believed Brenda was like a virus in that she latched onto Carlos and wouldn't let go. She would be a plague to Mike and use and abuse him if he got in her way. The sad part was that she had no idea of what was morally right, and what to teach a child.

Joe called to tell me that he knew Brenda didn't show for the hearing, and she was going to talk to her attorney and have him turn her in within a few days. Joe spoke to the attorney and found out that she didn't pay him what she told Joe she did and the attorney was not happy with her.

In the meantime, Mike was adapting very well to his stable situation. He was playing soccer and ice hockey, doing well at school, playing on his computer, and gaining self-confidence. He knew that he had to listen to and obey rules and he had chores to do. We wanted to continue to give Mike responsibility. He was taking out the trash, cleaning up his room, and taking his dinner plate to the sink. We wanted to do something special for him. We didn't tell him anything except to get into the car with Linda, Cindy, and me because we had somewhere to go. We went to a special pet shop that had the dogs running loose. Mike picked up one of the puppies and was in love. It was a cute little beagle puppy, but aren't they all? We told him that since he had done so well, if he took care of it, it could be his. He was flying with enthusiasm! We told him since it was his puppy, he got to name it. He named her Terry. We had no idea where he got that name, but that was the puppy's name. We were always used to having dogs, even though they tied us down. Since we felt that Mike wasn't going anywhere soon, we felt that he should have his own dog, which would be walked by me, fed by Cindy, and played with by Mike.

Joe came in to see Mike play two ice hockey games. He stayed with us and again, as usual, things were amiable. Joe knew that we would not allow him to take Mike to see Brenda. He was told that if he did that, he would draw the battle lines between us. Joe knew and told me that Mike was very happy and that Brenda was no good for him. It was something he seemed to be realizing, after all this time.

Later that evening, Joe went to see Brenda at work without giving her notice. She told him that Carlos was in drug rehabilitation and she was staying at his house just to take care of his dog. She added that she was totally through with him. When she finished making that statement, Carlos walked in the door, right in front of Joe. Once again, Joe caught her in a lie. She told Joe that he misunderstood what she said. Joe was furious and wanted to punch out Carlos, but Brenda talked him out of it.

This was the sort of logic that this family used in their everyday life and that was very difficult for us to deal with. Joe came back and told us what happened. We just listened. We would have liked to say, "Are you a total idiot? What don't you understand about lies and the welfare of your grandchild? When will you understand that you are being suckered?"

He only stayed for one game, instead of two, and he left to see his friend in New York. Joe was not our favorite person, but he supplied us with a lot of information that we had no other way of getting and he didn't even realize it. That was the reason that we allowed him to stay at our home.

Carlos could not afford a problem with police because he was still on probation. Later that week, we got a call from Carlos, to get Joe's phone number, which we thought he already had. He proceeded to tell Cindy how depressed Brenda was and that she'd had just been in an accident with Carlos' car and hadn't come home. She was depressed because some of her past was catching up to her. She was still wanted by the police for not showing up at her hearing and now, she avoided the police by leaving the scene of an accident. In the meantime, Brenda's attorney made the deal for her to turn herself in, which she did. Since she was not a good risk for a bail bondsman, she remained in jail. Joe called our home to speak to Mike and also told me that Brenda was 'on her own.' She was being taken care of by her boyfriend and he wasn't doing a very good job. I checked with the prison every few days to see if she was still there, which she was. Actually, there was more hate in our lives than we thought we were capable of having. Our hate was out of fear for Mike. What did we have to do to protect Mike? Were we protecting Mike by hoping his mother was out of his life? The answer was a definite 'yes!' Would there be explaining to do later? Would he have psychological problems since he was without a mother and father? We made the decision that a bad mother was worse than no mother.

After two weeks, we found out that Brenda was not in prison, but we didn't know where she was. Joe called me and said that he guessed that we knew that Brenda was out of jail and in Boston. I said that we didn't know that. Joe then told me that she was getting help and she was getting her act together. Also, she "came clean" on all of her lies. Hell, when you were caught, why not come clean! He told me that Carlos picked up her paycheck at the restaurant, cashed it and went to New York and partied with her money. Joe said that he told Brenda to come directly to Boston from jail when she was bailed out. Joe neglected to tell me that he bailed her out. Joe did say that he was consumed with her and her plight and couldn't think of anything else over the past two weeks. When Carlos, who was at the bail office talking to Joe, said that she was staying with him for a few days first. Brenda's father said to put her on a train now or he would have her bail revoked. Carlos wanted some action first, but her dad wanted to get her away from him. Now there was a lot of stress in our home. Mike still didn't have a clue as to all of the ramifications of what was going on.

Brenda called the next day to speak to Mike and I put Mike on the phone, but advised her that I would be listening in.

The conversation was ok, except Mike didn't want to talk to her. He had been taught to be polite and he was at a conflict, which was tough for adults, let alone a 5-year-old. Brenda said that she loved him and was waiting for him to say it back, as he did with Cindy and me. His response was "ok." If she never called, he would not be faced with a head-on conflict. We were thinking of what, in the opinion of a psychologist, would be worse: bad mother in and out of your life or no mother and no stability? Brenda told Mike that she would be back in town in a few weeks for his birthday and asked him to invite her to his party. Mike said nothing.

Our thoughts were that there was no way to allow her into our home unsupervised or with other people. We knew there would be many opportunities for her to steal from the pocketbooks of the parents attending the party. We couldn't watch her, and didn't want to have to worry about her during Mike's party, so it was best that she not be there. We also had just been informed that her criminal trial was coming up in six weeks. There was a good chance that she would go to prison very shortly thereafter. We wrote up a summary for the judge that, as victims, we were able to read prior to sentencing.

Our other thoughts were simply that she wouldn't show up again. If it was me, and I just spent two weeks in jail, dreading the fact that the cell might be my new home for the next 16 months, I wouldn't be going to a party.

We also had a problem we needed to face. Mike was supposed to go to visit Brenda's father for three days in Boston. Knowing that he could fill Mike's head with propaganda about how good mama was, which could confuse Mike, should we let him go? Were Cindy and I over stepping our bounds? Granted, it was Mike's other family, but they certainly were a dysfunctional bunch. I knew that when the trial came, Brenda's father was going to have to take sides. We wouldn't let him play both because Mike would be affected. Joe would have a difficult decision to make. If he went against Mike, and if we won, Joe would be totally at our mercy and we would not allow Mike to go to

Boston unsupervised for fear that Joe, or the relatives, would confuse Mike about mama. If Joe went with us, he would have to divest himself from Brenda, who wouldn't allow her dad to be in a relationship with Mike if she got him back.

Cindy and I decided that we would drive Mike to Boston to see the rest of his family. We did it for the courts, so they could see we were making an effort. We drove up in the evening so Mike would sleep in the car. We arrived at Joe's house about midnight. We carried Mike up the outside steps and knocked on the door; we exchanged cordialities and then Mike woke up. We told Mike to have a drink and get ready for bed. We told him he could sleep in Joe's room if he wanted, but he was in our bed twenty minutes later.

In the morning, we allowed Joe to take Mike alone to the Renaissance Fair, while Cindy and I went to Fanuel Hall in Boston with Joe's wife. We felt that if they were on their own, it would be a good opportunity for Joe to see how happy Mike was. It was a totally wasted day of doing nothing that Cindy and I would have rather done without. We were nervous, and we kept watching the clock. When Joe and Mike got back to the house about 6 p.m., Mike had a hunting knife in his belt. We were flabbergasted! It had an eight-inch blade and four-inch handle! When Joe saw our expression, he said to Mike that he could only play with it when we were with him.

He kept giving us more ammunition against his side of the family, but we didn't know if the courts would let us use it. We sat around and Joe bought Chinese take-out food, which we ate. We asked if the "other side of the family" was coming over and he said he called them. Brenda's aunt and cousin came over, but Brenda's grandmother didn't. They only lived fifteen minutes away, but the grandmother hated Joe's guts and she hated Cindy and me even more. Mike didn't care. He was amiable with everyone who came over because he realized that he was the 'star' of the show. We stayed over that night and left at nine the next morning.

If Joe went against us in the custody hearing, we would bring the knife that he gave to Mike into court. Seeing that knife would absolutely kill any credibility that Joe had, unless the judge was an idiot. This was an on-going stressful situation. There was still no answer to jail or custody at this time and we wanted things to be settled so we could get on with our lives.

Cindy just received a letter from our attorney stating that she was hoping to have full custody for us in about six months. We had mixed emotions because we didn't know what that meant. Did Brenda get visitation rights? Were we forced to tie up our lives again for planning because the judge didn't have a clue as to what Brenda had put everyone through? It was like me describing what it felt like to give birth; especially since I was a guy! I couldn't do it well!

The files on Brenda were getting huge and we couldn't even begin to sort out what should be brought into court. Our attorney was the best in the area and was very high profile, which meant costly, and she couldn't know every nuance of the situation. She had tremendous experience with family law and realized what we were dealing with in Brenda and Joe. Our friends said that we should offer Brenda money to go away. They didn't understand that could not only lose the case, but also destroy our credibility with the courts? We knew that was not the answer. A move like could put Mike right back into her hands to be led to the slaughter, without any visitation by the grandparents. Buying and selling children was, and still is, to the best of our knowledge, illegal. People meant well by saying that, but no one was in our shoes, except us.

It became another waiting game, but every day that Mike was in a stable atmosphere of love and warmth, he was ahead. When he was in the car with me, he demanded we play math games by saying, "give me a math problem," with his chest puffed up with pride and a grin from ear to ear. That was what made it all worthwhile to be in the war to protect Mike. The ironic part about all of these past and future battles was that the judge went home to his family after seeing only the tip of the iceberg, and the attorney got big bucks and felt that she would either win or lose the game.

The problem was that the judge and attorney would play another game tomorrow, but today was the beginnings our lives!

We were out of our league in the family courts, but we knew damn well what was going on and the real dangers. How could that be conveyed? We had to keep the criminal and custody trials separate, but they were related because it was the same individual who could control this child's destiny. Should we now ask Brenda for child support just to prove she had no way to support him? If we did that, did that show we couldn't support him? Why couldn't logic prevail, as she had not shown any responsibility in ANYTHING!

Chapter Twenty-nine

Over the next few weeks, Mike was finishing up playing ice hockey and starting little league. He was very excited because he knew how much better he got by trying and giving 100% and never quitting in hockey. It was amazing to watch the little guys learn a sport from scratch and in this case, from stepping on the ice and falling on his butt to skating backward with ease in one season. At the same time, he learned the game and its rules and learned to appreciate watching a professional game on television. He was enjoying himself. He had no idea Brenda was in jail, although we kept wanting to ask him if he knew what a jailbird was, but we didn't. Certain things always brought mixed emotions to us. Mike usually took showers, but sometimes, including that night, he would take a bubble bath. The bathtub was where Mark initially started his physical march to death with the razor. Mike always had a smile on his face and was a very happy kid and as we watched him playing and laughing in the tub, we were both sad and happy. We conjured up a picture of Mark in his last minutes, but we also felt this tub brought Mike and his father together, in a spiritual way, since he used to take Mike into the tub with him. Cindy and I would have to wipe our eyes periodically during these pensive times. It allowed us to think his father still had some indirect input without Mike realizing it. It also relaxed him before bed.

Now we were again waiting to see if Brenda would call, which she didn't so far. That meant that she now had not seen him, except for Christmas day, since December 5, and it was now March 24. We were waiting three times a week for the court ordered visitations and videotaping each non-visit without telling Mike why. After a while, Mike was telling us that it was time to tape the weather station and read the time, date, and tell who he was with. Mike considered this a learning game that we played. We were getting stressed out knowing that the trial was coming up. Cindy's father was still living with us, with dementia, and we were still working to make a living. As things developed, more notes and filing took place, as did communication with our attorney. I wanted to fight without gloves and the attorney was saying to let things develop, as Brenda would again screw up. She couldn't change her life. She couldn't change her work ethic. She wouldn't give up Carlos. She couldn't stop doing drugs. She wouldn't stop stealing. Why should she? No one was keeping her on a leash to train her. She wouldn't be trained! She wouldn't listen to the judge, so what was left. Any threat by the judge would be taken to heart by anyone else with fear or respect for the law.

We tried to put ourselves in her position, to try and understand what she might be thinking. She never had money. She was active sexually. She stole what she wanted. She slept all day. She sometimes did waitress jobs, but after a day or two, the novelty wore off and she quit. She thought she could do anything she wanted to do in the drug zones because she was comfortable being there. The threat of jail must exist, but she must not take it very seriously. Her friends told her the jails were too crowded and she won't spend any time there. But she must have been a little scared. She was already in jail because of a bench warrant. Was she thinking about her future? Was she thinking about her son at all? Why didn't she call? Why didn't she at least write him a letter? Did his welfare ever enter her mind, or was her whole life centered on her wants and desires? From our experience with her, we would have to say she lived in an "I" only world.

The way to approach any fight was to be so right that there was no other view. Cindy and I were right, but we were not the 'biological mother.' We had to guess what Brenda's moves would be and defend against them. The sad part is that we knew Brenda had no idea what her moves would be; we had to guess what impulsive move she would make. We were like prizefighters reviewing tapes to know our opponent's next move so we could counter it. Would she have an attorney and what moves would he or she make that were a legal ploy to catch us off guard? The one move that we knew would be brought up was that she stole only once and regretted doing it. Brenda would have tears in her eyes and say how much her baby needed her. She would also play on the theft being her first offense. How could we prove that she stole six times? We knew her and she couldn't hold a dime without spending it. When she came over to the house, if she came to the house, we wanted to wash everything she touched or sat on. That was hate! We felt as if the showdown was coming and we weren't sure if our gun was loaded. If she went to jail, Mike got a reprieve. We felt like prisoners on death row, waiting and counting every second. If a balloon burst near us or a car backfired, it was heart attack time! It wasn't fair that she did the crime and we got the stress. Well, as the saying goes, no one said life was fair. It sometimes made one wonder if the so-called backward countries were wrong when they cut off the hands of thieves! We got ready for the criminal trial as the date was fast approaching. We called the D.A.'s office to see what jobs we had to do and were told our job was to be at court and shut up unless we were called upon. The night before the hearing, Brenda called and came to the house to see Mike with her relatives from Boston, who came in to give her support. A taxicab came to our home and Brenda, her grandmother, her cousin, and the cousin's boyfriend got out of it. Since Brenda's Grandmother was frail, we asked if they wanted to come in. The grandmother never acknowledged Cindy or me. They just stood outside in the driveway. Her cousin asked if she could see Mike's room, and we told her to go upstairs and it was on her right. We still had Brenda's picture in his room. They stayed about one hour and were bored and wanted to go to dinner. Mike had no reaction to Brenda and didn't want to hug her. If only the custody judge could have seen that, and what the child's true feelings were, but he couldn't, so that part was on hold until the criminal proceedings were complete. We sent the D.A.'s office some facts that included the following topics, since we knew the effort, or lack of, that probably would go into the D.A.'s research:

Details of the theft, actions at the pawn shop, relationship with us, her credit card record, drugs, theft of other items in the house, relationship with Mike, gifts she was given by us, and anything else that would put her in a position to defend herself.

We hoped that these topics would make our life easier, and get the points across, without the D.A. getting annoyed and thinking we overstepped our bounds by doing his job. All courts appearances were scheduled for one room. We waited for them to assign us to another room for the hearing. We went to the newly assigned room, but we couldn't find the assistant D.A. that we had already met with earlier. The hearing started and we had no idea where our prosecutor was. I went to a pay phone and called the D.A.'s office that was somewhere in the same building. I found out our guy was out sick and one of two people took the file and was going to handle the trial. Catch this new scenario. We now had a reason to worry; $100,000 stolen jewelry, thief caught, substitute prosecutor picking up file at the hearing. It didn't give us a good feeling about prep time! Brenda didn't realize that the prosecutor had no idea about her case. We were lucky because Brenda admitted to the crimes and figured that she was getting off. The judge looked half asleep and as if he could care less. I went up to the railing separating the attorneys from the gallery and asked to speak to the prosecuting attorney. The new prosecutor blew me off when I tried to talk to her. I wanted to see if she had a clue about this case that was just dropped into her lap. We were sweating and our two neighbors and friends with us were in shock watching this nightmare unfold. We were thinking the courts were going to give Brenda a medal!

The entire time, we kept thinking that these enforcers of rights and justice were giving Mike the death penalty by allowing her to get out. All of the preparation was wasted and we had no control since it was the county against her, not us.

As it turned out, Brenda was warned that she could go to jail, but she knew if she had a real trial, it could be worse. She plead guilty to theft. I asked what happened to the drug charges. During a break, we caught up with the prosecutor in the hallway who said those charges were not as important so they dropped them, but they would be on her record. This was out of control. How could drug charges be dropped when a child's life was in danger? Who would want a child to be raised by a druggie? We were outraged and this whole scene was beyond our comprehension. When the hearing was over, we cornered the acting prosecutor and inquired as to what the bottom line would be. She said that there absolutely would be jail time and we should check with the other prosecutor when he came back. Brenda was told to come back for sentencing when she received notice of the date. We were told it would be about three months.

In the meantime, we had three months to sweat out this situation. The possibilities of what could happen were our every thought. Brenda went to Boston, Mike went to school, and Cindy and I worried about Mike and his psychological mindset. He didn't know that she was ever in jail. Mike did know that "momma did some bad things," but he never asked about her and we never brought it up. The few times that Brenda was with him, we made sure that one of us was within hearing distance. We knew from experience that

Brenda would not think of Mike's future, but would lie to him and say things to confuse him. Things register with five and six year olds that one doesn't realize until they ask questions days or weeks later. Things adults might think passed by them.

Joe told us that she now had a job in a day care center in Boston. That didn't sound right. If she was honest on her application, she would never be hired to be with kids. Drugs and felony theft were not the influences that owners of daycare centers were looking for in the people they hired to care for the kids. We were also told that she was going to A.A. meetings every night and doing great. We listened and were told those things when there were calls from Boston. Joe also told us, with no uncertainty that she was done with Carlos.

The system was not at all interested in helping either the parent or the child. The system was set for reaction rather than action. While all of this was going on, did anyone realize that a now six-year-old child no longer had a mother or a father?

If it is at all possible for you to put down this book, sit in a dark room, evolve yourself into the mind set of a child, see yourself happy with grandmom and grandpop, and wonder what it would be like to have a real mommy who cared and a daddy that came home from work and played with you. Picture your friends talking about mom and dad and you talk about your grandparents; we did.

When we did it, there were a lot of questions: " I thought that I would talk to my dad and ask him why he died and didn't stay with me because I loved him and now I love his picture. I don't really understand death, but my grandmom says daddy is watching me from heaven with God. Why can't God send my daddy back to talk to me and play with me? Mom comes around sometimes, but I know she does bad things; she told me that. Why can't she just stay with me and do good things? I know mom goes out and takes me places that I don't want to go, but she always says that she will buy me something, but she doesn't. I really love my grandmom and grandpop and they do all the stuff with me, but that's not the way my friends live. My grandpop is strict, but he plays with me when he is not working. He helps the coaches out on my baseball team, but he has white hair. Why are things different? Oh well, I'm having a good time and I know that I am doing good because my grandmom and grandpop said they are really proud of me and my daddy talks to them to from heaven and says he is proud too."

We were sad about Mike's potential state of affairs. We knew the situations he had to deal with in his young life made him different from the other children. While other kids in school talked about their parents, he would automatically be excluded from the conversation. His dad is dead. This fact alone is hard for a kid to live with, but the way his father lived and died is also a stigma that Mike will carry with him forever. Although Mike has his picture, and some distant memories of his father, this will never take the place of a father that plays and nurtures and cares for his son.

In many other situations like this, the child at least has the mom to cling to, someone to help him or her get through the difficult years. But this child is also denied the nurturing of a mother who cares about his well-being. His mother is an admitted druggie and felon. A woman who wanders in and out of his life, offers no stability, and breaks countless promises. A woman who is facing a prison term for things she did to people who tried to do all they could to help her get on the right track of life.

We also did all we could to make up for the life Mike was thrown into at such an early age. Trying to keep him safe and secure, through a system that only seems to work after a tragedy occurs, is the most frustrating of all. We knew in our hearts that we could give him a better life than Brenda could. All we need is for the courts to see the situation through our eyes. This three-month waiting game we were playing with the court system was like living with an axe above our heads, and holding our breath, waiting for it to fall.

During this three month wait, Brenda showed up after saying she was coming to town to see Mike for his birthday, which was six weeks earlier. She got to town Friday night, and finally came to see Mike at 6 p.m. Saturday, watched his Little League ball game, and said she would see him Sunday. She came to the game with Carlos, who Joe said was out of the picture. She talked to Mike for five minutes after the game, and never saw him the rest of her stay. She never showed up at his soccer game, which she said she would do on Sunday.

The laws in this state allowed for custody to be given to someone other than the parents if it was in the best interests of the child. The courts had to decide how to interpret that phrase. Do words like security, safety, prevention; love, stability, etc. ring a bell? As decent citizens who obey the law, the answer was fairly simple for us. While all of these discussions were going on, what about the child? Health insurance for the child was difficult, if not impossible, to get. If an operation were needed, whose approval was required? Many things that parents take for granted were not the case here with us, as his grandparents. Why even have custody laws, if by the time the case is settled, the child is old enough to be married by the same judge who was to render a verdict on the custody case! Time goes by quickly for children and slowly through the legal system. That is a bad match!

The trial was approaching, and we were afraid of what was going to happen. We had already seen first-hand that the courts seemed to want to toss out the cases where there was no physical harm involved. Mere loss of valued possessions didn't seem to be such a big deal. But since it was Cindy's value, she looked at it differently. I called the D.A.'s office to see what direction they were heading and they said that they were looking for work release, restitution (right!), and probation. I asked about jail time and was told they weren't sure since it was her first offense. I again laid out the entire scenario, including all of the lies to the courts, the D.A., the probation officer, and the prosecutor. They seemed to realize that this was not a virgin "bad girl." I told him, in my opinion, she should go away for a while; she will either get worse or straighten out. Either way, it was better than what she was doing. The prosecutor agreed. He said he would ask for state time, possibly two-five years. We felt this was a good sign. We also were trying to figure out if she would show up knowing that she was going to jail. If it were someone intelligent, would he or she stay in the area to be locked up after all of their freedom? For this type of crime, no court would make anyone leave the state if they were picked up. What if she said she was not guilty? What witnesses should we have at this hearing? How many people should we inconvenience and how many times? Should the psychologist be there? Should we put an investigator on Brenda now? How much money was left to spend when lawyers cost so much? How will her lawyer try to get her out? Would her lawyer use the poor, single mother raising her child routine? That was stress as no one knew and very few cared about! Brenda's lifestyle provided no stability for Mike or herself. How was this going to be played to her favor by her attorney? Was this just sentencing or would it turn into a trial? We still didn't know all of the rules.

The judge sat on the bench and the original assistant D.A. was there. Was Brenda just going to be told to stand up and hear the sentencing? We quickly found out! Our jewelry appraiser was called to the stand and Brenda's attorney tried to discredit him. He was one of the most respected appraisers in the entire area and had a reputation, even among the courts, as a very credible expert. Brenda's attorney was trying to lower the value of the jewelry to reduce the recommended guidelines for sentencing. The appraisal witness was accepted after about five minutes because with each question Brenda's attorney asked, the witness became more creditable. He was on the stand for over ½ hour and Cindy was getting uncomfortable because things were dragging. We were there with two neighbors and Linda. We kept looking at each other, especially when Brenda was on the stand. She was lying and it wasn't getting caught by anyone except us. She said she was never in trouble, all of the jewelry was recovered, she was in drug rehabilitation programs, and she didn't did heroin daily, etc. You would have thought that she was the coming of the Virgin Mary and we should be hung for the treatment that we gave her.

I couldn't take it anymore. I approached the prosecutor's table in the courtroom and told him of all her lies. This prosecutor read the notes that we made as we listened to her false testimony. Thankfully, the facts were once again discussed, with Brenda finally admitting to lying. Next up was Brenda's father, who offered the court letters from four rehabilitation centers. He told the courts how Brenda made a mistake, but was doing great now. The DA then read each of the four letters and each stated that she didn't go, nor did she complete any type of training. Joe lied as much as Brenda!

It was my turn on the stand. I was asked how we were affected by the theft. I told the court about the empty feeling Cindy had every time she dressed to go out, realizing that the jewelry that she would have worn from her mother and grandmother were gone. I told about how Cindy would just think about it and cry because the items, when worn, made her feel as if her mom was with her. Suddenly, the judge said that it was his time to give the sentence. He first stated that Brenda was not a credible witness and she was going to have to serve time in jail. With that, he sentenced her to ten-twenty three months in county prison. He then said she was eligible for work release, and could get credit for good behavior. He also gave her five years probation upon release, and said she had to pay restitution for the value of the missing jewelry. Upon completion of the sentencing, Brenda was handcuffed and led away. As she was walking past her father, Joe said to her that Mike would be back in Boston before she got out of jail.

As we were leaving, the prosecutor came over to us, sat down, and apologized for the weak sentence. We honestly felt that he did a great job presenting and proving the case. The bailiff seemed as shocked as everyone else as he came over to us and voiced the same opinion. The judge appeared to surprise everyone with his lenient ruling, but that was the law. When we left the courtroom, we went to the custody attorney, who had an office across the street from the courthouse. We told her what happened so she could decide how the custody would be affected by the criminal decision. She said nothing would happen until Brenda got out of jail, but Joe, now filed for visitation and partial custody. We felt he probably had no standing to file, according to state law. This meant we had more filing to complete, but that was the law. We drove home and had a feeling that Mike was safe for a while. The best part of all of that was that Mike's attitude was not affected and he had no idea that anything out of the ordinary was going on.

When Joe called to speak to Mike, I advised Joe not to mention anything to upset him about what happened and don't tell him that his mother was in jail, coming, loved him, or was going to do something for him. I asked that he just talk about Mike and things that would interest Mike. I was specific and said don't tell Mike that he is going to Boston because, as far as we were concerned, he wasn't going to be out of our sight since Joe filed papers with the court. Joe was livid, but I told him that Mike didn't need to be involved and I was going to listen on the phone to be sure Joe didn't upset Mike. Joe was still welcome to come visit, but he had to stay somewhere else. Joe was getting more agitated with each word! Before Joe filed the petition for visitation and partial custody, we said that we would bring him up to Boston for two long weekends, but Mike would be supervised at all times around Joe. Of course, Joe didn't like that either.

I wanted to go to court, but our attorney said no. We wanted to bring to court the knife with the 8" inch blade that Joe bought him the only time Joe was alone with him. That would have knocked him out of the case forever with only visits with supervision. We were imagining the headlines if Mike took that knife to school. The only thing that put knots in our stomachs was when we envisioned Mike being raised in that environment.

That same week of the trial, Mike started his day camp and was having a ball. He got to play all types of ball games, twice-a-day swimming, fishing, archery, great food, and then came home at four o'clock to play with the thirteen kids in the immediate neighborhood.

At the same time, within five days of Brenda's incarceration, we were told Brenda got out on a work-release program in a fast food chicken restaurant in a mall. Imagine one week in jail, admitting to a daily heroin habit, and jail releases you and says come back after work.

Were we stupid or doesn't a drug addict need more help than to be put back in public, especially at a fast food restaurant with kids? One week later, she was taken off work release and was being reevaluated. She didn't go to work one day and told the warden that she went shopping. Did they believe that? What does one shop for; decorations to a jail cell and orange overalls?

In the meantime, Joe's effort to get control of Mike was too scary to think about so we did some investigating of him. Beside the old charges of forgery and assault, there were newer violations of trying to cause accidents on the freeways to collect insurance money. Joe got caught because a cop was following him and saw the scam! Of course this was not supposed to be admissible in court unless he said his background could be checked. There were about fifteen other things on his docket, but none as bad as those and many were dropped. We knew the feeling we had was true concerning Joe's morals and what type standards he set for his kids. Didn't he realize that someone could have been killed on the highway just for him to scam some insurance company for money? We apologize because our prospective was from this side of the law. I'll bet yours is too. We needed questions answered so, although we believed we knew the answers, we needed either reassurances or someone to tell us that we were being selfish assholes. We still couldn't understand why the process would probably take years to resolve, when a child grew up in less time. Why jam a child down a mother's throat when her actions said she didn't want him?

Since we were new to this situation, and didn't want damage to Mike, we needed advice. Our concerns needed answers, so we wrote a letter to the psychologist who did the studies on Mike, Cindy, and me:

Please take two minutes to help us out if possible, since you know us and our grandson and the situation, which I will recap briefly:
Referred to you from --------- for evaluation for custody
You did work-up on Mike, Cindy, and me. Brenda never completed study
She is now in jail for grand larceny and will be out in February at the earliest. She admitted to daily heroin use and screwed up her first work release within one week of incarceration.
Her father in Boston (same type record as his daughter and is trying unsuccessfully for partial custody)
Mike is happy, never asks for anyone from Boston, and is very active in sports and education.
We are trying to "guess" what would be best for Mike, but we have concerns as follows:
Should Mike be told, "momma is in jail?"
When Brenda's father calls, he lies and says "she is sick and will see him soon" Mike and the grandfather were told we listen to the conversations, because the grandfather confuses Mike. He told Mike he was going to Boston (Mike wet the bed after that and still does periodically after he speaks to him.)
We don't trust her father alone with Mike so we believe we should allow him to visit, with us present. If he doesn't accept that, then that's his problem
Her father reinforces that "momma loves you" when momma never cared about anything but momma.
Mike saw Brenda steal money from his piggy bank and hides it if he thinks she is coming. He speaks to her about once a month for two or three minutes and seems confused for about 15 minutes, but we're not sure why (security, relationship, etc.)
He gets confused, but says nothing every time we allow him to speak to Boston family.

We want to do what is best for his head, even though the Boston group is mostly ex-cons (forgery, assault, drugs, theft, etc).

Any thoughts, advice, or general guidance? We have full, temporary custody so this is not a legal concern.

Thank you

Cindy and Ed

With the above letter waiting for a response, Cindy decided to call a friend who was a psychologist. She was very blunt about Cindy telling Mike the truth. "If he can't trust you guys, who can he trust?" She made sense! She said that we were right on target with honesty, giving 100% on everything that he did, and letting him know what responsibility was involved and that Mike must be part of it. When we thought about that, it was darn good advice! We believed these words were the best advise for raising a well-functioning, healthy child.

The response to the letter came back the next day, which was well appreciated. The psychologist said, "that he would not lie to the child, but don't go to him and push the news of his mother." He said that Brenda's father was difficult to comment on except that since Cindy and I were his security, keep the visits supervised. We would not allow Brenda to be put up on the pedestal by Joe. We would not permit Joe to lie to Mike by telling him that his mother was sick and wanted to be with him, and when she got out of the hospital, she would be with him. With television today, these kids knew what jail was, even if it was not a full meaning.

At this point, I was thinking of all that has happened to us; where everyone was at this stage of the game.

Living at home with Mike was Cindy, Linda, Cindy's father, the nine-month-old puppy, and me;

Living in Boston was Brenda's father, stepmother, grandmother, aunt, brother (girlfriend and baby) and cousin;

Living in jail was Brenda on a work release again (now at a pizza shop in the same mall);

Mike was in day camp, Cindy and I were working out of the house, and Linda was going to school;

Cindy's father had dementia and was equal to a pet that ate, slept, went to the bathroom, and said hello;

Joe was trying for partial custody and visitation;

Cindy and I were staying very close to our legal counsel to protect Mike's rights;

We were still working on publicity for grandparent's rights through AARP and the media;

We were closely watching Mike to see if he was affected by the situation;

Mike was signed up for another year at the private school;

The entire neighborhood kept a special watch for Mike in case of a kidnapping attempt;

Linda was like Mike's big sister; she was from a broken home so she watched Mike's reactions;

Brenda's mother was in jail for theft and heroin;

Cindy and I were working on three cases: two custody and one criminal.

There were more questions being asked by us and to us on a daily basis:

When will these situations end?

When will the court take their heads out of their butts?

What effect will Brenda have being in and out of Mike's life?

How can we not portray the hate that we had for Brenda and her actions?

Why didn't we feel sympathy for a drug addict and why should we?

Why did we have to prove to everyone that Mike was not safe with momma?

Why didn't Brenda keep in touch with her son?

Why was every day an adventure; we never knew who would call or what would happen?

What if Mike got hurt in camp; would we be blamed for not being responsible?

When Brenda gets out of jail, why would she try to take him

knowing she couldn't support him?
When will Brenda screw up next and how?
Why doesn't the prison test her for drugs?
Why doesn't Mike even ask about her?
Why does Joe think that he controls the situation when he has no authority?
What should we do on visits from anyone in Boston, since we trusted no one?
Why didn't Brenda give Mike up on the condition that she could see him when and if she straightened out?
Why did everyone keep telling us to buy her off?
Why didn't the courts end this when she defied every order she was given and she jumped bail?

Chapter Thirty

The jail discussion bothered us so we discussed it with Mike one more time. We sat Mike down and said, "Have we ever lied to you?" He said no because he knew how we stressed the truth. We told him that it was important that he listen and understand, which he said he would. He knew that Brenda did bad things, from her theft of his piggy bank money to lies. We asked Mike what happened to people who did bad things. Mike said that they went to jail. We said that he was right and that's where momma was. I told him that he was good and the judge said Brenda had to stay there until she learned her lesson, like a long time-out. I said it was nothing that he, Cindy or I did, but it was her choice to do the right thing and she chose not to on purpose. We asked if he understood or had any questions. He said he understood, had no questions, and could he go out to play?' Cindy said, "yes, and if you ever wanted to know anything or were confused, ask and we would tell you the truth." We weren't sure if it registered, but we think it did.

We knew that more hearings were coming up, including Joe's, who had filed papers to get some control of Mike.

Now we were faced with two more hearings on custody; one with Brenda eventually and the one with Joe coming up soon. Our relationship with Joe was gone. We filed papers to take Mike on vacation to Florida because the order for Brenda to visit three times a week was still in effect, even though she was in jail and was not able to get out until February of next year, and we were going away August and December of this year. Joe insisted that Mike be allowed to go to his house in Boston for two weeks. We asked Mike about that to see his reaction. Mike said that he would like to go for a day and then come home. Mike said that he wanted us to go, too. We dropped that issue because it was not going to be an issue! At our request, we were scheduled for the hearing to go to Florida, which everyone thought would be a quick in and out a situation.

We assumed that the judge would just say that even though the other order was still in effect, it was a technicality. We arrived at our attorney's office at 9 a.m. for the scheduled 9:30 hearing. We gave no thought to this hearing and were relaxed. We proceeded across the street to the courthouse. As we walked up the steps, our throats tightened as we saw Brenda and Joe standing at the front door. I leaned over to our attorney and told him who was in front of us. He was as surprised as us. No one acknowledged anyone and we proceeded to go through the doorway as Joe and Brenda followed.

The hearing started and the judge asked if there were any objections to our going away and Brenda and Joe both stood up and said "yes." With that, the judge ordered everyone out of the courtroom to discuss the matter to see if a compromise could be worked out. Our attorney went out of the room with Brenda and Joe. Cindy and I stayed in the courtroom at the request of our lawyer. They came back about fifteen minutes later and said that Joe called his attorney in Boston who said to seek a hearing on the matter. Our calm demeanor was gone. We were very confused and shocked. Brenda was supposed to be in jail, and Joe was going to force us into a hearing before a judge who never saw this case. Cindy asked our attorney what happened outside and he told us that Joe wanted Mike in Boston for two weeks. The attorney told Joe that we would consider it depending on the results of the present hearing.

Two hours went by and the judge finished the other cases and said he would hear our case now. He proceeded to tell Brenda that there should be a good reason for her to object to us taking Mike to Disney World. He didn't see a reason why not, and he believed he would rule against her. With that, Joe stood up and said that they are withdrawing their objection. The judge asked about the custody rulings so far and was given the transcript, which he took to his chambers. He came back ten minutes later and said that he was ruling in favor of the grandparents, and the record should read that both sides mutually agreed to the decision, which was not the case, but we had no say. The judge then told Brenda how she didn't show up for her court ordered psychological testing and that was her responsibility as a mother. He said he would not do it for her, but if she called the psychologist, made the appointment, and advised the his office of the appointment, he would make sure that the court would allow her to leave jail to go get the tests. Was someone going way beyond their duty as a judge when she had the opportunity to get the tests for the prior eight months, especially since we had to pay for them eight months earlier?

The judge then proceeded to tell her that he believed that a child should be with his mother and he would do everything in his power to make that happen. He sounded like her attorney. I looked at Cindy and our hearts sunk. Here was the man, a judge, who was going to make the decision for Mike's future and he basically told everyone his ruling. As we left the courthouse, Joe came over and asked me if we reconsidered and would allow Mike to stay at his house for two weeks. I quickly answered, "No," when I should have said, "talk to my attorney." With that answer, Joe said that he would see us with the conciliator next week, when it was scheduled. We tried to cover all bases, except Joe was right; he would see us in court the next week.

Mike was ready to go away with our family to Disney World and we were going with another couple who had a daughter that Mike was friendly with. We were extremely excited. The kids talked about what they would do and we told them how they would have to sleep in the car when we told them to. We were driving non-stop through the night, leaving at 5 p.m. and arriving there by 9 the next morning. It was going to be very easy as there would be four drivers. The only problem was that we had to be at the conciliator's hearing the day before we left. We got to the hearing and Joe was there with his wife. There was no way Brenda could be out of jail for a hearing that was more of an information hearing, but we were on edge after the last hearing.

The rules were that we had to bring Mike to the hearing. We parked the car in front of the attorney's office, which was also in front of the storefront conciliator's rooms. Joe saw us pull up and walk past the office toward our attorneys'. As we approached the attorney's door, Joe came out of the conciliator and yelled to Mike. We stopped as Joe approached us. Joe picked Mike up and asked how he was. Joe hugged him, but it was very obvious that Mike wasn't overly thrilled to see him because he backed away. Joe put him back down and said he brought Mike a few baseballs. Mike said nothing to him.

I said we had to get up to our attorney's office. Joe asked if Mike could stay with him and I said, "no, I had to see if the attorney needs Mike." I prepared a one-page outline for our attorney giving the facts about the investigation we had done on Joe. The attorney said that she didn't need that, but she did read it. I realized that it was unfair to the attorney for us to expect her to know the details I gave her. The attorney said it wasn't needed because the meeting was to assure everyone that a compromise could not be reached. When that decision was made, then a date would be set in court. Cindy and I went to the conciliator knowing that we did not want to expose the knife situation because our attorney assured us this meeting was only to try to work things out, and there would be no major decisions. I wanted the knife to seal the door shut for Joe if we actually ever got into the courtroom! Our minds were working toward the actual custody since there was no possible relationship we could now have with Joe. After about twenty minutes in her office, our attorney said that we should go to the hearing.

We went in the storefront and through the metal detector and saw Joe and his wife. Joe asked if he could see Mike. Mike was going into a room off the main lobby that was full of kid's toys. With Joe's request, our attorney asked Mike, so that Joe could hear it, if he wanted to come out and see Joe. Mike said maybe later he would, but he didn't want to now. That couldn't have been better since Joe was thinking he would be warmly greeted. If the conciliator had pressed Mike as to see if he was pressured to stay away from Joe, that would have been the best. Throughout all of the cases, neither of us ever pushed Mike away from the "other side." We always asked if Mike wanted to go, talk, or anything when the situation arose, and we made sure Mike made his own decision on what he wanted to do. The hearing got nasty. Joe did not have an attorney, but his wife worked in the legal field so she did a lot of the talking. Joe had a temper so she had to keep him under control. The conciliator had Cindy wait in the hall with Mike while things were being discussed.

The attorney almost went verbatim off of my notes and she put Joe on the defensive from the start. She nailed his character from the rap sheets and his wife said that was history from twenty years ago, and she was right. But that lead to the current insurance scams that he tried on the freeways and his wife said that was a mistake by the state police. At that point, everyone realized this hearing was a waste. Joe said he would put the case in for a hearing date, if he was legally allowed to be heard, based on the requirements needed in Pennsylvania on these laws. That was also a controversy. Our lawyer said Joe had no standing to bring the case up. When the hearing ended, and everyone went into the hallway, Joe again picked up Mike who again arched his back to pull away from Joe. At that point, the attorney and Joe started getting into it again and she said, "Do you want to buy him another knife?" I tried to pass that over as that was supposed to be the trump card if and when we hit court. Everyone left with bitter attitudes against each other and Mike was fine, even though that was the first time he ever heard any of the conflict. Our attorney realized the type of people we were dealing with and knew she had to get down and dirty when we all got into the courtroom.

We walked back to the attorney's office and talked to Mike. He was fine and wanted to go home and play with his friends, but he had a strange look. We asked him if he knew what just happened. That was the first time that Mike was in a situation that was foreign to him. We were not comfortable with the situation, but we were in it. We didn't want that confrontation in front of Mike. It wouldn't do any harm for Mike to hug Joe, or would it? Would he be afraid that he would have to go with him? Cindy asked him if he had any questions. To our surprise, he said that he did. He looked confused. He said he was trying to figure out a way to ask why Joe was there and he wasn't sure what was happening because we always protected him and wouldn't allow anyone to control and dominate him. He felt that I allowed it there when Mike refused to hug Joe. Mike wanted me to tell Joe to leave him alone. Did we fail him? Would he lose his faith in us? What should we do the next time, and there would be a next time? Was Mike going to wet the bed that evening? Was his security blanket tarnished? Cindy felt badly for him. She explained that nothing changed and he could live where he wanted and we were still in charge. He bought it, but he stayed real close to Cindy until we got home.

That night, Joe called and asked why Mike was afraid of him. I decided that it was best to act dumb and just say, "I don't know." Joe had figured that his attorney was coming in from Boston and no one knew for sure if the case would be heard, even though a hearing date had been set.

The time for the Florida trip arrived. All of the adults had been under a lot of pressure, so just being away calmed everyone. It also allowed Cindy, Mike, and me to be without the stress of who was coming over or could someone try to kidnap Mike. The trip to Disney was wonderful. Mike had a familiarity with the restaurants and facilities in general. He took so much pride because he knew where to go and he was the leader. He was beaming with pride. Disney was a place where even obnoxious children were tolerable and fortunately, these kids were great! Their favorite expression was "Let's go!" We went to all of the parks and water rides. We rested by the pools in the afternoons and stayed out late in the evenings. It was like there were six kids with no worries in the world. We saw all of the main characters at dinners and basically, didn't look at any clocks. Linda was home taking care of Mike's puppy and Cindy's father, who was now going to adult daycare. The time went quickly, but we were so upbeat that coming home was fine. When we got home, the only thing we had to do was check in with the attorney.

The attorney already filed saying that Joe should not even be heard as Joe had no standing, but that had nothing to do with the conciliator. In the meantime, we had to figure out what to do with that idiot judge who gave us a preview of his ruling involving the custody procedure with Brenda. Didn't the judge consider things such as drugs, theft, support, stability, etc.? Was he trying the mother or sentencing the child? Should we try to have the case heard by another judge since that one went out of his way to pre-judge, which was a questionable call on his part. Should everyone wait to see if another judge was appointed? If one judge were removed, would the others be vindictive toward us for trying to make one of their brethren look bad; politics or righteousness?

Our attorney decided that there was a new rotation on the bench in three months and the case was not going to be heard in that period of time so we should wait it out. It was possible that a new judge would be assigned to our case. It was also possible that this same idiot would keep the case. We figured that we better get the questions ready for the case with Joe, and not Brenda, just in case we were surprised again! The questions revolved around his drugs, the knife, his losing custody of his kids, scams on insurance companies, his former wife's jail time, and other things that would piss him off and get his temper in full gear.

We felt that Joe would be uncovered with these topical questions. He would be so busy trying to defend his actions that Mike would never be an issue. Every action that was being taken was to secure the best interests of Mike. On the other hand, was it possible that we were being too over protective and defensive of his rights? The court said Mike had no rights unless the court gave it to him. Cindy and I raised him, but the court decided what was best for him. This custody court, so far, had not seen him or heard any of the sagas that have occurred. What if the court saw an act of Joe saying how much he loved Mike and the knife was a mistake made out of love? The judges didn't always go on case law in family court. The gut feeling of the judge and his instinct played a major role. We had seen this in the non-hearings through two judges already.

In the meantime, based on the judge pushing Brenda to see the psychologist, she made her appointment from jail and took the tests. We got a letter from the same psychologist who said that Cindy and I had to be evaluated again since it was a year since our last visit. At our ages, did anyone think that we were going to change in a year to become irresponsible? We went and met with the psychologist and were reevaluated. This time, we were more aggressive and basically said, "let's cut the bullshit, she is conning the judge and you!" The psychologist kept his cool and said that he was not conned and she lied on 90% of his questions. Those were tests proven to bring out the truth in these situations and the tests were standardized. We shut up as we realized that the shrink knew his stuff and Brenda was not helping her cause. That was good because it give one professional view, but it was not the view of the judge, who would ultimately make the final decision. We also were aware that the courts like to use the psychologist's report, because it takes pressure off of them when they can listen to the experts.

The attitude of the judge in the prior hearing had placed us on edge. We were frightened, so we made up a list of more custody questions for the attorney to use, if and when the custody trial with Brenda came up. It would also serve as the paper that could tell everyone the situation. We suggested topics that included all of her jobs and subsequent firings; harmful actions that caused injury to Mike; drugs; lack of financial responsibility; breaking court orders; running with known felons and druggies; number and length of time she lived at various areas; auto accidents; lack of reasonable morals; physical confrontations that Mike witnessed, etc.

We then had to go over some questions that were redundant, but penetrating and showing her personality:

With your first car, were you given notice that the police were going to boot your car in Philadelphia and you said, "Fuck them, I don't got that car no more?"

Were you involved in an accident in the older (car VW Jetta-88) when you got mad at Carlos and purposely banged up both cars by hitting the one car with the other?

Did you sideswipe an older woman who sued you for damages, and you had no insurance, told them you have nothing, and said you won't pay?

Did you tell me that you hit a young boy in your car and he was limping, but the mother told you it was ok to leave?

Did the police investigate you hitting a motorcycle at the corner of my home and leaving the scene?

Has Mike ever seen you or Carlos or any of your friends do drugs or has he seen you buy drugs?

Does Mike know the smell of drugs?

Has Mike ever seen bloodied people in the car that you drove to the hospital?

Has Carlos ever hit you? Did you file a report to police that he threatened you and pushed you around?

Has he ever strangled you? Has Mike ever seen violence with you and Carlos?

Did you ever have a restraining order against Carlos? Did you tell the judge you got counseling? Where? Did you lie to the judge?

Has Carlos ever been arrested for violence or for a weapon offense? Is this the same person who you want to live with and have your son live with?

Did Carlos break into Tristen's house and you filed a police report? Were you hit or pushed against the counter in her kitchen?

Did you use a credit card that you lied to get (application said working at Carlos' mother's hair salon) and buy a $2,000 stereo system for his car?

Did you sleep away from Mike (out of the house) 50 out of 55 nights in April, at Carlos' house?

Didn't you go out seven nights out per week? Didn't Cindy beg you to at least try to put Mike to bed before going out?

After the shooting on Carlos' block, did you swear to Cindy that your child would never go down there again?

Have you ever told Mike not to tell Nanny and Papa certain things about your activities? Did you walk into the house about 9 p.m. and Mike ran over to you so proud and said "See mama, I didn't tell Nanny and Papa that you were with Carlos?" Do you think it is good to teach a child to lie? Do you lie?

Did you take a happy child from his playmates many times, tell him he was going to North Philadelphia, force him to his room and pinch, berate, and verbally abuse and punish him until he was screaming and crying uncontrollably, then walk him downstairs with his head buried in his chest and say to him "tell Nanny and Papa that you want to go." At that point, barely audible, without looking up, he says, "I wanna go." The child was frightened and confused why he was being taken somewhere where he feared.

Many weekends, you had Mike sleep in North Philly so you could play with your boyfriend. Was that in his best interests? Was he afraid of the rodents in the house? Did you care? If you cared, why did you take him out of his safe environment?

Did Mike ever see sex movies with you and Carlos?

Does your boyfriend have another child? Does he see him? How old is he and what is his name? Has he always paid support or is he behind now?

Is Carlos your fiancé? Where did he get the ring or did YOU buy the ring right after you pawned more jewelry three days after we came back from taking you on a family vacation to Las Vegas?

Were you engaged when you went to Las Vegas? Were you picked up by a guy named Gary in Las Vegas within three minutes from the time it took to walk from the show exit to the front door? Could you have gone back to the hotel like us to meet with your son who was with friends in the room waiting for your return?

Weren't you picked up by two guys in Disney World from New York, who you went to see at 1 a.m. in the morning? Didn't you walk 3/4 of a mile and take a cab to their room to be alone with them? Does the name Rodriguez sound like the name of one of them?

Did you break every rule on your Contract for a new VW Beetle bought for you? Isn't it your lifestyle to take, take, and never give anything in return?

Were you proud that you portrayed your way of life as a thief to a young child?

Do you feel you can take care of Mike and his hygiene? Can you take care of your own dental hygiene?

Do you feel it was in the child's best interest to take him from a sound sleep in his own bed to your bed every night somewhere between 2 and 3 a.m., and then tell Cindy that he walked in himself when they saw you take him? Was that for you or for his benefit?

Did you have at least three abortions 1-from Mark; 2- Cindy drove her to one clinic; 3- Tristen drove her to another. (Tristen told us that it was six abortions by the time Mike was three)

Did you agree with all of the points on the custody petition for Mike?

Did you receive SSI for Mike and is it now about $171/month? Has Mike received any of that money, since Cindy and Ed paid all of his expenses for the past four years? Did you put his money in a savings account? Do you

386

realize that you spent Mike's money, over $8,700 on yourself? With interest, he would have over $10,000 today instead of nothing! Weren't you told that was money for his best interests, not yours?

Didn't you tell us that you were scamming the insurance company because the guy who backed into you at KFC was a kid and his father was trying to protect the kid and take the blame and he said you could get the car Carlos was driving all fixed for free?

Did you tell the court at your criminal trial that heroin addicts could raise children if they weren't really bad?

History of Physical abuse that was in Brenda's immediate circle:
Brenda's mother with boyfriends
Brenda with Mark and their family accepted that in Boston!
Brenda with Carlos

Family history with jail:
Mother
Mother's boyfriend
Father (when younger)
Brother charged with selling drugs in a school zone
Aunt

Our other observations of Brenda are as follows:
The mother who thinks he is a possession is neglecting this child. She believes that she can control this child to accommodate her needs and no one can do anything about it. She doesn't care about his best interests. She believes the law can't do anything because she is the mother (biologically) and she will do anything she damn well pleases!

She does not realize that the law does not necessarily believe that the biological mother's actions and judgment are in the child's best interests. She was arrested for criminal charges of theft and told everyone that she would beat the law, get probation, and get Mike back. She was so sure that she brought over a puppy (pit bull) June 28, and told Mike it was his when they get to their new home. That was very confusing to a child. She disposed of the puppy about two weeks later.

The above questions and comments were self-explanatory, but hopefully, would they be enough to scare the judge into thinking safety for Mike? We were driven by the thought of Mike being in Brenda's lifestyle for even a day, let alone a lifetime! The above was the entire case laid before the court.

While those thoughts and actions were going on, we decided to check on the status of Brenda, who was still in jail on work release. We found out that she screwed up twice and still hadn't paid any restitution. She lived in a cottage setting at the jail and was cocky as hell and still refused to listen to the county correction authority, but didn't go far enough to get disciplined. In her reality, she was right to do what she wanted. She stole, did drugs, disobeyed at least three court orders, didn't obey jail rules and she was still not being punished much. We also found that she was still working at the same fast food store in the mall. Why would a convicted felon be allowed to work so close to the public, one week after being convicted? Shouldn't the public have some idea who was either preparing or associating with them? If someone said, "we are having a party and we pulled five convicted felons to cater it at our home," how anxious would a guest be to attend?

The weather was losing its summer warmth and it would now be harder for Brenda to get to work. September also had less daily activity at the mall, so her job and hours were changing. Kids were in school during the day so lunches were less hectic.

Mike was excited about going to school because he was now a big first grader. He started school two days after we returned from Florida. That meant that he was in the main building and he knew most of the teachers. He knew the system from day one. He was ready for learning. The school, as well as Cindy and I, had emphasized to him the importance of learning and how proud he should be when he was aware of the news, speaking another language, getting the right answers doing math problems, etc. Mike was driven by self-satisfaction. He was proud when he learned to open doors for people and shy when they said thank you. The year started with Mike seeing his friends, both boys and girls, and playing with them at recess. They seemed to have a genuine liking for each other, and no one ever picked on anyone. It was very positive. The year went on and there were the school events including cocktail parties for adults for fund-raising, and sock hops for the entire school, which included the slicked down hair to poodle skirts and T-shirts with rolled up sleeves. Mike was the most athletic in his group, so he was very popular with the kids. His only weakness seemed to be that he was stubborn when he wanted to do something that was not what the class was doing. He would connive and even make up excuses, which he learned were going to be exposed quickly. School and home would keep reinforcing that listening, learning, and telling the truth were key elements that made up a good person. It took about a week to get Mike back into his school schedule, since he was used to staying up later at night and playing with all of the kids in the neighborhood. Mike was doing well with his soccer and ice hockey, except he was growing all the time and it was difficult to keep him in equipment. The year was uneventful and running very smoothly for Mike. He never asked about Brenda.

Brenda would call at odd hours and very rarely speak to Mike. She would leave messages on the answering machine. We played the messages for Mike and asked if he wanted to call momma. He would say "no" or "not now." She was getting ready for her release. I was not kept informed about her activities in or out of jail when she was out on work release. The prison had a confidentiality policy. The only things that we were told were that she was not the "prisoner of the year." She still had her attitude, but the prison was just as happy to get rid of her. The constant phone calls I made were to see if any restitution would be forthcoming and during those conversations, I would get comments or tidbits on information that allowed me to know she lied to everyone in the prison, so that hadn't changed. Brenda hadn't worked a lot of hours, but we didn't know what the reason was. We were still betting that she would get knocked up during her prison time. We didn't know if Carlos was still seeing her, but he could very well could have picked her up at the prison, had sex with her in the car or in an hourly motel, and dropped her off at work.

We were still under her visitation orders from the court from over a year ago, even though she realistically could not visit. We did not volunteer to take Mike to jail to see Brenda, although we did ask him if he wanted to visit her. Our opinion was that jail was a place to fear, not feel comfortable since momma was there. We still didn't understand why some courts order the children be taken there to visit.

In the meantime, Joe was calling about every two weeks to talk to Mike. The last time he called, Mike spoke politely for about one minute and then handed the phone to Cindy and said "you talk nanny," and he went out to play. That shocked both sides because neither wanted to speak to each other. Joe was not anxious to come down to visit. Joe still had to decide what to do with Brenda, since he put himself into the fray. Since she was getting ready to be released, what would the probation officer allow her to do? He could try to switch the probation to Boston, but then Brenda would be away from Carlos and Mike, in that order, or she could be forced to stay in Philadelphia to finish out the 5-year probation. She would try to have it both ways, but no one was sure how the situation was going to work. Brenda didn't want to be under Joe's control, and Joe's wife didn't want Brenda in her life, but she was only trying to appease Joe. She also realized that Mike was intertwined in this mess and until something was resolved, Joe's wife thought she better leave all doors open and not be the decision maker. The ironic aspect of this entire situation was that the most stable person was Mike!

The day arrived when Brenda was supposed to get out, but the officials decided that she would remain another two months, which was her actual scheduled date of release. The earlier release date would have been for good behavior. She took the news of the extension with annoyance, but not anger. Joe was annoyed because he had set up his work schedule to come down to meet her and he planned on seeing Mike at the same time. We were considering having the county set up a special room and an individual to supervise the visit, but that would not be fair to Mike. At least at home, Mike knew that his friends would be around when he was done. The only thing that we were concerned about would be that the filing of petitions to get Mike back would start coming all the time, since Joe would be pushing for custody. Joe's attitude was that Mike needed his mother, although he stated many times that she was no good for him now. Joe just wanted access to Mike to show off for Mike to build his own ego. He never asked Brenda what she wanted. He never asked Mike what he wanted. We were all too busy fighting. Everyone was walking a thin line because each one was one mistake from losing Mike. Brenda was the biological mother and that carried a lot of weight; Joe thought he carried more weight than he did.

Two months later, Brenda was released. She called Cindy to say she was coming to see Mike in two days. We wondered why in two days, since she hadn't seen him in nine months? That behavior told us some things never change and she was a prime example of that!

Joe did not come down, although he hadn't seen Mike for four months. Brenda was released and went straight to Carlos' house. I was thinking, "How did one say party time!" Brenda was probably going to enjoy her new freedom and worry about jobs and responsibility later, much later. Two days later, we were waiting for her to arrive. She called and said she would be an hour late, because her ride didn't get there yet. The routine had started! I told Mike to go out and play, but tell us whom he was with so that when Brenda got to the house, we would call him. We told Mike to do what he felt. If he wanted to hug her, kiss her, not hug her, etc, it was up to him.

Brenda came over, with Carlos, two hours late and I called Mike. Mike asked if he could go back to his friends after momma left and we said he could. He came home within two minutes after we called him and Brenda started the same routine; "give momma a hug, momma loves you, momma missed you, my baby's getting so big, tell momma that you love her." Mike kept his hands by his sides and allowed Brenda to hug him. He turned his head away when she tried to give him a kiss. That was the extent of his reaction, other than saying "hello."

He asked her to watch him roller blade because that's what he was doing with the kids and he wanted to show off. She watched and made no eye contact with either Cindy or me. Carlos just tried to stay out of the way after saying hello. Brenda whispered something in Mike's ear and saw me getting ready to reprimand her. She then backed away from whispering and spoke normal. She asked him to sit on her lap and he said that he wanted to skate. I let them have their own interaction, which did not seem to be a warm and fuzzy feeling for Mike. Mike didn't realize that I was supervising, because I did try not to be obvious. After about an hour, she said she was leaving and would be back to see him soon. Mike went back to playing with his friends.

We had to worry now about her next moves, which we knew would be to petition the courts for custody of Mike. It took about six months, but the papers did come in. When the court papers came, we knew that we were within six months of the final hearing. Mike was now seven and a half years old and he knew what was going on. He was aware that no love was lost between among the Boston family and us. He still didn't totally understand what the finality could mean to him. The activities were still going on in Mike's life and most things were still very scheduled for him. We were traveling with him to ice hockey games within one to two hours away, and he was developing a wonderful camaraderie with his team.

Things were going fine with him. He was a normal 7 year old!

Joe was pushing Brenda to stay straight. She stayed with Carlos, but we were not sure if she was forced to stay in town from the courts or whether it was her choosing. She was working as a waitress at a local franchise restaurant; Cindy was told it was her third job in more than six months. Brenda visited Mike about once a week, saying her work schedule wouldn't allow her more time. Also, she said that to get to the house with public transportation was very difficult. We had no idea what was happening with her probation situation.

We received a total of $75 restitution toward the $60,000 debt, which was reduced since we recovered the five items. According to my calculations, we would be fully paid for our loss in a mere 166.6 years! It was a good thing the courts didn't add interest or it would take her several lifetimes for her to repay the money! The courts wanted to be sure that she had enough to live on, as well as repaying court costs and room and board at the prison. We realized that Brenda would never pay us, so we decided that we would go after the pawnshop. We knew they were "dishonest," and we knew we could go after them anytime within two years of the crime.

The reason for waiting to press for restitution was because we wanted to see if we needed the pawnshop owners to be witnesses at Brenda's criminal trial, which we didn't. We called an attorney that we knew who was in litigation law. We figured that he would do a contingent case. He said that his partner felt it should be an hourly rate. I thanked him for his time and said, "We'll do it ourselves." I went to the law library and found the format to use to submit the civil suit. I didn't want to go after them for criminal because their insurance wouldn't cover that. I stayed two hours at the law library looking up cases and buzzwords. I came home and wrote up the documents within two hours. Cindy proofread them and we went to city hall and filed them. That saved us a few thousand dollars!

We figured that the insurance company would pay us eventually, and then go after Brenda to recoup their loss. The judge gave her five years to pay us back, yet he had no clue what she would pay. The question came up that what if she didn't pay it all back in five years? We were told that we could file a civil suit against her.

That would be a waste of time! Let the insurance company go after her for the rest of her life or else they would just have to write it off! The buzzwords were nasty; acting as a fence, reasonably should have known the goods were stolen, receiving stolen merchandise, etc. This suit will eventually see the state banking commission floor! We now had all of our cards on the table; four different hearings based on her theft!

The date for the custody hearing with Brenda was one month away. We had four meetings with our attorneys and were helping them to prep the case. We already knew in our minds what Brenda's case was going to be. She was going to say she was a single mother who made a mistake; she loved her child more than anything; she was working to pay off her debts; she was in a position to care for her child as only a mother could do; Mike needed her since he didn't have a father; and she was making enough money now to support him. She never physically abused him, and her son was stolen from her. He has so much family in Boston that wants to help care for him, and give him all of their love. She would say that she didn't have as much money as Cindy and I, but she could give him more love. For effect, she would start to cry half way through her speech describing her love for Mike.

We were using a more sophisticated and realistic approach, one that was a less emotional plea. We would say Mike was happy, stable and loved; he was getting a great education and was thriving; he enjoyed his extra activities and his many friends. We would attack her background, her past history of showing she had no idea what responsibility was, and why should anyone, especially a court of law, experiment with Mike's life. We would make it very clear, with all the past

394

history that had transpired, Mike's entire existence would drastically change for the worse. Brenda had proven, over and over, that she had no future and couldn't even take care of herself. We would stress that children are the future, and the system owes Mike a chance to have a descent one. We will show that she is in poverty and won't get out, because she proved she had no interest in working toward any worthwhile goals. We will show her record as a felon and a heroin addict. We will stress that Mike can break the poverty line by getting an education. We will bring forth witnesses that will attest to the non-motherhood role she had played since Mike was born. We will get to the point in the saga where the judge will be able to write the rest of the script.

Chapter Thirty-one

The day of the hearing arrived. It was scheduled for two full days and everyone was very tense. Cindy had bitten all of her nails and I hadn't stopped eating in a week, out of nervousness. We arrived at our attorney's office a half hour before the 9 a.m. hearing. We had Mike dressed casually, but nice. One of our neighbors stayed with Mike in the attorney's office while the rest of us went across the street to the courthouse. Mike had to be with us, in accordance with the court order, but no one believed the judge would put much weight on anything that he said because of his age. Cindy was actually shaking. The next two days would give us the most important decision in the life of Mike and only we, fully knew all of the proven and unproven facts.

The hearing started and was true to form. Our attorney called Brenda to the stand and absolutely ripped her apart. Our attorney was good, almost too good. We were starting to feel as if the judge was becoming sympathetic toward Brenda. He kept interrupting our attorney to give Brenda a breather. We were nervous because this was the same man who told everyone, in that prior session, that he favored keeping the mother and child together, if it was at all possible.

The case was pretty well laid out. Brenda was the biological mother, who we felt the judge was helping, because she did not have an attorney representing her. Joe was sitting with her, and giving her guidance. The hearings went on for one full day, without any interruptions. Mike's teacher from school testified and was followed by a minister who was a personal friend of our family. He offered to have his Church sponsor Brenda in one of their affiliated drug counseling centers. One of our neighbors testified about Mike's care and who was giving it. Brenda said that she loved the child and cared for him most of the time. We brought up her moral standards and were shut down by the judge. In a surprise move, the judge asked to speak with Mike in his chambers. Someone from our attorney's office went across the street to bring Mike back as we took a short break. We had no feel where the judge was going. When Mike came back, he and the judge walked past the bench and into his chambers. When he passed Cindy and me, he gave us a forced, scared smile. Ten minutes later, they came back into the courtroom and Mike was taken back to the attorney's office. Finally, the judge said that he had heard from both sides, and there was a decision that he would have to make quickly, but it was not going to be an easy decision. He begin with 'each party stated their case in a very clear and understandable manner, and he didn't feel that he had any questions he needed to ask.' He said that he had read the other information from outside sources and had read other cases that were referenced during the hearing.

To everyone's surprise, he asked that the court be recessed for one hour and he would come back in with his decision. He told our attorney to bring the child back to the courtroom when we were to reconvene. We went back to our attorney's office to wait. It was a horrible feeling to go back and we just stared at Mike. Both of us had tears in our eyes; we had to turn away so Mike wouldn't see us. This could be the last few minutes that we ever spent with Mike.

Our attorney was very nervous. She knew her presentation

was good, but she was concerned that the judge may have preconceived notions about motherhood. Did we or didn't we make him realize it was going to be a life or death decision, or was he still thinking momma should have her child just like a regular family? We got back to the courtroom five minutes before the scheduled start. Brenda and Cindy exchanged glares. I could tell from their expressions that they both had the same thought; both sides wished the other one were dead. There were no thoughts of compromise. Mike was sitting with our neighbor in the back of the room, and we all just kept glancing back. Mike smiled back at us, but it was the same scared smile. He looked upset; it was as if he understood that the most important ruling in his entire life was about to be determined by a total stranger.

The judge walked into the courtroom and sat down. He said nothing. The room was absolutely still. He looked down at his papers, and then looked up.

"This is a very difficult decision that has to be made. I understand that one of the parties will be devastated from this decision. The well being of this child is of the utmost importance. A decision of what is in this young child's best interests is a decision that will be made today," he said. "This child has lost one parent and could lose another. A child's life without the father could have a major impact on his life, but without both parents, it could be devastating!"

As we were listening to this, our hearts were in our throats. Was he telling us what he already prepared us for in earlier statements?

With that, he raised his head to show that he was the authority, conveying the message that his decision was final.

"It is my decision that this child, Mike, ..."

With those words, I reached for Cindy's hand. I felt her trembling, and I knew she could feel me doing the same. We held our breaths. It seemed to us as if time had stopped; everything became frozen and still. I was afraid to look back at Mike. I was afraid to let him see the fear that had griped my very soul. If he was to leave our lives and get sent back to Brenda and her family, I didn't know how we would handle another devastating blow. How would Mike adjust to living with a mother who he feared and had no clue on how to be a parent? Just envisioning the scenario turned my blood cold.

Those split seconds, waiting for the judge to finish his statement, felt like hours. He voice brought me back to reality ... "should stay with the grandparents who have loved and nurtured him for most of his life. They have proved to this court, that they have only the child's health and well being as their primary concern. His biological mother, through her actions and behavior, has proven the exact opposite. My ruling stands." With those brief words, words that will literally changed our lives, he stood up, gathered his papers and left the room. I gave our attorney a big kiss and whispered "thank you" into her ear. I whispered because I couldn't speak.

It was as if fireworks where exploding above our heads. The years of pain and suffering were being washed away, and sunshine was gloriously breaking through the clouds that have darkened our lives.

We looked across the room at Brenda. She had her head down, and her father was saying something to her. It was a good feeling to know she couldn't hurt Mike anymore.

Together, with tears in our eyes, we looked back at Mike. He had a smile that stretched from ear-to-ear. "Let's get our little guy and go home," I whispered to Cindy. She looked at me and smiled, and for the first time in years, I saw peace in her eyes. Together, we walked to the back of the courtroom, each of us taking one of Mike's little hands into ours, and we started out of the courtroom.

We gained our composure after about five minutes and asked our attorney if it was over? She said, "It is for a while, but she can come back at some future date and file for custody if she ever gets her life together."